Noodling for Flatheads

Burkhard Bilger

SCRIBNER

New York   London   Toronto   Sydney   Singapore

SCRIBNER
1230 Avenue of the Americas
New York, NY 10020

Copyright © 2000 by Burkhard Bilger

SCRIBNER and design are trademarks of Macmillan Library Reference USA, Inc.,
used under license by Simon & Schuster, the publisher of this work.

DESIGNED BY ERICH HOBBING

Set in Adobe Caslon

Manufactured in the United States of America

1   3   5   7   9   10   8   6   4   2

Library of Congress Cataloging-in-Publication Data
Bilger, Burkhard.
Noodling for flatheads : moonshine, monster catfish,
and other Southern comforts / Burkhard Bilger.
p.   cm.
1. Southern States—Social life and customs—20th century.
2. Eccentrics and eccentricities—Southern States. I. Title.
F216.2.B49 2000
975'.043—dc21   00-030107

ISBN 0-684-85010-9

"Noodling for Flatheads" and "Send in the Hounds" originally appeared,
in altered form, in *The Atlantic Monthly*. "Enter the Chicken" originally appeared,
also in altered form, in *Harper's Magazine*.

Text permissions can be found on page 253.

For Jennifer

CONTENTS

The Mall of the Wild 133

IN WHICH A GEORGIA MAN, DREAMING
OF THE ULTIMATE GAME FARM, CALLS FORTH
A PLAGUE OF FROGS.

Send in the Hounds 157

IN WHICH DOGS CHASE RACCOONS,
HUNTERS CHASE DOGS, THE AUTHOR CHASES HUNTERS,
AND NO ONE KNOWS EXACTLY WHY.

Low on the Hog 181

IN WHICH A COOK'S SOUL IS TESTED BY A PLATE
OF STEAMING INTESTINES.

The Rolley Holers 205

IN WHICH A FEW GOOD MEN, ARMED ONLY
WITH THEIR THUMBS, CRUSH THE BRITISH
AND MAKE THE FRENCH CRY.

Noodling for Flatheads

INTRODUCTION

BOOKS ABOUT strange obsessions, like the obsessions themselves, tend to grow out of chance encounters. Mine began, like an old Jack London story, with a search for a dog.

I was living in Cambridge, Massachusetts, at the time, learning to play country blues guitar and thinking it would be nice to have a lazy coonhound for an audience. In Oklahoma, where I grew up, coonhounds seem to haunt every paper route and country road, to lurk in querulous packs down every gravel drive. Most of my childhood had been spent trying to dodge their teeth, whether on foot or on my blue Schwinn bicycle. But now I found, after years on the East Coast, that I missed their voices.

That fall I started calling the AKC and the ASPCA, scanning ads in local newspapers and consulting dog trainers, all to no avail. In New England coonhounds are about as common as wolves. A few people had heard rumors of such dogs, but none had actually seen one in the flesh. Why not a pug, they said, or a nice Brittany spaniel?

Finally one day, weeks into my search, I managed to track down a breeder of blueticks. At first, as I stood on his front porch explaining what I wanted, I could see his smile fade through the screen door: his puppies were all spoken for that season, he said. But then, as we talked some more, he suddenly held up his hand. "Hold on a second," he said, turning and disappearing into his house. A moment later he emerged from the shadows with a rumpled document: *American Cooner* magazine.

It was the strangest publication I had ever seen.

After half a century of television, it's easy to mistake our sitcoms for ourselves—to imagine that there's no more to popular culture than Barbie dolls and TV theme songs. But *American Cooner* came from somewhere beyond the range of most antennas. Its closely typeset pages contained dozens of articles about coon hunters and their exploits, interspersed with snapshots of the hounds in action: front paws high up on tree trunks, eyes gone white from the photographer's flash, mouths bawling hysterically at a coon somewhere above. Here and there, advertisements for kennels referred cryptically to "Grand Nite Champions," "cold-nosed, chop-mouth dogs," and "chilled semen for sale." I had no idea what they meant, and it was hard to imagine that thousands of people out there did. Yet *American Cooner* was a fat, glossy monthly, chock-full of ads.

Leafing through page after page of coonhound arcana, I realized there was a side to Oklahoma that I had missed growing up, a hidden history and landscape that even locals might not see. While I had moved about in what seemed a nine-to-five world—where dinner was always at six and every porch light snapped off at ten—a few of my neighbors spent half their waking hours in the woods.

When the rest of us went to bed, the coon hunters among us were just fully awakening, keyed to their dogs' unearthly voices and the forest's nocturnal pulse.

The wonder, to me, wasn't that people did such things, but that they published magazines about it and compiled coon-hunting histories, maintained century-old blood-lines, and held week-long competitions. Here was a full-blown subculture—one with its own rites, rituals, and deeply rooted lore. And I had heard of it only when I moved a thousand miles away.

In years since, I've come across even more obscure publications—a cockfighting magazine called *Feathered Warrior*, for instance—each of which speaks to a clandestine culture of its own. Few of them can be found on news-stands, just as their virtual alter egos can't be found on lists of hot Internet links. But like samizdat publications in the former Soviet Union, they reach their audience just the same.

This book explores a few of those hidden worlds—worlds that exist just around the corner, through the look-ing glass of American life. Each chapter circles in on a specific southern tradition: cockfighting in Louisiana, moonshining in Virginia, soul-food cooking in Georgia, and so forth. The book as a whole, however, is less about the traditions themselves than the hardy, tenacious communi-ties that have come to entangle them, like wild vines around an underground spring.

I won't pretend that the result is a comprehensive por-trait, or even an internally consistent one. Religion isn't here, for one thing, and race only briefly. Some of these traditions are illegal, others merely obscure; some ancient, others ultramodern. But the people who practice them share an undeniable kinship. Unlike so many of us, bent on wealth, promotion, or a few seconds of prime time, they cling to dreams that force them ever deeper underground. They hide their liquor under floorboards, make chitlins late at night when the family is asleep, or practice marbles in forest clearings. The more chilling their isolation, the brighter burning their obsessions—and their loyalty to those who share them.

I now think that rumpled copy of *American Cooner* was less a magazine than a secret handshake, the opening clue in a scavenger hunt. It eventually led me to a half-lame coon hunter in western Massachusetts and through him to a six-month-old redbone, the lonesome runt of a broken-chain litter. Hattie is a dead ringer for the dogs I grew up with (though her disposition is sweeter) and sometimes she even howls on pitch when I play the guitar. But if she helps dispel my homesickness, it's not the way I imagined. Home, she reminds me, is a place as foreign as it is familiar—one you can go back to again and again, as if for the first time.

Noodling for Flatheads

The great river was very dangerous [the Indians said].
There was a demon . . . who would engulf any who
approached in the abyss where he dwelt.

—JACQUES MARQUETTE, 1673

I have seen a Mississippi catfish that was more than six
feet long and weighed more than 250 pounds. And if
Marquette's fish was the fellow to that one, he had a fair
right to think the river's roaring demon was come.

—MARK TWAIN, *Life on the Mississippi*

GROWING UP with Lee McFarlin, I never took him for
someone with odd and intimate dealings with fish. In our
high school, in north-central Oklahoma, Lee was one of
those kids who sort of drifted from view: cutting classes and
tooling around in his '62 Chevy Impala. When I looked him
up in my senior yearbook recently, he had a single picture to
his name—no sports, no clubs, no academic honors. Back
then, the only clue to his secret life was the faint tracery of
scars along his forearms.

Late in the spring, when the rest of us were thinking about the prom, Lee would head to the Cimmaron River. As soon as the chill comes off the water, he knew, catfish look for places to spawn. Hollow banks, submerged timbers, the rusted wrecks of teenage misadventure: anything calm and shadowy will do. Once the eggs are laid, the male chases off the female with a snap of his jaws. Then for days he hovers over his glutinous brood, waiting for the first fingerlings to emerge, pouncing on any intruders.

That's when Lee would find him. Wading alongshore or diving to the lake bottom, Lee would reach into likely nooks and crevices, wiggling his fingers and waiting for a nip. When it came, he would hook his thumbs into the attacker's mouth or thrust his hand down its throat, then wait for the thrashing to stop. If he was lucky, the thing on the end of his arm was a fish.

Now, your average catfish is an innocuous thing: farm fed, soberly whiskered, tender as an earlobe. But inflate that fish a hundredfold—like a flea seen through a microscope—and it becomes a true American monster. When it lunges from the river bottom, opening jaws the size of dinner plates, the suction may pull in almost anything: shrimp, fish, snake, or rat, baby duck or beaver. According to one old story, when pioneer mothers did their wash by a stream, they sometimes heard a splash and a muffled yelp: where a little boy had been playing, only a few bubbles were left.

It's been a long time since catfish were the stuff of children's nightmares—the troll under the bridge, the thing at the bottom of the well. But by all accounts they're only getting bigger. In the 1990s more than forty-five state records were set for catfish, including one for a 111-pound blue cat. People spear them with pitchforks or snag them with hooks spooled in by lawn-mower engines; some use boron rods with titanium guides, ultrasonic lures, or baits spiked with amino acids that seize control of a fish's brain. But a few, like Lee, still dispense with equipment altogether.

"I'll tell you what it feels like," Lee says. "You know little puppy dogs, when you shake the fire out of them when they're teething? That there's exactly how it feels." Catfish may not have fangs, but they do have maxillary teeth: thick rows of inward-curving barbs designed to let food in but not out. When clamped on your arm, catfish also have an unfortunate tendency to bear down and spin, like a sharpener on a pencil. "It ain't nothin' but sandpaper—real coarse sandpaper," one hand grabber in Arkansas told me. "But once that thing gets to flouncin', and that sandpaper gets to rubbin', it can peel your hide plumb off."

A second-generation hand grabber, or "noodler," Lee caught his first fish that way at the age of eight. Though the bite didn't break his skin, it infected him like a venom. He's married now, with two children and a plumbing business, but he still starts noodling when the wheat turns golden brown, switching to even bigger game at summer's end. His house, plain enough on the outside, is appointed in high atavistic style on the inside: heads looming from every wall, giant fish twisted in desperate poses, freezers full of strange meats. (Once, when a deer wandered through his sleepy neighborhood, Lee grabbed a hunting bow and chased it through his backyard.) Last spring, to make the place a bit more cozy, he brought home a baby bobcat.

Today, noodling with his family and me on a lake just west of our hometown, Lee needs less than five minutes to launch his boat, gun it across the lake, and leap into the water as we drift to a stop. A few seconds later he calls me over to a crumbling pier. "Sit here," he says with a weird grin, "I want you to feel something." I scoot onto the concrete, trying to look nonchalant. If Lee was enigmatic in high school, I was something worse: bookish, bilingual, taught to be terrified of the outdoors. ("The bones of drowned boys," my mother was fond of saying, "lie at the bottom of every farm pond.") While he was trapping muskrats and skinning wild pigs, I learned about the American wilderness by reading James Fenimore Cooper in German.

Sitting on the pier now, I can feel reverberations of the old panic. Beneath me, all is quiet at first. But then, as Lee fumbles under the concrete with both hands, something begins to stir. Another dip of his thick shoulders, and the thing is fully awake, thrashing in the water six inches below me, thrumming the concrete with sharp cracks of its tail. We've found it—the troll under the bridge. All that's left is to reach down its throat.

The origins of noodling are difficult to imagine, much less prove. In North America archaeologists have found fishhooks made of bone, weirs of wood and stone, and perforated shells for sinking nets. But noodling leaves no traces; it is as ephemeral as some of the boasts it inspires.

Native Americans, by all historical accounts, had a peculiar genius for killing fish. Hernando de Soto's men, trudging through swamps in search of El Dorado, saw lines of Indians splashing in pools, scaring up fish and whacking their heads "with blows of cudgels." Others mentioned Indians attracting fish with torches, lassoing them by the tail, harpooning them with lengths of cane, and drugging them with buckeye and devil's shoestring. The most straightforward of all fishing methods, however, was first described in 1775, by a trader-historian named James Adair:

> They pull off their red breeches, or their long slip of Stroud cloth, and wrapping it round their arm, so as to reach to the lower part of the palm of their right hand, they dive under the rock where the cat-fish lie to shelter themselves from the scorching beams of the sun, and to watch for prey: as soon as those fierce aquatic animals see that tempting bait, they immediately seize it with the greatest violence, in order to swallow it. Then is the time for the diver to improve the favourable opportunity: he accordingly opens his hand, seizes the voracious fish by his tender parts, hath a sharp struggle with it against the crevices of the rock, and at last brings it safe ashore.

Most Indians, Adair goes on to say, "are in the watery element nearly equal to amphibious animals." By contrast, the first Europeans to try their hand at noodling must have been ungainly sights. Flailing out of the water, gasping for air, they may have tried to do justice to the experience by rebaptizing it wherever they went. In Arkansas they called it "hogging," in Mississippi "grabbling," and in Nebraska "stumping," though any given noodler might have two or three names for it. In Georgia it became "cooning," in Kentucky "dogging," and in Texas and Oklahoma "noodling." "The way you get ahold of that fish," Lee explains, "it's kind of like a wet noodle, squirming and squiggling."

As settlers drifted farther down the country's waterways, catfish stories sprang up with each new town and steamboat station. According to one nineteenth-century report, catfish would congregate beneath a dam on the Kansas River "like hogs in a hog lot," just waiting to be eaten. Sometimes the same men who searched for drowning victims by the dam would strap a gaff hook on one arm and dive for fish. At the turn of the century a man named Jake Washington went down and came up two or three days later—a drowning victim himself. "He hooked him a giant fish and couldn't get loose," says Tom Burns, a self-proclaimed "old man of the river" in Lawrence, Kansas. "They found them side by side on a sandbar."

Since the great dam-building years in midcentury, American rivers have grown less hospitable to catfish. Brushy snags have been yanked clear, mucky bottoms dredged out, banks scraped clean, till the Missouri River, where some of the country's biggest blues once lurked, has

become "a pretty swift ditch," in the words of one ichthyologist. If the catfish have gotten bigger lately, it's partly
owing to neglect: on the Mississippi Delta, where less
than 20 percent of all streams could support fisheries in
1979, the Army Corps of Engineers has nodded off just
long enough for some rivers to recover.

Like the black bears resettling once-ravaged parts of
the Ozarks, noodlers may be an indicator species of sorts
for healthy waterways. More often than not, though,
modern noodlers are less throwbacks than thrill seekers,
donning scuba gear, diving into reservoirs, and harvesting
fish from made-to-order catfish boxes—a southern varia-
tion on lobster traps. (One noodling pond I visited in
Arkansas had such clean, accessible catfish accommoda-
tions that it was called the "hole-tel.") In Mississippi,
once home to the scariest noodling waters in America, the
sport's best spokesman in recent years has been Kristi
Addis, Miss Teen USA 1987. One of her favorite pastimes,
Addis told judges at the pageant, is grabbling for flatheads
on the Yalobusha River. When pressed, she admitted that
the mechanics of grabbling were "really hard to explain."

tick tick tick

I'm nostril-deep in murky water, sunk to the calves in
gelatinous muck. Half an hour ago the troll got away,
squirming through an escape hatch beneath the pier. A
good omen? I'm not sure. Noodling, I know, is the fishing
equivalent of a shot in the dark. For his master's thesis at
Mississippi State University, a fisheries biologist named

Jay Francis spent three years noodling two rivers. All told, he caught 35 fish in 1,362 tries: 1 fish for every 39 noodles. Still, it's too soon to take comfort in such statistics. From this vantage, Lee still seems dismayingly confident. Perched on the nose of his boat, surveying the shore, he looks like some raw country god, an embodiment of the lake: hair red as a clay embankment, bright puddles for eyes, patches of freckles like sandbars across broad, ruddy features. "Yessir," he shouts, "I guarantee you we're gonna find us some fish." On his best day, he adds, he caught thirty-five on this lake, all of them by hand.

tick tick tick

In the evening's honeyed light, the boulders and tumbled-down walls alongshore look ancient as Troy. "Used to be a gas station here," Lee says, wading toward a collapsed slab. "They love to hang out under this old sidewalk." Behind us, his kids have set sail from the boat in their water wings, like a small flotilla. "Daddy, can I ketch 'im, Daddy?" one of them squeals, bent on making me look bad. "You promised I could ketch one, Daddy." We shoo him away and take up positions around the rock, ready to reach in at Lee's signal.

tick tick tick

I've never been so aware of my fingers as I have been these past few days. I've found myself admiring them in pictures of myself, flexing them in the mirror, taking pleasure in their simple dexterity. Catfish, I've been told, share their love for calm, shady places with turtles, electric eels, and cottonmouth snakes. "In almost any small-town café, you can find some guy who says he knows a noodler who lost three fingers to an alligator snapping turtle," says Keith Sutton, a catfishing expert and the editor of *Arkansas Wildlife* magazine. His father-in-law, Hansel Hill, who has been noodling in rural Arkansas for forty years, had an uncle who once reached into a hole and found a "no-shoulders." The snake's bite left a permanent crook in his right forefinger. Some noodlers wear gloves; others probe holes with a piece of cane. ("If it feels rough at the end of that cane, it's a snake; if it feels like rock, it's a turtle," Hill says. "But that catfish is just as smooth and slick as can be.") Lee is a purist. Better to reach in with bare digits, he says, "so you know where you're at with that fish."

tick tick tick

"What in the hell is that ticking sound?" Lee blurts, surging from the water for breath. "It sounds like a time bomb's about to go off down there." I glance blankly at him, still focused on my wiggling fingers. "That must be my fish locator!" some local angler yells from a nearby boat. He and his buddies have been floating alongside us for a while, hoping to get in a little rubbernecking before the sun sets.

"Well, turn that damn thing off!"

Catfish have the sharpest hearing in the fish world: an air bladder tucked behind their heads serves as an eardrum, sending vibrations down an arch of tiny bones to the fish's inner ear. In Florida the Indians used to wear such bladders, dyed red, as earrings. I'm busy imagining this when I see something odd in Lee's face—a sudden tightening around the eyes. Then, just as quickly, his features relax. "You want to see him?" he says, jerking to one side involuntarily. I follow his gaze down: There, frowning beneath the water's surface, is an eight-pound flathead catfish, clearly disgruntled, gnawing futilely on Lee's thumbs. A homelier sight would be hard to imagine.

"Catfish are the redheaded stepchildren of America's rivers," Keith Sutton likes to say. "A lot of people think they're above catching them." My brother-in-law, George, who will fish for anything that swims, goes even further. Fish, he says, embody our social stereotypes. Haughty, neurotic, and beautiful, trout are natural aristocrats. Largemouth bass, omnipresent and resilient, are the river's working class. Catfish, in this view, are true bottom dwellers (though George says that gar, moon-eye, and paddlefish are even lower—piscine untouchables). It's an arbitrary ranking, based more on a fish's looks and personal habits than on its taste and fighting ability, but it can change the course of a river.

In the late 1980s the Army Corps of Engineers finally woke up to the untidy state of the Mississippi Delta. Twelve miles of the Yalobusha River, they announced, would be cleared, dredged, and snagged. "They said it would have no significant impact on the fish," Don Jackson remembers. "I guess they didn't think anybody would care enough to check." Jackson, then a newly appointed professor of fisheries and wildlife at Mississippi State University, decided to see for himself. Even the muddiest reaches on the Mississippi, he found, were alive with flatheads, channel cats, carp, and smallmouth buffalo. When he told this to some of his colleagues, however, they were less than impressed. That's just fine, they said, but what about *real fish?*

Jackson and the Mississippi Wildlife Federation eventually forced the corps to scale back its plans. But most fishermen never bothered to get involved. It wasn't that they didn't care for catfish—even an ugly species can launch a thousand ships. According to the last national survey, nine million Americans catch catfish, more than fish for trout. "But the people running trotlines and hand grabbling are kind of backwoodsy," Jackson says. "They can lose things that are very important to them, and they still don't speak out." There is no environmental organization named Catfish Unlimited, no catfish-ecology chat group on the World Wide Web. Catch-and-release, an ecoreligion of sorts among fly fishermen, is practiced by only one in fifty catfish fishermen.

To born-again fly fishermen—some of whom write laws for state fish and wildlife departments—noodlers rank even lower than paddlefish. Not only do noodlers kill their fish, they grab them at their most vulnerable moments, sometimes leaving thousands of eggs behind to be eaten by predators. The fact is, however, that noodling poses little threat to the environment. A single catfish can lay enough eggs to repopulate a stream reach. Besides, noodling is just too unpleasant to become very popular. "I can't tell you how tough it was," says Jay Francis, whose 1,300 noodles had less effect on catfish stocks than did the weather. "Some of those fish were just incredibly, incredibly vicious."

If noodling is legal in only seven states, the reason has less to do with the environment than with ethics—and ethics of a perversely genteel sort. In the words of one ichthyologist in Missouri: "It's just not a sporting thing to do."

Stumbling across another muddy inlet, I have a hard time feeling sorry for the fish. In my right hand I'm holding a rope threaded through the gills of Lee's three catches, which swim along behind me like puppies on a leash. Blue cats have the worst bite, Lee says—"The difference between them and flatheads is like the difference between pit bulls and poodles"—but these flatheads look plenty tough to me.

A few feet from shore, the waves break across low, blue black humps, glistening beneath the water like a school of eerie, robotic fish. Two years ago Lee made these catfish dens out of sawed-up oil barrels. They were meant to be fully submerged, but the same drought that has been withering wheat crops in the Oklahoma panhandle keeps exposing these drums to the sun, forcing Lee to move them every few weeks. Wading over to one, I see that Lee has his right leg inside it, struggling to pin something against its inside wall.

"Owwwwwwwwww! That damn fish bit me!"

"Have you got him?"

"Not this one, that one! The one on your line!"

I glance down at my aquatic puppies. One of them has managed to dodge through my legs, sneak up on Lee, and chomp on his big toe. A bold feat, though hardly sporting.

"Hold on a second, just hold on."

By now Lee's eyes flash signals clearly as a lighthouse: He's found a big one. In a beat I'm crouched next to him, arms tangled with his inside the den, hands splay-fingered to stop the fish's charge. Somewhere in there, a fish is caroming off the sides of the barrel, ringing it like a muffled gong. And I realize, with a shudder, that my fingers are waving frantically, almost eager for a bite.

"He's on your side," Lee yells. "Can't you feel him?"

No. But how could I miss such a huge fish? A twitch of my right hand solves the conundrum: I can't feel the fish, it seems, *because my arm is all the way down its throat.* The fish and I realize this at about the same time, like stooges backing into each other in a haunted house. The fish clamps down, I try to yank free, and the rest is a wet blur of thrashing, screaming, and grasping for gills. At some point Lee threads a rope through its mouth, and for just a second I get a good look at an enormous, prehistoric face. Then, with a jerk of its shoulders, it wrenches free, taking a few last pieces of my thumbs with it.

Later, coasting toward our dock in the dying light, Lee guesses that our catch weighs twenty-five pounds. Out of its element, though, it looks sadly diminished: prostrate on deck, mouth working to get air, skin soft and pale as dough. At first the kids scream when the boat hits a wave and the fish slides toward them, mouth agape. Then the shock wears off and their voices turn mocking, exaggerated. Finally one of them gives it a kick: just another monster done in by daylight.

But not entirely. That night, when I come home from the lake, my son comes padding down the hall to greet me. He's been hearing bedtime stories about catfish all week—stories not so different, I'll admit, from my mom's macabre tales. Now he looks up with anxious eyes as I tell him about my day. And I feel a stab of recognition, watching his face contort with the effort of imagining. The troll, I think, has found a new haunt.

Enter the Chicken

⌒

Suddenly we noticed barnyard cocks beginning a bitter
fight just in front of the door. We chose to watch.
—St. Augustine, *De Ordine*

THE ROAD from Baton Rouge to Lafayette snakes through
the heart of Cajun country, barely elevated above the
swamp's reach. It's a dividing line of sorts between the old
Louisiana and the new, the puritan north and the licentious
south, and the land around it seethes with fecundity. Even
in the driest of seasons, the cypress trees are moss grown
and saturate, and when the rains come the ground convulses
like a living thing. Under the highway the earth shifts and
swells, cracking the cement along its seams till it feels like
a reptile's skin beneath your car's wheels, like the back of a
great, slumbering sea beast, easily awakened.

On the night that I arrived in Baton Rouge, southern
Louisiana seemed ready to cast loose from the continent
once and for all. Floodwaters from the north had already
strained the levees to bursting, threatening to capsize
chemical barges along the Mississippi; now a thunder-

storm swept in to finish the job. Driving west, beneath the phosphorescent plumes sprayed by passing cars, I felt the rain's nervous drumming in my gut. My plane had spent hours in a holding pattern above this storm, and the *kerschlick* of my tires ticked off every second of delay: midnight in the bayou seemed an inauspicious setting for a cockfight.

I was looking for a club called the Red Rooster, near a town called Maurice. A cockfighter named James Demoruelle had promised to meet me there, though I was three hours late by then and counting. Ours would be a perfectly legal meeting—cockfighting has never been outlawed in Louisiana—yet I felt as though I were going undercover. Cockfighters are strange attractors of vice, I'd been told, conduits for drugs and gambling and episodes of violence. They shun publicity like an avian virus, hide their meetings as assiduously as any drug cartel or pornography ring. A few weeks earlier I'd tracked down the editor of a cockfighting magazine at an unlisted number in rural Arkansas. When I called, she barked into the phone, "You sound like one of them animal lovers to me," and hung up.

If Demoruelle had agreed to meet me, I thought, it was because he was a little desperate. A few months before, a state congressman from New Orleans had written a bill to ban cockfighting in Louisiana. Though Demoruelle, as president of the Louisiana Gamefowl Breeder's Association, had managed to fight off "the humaniacs" for years, the battle seemed to be turning against him: cockfighting was a misdemeanor in twenty-nine states by then and a felony in sixteen. Arizona, Louisiana, Missouri, New Mexico, and Oklahoma still allowed it, but in Louisiana some of the sport's biggest boosters had been swept out of office, and in Arizona and Missouri animal rights groups were gathering signatures for state referenda on the sport.

At the same time, however, cockfighting had never been more popular. There were at least five hundred thousand cockfighters in the United States, and owing to the immigration of Asians and Latin Americans, the number seemed to grow every year. There were three national cockfighting magazines, with names like *Feathered Warrior,* and there were cockpits in even the most tranquil, law-abiding communities. When I told the name of my home-town in Oklahoma to a criminologist who specializes in cockfighting, he laughed. "Oh yeah. I know that place. There's a pit just outside of city limits."

Part of me wanted to go back and see that side of small-town life, to let it rattle my memories like the false fronts of a Hollywood set. But another part, Demoruelle must have known, was just looking for a thrill. When he wasn't fighting chickens, Demoruelle worked in a drug rehab center, and he knew all about forbidden pleasure. "Be careful," he'd told me, only half-joking. "If you get into this thing, you might really like it. I can get somebody off drugs or alcohol better than I can off of chickens."

Had I come to Louisiana a century earlier, the warning would have been unnecessary: cockfighting, back then, was a perfectly honorable addiction. For hundreds of years, in England, it had been a sport of schoolboys, country squires, and kings. Henry II appointed a "Hereditary Marshal of the King's Birds" to take care of his gamecocks, and Henry VIII had a sumptuous cockpit built, encircled by coops belonging to the lords and princes of the realm. Even clergymen joined in the sport, holding cockfights at churches and, in one instance, awarding a prayer book to the winner.

In the New World, cockfighting would find an even better audience. Hungry for diversion, accustomed to the brutality of frontier life, the colonists took to blood sports with indiscriminate avidity. From the Dutch they learned gander pulling and snatch the rooster: you stretched a rope between two trees, hung a bird from it upside down, greased its head with lard, and tried to yank it off as you galloped underneath. From the British they learned everything else: bearbaiting, bullbaiting, wolfbaiting and ratbaiting, dogfighting and cat clubbing. When the first British colonists crossed the Atlantic to Jamestown, they brought fighting cocks with them.

Throughout the eighteenth century and most of the nineteenth, cockfights were a "fashionable amusement" in the North, a gentleman's pastime in the South. When cockfighting waned, in the late nineteenth century, it was out of concern less for the animals than for their audience. "By being spectators of these scenes of cruelty," one editorialist wrote, "the mind is imperceptibly hardened, and prepared for beholding, without disgust, scenes at which humanity must recoil." Others complained that blood sports sullied the national reputation or that Americans needed more fresh air, more group sports. "I am satisfied," Oliver Wendell Holmes Jr. wrote in the *Atlantic Monthly*, "that such a set of black-coated, stiff-jointed, soft-muscled, paste-complexioned youth as we can boast in our Atlantic cities never before sprang from the loins of Anglo-Saxon lineage." In 1867, New York, once famous for its cock-fights, became the first city to ban all blood sports. By the turn of the century, most of the country had followed suit.

These days, Holmes would be pleased to find, American pastimes are altogether more wholesome. But then, talking to cockfighters and sociologists, politicians and animal rights activists, I often felt as though there were two Americas: the one we legislate and the one just down the street, inside an abandoned warehouse or a neighbor's basement; the one on television and the one where Santeria rituals are performed and snakes handled, where moonshine glimmers and gamecocks fight.

As I drove past Maurice city limits, the night was nearly absolute. Only now and again did the lightning expose the skeletal landscape beyond my car's headlights. I was almost to the next town by the time a low, rickety building swam into view. Turning in, I saw a few dozen pickup trucks scattered across the mud and gravel, as if flung there by the storm. Off to the side, perched on the embankment, a portable sign flickered and buzzed in the rain: "R d R ost r."

Demoruelle was standing on the top rung of the bleachers across the room, arms folded over his beefy chest. Though

I'd only heard his voice, I picked him out of the crowd right away: silver hair, bullish features, melancholy eyes. Even at that distance he radiated a kind of sullen power, surveying the scene like Henry VIII himself, inspecting his troops.

A few weeks earlier a friend had sent me a farmer's cap with a gamecock stitched on it. Dressed in that hat, threadbare jeans, and a paint-spattered T-shirt, I thought I might slip into this scene unnoticed. But now, in the cool glare of fluorescent light, I could feel my joints stiffening and my eyes getting dodgy. I yanked off the hat and stuffed it in my back pocket.

I shouldn't have bothered. A few eyes locked onto mine as I came in, but when Demoruelle raised his hand and called me over, they drifted back to the fight. A moment later I was standing within his protective circle, shaking hands with two men who flanked him like lieutenants.

It was only then that I began to notice an odd thing: The Red Rooster was a fairly cozy place. Warm and brightly lit, high ceilinged and amiably sloppy in its construction, it seemed better suited to a Boy Scout jamboree than a cockfight. Over in the central tier of bleachers, a mother was tickling her toddler into ecstatic peals of laughter. A few rows down from her, a woman was nursing her baby within touching distance of the cocks, cupping her hands over the child's ears when their squabbling grew too loud. There were crawfish farmers in overalls and old-timers trading gossip, a woman hawking cockfighting T-shirts, and teenagers loitering in the aisles, flirting between sips of

Dr Pepper. It was two in the morning by now, and the Red Rooster looked as harmless as a bingo parlor.

Where were all the drunks and scofflaws, dope fiends and edgy hustlers? Where were the "vain, idle, and wanton minds," as William Penn wrote of cockfighters in 1682, who "gratify their own sensualities and raise the like wicked curiosity in others"? I felt like some South Sea explorer, making my way past spooky totems and grim palisades only to find a few peaceable villagers inside, eating roots and swatting at flies.

Cockfights, sociologist Clifton Bryant later told me, are like "a demographic frozen in time. The country changed, but they didn't." In 1974 and again in 1991 Bryant conducted a national survey of cockfighters. "They're mostly middle-class, from small towns or the country, more likely to be married, more likely to stay married, more likely to go to church, to be veterans," he said. "In fact, if you tried to go back and put together a typical American of the 1940s or 1950s, that would be a cockfighter."

Demoruelle's friends were typical cockers. Sonny Wabinga, to his left, was an army ranger on his third tour of duty. He had a moon-shaped face, wide, dreaming eyes, and a body as compact and lethal as any gamecock's. I'd once seen film clips of rangers on patrol so sleep deprived that they mistook tree branches for telephones and tried to call home. Surviving that sort of thing, and raising chickens, had given Sonny an oddly upbeat Darwinian outlook. "We've got the battle cross!" he told me later when I asked about his kids. "My wife's German and I'm Filipino, so my boys have the power and the speed." John Hickerson, to Demoruelle's right, was lanky and gray haired, with the loose, loquacious manner of a cowboy poet. He was from Michigan but had to come south to do his cockfighting. "Where I come from," he said, "it's a felony just to own cockfighting *equipment*."

They made a strange threesome, standing on that bench together, calling out their bets: a St. Bernard, a pit bull, and a bloodhound, all howling at the same moon. As Sonny put it, "If you have chickens, great, we can talk. Otherwise . . ." He smiled his strange smile and turned to the fight.

The cockpit rose from the center of the room like a minia-ture Thunderdome: a raised, octagonal cage, eight feet high and more than twenty feet across, surrounded on three sides by bleachers. The cage was meant to protect the audience, not to confine the birds, Demoruelle told me. "They say we're cruel, that we're making them fight. But I guarantee, if you put those chickens on either end of a football field, they'd crow and charge and end up fight-ing at the fifty-yard line." He spoke in a flat, faintly Gallic grumble, with flashes of local color but not much music—the voice of a man who'd never gotten used to defending himself. But I believed him. The two men entering the pit just then were cradling their birds like jars of nitroglyc-erin. The cocks' heads jutted from their owners' arms, wild eyed and quivering, desperate for release. From where I sat, they looked less like farm animals than birds of prey, barely a gene or two removed from gyrfalcons.

If cockfighting is still legal in Louisiana, if calling it immoral can still get your nose broken, this is why: Most blood sports are merely cruel; no bear or badger is baited willingly, and dogs rarely fight to the death. But chickens are different. Egg factories lose as much as 80 percent of their layers to cannibalism, unless they cut off the birds' beaks; and even on a free range, roosters are seized by blood lust now and then. "We call it comin' into their pride," one chicken breeder told me. "After a storm sometimes, you'll go out into the yard and it'll be littered with dead birds."

Still, a good gamecock is largely a human invention. Beginning three thousand years ago Asian cockfighters took the most unfriendly birds on the planet—jungle fowl, *Gallus gallus*—and proceeded to make them even meaner. They crossed them with Himalayan Bankivas for speed and flying kicks, and with Malay birds for stamina and wallop. They taught them to punch and feint and roll. They marched them through gamecock calisthenics, trimmed their wattles and combs, and stuffed red pepper up their anuses. A few thousand generations later this was the result: two birds programmed to kill each other, each a glimmering alloy of instinct, training, and breeding; each as exquisitely forged and lacquered as a Persian dagger.

Below us in the pit, the two men were standing side by side now, swaying toward each other like dancers bumping hips, holding their birds at waist level and letting them peck at each other. "Gamecocks are meant to fight," Demoruelle said finally. "Anyway, they were doing it when

Christ walked the earth, and he never said a word about it." Then he held up a roll of $10 bills and hollered, "Fifteen on the gray!"

Two rows down, a hairless old man with ears like flügelhorns turned and nodded.

Cockfighting, the *Kama Sutra* tells us, is one of sixty-four arts that every sophisticated woman should know. The rules are simple: Two roosters are matched by weight and given identical weapons (wild cocks use their bony back spurs to fight, but cockfighters cut these off and strap knives or gaffs, like curved ice picks, onto the stumps). Once armed, the birds are placed in a ring and launched at each other like self-guided missiles, exploding in a flurry of beaks and feet. The fight is no-holds-barred, but it's a controlled sort of mayhem, full of stops and starts and odd points of etiquette. When a cock stops fighting, the referee counts to twenty and then calls a twenty-second break. (In Bali they drop a pierced coconut into a pail full of water; when the coconut sinks, the birds fight.) If a cock goes down for three counts of ten and one count of twenty—or if he runs away or simply dies—the fight is over.

The whole thing can look a lot like a boxing match, but with one essential difference: Here, "gameness" matters more than landing punches. Your bird may be mortally wounded—he may even drop dead while chasing the other bird—but if he's the last one to show some fight, he wins.

Those are the basics, and any young adept could learn

them in a day. But in a cockpit everything bristles with hidden meanings. Before a cock steps into the pit, for instance, the owner may lick his bird's weapons, or the referee may swab them with wet cotton and squeeze the water into the bird's beak. Both acts have a certain strange sensuality, a symbolic aptness, but the reason behind them is prosaic: Some cockfighters have a fondness for poison. On the Venezuelan island of Margarita, for example, the locals like to coat their knives with stingray venom before a fight, or they may spread a foul-smelling ointment beneath the bird's wings—when the opponent runs to escape the odor, the referee will disqualify him. Some cockfighters have been known to poison the other bird's food or else reach over and snap a small bone in his back when no one's looking.

To protect their birds, most cockfighters keep them hidden until just before a fight and sometimes put them under guard. But nothing can thwart the most determined cheater. In one famous case in the Philippines, a local mayor was at a cockpit when his bird began to lose. Rather than wait for a decision, the man pulled out a forty-five and blew the other bird away. All bets are off, he declared, since the fight never officially ended. His armed bodyguards, it seems, agreed.

At the Red Rooster the betting was a tad more casual—Demoruelle was the highest roller here, and he was sticking to twenties—and cheating was a rarity. Once the voices died down, the handlers set their birds behind lines of white cornmeal, eight feet apart in the dirt, and waited for the referee to shout, "Pit!" To the left was a "gray," in cock-fighter's terms: a tall, lean bird with creamy hackles, gray green legs, and auburn wings. To the right was a stockier "red" with crimson hackles, yellow legs, and dark wings, his tail iridescent with ruby and turquoise. Like warrior monks, they'd both spent two days fasting, in darkness and isolation, preserving their strength and coiling their frustrations. Depending on their owners, they might be fueled by injections of testosterone, vitamin K to clot their wounds more quickly, and digitalis to speed up their already racing hearts. Now the bright lights and shouting faces were sending them into overdrive. "A bird should have a little nervousness to him right before a fight," Demoruelle said, watching them squirm, "a tremble, a twitch to him, like a boxer."

What came next, to my eyes, was an almost meaningless blur. To Demoruelle, though, it seemed to unspool in slow motion, every frame distinct: the referee's hoarse shout, unnaturally drawn out in the sudden quiet; the handlers watching his mouth, pulling back their hands as his lips pursed to speak; the cocks gathering themselves to leap, unfolding their wings as their necks strained upward; their legs driving toward each other, at the top of their arcs, talons spinning like teeth on a chain saw. And then the tumble, the scramble for footing, and another rattling clash.

"Oh. That was a good hit," Demoruelle said when the red connected with a kick to the head. "The gray's hurt." Although most hits with a gaff aren't fatal, a good cock can do plenty of damage with it. "Oh hell, yes," Hickerson said. "If you hold a plastic milk jug up to them, they can punch eight holes in it before you can pull it away."

It was all a matter of opposing forces, Demoruelle explained. "When a rooster has his wings back, he brings his feet forward and his tail down like an air brake." He raised his hands and made a few quick jabs in the air. In his twenties, he went on, he was expert at the martial arts—"135 pounds and greased-chicken-shit fast"—and I could almost see the young fighter moving beneath his middle-aged bulk. "When you're watching a cockfight," he said, "you're watching pure karate."

Both roosters were striking home now, spraying the referee with blood and bits of down. They hurled themselves at each other in weary spasms, biting each other's necks and windmilling their feet, until their gaffs snagged and the handlers rushed in to separate them. Demoruelle had hoped the gray would gradually gain the upper hand—green-legged birds have more "bottom" than yellow-legged birds, he explained—but that didn't seem to be happening. After five minutes of fighting, both birds were wounded, though the gray looked worse: one eye dim, the other destroyed, pale feathers matted with blood, beak trembling with every breath. Between rounds his handler held him close, swabbed his head with a wet sponge, and whispered to him urgently. When that didn't work, he put the bird's whole head in his mouth, sucked the blood from his throat, and then spat saliva into his beak. Little by little the gray revived, twisting his head to glare across the ring.

• • •

A rooster's rage is a simple thing. His courage is more complicated, and only certain weapons truly test it. So some cockfighters say, at least, and their choices divide them into camps as ardent and contrary as religious sects. In the Pacific Islands and most of North America, cockers prefer the clean, quick kill of a knife fight. (Filipinos, who like their knives especially long, sometimes forge them from armor-piercing bullets.) In India and Pakistan they breed huge, powerful Asile birds, wrap their feet to form miniature boxing gloves, and fight them for days on end. In the Caribbean and Louisiana, cockfighters tend to prefer gaffs, but even gaff fighters split into factions. Puerto Ricans cut off a bird's spur, scrape and varnish it until it's needle sharp, and strap it back on. Most Cajuns prefer their gaffs made of surgical steel, with a pointy end, but others favor a blunt gaff known as a peg awl.

Like a bullfight without a matador to finish the job, a gaff fight can go on for hours, the cocks goring each other again and again until one surrenders from blood loss, exhaustion, or fear. On this night the gray and the red were soon lying side by side in the sand, chests heaving. But even then the gaff fight was far from over. After a moment the gray staggered to his feet and flailed about blindly, delirious with anger and pain.

"Now, that's heart," Hickerson murmured next to me. I looked over at him: shoulders hunched tight, eyes squinting slightly, a twinge of pleasure to his lips. Like most gaff fighters, Hickerson was a throwback, a believer in the ancient, primal meaning of the fight. Gaff fights are long and brutal, he admitted, but the anguish was worth it, if only for that one moment when two hearts are put to the test. "At least with the gaffs, you're really only replacing their natural spurs," he told me later. "And a gaff fight doesn't rely on a few good kicks, it relies on this." He pointed to his chest.

Over on my other side, Demoruelle started to chuckle when the red dashed away from the gray. "Did you see that guy's butt start to pucker?" he said, jerking his head toward the red's embarrassed owner. Gamecocks, for Demoruelle, were more than symbols of courage, they were stand-ins for their owners ("detachable, self-operating penises," in anthropologist Clifford Geertz's great phrase, "ambulant genitals with a life of their own"). When they collided, he didn't just see windmilling feet; he saw converging plot-lines, intersecting histories: a whole community crystal-lized in an instant.

The gray eventually won his match and died in doing so. But the crowd barely seemed to notice. Most of them weren't here for the gambling, or the spectacle, or some ter-rible communion. They were here for something more mundane: a sense of community—one drawn all the tighter by secrecy and persecution. "So what do you think?" Hickerson turned and asked. I shrugged, feeling uncom-fortable. "If you think it's hard for you to watch, think how it is for me," he snapped. "I've raised chickens from birth, and they're damn cute when they're little." He paused for a second, then added: "I'm a compassionate man. I have a lot of crippled roosters running around my yard that I should have gotten rid of a long time ago. It's bad business, really." Then he turned to watch the next fight, the same hungry look in his eyes.

Driving around Louisiana with Demoruelle and talking to him over the following months, I began to fill in the outlines of his double life. It had started, oddly enough, overseas. Although he grew up in the Mecca of American cockfighting, he discovered the sport in 1960, as a nineteen-year-old navy corpsman stationed in the Philippines. "There was this beautiful girl," he told me. "I wanted to date her, but when I finally worked my way around to asking, she said I had to meet her family first." The visit wasn't quite what he had expected. "I walked out into the courtyard and there all the men were," he remembered, "a beer in one hand, a rooster in the other."

Ever since the 1930s, when some airmen from Texas had brought their gamecocks to Manila, American birds had earned a certain mystique among Filipinos. Compared with the gaudy local strutters, the "Texas" birds were homely as could be, but they were fast and gritty, and they whipped birds up and down the island. Soon rich Filipinos were flying to Georgia or Louisiana for fresh stock, and American cockfighting magazines were worth half a bottle of Scotch. "When these guys heard that I was from New Orleans, they just went nuts," Demoruelle remembers. "They wanted to know if I knew such and such—all famous cockfighters. But this was the first time I'd ever heard of it."

He forgot about the girl eventually, but he fell in love with the birds. "Gamecocks will fight for their territory and defend it to the end," he told me. "They have a spirit about them that's very gallant." American men have very little of that spirit left in them, he says, but wherever he was stationed, he found it among cockfighters. He could stand on a hill in Borneo and listen to a rooster crow on another hill. If it was a gamecock—and he could always tell—he would knock on its owner's door, knowing he would not be refused. "I used to go out to the jungle to see fights between operations in Vietnam," he said. "I never worried about being kidnapped by the Viet Cong, though I'm sure they were there. I was a cockfighter like them."

It was back in the States, between tours, that he had to be careful. During the day he worked at Camp Pendleton in California, but evenings and weekends he gave to game-cocks, training them in secret for airline executives and others with a taste for the transgressive. Real cockpits were hard to hide from the authorities, so he would set up in local hotels. "We used to go up the service elevators real early on Sunday morning," he remembered. "We'd fight them in a suite with a tarp thrown over the floor, a few inches of dirt on top. By noon we'd be out." Some say that cockfighting is more orderly where it's illegal, that codes of honor are more binding when they're a fighter's only guarantee. But Demoruelle disagrees. "In illegal states," he told me, "a lot of the people who do it are bad apples." Finally, in 1980, he went home to Louisiana, where he thought he had nothing to hide.

•   •   •

He lives and works back in Ville Platte now, not far from where he was born, and directs 156 employees at Evangeline Psychiatric Care. On the surface he could be a poster boy for the Louisiana tourist board: farm owner, Cajun song composer, consumer of vast racks of baby-back ribs—*"Laissez les bons temps roulez!"* Yet his double life continues. Demoruelle's posh suburban house feels barely inhabited: its oversize rooms echo beneath their cathedral ceilings, and his wife and children seem to float through them like extras on a set. "Cockfighting wives tend to be either supporters or tolerators," he says. "Mine's a tolerator—and not much of one at that."

Standing in his driveway one morning after a cockfight, I felt oddly at home. Surrounded by trim lawns and quiet neighbors, I could have been in any suburb in America. But fifteen minutes away, among rolling hills blanketed with pine, white oak, and magnolia trees, lay his game farm. And it was unlike anything I had ever seen.

When we stopped by, it was still early morning. A-frame huts, fashioned from cement or corrugated metal, marched across the weed-choked yard like miniature missile silos, their launching strips stretched out in front. Near each one a lone rooster kept vigil, often from the top of his hut, bound by one leg and screaming out challenges in ragged counterpoint to the others. "The crowing?" Demoruelle said. "That's all day. I don't even hear it anymore."

Although the farm looked like an army bivouac in miniature, these birds were more pampered than any soldier. The average broiler chicken lives for six weeks, wing to wing with tens of thousands of others. These game-cocks, by contrast, typically lived for two to three years. And they lived like pashas. Every day, from five-thirty in the morning till sundown, three employees tended to their every need. They fed, trained, and vaccinated the birds; trimmed their feathers and searched their droppings for worms; put them on trapezes to strengthen their legs and slowly stroked the twitches out of them. If the birds still went a little stir-crazy, the trainers might even bring around some nice, plump pullets to calm them down. "The prisons could learn something from us about conjugal visits," Demoruelle said. "The cocks won't fight as much if they get to see a female occasionally."

We walked around to his training room, crudely built of fiberglass and steel. An adolescent bird, or stag, begins his schooling at around nine months, Demoruelle said, when he grows his spurs and starts to show some fight. He grabbed a scruffy red bird from one of the cages lining the wall. "First we'll put sparring muffs on 'em and let 'em hit each other once or twice," he said. "Then, about six weeks before their first fight, we'll start taming 'em and workin' 'em on the bench." He walked over to a table the size of an executive's desk, padded with foam and carpet, and ran the stag through a series of drills. He shoved the stag back and forth between his hands, making him sidestep as delicately as a dancer, then pressed him down to strengthen his legs. He rolled him on his back ("that's not a natural position for a rooster") and flipped him backward through the air in a fluttering pinwheel. The bird landed deftly on his feet. "You can't train a rooster to fight," Demoruelle said. "But you're always looking for that little edge."

Every culture has its tricks for training cocks: In Louisiana old-timers feed their birds sulfur and gunpowder. In Martinique they rub them with rum and herbs every morning. In Brittany they give them a sugar cube soaked in cognac before a fight. In Argentina, when a bird is wounded, the gauchos will rub his genitals until he ejaculates; if the sperm contains blood, the bird is retired. The one tradition that seems to cut across cultures—the one downside of training from the cock's perspective—is celibacy. Aside from the occasional conjugal visit, sex is universally believed to sap a bird of its fighting spirit, especially before a fight. In the Philippines the mere touch of a menstruating woman is said to spell doom.

Demoruelle had his share of tricks—to increase his birds' appetite, for instance, he gave them a little strychnine, which acts as a stimulant in low doses. But for the most part he put his money on exercise, nutrition, and breeding (like most American cockfighters, he could talk genetics like a postdoc). If a stag showed promise, Demoruelle would start fighting him at around eighteen months and keep on doing it for another two or three years. Then, if the bird was very lucky and survived, he would come back to the farm to stud.

Demoruelle had a few chickens in his yard more than six years old. One of them, a dark red bird with green legs known as Crooked Toe, was nine years old and had won seven fights. "I'd love to have five hundred like him," Demoruelle said. "If I did, I'd have a Cadillac in every garage." As it was, he barely broke even, selling birds to Hawaiian businessmen at prices ranging from $75 to $500, though a champion bird could fetch up to $25,000. "If I quit everything else, I could make a living at it—an old man's living," he said, "but I wouldn't get fat."

John Hickerson, walking next to me as we entered the feed shed, glanced around with unvarnished envy. "You have to understand that for 90 percent of cockfighters it's a losing proposition," he said. He scooped up a handful of greenish feed—a mixture of Canadian peas, corn, milo, oats, red wheat, and soy beans—from a drum the size of an oil barrel. "Look at this: nutrients. Not cheap." (Last year alone, Demoruelle's three hundred gamecocks and chicks went through some seven thousand pounds of feed.) Hickerson went over to another drum, this one filled with a pink powder. "Oyster shell and granite for their beaks and gizzards. Not cheap." Then he swept his arm in a circle, pointing to the farm, training rooms, cages, and surgery rooms. "Look around here and see the amount of work that goes into this each and every day and you'll realize that the cockfight's only the culmination," he said. "It's only the last of things."

"And you can't be a drug addict and do that," Demoruelle added. "You can't be an alcoholic."

"You have to be a workaholic."

"That's right."

When I met Hickerson, he had left behind his family,

his job, and old roots in Michigan just to live in a house next to Demoruelle's farm and raise birds. More than for any of the others, cockfighting was a way of life for him— one he had been denied up north. "We are the keepers of the chicken's genetic pool," he declared as we climbed in the van and headed for another cockpit. "We can't afford to lose this stock." Wabinga nodded quietly in the front seat. "We are the keepers of the flame."

Outside our windows, beneath a lowering sky, the swamp forest was luminous green, its trunks and branches still black from recent rain. Hickerson popped in a tape by Woody Guthrie and told me about the Calumet copper strike of 1913. When the next song came on, he stopped in midsentence and began to sing along, half smiling at the melodrama of it:

> *I ain't got no home, I'm just rambling 'round*
> *Just a wand'rin' worker, I go from town to town*
> *The police make it hard wherever I may go*
> *And I ain't got no home in this world anymore*

If ever there was a home for cockfighters, the cockpit we were visiting was it. Known as Sunrise, it was tucked along the border between Louisiana and Mississippi and drew cockfighters from the entire region. Other pits were larger: Sunset, in western Louisiana, had air-conditioning, plush seats, and a history of hosting the most famous cockfighters in the country; Texoma, on the southern Oklahoma border, had given away $150,000 at a single fight the previous year, along with a new truck for the "Cock of the Year." But as a symbol of big-time cockfighting—of what the sport might look like if it were widely accepted—Sunrise would do.

"From the sand lots of Florida to the bayous of Louisiana to the cotton rows of Mississippi and Georgia," Hickerson was saying as we passed some trailers in the parking lot, "these are some well-traveled chickens." Those at the Red Rooster, Demoruelle added, were a kind of avian underclass, poorly conditioned and sloppy in their attacks. These birds were in a different league. Each owner had paid $300 for the right to enter six of them in the derby. Because 150 owners were signed up in all, that came to nine hundred chickens fighting for one $45,000 pot. "That guy over there?" Demoruelle said, pointing to a middle-aged man in jeans and a sport shirt. "He's the largest fish wholesaler in Mississippi."

The whole scene reminded me of Samuel Pepys's description of a cockfight in seventeenth-century London: "But Lord! to see the strange variety of people, from Parliament . . . to the poorest 'prentices, bakers, brewers, butchers, dairymen, and what not; and all these fellows one with another cursing and betting." And yet I kept coming back to those nine hundred chickens. A cockfight, as I understood it, was a single combat between lone fighters. But this sounded more like a mass slaughter, a battle royal. True, not all nine hundred birds would fight: a cockfighter would stay in the contest only so long as his birds were undefeated. (In Martinique the list of matched roosters is called a *tableau de mariage*.) Still, a good half of the birds would enter the pit tonight, and half of them might die.

Sunrise, at first glance, hardly seemed the place for such epic carnage. Slapped together of corrugated steel, painted sky blue, and thrust into a patch of scrub oak, it had an almost deliberate impermanence about it, as if it could be disassembled with a moment's warning and spirited into the woods. As we shouldered our way through the front door, one of the men we passed shook his head and said, "It's a madhouse in there. You can't even get a seat." But we pushed ahead anyway, past concession stands, surgery rooms, and bloody drag pits where the endgames of the longest fights were played out, past walls of raw particle-board and through leaning, unsquare spaces. Though we never descended any stairs, we seemed to be tunneling underground, the heat pipes like earthworms glistening in the walls. When a long corridor opened at last onto the cockpit, it felt like an animal's burrow, spacious yet claus-trophobic.

The bleachers rose in a steep-sided bowl around us, two stories high and bristling with spectators. This was no neighborhood social club, like the Red Rooster. These people had paid $16 a seat and traveled hundreds of miles to be here, and they focused on the pit below with clenched jaws. There was a sense of volatility in the air, of minds at the edge of ignition, and I kept imagining the chaos if a grease fire erupted in the concession stand and we had to claw our way back through those tunnels.

The pit itself, by contrast, was a model of neatness and

grim good order. Most of the birds wore one-inch Spanish knives or three-inch Filipino knives on their heels, and their bouts were often over within seconds. A Filipino knife, driven by a powerful gamecock, can split a bird's head in a single stroke, and Spanish knives are nearly as deadly. ("I know a thoracic surgeon who handles his own chickens in the ring," Hickerson had said on the ride over. "Now, how can you be that smart and that dumb at the same time?") The referee would cry, "Handle!," the birds would flurry in the air a few times, and then one or both of them would lie dead. No bludgeoning brawl, no show of courage or fear, surprisingly little blood.

Should cockfighting ever make it onto *ABC's Wide World of Sports*, I thought, this was how it would be: a little trash talking between the handlers, a little fancy footwork by the birds, and then the knockout blow. Watching a gaff fight required a nearly religious devotion, a hard slog toward an uneasy enlightenment. But a knife fight offered instant gratification. It was all highlight film and no story. Throw in a few bets, to give yourself a stake in the outcome, and you had the ultimate in guilty pleasures.

Now I could see why Demoruelle had thought cockfighting might seduce me. If he preferred knives to gaffs, it was partly because the fights were shorter and they gave him more chances to gamble. But part of him, too, had come here to see something killed. "Man is born a warrior," he told me later, "and the more we constrict his natural tendency to hunt and to kill, the crazier the world seems to become." After ten or fifteen bouts, though, Hickerson began to fidget. "Knives are going to kill this sport," he muttered. These cocks weren't bred for courage, they were bred for speed and power. Knife fights were mostly about luck and getting in the first punch, Hickerson said. Knife fights were a crapshoot.

As for the crowd, a crapshoot was exactly what it wanted. Whenever a gaff fight began, people's attention went slack, and they drifted into small talk. But as soon as two knife fighters came out, they seemed to hold their breath. Soon the bets began to ring out, shyly at first, then with more urgency as some failed to find takers: "Ten on the red!" "I'll take twenty on the white shirt's bird!" A few rows over, a man handed some bills to his skinny boy and whispered instructions in his ear. The boy jumped on his seat, screwed up his face, and screamed an octave above the rest of the crowd: "Twenty on the red! Twenty on the red!"

This was where things got interesting at many Asian cockpits. Small-time fights were merely about money, but bigger ones were about status and kinship—you always bet on your kin group's cock, and you did so for prestige, not winnings. But the bets at Sunrise, unlike those at the Red Rooster, were as impersonal as coins tossed into a slot machine—six roosters in a row and you hit a jackpot. Hickerson, for his part, hardly bothered to assess the birds. When knife fighters came into the pit, he almost always stood up and yelled, "Twenty-five–twenty! Twenty-five–twenty!" meaning, "You choose the bird, but I get twenty-five dollars if mine wins, and you get twenty if yours wins." As long as a cockfight is just a game of chance, he said, you might as well play the odds.

The fights would go on like this till dawn—there were a lot of chickens to get through. At one point I stepped into the bathroom and found a referee scrubbing the blood from his face while a line formed behind him. He kept squinting into the mirror, face sopping wet, and then bending down to scrub some more. Finally he glanced at my reflection and laughed.

"Stuff still isn't comin' off!"

"Must get pretty thick by the end of the night."

"Heck, yeah, I'll be covered in it head to foot. These white stripes won't be white no more."

The owners were honor bound to stay till the end, but we were only spectators, so we slipped out before midnight. By then there were dead cocks lying in the hallways and heaped in trash barrels, their bodies twisted and brittle, their once-brilliant feathers dimmed by dried blood. "We used to eat the losers after a fight," Demoruelle said in passing, "but the dewormer some people use now makes the meat carcinogenic."

Surreal as it was, the scene made a certain sense. At pits like Sunrise, cockfighting was big business—less folk tradition than mass-market entertainment—and the audiences were hardly different from those at riverboat casinos in Baton Rouge. The cocks we had seen, impeccably trained though they were, had lost much of their glamour to commerce. Elsewhere they might be symbols of sin or sexuality, courage or betrayal, stand-ins for their owners or for the devil himself. But at Sunrise a gamecock was just another form of disposable culture.

In Bali, Clifford Geertz one wrote, a cockfight is a story that people tell themselves about themselves. For more than two centuries the same was true in this country. Long before the Revolution, George Washington loved a cockfight for the spirit of anarchy that it embodied, and he once invited Thomas Jefferson to Mount Vernon to see his "yellow pile" gamecocks. By the 1830s Andrew Jackson was fighting cocks on the White House carpet, and cockfighting was a national pastime—an embodiment of the country's new arrogance. Three decades after that, Abraham Lincoln, a former cockfighting referee, saw something darker and more ambivalent in it: "As long as the Almighty permits intelligent men, created in His image and likeness, to fight in public and kill each other while the world looks on approvingly," he is reported to have said, "it is not for me to deprive the chicken of the same privilege."

But nowadays blood sports are a story we would rather forget. In the fall of 1998 volunteers with anticockfighting groups in Missouri and Arizona managed to gather 136,000 and 189,000 signatures, respectively, forcing state referenda on the sport. In early polls, 88 percent of Missourians said they were against cockfighting, and 87 percent of Arizonians, but in the privacy of the voting booth, many must have had second thoughts: only 63 percent voted against the sport in Missouri and 68 percent in Arizona. Still, today, hosting a cockfight is illegal in both states, and as I write, Oklahomans are petitioning for a referendum of their own.

Only in Louisiana, where the sport once seemed most vulnerable, do cockfighters feel a measure of security. Twenty years ago, when Louisiana passed a new set of animal rights laws, cockfighters had to dabble in taxonomy to avoid them: chickens are not animals, they declared in an amendment pushed through at the eleventh hour; they are birds. Since then, cockfighting has never been seriously threatened: the anticockfighting bill that Demoruelle feared never even made it past committee. The next year, when an anticockfighting amendment reached the floor of the house, it was defeated by a vote of 22 to 5.

Nevertheless, most observers say that legal cockfighting will be gone within the next ten years. Even in Louisiana, a single election and a new crop of legislators could consign cockfighting to the chopping block. "I think the forces of modernity and New South boosterism are just going to do it in," says Frederick Hawley, a criminologist at Western Carolina University who wrote his Ph.D. thesis on cockfighting. "And if I'm wrong now, it won't be long before I'm right."

Animal activists will tell you this fight is all about morality. Cockfighters will tell you it's about individual liberty. Most legislators, if you catch them in an honest moment, will tell you it's about economics—about the South reinventing itself to attract investors. But mostly it's a matter of demographics: the more urban an area is, the more likely it is to ban the sport. And though country values have given way to city values, cockpits to Kentucky Fried Chicken, the sum total of bloodshed has hardly been diminished, only swept out of sight.

Not long after I left Louisiana, I went to visit a chicken factory an hour south of Little Rock, Arkansas. One of forty-one "vertically integrated" operations owned by Tyson Foods, this one took in 1.3 million birds a week and spat out an endless stream of chicken parts and precooked wings. A mill, a hatchery, and dozens of feed sheds lay around it like spokes on a wheel, and most of the work was automated (when a chicken laid an egg, a tiny conveyor belt beneath the roost trundled the egg off for incubation). Thanks to such efficiencies, American factories slaughter some seven billion chickens a year, and chicken meat, once more expensive than filet mignon, has become blandly ubiquitous—poor man's fare. Breeders, meanwhile, keep picking up the pace: a century ago a broiler needed sixteen weeks to reach two pounds; today they reach four pounds in six weeks.

My guide at the factory, a man named Archie Schaffer III, was a rare believer in full disclosure (the public relations people at Perdue wouldn't let me near their factory). "Nobody has any idea in America where their food comes from," he told me, "and the reason is people like me." Schaffer was more than happy to show me the hatchery, where eighty-five thousand chicks tumble down chutes every hour, like cotton balls at a cotton ball factory; the vast hangars where the chicks grow into broilers; the trucks that haul the broilers to the factory seven thousand at a time. Yet when I asked to see the killing floor, he nearly refused.

I could see why. If a broiler's life sometimes looked like a trip to the amusement park—careening up and down conveyor belts, standing in crowds, watching gizmos pop and whir—this was the nightmarish finale, the tunnel of fear. After their wild ride in the truck, the birds were dropped onto a broad belt that rolled into the dark mouth of the factory. Inside, most of the room was bathed in black light—it calms the birds down, I was told—and the stench of spilled intestines was overwhelming. Assaulted by screaming machinery and Top 40 radio, the birds were jerked from the belt by a row of eight workers, wearing black goggles and industrial tunics, and hung by their feet from a running chain overhead. "The live hang job is about the nastiest job in the business," Schaffer shouted. "But a lot of people seem to like it."

Next door was a room of raw concrete, lit like an old Dutch painting, with a bright, bloody trough snaking along the wall. "First we stun 'em over here," Schaffer explained, pointing to the first of two mechanical bottlenecks through which the chickens' heads had to pass. "Then we slice 'em with a rotary saw over there." Most of the birds stretched their necks obediently. But every so often one would crane his head to see where he was going—and inadvertently avoid the saw. When that happened, a nearby attendant, sitting on a stool, would reach over and slit the rubbernecker's throat.

These are things we don't want to know, that we zone

away beyond city limits, and most meat producers are happy to oblige us. Every year we eat more chicken meat and see less and less of the living birds, and this strikes us as right and normal. Animal rights activists, of course, condemn poultry factories as well as cockfighting, but most of us aren't that consistent. We're appalled at blood sports, yet when activists picket slaughterhouses or send lurid photos to the media, we resent them, deem them unrealistic. Like cockfighters, they threaten a cherished illusion: that society, in growing up, has lost its taste for blood.

When I was nine years old, and the only blood sports I knew were those my brother had invented, my family rented a house with some chickens in the backyard. It was a crumbling old adobe in a quiet part of Pasadena, where my father would do research in the summer, and the chickens seemed to have been there forever. After a while I got used to their sudden flights of rage when I fed them, their strange, hysterical secrets. But I never got used to the dawn. In suburbia, more than most places, a cock's crow can sound like the end of the world.

One afternoon, when my mother answered a knock on the door, she found a policeman standing awkwardly on our stoop. "It's about your rooster, ma'am," he said.

My mother stared at him blankly for a moment. Then, with a twitch of a smile, she asked: "What's he done?"

Our bird was arrested for disturbing the peace. After the Humane Society dragged him away—kicking and screaming as only a chicken can—we never saw him again. Looking back, we always laughed at my mom's reply and at the rooster in the paddy wagon. But the funniest part, we thought, was the fact that we had a suburban chicken coop in the first place. Now I think that the joke was on us. We thought of our neighborhood as an ideal of sorts, clean and safe and free of life's old brutality. But we lived in a glass bubble, one so fragile a rooster's call could shatter it.

These days the stories we tell ourselves about ourselves grow ever more polished and predictable. We play out our primal urges on the Internet, in cineplexes, or in therapy rather than in the town square at midday. Yet cockfighters still stir in the dark, incubated by secrecy and the heat of resentment. Judging from the pits I visited, the twilight suits them best. "You can't stop us," Demoruelle says. "We have more gamecocks being fought this year than we've had in the history of this country." If they jangle a few nerves, so be it: disturbing the peace is a rooster's business.

Moonshine Sonata

SMITH MOUNTAIN LAKE lies in the foothills of the Blue Ridge Mountains of eastern Virginia, an hour's winding, tumbling drive from convenience store or neon sign, fast-food joint or freeway. On still summer days millworkers and tobacco farmers from Roanoke and Danville like to go there with their ice chests and portable TVs, pitch their tents among the dogwood and magnolia, and imagine what it might have been like to carve a living from country so rough, to raise a family and erect a cabin and hunt for food among the parsimonious trees. At the lake's visitor center, perched on its shores, they can see sepia photographs of their ancestors and a few examples of the tools they used, now weathered and gray. There is a wooden scythe and a handmade lathe, a corn cutter, a rusted sausage stuffer, and a wooden trap for catching small mammals. And over in the corner, seemingly more ancient and obsolete than all the rest, stands a small still used for making moonshine.

Press a button on the oak barrel, cup the old-fashioned ear horn to your head, and you'll hear a running stream and a lazy banjo, footsteps splashing stealthily through a swamp, and waterbirds squawking at their approach. A voice will tell you that the dictionary defines moonshine as illegally distilled whiskey and that it earned that name because it was often made under cover of night. You'll learn that moonshine is made from a mash of grain, yeast, sugar, and water, that this mash is fermented and boiled, and that the alcoholic fumes are cooled to liquid in a long, twisted copper pipe known as a worm. You'll learn that making moonshine is an ancient, exacting craft, but it was outlawed in 1791, when the federal government under George Washington imposed a tax on all liquor.

Most of what you'll hear is common knowledge, long ago passed into folk tales and history books. But if you had come to that same place one winter morning in 1993, equipped with a high-powered telescope, you might have gotten a more up-to-date education. Training your scope across the lake's clear waters, toward a steep hill that looms beyond the southeastern shore, you would have made out seven figures huddled in the snow, barely discernible in their camouflage parkas, patiently watching a long silver shed below them.

Just a few days before, on Christmas Eve morning, J. E. Calhoun, then a special agent with the county sheriff's department, had gotten a call from a local farmer. "It sure smells sweet down here," the man had said. "I ain't never been around no liquor still before, but if I had, I'd swear it would smell like that." When Calhoun came around later that day, he caught the scent right away: a heady, yeasty presence in the air, as if every cook in the neighborhood had decided to bake bread at the same time. The smell had a hint of malt to it, like a strong beer, and just a trace of bitterness—of something slightly rotten at its core. Somewhere close by, it told him, some mash had just finished fermenting and bootleggers were running their still.

For the next two weeks Calhoun spent nearly every night on that hillside, sipping coffee and soup from thermoses and scanning the valley with binoculars. Because bootlegging is a tax violation rather than a criminal offense, he was joined by four revenue agents with the Virginia Alcohol Beverage Control Board as well as a local sheriff. "The still was runnin' that first afternoon," Calhoun says. "But before we could make a move on it, they was shuttin' down." When the search warrant was finally ready, and the agents came rushing down the hillside with their walkie-talkies and guns at the ready, the moonshiners had taken off. Yet what Calhoun found left him dumbfounded.

Inside the forty-five-by-ninety-foot warehouse were thirty-six 800-gallon pots, each nearly filled to the brim with fermenting mash. There was so much mash that the smell had carried through six inches of insulation and tar paper; so much mash that Calhoun and the others were afraid that dumping it might disturb the pH balance of the lake. (In the end, they pumped it out and shipped it to a water-treatment plant.) Four submersible pumps ran water to the still from a nearby pond, stacks of sugar and yeast fifteen feet high kept the fermenting mash well fed, and bales of shrink-wrapped gallon milk jugs stood ready for transport. Altogether, the setup was capable of producing some four thousand gallons of whiskey every seven days—more than enough to keep a small city inebriated.

The Smith Mountain bust was the single largest in Virginia history, yet its details feel somehow anachronistic, like the herky-jerky footage from an old newsreel. In weeks of traveling through the South researching moonshine, I was told again and again that moonshining is a dying art, too demanding and unprofitable for modern criminal tastes. Federal statistics bore this out: In 1970 the Bureau of Alcohol, Tobacco, and Firearms seized 5,228 stills and 86,416 gallons of liquor; by 1996 those numbers had dropped to a single still, and it was bone dry. "It used to be our forte, sitting on stills," a publicity officer for the bureau told me, "but by the time I got here it was long gone." The note of nostalgia in his voice was unmistakable.

When I talked to local revenue agents, though, I got a very different story. There may be more moonshine in circulation today than thirty years ago, they said; the feds simply ignore it in favor of the war on drugs and terrorists. Gone are the Eliot Nesses, busting up stills with religious zeal; in their place are working-class detectives on tight budgets, squeezing in a few moonshine raids now and then between shipments of cocaine. Even so, between 1985 and 1998 agents in six Virginia counties alone seized 538 stills. "People keep saying that the moonshiners have gone, but we keep finding more stills," one agent told me. "I guess if no one prosecuted murderers, they wouldn't exist, either—there'd just be a bunch of dead people lying around."

•   •   •

It was neither a revenue agent nor a publicity officer who took me to see the site of the Smith Mountain still, but a local moonshiner I'll call Jim Stoat. We drove there on a dreary October morning, when the leaves of the surrounding forest were as faded and lifeless as spent mash, but to Jim the place still held a glamorous glow. Parked at the foot of the mountain, we looked up at the slope where the agents had done their stakeout. A tall wrought-iron gate, surmounted by gilded eagles, fronted the property, a white gazebo stood in the middle distance, and the silver shed glimmered beyond it. Everything about the place was contrary to the old moonshiner's creed, which preaches mobility over permanence, humility over ostentation, yet Jim couldn't help but admire its scale, its chutzpah. The shed was snugly built, there was enough water to supply a hundred distilleries, and the owner bought his grain from a hog farmer who lived down the road. "Thirty-six pots," Jim said, pausing to do the math in his head. "That's fifteen thousand pounds of sugar alone." Standing there gazing at the golden eagles, he looked like a small boy at the gates of Xanadu, dreaming of his own mansion on a hill.

In most ways Jim ran his business like any other young entrepreneur. He kept track of the moonshine market and adjusted his prices accordingly, monitored product quality and looked for ways to streamline production. While others scanned the *Wall Street Journal,* he kept a file of clippings from local papers, noting which colleagues had been busted, what kinds of sentences they were given, the size of their stills, and where they were established. He knew which cars the local agents drove and kept track of their movements whenever he was running a still.

The differences were largely a matter of style and degree of risk. Instead of three-piece suits, Jim favored T-shirts and baseball caps; instead of lawyers, he tended to back up his deals with firearms. Rolling around on the floor of his car were two boxes of hollow-point .357 cartridges for his snub-nosed Smith & Wesson revolver, along with copies of *Guns and Ammo* and *Shooting* magazine. Propped next to his seat, like a second gearshift, was the tarnished bronze handle of a long, medieval-looking dagger. "They call this an Arkansas toothpick," he told me as we drove. It was meant for whacking, not stabbing, he added reassuringly, but I knew that this part of Virginia had had its share of moonshine-related killings. "They have got to be the most paranoid people in the world," one agent told me. "They're always thinking that somebody told on them, and that fuels the cycle of violence." Only a few months earlier, two bootleggers from the same family had shot a third to death; two years before that, Jim's own mentor had been gunned down in his car.

These facts made me nervous, but not nearly as nervous as I made Jim. Under other circumstances, I think, we might have taken an instinctive liking to each other. We were both in our early thirties and both had three-year-old boys. Jim liked to talk, I liked to listen, and we both had a love for the detailed inner workings of a craft and a business like moonshine. Still, the fact was that he was a felon, in a business rife with undercover agents. And though I had no intention of giving him away, I was dividing my time between him and the revenue agents bent on hunting him down. He was savvy enough to suspect as much—he'd even given me the local sheriff's name, in case I wanted to interview him—but the situation made him justifiably uneasy. "Never sell to someone you don't know," was the first rule of moonshining. Or as Jim's father, a moonshiner himself, put it: "Dealin' with strangers is like bitin' a persimmon. If the fruit ain't ripe, it'll turn your mouth inside out."

I first met Jim at a "moonshiners' reunion" in northwestern South Carolina, in an area known as Dark Corners. We had both heard of the event through the Internet, while doing random searches for the keyword "moonshine," and had both come with a certain skepticism. The organizer, a grizzled hippie musician named Barney Barnwell, claimed to descend from a long line of moonshiners, and he promised that plenty of ex-moonshiners would be in attendance. But at first glance the moonshining theme seemed largely a marketing ploy. There were crafts booths and barbecue stands, bluegrass concerts and tours of defunct stills. Though Dark Corners, with its dense forests and secret glens, was once a notorious haven for bootleggers, these days most people made their living from the BMW plant in Greenville.

At night, when the last band left the stage, we'd retire to campfires in the woods, among the creepers and crickets and trees hung with Confederate flags. The guitars and mandolins would chime on till morning, and people would pass around the old stories—of stills hidden behind false walls and under cemeteries, of car chases through the ivy-hung Carolina hills, of judges going home from court half-drunk on "corn squeezin's." But the heroes were invariably neighbors, or relatives, or men long dead, and there was more marijuana smoke in the air than illegal spirits. When I asked one supposed bootlegger for a taste of his wares, he gave me a half gallon of pickled peaches instead.

Only late in the reunion did I get stronger proof of a living tradition. Up on stage, Barnwell's heavy-metal bluegrass group, The Plum Hollow Band, was finishing its last set. "I used to hate my daddy's music," he said before launching into a medley of "Rocky Top" and a Black Sabbath song, "but now I think we have some common ground." When it was over, and the crowd was whooping and laughing and lifting its lighters in mock tribute, he went back to the mike and announced an impromptu "'shine-tasting" contest. "It's illegal as hell," he said. "But what are they gonna do, arrest five hundred of us?"

It was as if some silent code had been broken. Within a matter of minutes mason jars were making their way through the crowd from every corner: some filled with moonshine clear as water, others afloat with strawberries, blackberries, scuppernong grapes, and native peaches. Barnwell entered a little white lightning, a little peach, and a little wild muscadine. Another contestant walked past me balancing half-gallon jars on each shoulder. "I've got to mail these to California tomorrow," he said, "but I might as well have a taste first."

Word had gotten around, over the previous few days, that a clan of bootleggers had come down from Franklin County, Virginia, and that moonshine was still serious business up there. To guard against charges of nepotism, and to give the contest a somewhat cosmopolitan flavor, Barney chose the patriarch of their clan, Jim's father, Willard, as the judge. (I've changed the names of Jim's family members, as well as some identifying details about them.) Willard was a short, wizened septuagenarian, with gnarled hands and lidless, protruding eyes. As he lifted each entry from a row of numbered Dixie cups, his eyebrows would arch and his eyes would go wide. "Ah-ooooh," he'd say, smacking his lips. In the end he declared Barnwell's white lightning the best straight moonshine and Barnwell's cousin's peach the best of the fruits.

Afterward, I cornered the old judge, hoping that the tasting might have loosened his tongue. At first I found him more than accommodating. He told me how to make peach brandy and how to test moonshine for quality: "Strike a match to it and look at the flame: if it's blue, it's all right, but if it's yellow . . ." He told me that homemade liquor has fewer chemicals than store-bought, that the body naturally manufactures a quart of alcohol every day, and that moonshine could help you pass a kidney stone. But when I asked him about his own stills, he drew back into his shell like a snapping turtle. "I never have made any liquor," he said, glaring at me from beneath the shadow of his cap. "My mama used to give it to me for the whoopin' cough, with a spoonful of sugar, but that's about all."

I might have given up then, if Jim hadn't suddenly appeared, bobbing his son on his knee. He'd come to Dark Corners to check out the competition, he said, and he wasn't too impressed. The few active moonshiners around were mostly home brewers, and after days of their tall tales and empty boasts, Jim positively fidgeted with the need to set the record straight. Every time the old man tried to duck a question, Jim would jump in with the answer: market prices, manufacturing methods, preferred means of camouflage. "This ain't nothin'," he said, glancing at the two rusted stills on display beside us. "This ain't nothin'."

In the background I could hear four singers patiently build their harmonies, while a fiddle and banjo tripped madly along behind:

> Now pour a glass of 'shine to fortify your soul.
> We'll talk about the world
> and the friends we used to know.
> Well, I see a stream of girls
> who'll put me on the floor.
> The game is nearly over, the hounds are at my door.

Franklin County, Virginia, unlike most places renowned for their moonshine, seems at first glance to have nothing to hide. Compared to the huddled hills of Dark Corners, the landscape here is open armed and welcoming, lush with tobacco and spreading oaks and braided by slow-moving streams. In autumn the county roads burrow through the forests like children in a leaf pile, leaping up into sunlight on the other side; the mountains hover above the horizon in pale blue outline, and curing barns keep watch from every hillside, their timbers warped and cracked and mortared with red earth. It's a landscape as lovely as it is innocuous—one that's easy to hurtle past as you head toward some more dramatic vista—and the locals like it that way.

The town of Zenith, where Jim lives with his wife, Kelly, and his boy, Audie, is hardly less humble, its name notwithstanding. Whether it's really a town or just a mini-mart at a fork in the road is a matter of some local debate. Maps don't show it, phone operators don't list it, and letters come addressed to a larger town, twenty-five miles to the west. The surrounding area is so sparsely inhabited, and so many turns from a well-traveled highway, that people invariably wave to every passing car—not just to be friendly, but because they assume that they know the driver.

Jim's double-wide mobile home sits about five miles from the minimart, a stone's throw from a Presbyterian church. Unlike his neighbors' houses, it's placed far back from the road, screened from view by a row of white pines and guarded by a myopic, mean-spirited dog named Goober. From his front window you can see his father's house—a yellow, three-story structure slightly a-kilter from when it was moved from beside the church—and through his back window you can see the remains of the log cabin where his mother was raised. For at least six generations, he says, his father's people have lived within thirty miles of this place, marrying next-door neighbors or cousins as often as not. And though, for a time, Jim wanted nothing more than to get away from Zenith, he eventually married the girl next door as well.

Jim's people have been making liquor since as far back as Willard's limited recall will allow, and the outline of their history is roughly that of all moonshining in America. There were three Scotch-Irish brothers, family legend has it, who came first to Pennsylvania and then moved south to Virginia, making whiskey as they went. Just when they arrived is unclear, but they most likely belonged to the great wave of Scotch-Irish settlers that flowed down the Great Philadelphia Wagon Road between the 1730s and the 1770s. Known as Ulstermen, after the part of Northern Ireland from which they hailed, they had come to America fleeing smallpox, sheep rot, drought, and winter fevers, but especially repressive land policies. Tireless farmers, they had introduced the potato to Ireland and turned miles of bog into productive farms, only to have their rents doubled or tripled when the leases ran out. Great lovers of "ardent spirits," they had refined the arts of Scottish and Irish whiskey making, only to have a crushing excise tax placed upon their wares. Once in America, they were hungry for their own land and positively allergic to government. They gravitated toward the wildest, roughest sections of land, tamed them as they had the Irish bogs, and kept their own counsel. When Pennsylvania grew more crowded and less welcoming, they headed south across the Susquehanna

River, along the Alleghenies, and down the Shenandoah Valley, dropping off Jim's ancestors along the way, presumably, before moving on to the Carolinas.

American history, some say, could be written in terms of whiskey as well as wars and wandering tribes, and the result might say more about the American character—about the perennial battle between liberty and the rule of law. Since the beginning, liquor making was an essential frontier enterprise, whether in the Caribbean, where rum fueled the economy, or in the early colonies, where newcomers were advised to distill liquor until their stomachs got used to the water. To a farmer, a still was the ideal instrument for concentrating profits: a horse could carry only four bushels of corn at a time, but it could carry twenty-four bushels in liquid form. And to every colonist alcohol was far more than a means of getting drunk. It was a disinfectant, a tranquilizer, and a medicine for countless ills. It was an anesthetic, a solvent, and an admirably stable unit of currency.

No wonder, then, that the liquor tax of 1791 provoked the first armed revolt in the young country's history. (Alexander Hamilton, the architect of the tax, seems to have intended just such a reaction, if only to give the government a chance to prove its mettle.) Though the Whiskey Rebellion was soon lost, the same battle would be fought again and again on a lesser scale. Thomas Jefferson repealed the tax in 1802, bringing on a brief golden age for small distilleries, but Abraham Lincoln reimposed it in 1862 to raise money for the Civil War. That act also created the Internal Revenue Service, with whom moonshiners have been at war ever since.

In his 1974 book, *Mountain Spirits,* writer Joseph Dabney pegged Dark Corners, Dawson County, Georgia; Cocke County, Tennessee; and Wilkes County, North Carolina, as the historic moonshine centers. But in the past twenty-five years that geography has shifted. While some areas have stepped up production, others have switched to more profitable poisons. When Barnwell went to jail in South Carolina in the 1970s, it wasn't for making moonshine, like his grandfather, but for growing marijuana. (After that, he grew hallucinogenic mushrooms in the same mason jars his grandfather used for moonshine.) When I interviewed the grandson of Dawson County's most famous bootlegger, he was in county jail for possessing methamphetamine with intent to sell.

"I kind of went from moonshine to marijuana to crank," he explained one morning, sitting across from me at the police station, wearing bright orange coveralls from his work-release program. "When I was a kid, I used to tote sugar for my grandpa's still. Then I ran the ground crew for my dad, when he'd fly in his crop from Honduras—two-hundred-pound bales of marijuana comin' out of the sky, right here in the foothills of Dawsonville." Methamphetamine, or crank, was now the drug of choice in Dawson County, he said, and so many people were making it that the quality was getting dicey. "I guess you could say liquor was the root of everything."

Franklin County may be the last of the old watering

holes that hasn't gone dry. During the 1930s nine out of ten people in the county had some connection to illicit alcohol, a federal commission reported, and author Sherwood Anderson based a short story on a famous moonshine conspiracy there. Now local moonshiners have taken the lessons of that era to heart, preselling their liquor to networks of shot houses, mass-producing it, and keeping the quality just high enough that it won't kill people. Though the landscape may not lend itself to secreting stills and running from revenuers, major moonshine markets encircle it like spigots on a keg: Philadelphia to the north; Washington and Richmond to the east; Raleigh, Greensboro, and Charlotte to the south; Charleston to the west—most of them less than three hours away. Moonshiners in Virginia produce close to a million gallons a year, the lion's share of it in Franklin County. Yet according to the Virginia Alcohol Beverage Control Board, 60 percent of local moonshine is sold out of state, mostly to inner-city blacks, and almost none of it is sold within the county. Homemade liquor, these days, is meant mostly for strangers.

Jim rubs his eyes and goes over the numbers one more time, whispering so as not to wake Kelly and Audie in the next room. The early morning light, filtering through the room's dark blue curtains, gives the air a spectral glow, but Jim has nothing hazy or indeterminate about him. He came home at one A.M., after working the late shift at a paper mill, but woke me before dawn with moonshine on his mind. "I shouldn't even be talking to you," he said again as I sat blinking on the couch, but he couldn't resist a captive audience for long. Now he sits shirtless next to me and offers a lesson in economics, tracing diagrams on his open palm.

"In a normal operation," he says, "we use six eight-hundred-gallon stills—we call 'em black pots—each of which can make about a hundred gallons of moonshine. A black pot is really just a four-by-eight strip of stainless steel with its ends nailed together. You make the sides out of poplar or oak and cut a fourteen-inch hole in the top. Then you take that, set it up on cinder blocks in a shallow trench, and slide a propane burner underneath. The flames are about ten inches high, and it sounds like an engine runnin' real loud. When the mash starts boilin', you put a copper cap over the hole, seal it with some rye paste, and pipe the fumes to the doublin' keg—some folks call it a thumper—and then a two-inch copper worm. By the time the whiskey comes out, it's close to 200 proof and flowing about as fast as the faucet on your sink. You put that stuff in your car and it'll run it."

A tractor rumbles past on the dirt road below the house, though in the morning's foreshortening silence it sounds much closer. Jim steps quickly to one side of the living room window, peers through it obliquely for a moment, and then returns to the couch. "The name of the game is speed," he continues. "The faster you can ferment the mash, the faster you can make money, and the less chance you'll get caught. So you ferment and boil the mash in the same pot. While you're runnin' one still, you're already heatin' up the next one and adding new ingredients to what's left of your last—what they call the backin's, or sour mash."

The recipe Jim uses is 75 or 80 percent sugar—about four hundred pounds per pot—along with cornmeal or horse feed, malt, and Fleischmann's yeast. The resulting "sugar liquor" isn't quite as smooth as his father's corn liquor, but Jim can't afford to be an epicure. "It takes us about a week to get the operation set up and workin' perfect and about three weeks to work it. We run two stills a day, four runs per still. Then we mix the runs together in a barrel, get it down to around 100 proof, and put it in those gallon milk jugs. Most of the time it's out of the state the same day."

At first the facts and figures have a hard time seeping in. My mind is still cloudy from sleep and clogged with half-remembered nightmares—of guns being put to my head; of a silent, grim-faced circle of bootleggers waiting in the forest. But Jim, I know, is nothing like those men. He speaks quickly and accurately, in a voice like honey mixed with seltzer—more crisp and dry than an east Virginia drawl has any right to be. His hazel eyes are small, watchful, and unclouded by resentment; his beard is trim and well kept; and even after a night's sleep, his short black hair lies molded to his scalp, as if gripped by an invisible skullcap. Years in the military have given his body a lean, knobby look, and he sits with a certain stiffness, as if watching himself from a slight distance, constantly correcting his posture. "I like to live my life wide open," he says, and at first this seems almost comically inapt—I've rarely met someone so guarded, so calculating. But then I think that by "wide open" he means open to any possibility, and that much, certainly, is true.

Seen in retrospect, Jim's life has been like a bumper-car ride with the pedal always to the floor: full of drive and nervy self-confidence, but marked by jolting, split-second redirections. The first bump he hit was of a genetic kind: He was born severely color-blind, unable to distinguish between a red and a blue, though he does perceive color after a fashion. The next bump was clerical: Despite the fact that she was married, his mother chose to give him her maiden name—a reminder, perhaps, that he shouldn't always follow in his father's footsteps.

There wasn't a time in Jim's life when Willard wasn't involved in moonshine—either making it, hauling it, or selling it—and on at least three occasions he was arrested for it. The first raid Jim can recall was when he was seven or eight years old. There were sheriffs and deputies all through the house, and his mother was sitting with him at the kitchen table, explaining what was going on. When she was done, Jim reached under the sink, picked up a gallon jug of moonshine that the police had overlooked, and carried it calmly through the crowd to his bedroom. Then he hid it in the toy box that his father had made for him.

Like Willard, Jim can do almost anything with his hands: weld a still, construct a house, rebuild an engine. And like Willard, he joined the army when he was eighteen, hoping to put his mechanical gifts to use. Unfortunately, the army had other ideas. They had no need for a color-blind mechanic, they said. How would he tell the differences among wires? So they shuttled him off to southern Germany to study military intelligence. "It was just a desk job," he says. "Followin' paper trails, findin' out what was bein' bought that shouldn't be bought, rattin' on people. But it taught me how the system works, and that comes in handy with moonshinin'."

Jim rose steadily up the ranks, from corporal to lieutenant to captain, earning commendations at every step. A month after Kelly turned eighteen, he married her and brought her to Germany. By the time Desert Storm was gathering, he hoped to be among the first to fly to the Middle East, perhaps staying on for a full career in the military after that.

Then came word from his father: His mom had suffered a stroke and had less than a year to live. Jim was needed back home. "Me and Jimmy, it was the same thing," Willard told me. "I wanted to fight in Korea, like he wanted to fight in Saudi Arabia, but I got a hardship discharge, too. Had to come home and take care of my father. Same damn thing: hung between loyalty to your country and loyalty to your parents."

It was back home, living in an old trailer and watching his friends march to Kuwait on TV, that Jim fell into moonshining. Perhaps it was unavoidable, living where he did, with his father still in the business and good money to be made. Or maybe he needed some sort of adventure, some keen risk to compensate for the war he wasn't fighting. At first, he says, he considered going over to the other side—joining a SWAT team or the revenuers themselves.

But their uniforms must have been a little too close to home. So he started setting up stills instead.

Special agent Gerald Joyce swings his van into a narrow country road and slows to an easy, drifting pace. "That's the place," he says, jerking his chin toward a white, one-story farmhouse. "The source said it was in a tobacco barn, at the back end of the property." Behind him all banter suddenly ceases. The other members of the moonshine task force scrutinize the roadside through tinted glass.

"He said there'd be pumpkins, didn't he?"

"Yeah, a wagonload of pumpkins and a two-ton Dodge pickup truck."

"Well, there are the pumpkins, anyway." Joyce continues to the next section road and turns right, slowing to a crawl as he scans the landscape. At fifty he's the oldest member of the task force and the only one in civilian clothes. He makes a natural front man, with his graying temples and square-rimmed glasses, jowly cheeks, and smooth, articulate manner, and on days like today he's happy to be the designated driver. "I like raiding stills," he says. "But I don't like creepin' out there in the bushes during hunting season. Some of these guys will shoot at anything that moves." The others are already hustling into their gear: camouflage jackets and overalls, billy clubs and forty-caliber Beretta automatics. J. E. Calhoun, who joined the group soon after the Smith Mountain bust, glances at my burgundy T-shirt and red sneakers: "You expectin' to do some runnin', boy?" I glance up at him, wide-eyed.

"It's been several people shot wearin' red," Bev Whitmer explains, handing me his camouflage jacket. "They say it looks like a wild turkey's neck."

After a quick conference with Jimmy Beheler, the group's leader, Joyce decides to drop us off about a half mile to the side of the farm, where we can hike in unobserved. Calhoun grins up at them as he checks his walkie-talkie: "Once the two brains formulate what to do, they stop and throw our asses out."

"We're just the worker bees," Whitmer adds.

"The low men on the totem pole."

Beheler turns and glowers. His drooping mustache and duckbill hat, sullen, watery eyes, and low, grumbling voice make him look like an old, ornery hound snapping at some unruly pups: "Let's get ready to move."

It's been twelve years since Beheler started the task force, and in that time it has become the most successful group of its kind in the nation. That fact has hardly made him a local hero, however. Moonshiners may have the most violent history of any group in the country, yet it's a peculiar fact that Americans seem incapable of harboring bad feelings toward them. Homemade liquor has been illegal, off and on, for more than two centuries, but the courts still go easy on those who make it. Though it can be as addictive and debilitating as most drugs, few think to call it one. Alone among the old vices I've revisited, moonshine still claims a place in our cultural inheritance, though it long ago ceased to be quaint, or traditional, or even well made. In Franklin County moonshine memoirs fill the local paperback racks, the convenience stores sell moonshining T-shirts, and a county fair isn't complete without its copper-pot still. For a while, a local business-man even put up a billboard that declared Franklin County the "Moonshine Capital of the World."

Beheler's task force gets its share of tip-offs from ex-wives, jealous rivals, and disgruntled relations. But when most people get word, or whiff, of a still, they keep mum. The thirty-six-pot operation at Smith Mountain Lake had 150 mobile homes within eight hundred yards of it, Calhoun estimates, yet only one man bothered to report the smell. Even the local Baptist ministers tend to wink more often than thunder. "Some of these moonshiners make real good-quality stuff," one of them told me. "And if you follow Scripture straight, it does say, 'Take a little wine for your stomach's sake.'"

Beheler's best answer to such apathy is a dogged work ethic and a love of the chase. Because moonshiners tend to distill during the day and deliver at night, the task force is on call twenty-four hours a day, and there's no such thing as a weekend. One Saturday morning about ten years ago, Beheler was driving in the country with his eleven-year-old son when he stumbled on two men run-ning a still. "I just bailed out of the truck and told my son to stay right there," he remembers. "I ended up catching both those guys."

Jim will never get caught that easily—or so he says. From the very beginning he has done things differently from his father. Old-timers like Willard always lived like paupers, if only to keep from raising suspicions. They might have $150,000 in the bank yet live in a shack and drive a pickup with one door missing. Jim had no patience for that. He took a full-time job as a maintenance man at the mill and built a fully equipped, two-bay mechanic's garage behind his house. He tried his hand at corn farming and raising hogs. He scattered his hundred acres with fragments of his daydreams—tractor parts, still caps, a trailer concession stand, and dozens of used cars—and year by year he cobbled together a life from them, testing it constantly for speed, power, and reliability.

Moonshine has never been more than a side business for him, though a lucrative one. He sets up a still once a year in the fall, runs it for a month or so, and then dismantles it, keeping the copper cap and worm for the next go-round. The materials for six black pots will run him about $2,000 and the ingredients to fill them about $1,200. (He buys his sugar wholesale, in large pallets from the local SAM'S Club—"Them high school kids never ask any questions.") He'll usually hire two still hands, at $125 a day, and a cook at $200 a day, and together they'll produce around two thousand gallons of liquor before they're done. In the end he'll net around $10,000 for about 120 hours of work— about six times the hourly rate he gets at the textile plant.

The real profits, of course, lie further up the food chain. Jim may sell his liquor at the still site for $15 a gallon, but the distributor sells it to the shot houses for $30, and the customers there pay $1 a shot. "Course, you can make the most if you own it, and haul it, and sell it yourself. But I don't need that kind of risk," Jim says. So he doesn't even know the men who haul away his liquor. "They just show up with an empty truck, we fill it up, and the cycle starts over again."

Agent Joyce brings the van to a sudden, grinding stop, Calhoun flings open the sliding door, and everyone barrels down the embankment. For just a moment we huddle in the shade of a pine tree to get our bearings, then we veer off into the forest in single file. According to Joyce, the tobacco barn in question has a shiny new chain and lock, some freshly cut sticks by the door, and a stash of moonshine inside. But there are no barns in sight yet, only acres of thorny bottomland.

"This is gonna be fun."

"And we ain't got but a quarter of an hour to get through it."

Calhoun flips his hat around backward and surges into the brambles with a grunt. To guarantee a conviction, they not only have to catch their man red-handed, they have to physically restrain him—juries don't always trust an agent's eyes, and alibis are easy to come by. Over the years they've all suffered their share of lacerations and bruises, poked eyes and twisted knees, from stalking, chasing, and wrestling moonshiners. Beheler once needed eighteen stitches after running headlong into a barbed-wire fence during a raid. But no one here has ever been shot. Possessing firearms at the scene of a crime carries a much stiffer penalty than making moonshine, so most bootleggers do without them. And though the agents carry guns, firing at a fleeing bootlegger is out of the question. "I wouldn't even carry this damn heavy thing," Calhoun says, patting his Beretta, "if it weren't for the possibility of a booby trap." The gun that comes in most handy, Beheler adds, is loaded with BBs: "Keeps the dogs quiet."

We work our way through a patch of bloodred sumac, the greenbriers catching at our clothes as we pass. After a few hundred yards we reach a winding creek, thick with algae, and then a steep slope that leads to an airy grove of white oak. It's a cool autumn day, with clouds racing across the sun, but by the time we reach the back side of the house, I'm sweating beneath my fatigues. Crouching to catch our breath, we agree to split into two groups. Whitmer peels off to follow a path into the woods, while the rest of us pass through a small stand of pines and across a meadow covered with spindly black stalks of ragweed. A deeply rutted road skirts it on the other side. "Too rough for a car," Calhoun says, looking down. "But a four-wheeler could make it."

By now there are tobacco barns every hundred yards or so, and we begin to check them one by one. At first no one says a word, and we slink around as delicately as cats, prying open doors, peering under tarps, and squinting through chinks in the barns' wooden walls. At one point Calhoun sees me walking down the center of the road and shoos me to the side, then walks over and scuffs away my footprints. Still, after half a dozen empty barns, even his commando form starts to go slack. When Whitmer rejoins us, his slumped shoulders tell the same story: no shiny new lock and chain, no fresh tobacco sticks, no booze.

"Well, well, well."

"I think this is what's known in the business as a dead end."

Beheler spits in the bushes. Then he calls Joyce on his walkie-talkie, and we head back toward the road. Four out of five leads end up this way, I know. But there's an odd feeling, when you've been running around in the woods with funny clothes on for no reason, that you've been the butt of an elaborate practical joke. Moonshining is a cat-and-mouse game, everyone says, but it feels suddenly as if we're the mice: camouflaged like forest animals, skulking around in the underbrush, trespassing on private property.

Even Calhoun, standing there with his linebacker's build and Beretta automatic, is more vulnerable than he seems. He's spent his whole life in this area, and a good chunk of it crawling through the woods as a game warden or special agent. He knows the moonshiners' faces and their family histories, the cars they drive and the bars they frequent. But then they know him just as well.

Earlier that morning Jim took me out for a drive. About five miles from his house, he suddenly pulled up in front of a small ranch house with a silver trailer beside it. "You know who lives here?" he asked, smiling impishly. "Man by the name of Calhoun." He pointed to the front door and asked, half-jokingly, if we should leave him a note. Then, like a dog marking his territory, he drove up the driveway and spun around, spraying gravel from his back wheels as he left.

Moonshiners have always had to be stealthier than drug dealers; their product is so much bulkier, their manufacturing methods so much more complicated and conspicuous. But in recent years, prodded by groups like Beheler's, they've had to modernize their methods. When helicopters began to scan the forest, moonshiners camouflaged their stills with maple-leaf stencils. When motorboats puttered down streams in search of wood fires and exposed water pumps, moonshiners switched to propane and submersible pumps. When agents prowled the woods with infrared scopes, night-vision goggles, and motion-detecting cameras, moonshiners got the same equipment.

These days the biggest stills have moved indoors— whether in tobacco barns, chicken houses, or purpose-built structures—where water and heat are easy to come by. They're often hidden underground or behind false walls, and they may pump their liquor to a separate, inconspicuous building for loading. (A few years ago a still in northern Georgia was found in a basement, at the bottom of a hidden staircase. When you turned on the tap upstairs, moonshine came out.) But all those advances have come at a cost: moonshining, once the quintessential egalitarian enterprise, open to any hardworking man with a few dollars, now has its own class system.

"The big operators have brick houses," Jim tells me one

morning, walking around his place, waiting for another moonshiner to arrive. "They drive Mercedes. They have doctor's degrees. They've got, like, different lives." He stops and picks at the scorched remains of his mother's house, a few yards behind his trailer. "Now, this guy you're gonna meet, he's at the other end of it: he's a still hand. He doesn't even have electricity in his house, and he likes to live that way. He's like a modern bum."

There's something odd in the way Jim says this—as if he were shamed by it rather than amused—but I chalk it up to empathy later, when I meet the man. He sits on Jim's deck, eyes blinking in the sun, looking like a cross between Wild Bill Hickok and a forest gnome. He has a caved-in chest and shaky hands, shoulder-length hair, a scraggly mustache, and features flushed and bludgeoned by drink. His eyes are pale green, rimmed with black, his eyelids always at half-mast, and when he talks his tongue darts behind broken teeth, as if looking for a place to hide. He says his name is Leroy and that he's forty-eight years old, though he looks closer to sixty-five. He says he won't say anything about the living, but he's happy to talk about the dead. "You can't do nothin' to them."

From the time he was twelve years old, Leroy has made moonshine. He started out by toting sacks of sugar and scouting for signs of revenuers, then graduated to tending the still. He'd get up at three in the morning to light the fire and heat the mash, then head over to Zenith Junior High for classes. "My parents didn't know where I was; didn't care, I guess." His real father, you might say, was his boss: Aubrey Atkins, "Kingfish of the Franklin County Moonshiners," who would later teach Jim as well.

Aubrey was a rhinoceros of a man, only five feet nine but more than 230 pounds, with a single-minded love of moonshining. He was deaf in one ear and tended to bellow more than talk, and his irrepressible spirit—and above-average product—endeared him even to some judges. When the moonshining exhibit was built at Smith Mountain Lake, Aubrey was the only living moonshiner it showed, though by then he looked like a man from another age.

Over the years Aubrey put Leroy through a cooking school as exacting as Escoffier and an advanced course on camouflage as well. One of his favorite tricks was to cut down a few young pine trees and plant them like Christmas trees across the path leading to a still. Whenever a moonshiner arrived, he'd simply pull out the trees, drive on through, and then stick them back in the ground. "The first time I got caught in a raid I was just seventeen," Leroy says, "and everyone kinda left me there, with agents comin' in from every side. Well, I just ran over to a brush pile and pulled all them little pine trees over me. I must've laid there three hours, while they were bustin' things up. They never did find me."

As savvy as Aubrey was, his age and outdated methods eventually caught up with him. By his late sixties he'd lost a step or two to the agents he used to outrun, and the task force arrested him three times. In the end, the man who had outrun countless revenuers in the woods, who'd begun moonshining before the war and survived to the age of seventy-two, was caught short by a couple of teenage robbers with a shotgun. It took two blasts to kill him, Leroy says, and then his body was so heavy that they could drag it only two hundred yards off the road. A few days later a police helicopter spotted his shallow grave in the hard winter soil.

The killers are now serving extended sentences in the state penitentiary. But Leroy would rather not think about that. He'd rather think about the last time Aubrey was raided, when they were still together. "I'd just bruised my chest in an accident, so I couldn't run," he says. "But Aubrey, he just jumped over the top of that eight-hundred-gallon pot and ran right into the pines. They was yellin', 'Aubrey, we know who you is!' But he couldn't hear 'em, so he just ran on. I mean, it was like Alley Oop goin' through the jungle: you could hear the pines a-poppin'."

He hunches over then, as if in pain, his shoulders convulsing. I start to comfort him, then realize he's only laughing—a great soundless laugh, with his features bunching together as if someone had pulled a drawstring inside his skull. It's a startling sight, but after a while I can't help laughing along. "Oh man," he says, rubbing his right eye. "I wish I had me a jug of that moonshine right now."

Later I watch through the back window as Leroy helps Jim and his father dig a drainage ditch with a backhoe. Beside me, Kelly is sautéing some cabbage for lunch, keeping an eye on Audie, who's bent on cutting the kitchen table in half with his toy saw. Short and stoutly built, with curly brown tresses, a little girl's bangs, and a voice that rarely drops below a bray, Kelly seems as sweet tempered and uncomplicated as a Clydesdale. But when I ask her about Leroy, her eyes cloud over. "He's worthless," she says. "I know he's Jim's brother and all, but if Jim were anything like him, I wouldn't have him."

I stare at her blankly for a moment: Jim told me that they weren't related. "Well, he's his adopted brother, actually," she says. Then she jabs a finger at Jim's mom's cabin. "That's where he grew up."

Like most people in Franklin County, Kelly has her own deep history with moonshine. Her father was a great lover of it, though he never set up a still himself. "He was a real violent drunk," she says, "and my mama took a lot of licks to protect the kids. One time, I remember, she threw a big butcher's knife at him, and it stuck in the wood next to his head and just vibrated." She stops and looks up from the sizzling pan, the spatula suspended in midair. Then she continues in the same matter-of-fact voice. "He died in a car wreck when I was six," she says. "Took the top of his head clean off."

I ask if Jim's moonshining frightens her, and she says it does sometimes, especially now that Audie's around, but she tries not to think about it.

Outside, the others are hunkered down together in the ditch they've dug: Jim, giving orders and gesturing around the yard; Willard, already flushed from a few nips at his flask of Virginia Lightning; Leroy, looking surprisingly sturdy with his shirt off, his shoulders tanned and corded from years of outdoor work. While they talk, Audie squirts through the back door and careens toward them, waving a screwdriver. Before they notice, he's climbed into the ditch beside his father, only a few feet from the backhoe's gaping metal jaws. "Jim!" Kelly shouts through the window. But he just smiles and waves, climbing back into the driver's seat. As he guns the engine, Audie settles in next to his grandfather and starts to dig. In his element at last.

The bulletin board behind Jimmy Beheler's desk is crowded with yellowed newspaper clippings and curling snapshots. Though the backgrounds vary, the scenes are always the same: five barrel-chested men in camouflage, chopping up stills or posing in front of them, smiling for the camera like hunters with their kill. "Crime Does Pay," a bright red bumper sticker above the board declares, ironically. But when I ask Beheler about it today, he shakes his head. "Sad but true," he says. "Sad but true."

He's having a bad year. Though the task force will end up destroying some five thousand gallons of moonshine this year, that's only 1/200th of the illicit liquor produced in the area. And though they'll bust thirty-six stills—seven times as many as all the agents in Georgia put together—that's still a far cry from the hundred they busted in 1993. "I don't know," Calhoun says, leaning back and scratching his stomach. "We're doing the same things, but we aren't catchin' 'em as much as we used to. Which leads me to think that they must have changed the way they do business."

What galls Beheler's crew most isn't that some moon-shiners get away, but that they get away even when they've been caught. Possession of moonshine is only a misde-meanor in Virginia, whether it involves a gallon in the backseat or a thousand gallons in the trailer. And although making moonshine is a felony, most first offenders get off with a small fine. "They'll play that romantic, Depression-era thing to death," Joyce says. "You'll see him one day all slicked up, driving a $30,000 vehicle to pick up his girl for steak and lobster. The next day he's a hillbilly without a pot to pee in." A local man by the name of Elmo Bridges was arrested twenty-four times for making moonshine, yet he never spent more than a few months in jail.

Beheler says it doesn't get to him anymore—"You do what you can do, you do the best you can do, and that's all you can do"—but his mood, and frequent talk of retire-ment, suggest differently. Today he takes off early to play a round of golf, but the others stay behind a while longer, mulling over the empty afternoon, reluctant to emerge from their funk. They crack a few jokes about Randall Toney, the fifth member of the crew, who's off today. They talk about the economics of moonshine and how it often destroys those who most profit from it. They agree that it's nasty stuff, but that in eighteen years they've confis-cated only a handful of dangerous batches. Then Joyce reaches under his desk and pulls out a half-gallon mason jar filled with white lightning. "We got this a few weeks ago," he says, unscrewing the lid and handing me the jar. "Go ahead," he says. "Taste it."

• • •

Moonshine, I've been told more than once by now, is just another word for poison. A hundred years ago, perhaps, some people made it the way they made fine furniture. But what pride it involved, what craft, was all but dismantled by Prohibition. As demand skyrocketed, some moonshiners began to throw lye, sulfuric acid, car batteries, or sacks of steaming manure into the mash to hasten fermentation. They cut their product with bleach, turpentine, rubbing alcohol, or paint thinner; stained it with tobacco juice or iodine. They cooked it in galvanized steel or distilled it in car radiators that gave off lead from soldered parts.

A few of the moonshiners I talked to said these were nothing but scare stories, passed around by revenuers. But others admitted that there have always been two sorts of moonshine: the decent stuff, which is kept at home and sold to neighbors, and "nigger likker," as they called it, shipped to anonymous shot houses and nip joints in the big city. It's in such areas that moonshine has taken its worst toll. In 1928 sixty died of wood alcohol poisoning in New York alone, and in 1930 authorities estimated that fifteen thousand people had been partially paralyzed by "Jake," a type of moonshine made with Jamaica ginger. "Buyin' moonshine is like playin' Russian roulette," Willard told me. "It won't hurt ya if it's good—I mean, you can drink that white lightnin' and go to work the next day. But the bad stuff, it's a killer."

Even a few sips of Jake, I tell myself, wouldn't be enough

to hurt me. But even so, as I lift up Joyce's jar, I feel like a kid in high school again, buckling under peer pressure. At first all I can sense are the fumes burning through my sinuses. Then, little by little, the air clears, and the taste that lingers is clean, sweet, and surprisingly mild, with a faint afterglow of formaldehyde. "Not bad," I say just to get their goat.

For a beat or two they exchange glances, and the room's pulse seems to quicken. "Shut the door," Whitmer says, opening a file cabinet beside him. And then, suddenly, it's as if I'm back at the moonshiners' reunion and the 'shine tasting has just been announced. From every drawer and cardboard box, it seems, mason jars start popping out, as if the room were full of jack-in-the-boxes. Jars of damson plum and jars of peach; jars of cherry moonshine and more jars of white lightning: the essence and fruit, perfectly preserved, of years of tailing moonshiners.

Joyce passes me a half gallon of liquor so purple it's nearly opaque. The taste is deep and musky and sweetly familiar. "Blackberry," he says, grinning. Then a jar of liquid sunshine emerges, eight pears bobbing happily inside it, and soon Joyce is telling us about the charcoal keg his father used to own. Calhoun remembers a still they once busted that smelled just like Jack Daniel's, and Whitmer reminisces some more about the Smith Mountain bust. "Do you have any connections to Hollywood?" he wants to know. "'Cause we're thinkin' of getting us some agents. I'm thinkin' about Stallone for my part."

"I'd be happy with Sean Connery," Joyce adds.

"'Course, Randall Toney, he'll have to be played by Tony Randall."

That breaks them up for a while: three big men in a tiny room, surrounded by mason jars of every color, imagining themselves in those actors' bodies, chasing down some hapless local citizen. And for a moment the retirement plans and lenient courts are forgotten, and moonshine seems like only a game again—neither poison nor birthright nor cynical livelihood, just an excuse for grown men to play hide-and-seek in the woods.

"You know what I remember best?" Calhoun says, wiping his eyes. "It isn't all the adventure or the busts, it's the funny stuff. The ridiculous situations you get into."

"Like the time that copperhead crawled over Butch Wright's foot and he killed it with his umbrella."

"Or the time Garry Thomas came with us."

"Gerald, tell him about Garry."

Joyce looks away for a second, his eyes fixed on some middle distance in his memory. "Well," he begins, "you have to know Garry to get it. I mean, he's the nicest guy in the world, but he's from the city and he's never worked liquor before, and he keeps buggin' us all the time to take him on a raid. He just has this thing about wantin' to bust moonshiners.

"So one day we're working and watching this place with Garry, when a truck comes by with a bunch of barrels in the back. Jimmy and Randall are close by, so they run up to it. But those guys must have seen 'em comin', 'cause the truck pulls away and goes up a gravel road and into a field. The guys inside just jump out and run."

"Turns out the barrels are full of spent mash."

"Now, you've got to understand that spent mash is about the sorriest-smellin' stuff in the world. Fresh mash may smell like a loaf of bread, but spent mash smells like a pigpen. So naturally someone asks Garry if he wants to taste it. 'No,' he says, he doesn't want to taste the mash. But he'll take the truck and drive it in." Joyce takes a breath and grins at the others, rolling the jar of pears between his hands. "Now, Garry, to get back to the road, he has to drive all the way around this field. But when he comes back toward us, there's somethin' wrong."

"The field's wet, and his brakes aren't workin'."

"So he's goin' faster and faster, and he can't stop. He hits the front fender of one of the police cars, and then he about runs over my toes. He goes all the way to the bottom, the truck bouncin' this way and that, and then he smashes into a ditch.

"Well, that's when the truck stops, but those barrels of mash in back, they just keep on goin': right through the back window and all over Garry.

"The rest of us, we're kind of in shock. We run up and say, 'Garry, are you okay? Are you okay?' And he says he is. But I mean, he's just covered in that mash. There are clumps of it in his hair and it's all over his face and it's dripping down his shirt into his pants. So we're all just starin' at him, kinda dumbstruck. And then someone breaks the silence: 'Garry,' he says, 'I didn't think you wanted to taste the mash.'"

"Jimmy, he laughed so hard, he peed in his pants."

"I about hyperventilated myself."

Joyce grins. "If we could just have been a little more quiet," he says, "I swear we would have heard the moonshiners laughin', too."

Mad Squirrels
and Kentuckians

A September dawn, windless and clear, with the sky going to lavender behind the high branches. At the bottom of a hollow, Steve Rector and I wind our way along an ocher creek bed, stepping slowly from rock to rock to avoid the crackling leaves. These beeches should still be cloaked in emerald so early in the season, this creek overflowing its banks, but western Kentucky is in the throes of the worst drought in half a century. The only puddle in sight has been claimed by a box turtle, and camouflage clothes are our only cover.

Rector crouches down ahead of me, balancing his sixteen-gauge Winchester on his shoulder, and comes up with a handful of broken shells: beechnuts, gnawed open by little mouths. "I came through here on Sundee, but there wasn't any cuttin's at all," he whispers, moving on. In the distance a woodpecker's hammering dopplers through the forest. Then it happens. Using his shotgun as a crutch, Rector tries to clamber up the bank, but his feet slip just as his body goes horizontal. He reaches for a sapling, but it isn't there, and all three hundred pounds of him come crashing down at once. For a moment he just lies in the dirt, his heavy jowls and drooping eyes looking more than usually defeated. "Well," he says, groaning back to his feet, "I guess I must have that mad cow disease after all."

How many other squirrel hunters, I wonder, are thinking the same thing this morning? True, England and its agonies are half a continent and an ocean away. The epidemic that killed fifty-six British people, sent two and a half million cows to the incinerator, and poisoned Europe's already queasy trade relations should be no more than a distant rumor. No American cow has died of bovine spongiform encephalopathy, and British beef has never found a market here. Still, panic has a way of finding new victims.

In August of 1997 two neurologists published an odd letter in the *Lancet,* a prestigious British medical journal. A disturbing pattern had come to their attention, they wrote. In the previous four years, five patients in western Kentucky had been diagnosed with Creutzfeldt-Jakob disease (or CJD), of which mad cow disease is a variant. All five patients had one trait in common: They ate squirrel brains. Given that some forms of CJD can be transmitted by the eating of infected brains, and that most mammals seem able to carry the disease, the connection made sense. "Caution might be exercised," the authors concluded, "in the ingestion of this arboreal rodent."

To a country primed for the next epidemic, this was

perversely welcome news. As the terror of AIDS slowly subsided in America, fears of future viruses were beginning to flare up. Books like *The Coming Plague, The Hot Zone*, and *Deadly Feasts* were joining best-seller lists, and disease movies weren't far behind. Now here was the perfect fuel for all that smoldering paranoia. Mad squirrel disease, if it existed, was as fatal and as exotic as any novelist could wish, yet most people were no more likely to get it than the plague. If AIDS once seemed an affliction cooked up by country Baptists to punish city dwellers, here was the urbanites' revenge: a disease, common only among squirrel-brain-eating hillbillies, that turned its victims into demented fools. What could be more appropriate?

The feeding frenzy was brief but exceedingly gleeful. The *New York Times* began by garnishing the story with some suitably gothic details. "Families that eat brains follow only certain rituals," the paper reported, then it quoted Eric Weisman, one of the authors of the *Lancet* letter. "'Someone comes by the house with just the head of a squirrel and gives it to the matriarch of the family. She shaves the fur off the top of the head and fries the head whole. The skull is cracked open at the dinner table and the brains are sucked out.'" Squirrels killed on the road, the *Times* added, "are often thrown into the pot." Soon Jay Leno and David Letterman were riffing on squirrel brains in their monologues, and columnists across the country were chiming in. "This report raises some troubling questions," wrote syndicated humorist Dave Barry. "1. Since when do squirrels have brains? 2. Have squirrels and cows been mating? How? 3. Doesn't a person who eats road kill rodent organs pretty much deserve to die?"

Steve Rector first heard about it in the coffee room at work. He was putting some squirrel heads into the microwave for lunch, he remembers, when one of the guys mentioned the mad cow disease story in the Owensboro paper. "I figured that if it was really bad, like the bubonic plague, it would be on TV," Rector says. So he started to watch the evening news, scan the local obituaries, and look for signs of strange behavior in local squirrels. Though he never saw or heard anything more, he was spooked enough to lay off brains for the first time in thirty years. But that was last year. Like most of the squirrel hunters I interviewed, he couldn't stay away for long. "I just thought, You gotta die of somethin'," he says. "First it was cigarettes cause cancer, then pesticides, and then the water you drink. But I been eatin' squirrel brains since I was six years old, and I ain't dead yet."

It's midmorning now, and our vest pockets have yet to hold any dead squirrels. But as we circle back to the truck, Rector stops suddenly and gestures for me to hang back. Peering at the crest of a distant hill, he slowly raises his shotgun to his shoulder and shoots twice in quick succession, the reports ripping the air around me. Then he hustles up the slope toward a skinny maple tree.

Rector is no champion marksman. At forty-four he has developed astigmatism and can't use a rifle without a scope. His reflexes have slowed down, his heart beats irregularly, and his fingers go numb in the morning cold.

Yet when he reaches the tree, his face breaks into a boyish grin. "That was a hell of a shot," he says, reaching into the leaf litter, "sixty yards if anything." He pulls out a young squirrel, its tiny chest still heaving. "Smell of 'im," he says almost tenderly, lifting the warm body to my nose. "Isn't that just like . . . the woods?" Then he takes the animal by the tail and beats its head methodically against the tree. "Don't want to do that too hard," he says after a couple of whacks. "Else I'll spoil the best part."

If hunters around here seem uncommonly suspicious of authority (medical or otherwise); if they clamp on to their traditions even at peril of their lives, they have good reason. Ninety years ago, when Rector's grandfather was cutting the giant scaly-bark hickories out of these bottomlands and rafting them to the mill, it was said that the land would make its people rich. But eastern land speculators reaped most of the timber and mining profits, and a tobacco monopoly took what was left. When the virgin forests were gone, Rector's grandfather went to work as a share-cropper and then a coal miner. When his son turned twenty-two, he joined him.

They dug vertical shafts back then, two hundred feet down and up to four miles long, with thin wooden props and little ventilation. They used black powder to blast out the coal and steel picks to chop it up, praying that their carbide lamps wouldn't ignite a pocket of gas. After as many as seventeen hours underground, they emerged black as crows and got paid in company scrip, redeemable only at company stores. The result was best summed up by Merle Travis, whose father and brothers worked in the same mine as Rector's grandfather:

You load sixteen tons and what do you get?
Another day older and deeper in debt
St. Peter, don't you call me 'cause I can't go
I owe my soul to the company store.

When Rector was a little boy, and a life underground seemed his inevitable lot, he used to have a recurring dream. He was standing on a high hill overlooking a strip mine, waiting for his father to drive by so he could wave to him. Far below, the mine pit had filled with rain, and the acids in the coal had turned the water bright blue. "I was always wearin' a red shirt and blue jeans, and every time I'd just fall off that edge toward that Bahama blue water," he says. "I'm terrible scared of heights, and I'm not too good a swimmer, so I swear that fall took forever."

Rector always woke up before he hit the water in his dream. But in real life it was the coal business itself that saved him. "Don't bother," the owners told his father when he went looking for a job for his son. "The mines are almost played out. You're better off lettin' that boy finish high school." So Rector took a job as a meat cutter at a supermarket, while his father stayed on at the mine. His grandfather would die of consumption eventually, exacerbated by black lung disease. "The last two years of his life he had to sleep sittin' up in a chair," Rector says. "Couldn't get his breath otherwise."

These days Rector lives just off Paradise Street, in the town of Greenville, in Muhlenberg County, Kentucky. His ranch house is small and nondescript—"just a plain old country house," as he puts it—yet to a fan of folk music, staying there is like staying down at the end of Lonely Street at Heartbreak Hotel. It constantly brings to mind the refrain of a song, this one from "Paradise" by John Prine:

> *And Daddy, won't you take me back to Muhlenberg County*
> *Down by the Green River where Paradise lay?*
> *Well, I'm sorry, my son, but you're too late in asking*
> *Mr. Peabody's coal train has hauled it away.*

There are three things that every Rector man has always done, an oral historian once told Steve: hunt, make moonshine, and play guitar. Rector never did take to moonshining (maybe it was seeing his great-uncle's pajamas with the small hole in front, where the bullet went in, and the giant hole in back, where it came out). But he more than makes up for it with his other hobbies. In a county that calls itself the "Thumb-Picking Capital of the World," Rector's command of the guitar has earned him an honorary street sign, and his love of hunting is nearly as legendary. At the age of six he went hunting with his daddy, carrying a BB gun to kill crippled squirrels. At ten he had his own shotgun. "And then pretty soon I was huntin' all the time."

In New York or Boston, where squirrels eat handouts and scamper impudently above park benches, squirrel hunting can seem like poor sport. But in Kentucky squirrels know the meaning of fear. They leap to the canopy at the first sign of movement. They *baaaaa* to one another, like lambs on speed, sounding the alarm. They flatten their bodies against trees, rotating slowly to keep the trunk between them and the hunter, or just dive into the nearest knothole. "I'd say they're pretty damn smart," Rector says. "I don't know how many pairs of my socks I've burned up trying to smoke 'em out."

Rector's father taught him a few squirrel-hunting tricks, but most of what he knows he learned from his cousin Jimmy Vincent. Tall, skinny, and agile as an otter, Jimmy was nine years older than Steve and half orphaned by the state: his father was in prison for killing a man. When he was ten years old, another boy shot him in the right eye with a BB gun. ("It didn't bust it," Rector says. "It just went behind the eyeball so he couldn't see with it anymore—it had a funny shine to it, like it was made of glass.") But Jimmy didn't let that stop him. He learned to aim over his left shoulder instead and still killed more squirrels with one eye than most did with two.

"Jimmy was like the Chet Atkins of squirrel hunting," Rector says. "He had a sixth sense about 'em. He could smell 'em through the leaves." If the woods went suddenly quiet, Jimmy would pick up a nut and scratch it with his fingernail—an "all clear" sign to the squirrels. If a knothole was within reach, he'd cut a cross in the end of a green stick, poke it in the hole, and twist until it got caught in some hair; then he'd pull out the squealing animal. If a squirrel was hiding on the far side of a tree, he'd tie a string to a sapling and shake it on one side while he circled to the other. "Back when I hunted with my daddy, he used to just say, 'Walk around there, boy, and check that bush,'" Rector remembers. "It wasn't till later that I realized he was usin' me as his string."

All through their youth, Jimmy and Steve kept the family continually supplied with squirrel meat. It was said, in those days, that squirrel soup could cure a cold, but its healing properties were mostly in the form of raw nutrition. What game there was in Kentucky was small, and coal company wages could pay for meat only once a week. So the two boys would get up before dawn, kill a mess of squirrels, and make it to class by seven-thirty. (In elementary school they hung the tails from their bicycle handlebars; in high school, from their car antennas.) "I remember one time Jimmy and I killed ninety-nine squirrels in a stretch of five days," Rector says. "My mom just pressure-cooked 'em all and put 'em in jars with barbecue sauce. That way, all winter long we could have squirrel sandwiches whenever we wanted."

Alien as they sound, such habits have shaped countless American boyhoods. Squirrels are usually a hunter's first kill, historian Stuart Marks writes in his book *Southern Hunting in Black and White,* and they nest in his memory ever after. "I'd rather kill me six fox squirrels than a ten-point Boone-Crockett buck," Steve says, and he'd rather see a squirrel run free than waste any part of its meat. Besides, he says, all of it tastes good.

After our first morning of hunting, we dropped by to see the owner of the woods, Juanita Adkins. Small and neatly put together, with wide glasses, bright white hair, and mischievous eyes, Adkins is eighty-two years old but sharper than most neuroscientists. She took up painting a few years ago, and her farmhouse is hung with skillful oils flanked by the blue ribbons she's won for them at county fairs. Standing in her living room, admiring her animal paintings, Steve asked her if she'd ever eaten squirrel brains. Adkins looked at him as if he were a little dim: "When I was growin' up," she said, "that's all I'd ever eat was the brain."

There was a time, not so long ago, when neurologist Eric Weisman would have laughed at the thought of eating squirrel brains; a time when he would have dismissed it as yet another puzzling local custom, in a state that seemed to have an endless supply of them. Then a squirrel-brain eater showed up at Weisman's Neurobehavioral Institute in Beaver Dam, Kentucky. And soon Weisman was asking all his patients if they had the same habit.

At the age of fifty-four, Marvin, as I'll call him, was still robust, articulate, and sharp enough to run his hometown as mayor. True, he'd gotten fired from his day job recently for forgetting to fill out the left side of sales forms. And yes, he did hit that nun's car. But these were all misunderstandings, he said. For some reason he just didn't see the nun coming from the left, even though it was broad daylight. The crash didn't hurt him much—just a fender bender. But when they took him to the hospital in Bowling Green, he couldn't seem to keep from nodding off.

"They did a sleep study on him after that, but the problem didn't go away," Weisman remembers. "They said it was a stroke at first, and then a brain tumor. Then they sent him to me." During the tests that followed, an odd pattern emerged: If Weisman asked Marvin to draw a clock, for instance, he would cram all the numbers on the right side of its face. "He had what we call a nondominant hemisphere syndrome," Weisman says. "The left side of the world just didn't exist for him." An EEG revealed a strange, periodic disturbance in Marvin's brain waves, and an MRI scan revealed that the right side of his brain had atrophied. But what was the cause? "I just didn't have a good answer," Weisman says. "And then I saw him jerk."

Some eighty years before, a German physician named Hans Gerhard Creutzfeldt had seen the same twitch in one of his patients. A twenty-three-year-old orphan, she had once cheerfully worked as a maid at a convent; now she refused to eat or bathe, grew paranoid, and assumed strange positions. And there was worse to come. Bouts of wild laughter grew into ceaseless screams; chronic tics amplified into waves of epileptic seizures; periods of stupor devolved into catatonia and then death. When Creutzfeldt autopsied the patient's brain, he found masses of fibrous brown glial cells—designed to repair damaged tissue—spread through it like spackling on an old plaster wall.

Even today, no one knows for sure what causes such damage. Most doctors blame bits of rogue protein called prions. But others finger stealth viruses, known as virions, or insidious, corkscrew-shape organisms known as spiroplasma. Whatever its origin, the disease that was eventually named for Creutzfeldt and his colleague, Alfons Jakob, is among the most mysterious in all of neuropathology. Invariably fatal, CJD chooses victims across gender, race, class, and geographic lines. It can incubate, unseen, for decades and predominantly strikes the middle-aged and elderly. Over the years, forms of it have been found in sheep (scrapie), cows (bovine spongiform encephalopathy), and certain cannibals in New Guinea (kuru). Mad cow disease and kuru have further been shown to infect those who eat infected meat, particularly brains. But true CJD strikes rarely and randomly, killing one person in a million. "It's like plane crashes," Weisman says, "it only seems to happen to nice people."

Not long after Marvin's first visit, his mind began to seize up with increasing violence, like an engine that first runs out of oil, then grinds down its bearings, and finally throws a rod. What had looked like hiccups gave way to full-fledged spasms, and his mental lapses spread to his whole brain. "If you said, 'With the pen touch the comb,' he could do it fine," Weisman says. "But if you said, 'Touch the comb with the pen,' he wouldn't understand." Meanwhile other patients were arriving with related symptoms. There were a few who couldn't walk straight, one with mysterious back pains, and two with full-blown dementia.

Over the next five years Weisman alone treated six people in the early stages of CJD.

"I don't even like to look at those charts," Weisman says. "It makes me want to cry." Yet there is something of the magpie in most neurologists—something that can't resist the odd mental disorder, the shiny fragment of a mind that somehow casts light on all of human consciousness. The coauthor of the *Lancet* paper, Joseph Berger, calls himself "a collector of unusual patients," and Oliver Sacks has made a career of the same pursuit. Weisman says he was never interested in publicity. But the eerie glow of these rare cases—cases related to a disease that was then much in the news—must have been hard to resist: will-o'-the-wisps beckoning him out of a long exile.

Born in 1957 to a Jewish family in the suburb of Peabody, Massachusetts, Weisman had once seemed destined to become a Boston intellectual, if not a Brahmin. His father was an artist and businessman who sculpted the heads of the swan boats in the Boston Public Gardens. His mother was a soprano with the Boston Opera. (When she retired she was replaced by her understudy, Beverly Sills. Later she went on to earn her BA in archaeology from Harvard—valedictorian at seventy-one.) By the age of six, Eric was drawing pictures of brains. By the age of sixteen, he was taking a course in neuroanatomy at MIT.

He entered Harvard the summer after his junior year of high school, dreaming of becoming a brain surgeon. But when fall arrived he declined to stay on. "It was so competitive," he says. "People were stealing my research, pulling pages out of reference books so no one else could read them." He enrolled at Bard instead, took up dance, and started a rock band. But his grade point slipped too low to get him into an American medical school. He toyed with going to a school in Belgium but decided on Grenada instead—just in time for the U.S. invasion. ("The local kids were throwing rocks at us, but we got to meet General Schwarzkopf.") In the end he earned his medical degree in Brooklyn. But though he went on to an internship and residency in Mobile, Alabama, and a fellowship at Boston University, he had long since ceased to be the golden boy. In 1987, when a headhunter offered him a job in rural Kentucky, he took it.

It was in Alabama that he overheard a conversation that would later change the course of his life. "We were cutting this brain from Texas or Oklahoma one day," he remembers. "It had CJD, so the pathologist turned to his resident and asked him what kind of history it had. Was its owner a farmer or a factory worker? Did he eat sheep brains, cow brains, or pig brains?" The pathologist, it turned out, was veteran CJD researcher Frank Bastian, the originator of the spiroplasma theory. When he got to the last question, the resident answered "yes." As a matter of fact, the patient ate squirrel brains.

Twelve years later, relaxing on a terrace overlooking the Ohio River, Weisman seems at first glance to have settled in quite nicely. His hair is long, black, and fashionably unkempt, his body stocky and sunburned. While jazz fusion pulses from massive speakers behind us, he pads around barefoot, in khakis and a striped cotton shirt open halfway down his chest. "I don't know if you know, but neurologists don't usually live like this," he says, gesturing back at his swimming pool and deck chairs, his two-story home with its skylit cathedral ceilings and mantelpiece hung with an English fox-hunting scene. "Guys like me, in New York, we usually have one-bedroom apartments."

Yet as breezy and sunlit as it seems, this house has become a fortress of sorts, and Weisman is in a state of siege. He may be a card-carrying member of the Kentucky Colonels, the state's prestigious fraternal organization, but he's been tarred and feathered by the local press. He may have one of the finest homes in Owensboro, but his own neighbor—an eater of squirrel brains, Weisman suspects—won't talk to him. He may be married to a former candidate for Miss Kentucky, but by now she's ready to move to Boston herself. "You aren't going to get me killed, are you?" Weisman asked the first time I called. "I've gotten death threats, you know." The next time, he answered the phone by saying, "Squirrel brains," as if uttering a secret password. When I asked him how he knew who was calling, he said he had caller ID.

All this trouble, Weisman says, all this bitterness and innuendo, is a result of good medicine and bad media. It began a year or so before Marvin died, when the other dementia patients were beginning to crop up. Weisman was in his office one day when Joe Berger called to ask him if he had seen any CJD cases lately. Berger, who is chairman of the neurology department at the University of Kentucky Medical Center in Lexington, had seen a few cases of his own by then, and he had a hunch that they might be tied to farming somehow. By then, however, Marvin had told Weisman that he liked to eat squirrel brains, which had reminded Weisman of the CJD patient in Alabama. When he suggested the connection to Berger, something clicked in the other man's memory as well. In the late 1980s, while still at the University of Miami, Berger had had a CJD patient who had eaten squirrel brains, too.

The coincidence, as it turned out, was not quite as great as it seemed. Nationwide, 3.2 million people hunt squirrels and twenty-five million of the animals are killed every year in Kentucky, Ohio, and Tennessee alone. (Burgoo, the Kentucky state dish, used to require squirrel meat.) When Berger surveyed one hundred local people, he found that twenty-seven had eaten squirrel brains. Given those numbers, one could argue that there should have been more victims if infected brains were the culprit. Besides, squirrels had never been found to carry CJD, and it's hard to imagine how they would have passed it on: they eat only fruits and nuts—not one another's brains.

Still, by then the mad cow epidemic had accustomed researchers to macabre, wildly improbable tales coming true. "All I know is, everyone with CJD I saw ate squirrels," Weisman says, "and not that many people eat squirrels, and not that many people have CJD." Squirrels may not eat meat in the woods, he adds, "but in the city they go after beef by-products all the time—like the suet that people put out for birds." As for the rarity of mad squirrel disease, that jibes with a long incubation period. The fact that most CJD victims in western Kentucky are elderly, Weisman told the *New York Times,* "makes me think there may have been an epidemic thirty years ago in the squirrel population."

There was only one way to test the hypothesis: capture some squirrels and check them for the disease. But even as state wildlife biologists were setting out traps, the squirrel-brain story was running wild—much to the state's dismay. It wasn't so much the threat of mad squirrel disease that rattled Kentuckians as the hillbilly portraits it inspired. Some admitted to eating brains, but few could remember presenting a squirrel head to the family matriarch, as Weisman told the *Times,* and fewer still remembered scraping squirrels off the highway for dinner. "Is there anything as gullible as a Yankee?" columnist Keith Lawrence wrote in the *Owensboro Messenger-Inquirer.* "Somebody start printing up the bumper stickers now. 'I brake for squirrels. Mmmm-mmmm good.'" The *Kentucky Post,* meanwhile, berated the eastern media for its "snobbish perception that the Bluegrass State is filled with shoeless, toothless, inbred, mouth-breathing, road-kill-eating hijacks so primitive as to chow down on anything that walks, crawls, or slithers." It wasn't long before Weisman's referrals were drying up, and the father of a hockey player he coached was taunting him during practice.

Sitting in his sunroom, recalling the controversy, Weisman hunches his shoulders and his features darken behind his glasses and beard. He doesn't like to talk about it, he says—this is the first interview he's granted since the story came out. But the words stream out anyway in a low, embittered monotone. He alludes to anti-Semitism and says his colleagues abandoned him. He calls parts of western Kentucky "strongholds of white supremacy" and asks if Rector is a member of the Klan. He insists that the *Times* misquoted him, that he never said Kentuckians eat roadkill.

"How could they say I don't know anything about local culture?" he says, jabbing a cigarette at a framed picture of a young woman on the wall. "My own stepdaughter was the first International Barbecue Festival Queen! I watched her put on her costume and makeup in this house before the parade." Then he leaps up and leads me to the foot of the staircase. "Look at this," he says, pointing to a stuffed red squirrel, slightly flea-bitten, standing there like a supplicant. "My wife bought that for me for my birthday." Then he adds offhandedly, "She grew up eating squirrel brains, you know."

Across the room Beverly sits primly on the sofa, as if patiently awaiting this revelation. When I first came she was wearing a T-shirt and jeans, but while Eric talked, she disappeared into the bedroom for a makeover. She has on green silk pants now and a purple batik blouse. Her hair is pulled back in an elegant knot, and rouge and fresh mascara highlight her beauty queen cheekbones, her kind, slightly asymmetrical eyes. "It's true," she says with a half smile. "I used to go squirrel hunting with my dad when I was a little kid. The brains were kind of a delicacy." She hasn't eaten them in thirty years, she adds, and she doesn't quite believe they can cause disease. But she helped Eric with his research anyway. When the letter was published in the *Lancet*, she was listed as a coauthor.

They make an odd pair, sitting on opposite sides of the room: New England intellectual and Kentucky farmgirl, gentile and Jew, yoked together by their dissatisfactions. When they met at the regional medical center, Weisman was living in a one-bedroom apartment, eager for his next move; she was an intensive care nurse, dreaming of medical school and the wider world beyond it. Instead of leaving after their marriage, though, they bought this house and opened the Neurobehavioral Institute. "The circumstances kind of set me up," he says. "I had to show people that I could set down roots." When Eric needed help, Beverly came on as nurse and sometime bookkeeper—deferring medical school indefinitely.

Every morning now he reads the *Boston Globe* and the *Boston Herald* on-line. Every night he watches the Red Sox on TV, noting the scores on sheets of paper taped to the refrigerator door. (Beverly has become a fan now, too, he says.) He plays drums in his music room, travels to conferences, and keeps Kentucky at arm's length. "If I didn't have cable TV and a computer, I probably would have moved by now," he says. "But this way, it's almost like I'm living in Boston. It's just easier to find a parking spot." Does he ever feel isolated? I wonder. No, he says, pointing his thumb across the river to Ohio. "I've got the North right there."

•   •   •

The day's kill has been skinned and gutted by now, washed clean of blood clots and flies, and soaked in water for a few hours. Standing at his kitchen sink, Steve Rector pats the pieces dry and salts them generously while his basset hounds, Buford and Macey, look on. They get to eat the tails but not the meat, he says, rubbing Macey's belly with his foot—"She's so fat, there's enough room in there to fit another dog." But hope springs eternal.

We killed two gray squirrels and one red squirrel this morning, though two of their heads were too shot up to keep. Glistening against the porcelain, the rest of their limbs could be mistaken for rabbit or dove, but never chicken: the bones are too delicate, the flesh too dark and tightly muscled. Rector coats them in self-rising flour, then fries them in an electric skillet filled with hot oil. When the squirrel is nicely browned on both sides, he moves the pieces to a pressure cooker. "This is the healthiest meat there is," he says, throwing a few handfuls of flour into the bubbling oil to make gravy. "It hardly has any fat or cholesterol at all." Then he adds more salt, shakes in a substance called Kitchen Bouquet ("just to turn it brown"), and pours it into the pressure cooker with the meat. When the top starts jiggling, he says, it'll be done in fifteen minutes.

Standing there, girding myself for the coming meal, I try to imagine myself as John Lawson, an early American explorer whose diaries I've been reading. In 1700, when Indian guides led Lawson through the Carolina wilderness, he happily feasted on raccoon, opossum, and bear fat. Beaver is "sweet Food," he declared, "especially their Tail," and skunk meat "has no manner of ill Smell, when the Bladder is out." Among the Indians, Lawson noted, a meal in great demand consisted of "two young Fawns, taken out of the Doe's Bellies, and boil'd in the same slimy Bags Nature had plac'd them in, and one of the Country-Hares, stew'd with the Guts in her Belly, and her Skin with the Hair on."

Squirrel meat is one of the last holdovers from those older, immeasurably wilder days. Until 1996 even the *Joy of Cooking* had some recipes for it, complete with a drawing of a boot standing on a squirrel's hide and a hand reaching down to yank out the meat. Now mad cow disease and other epidemics, real and imagined, are chasing the wild game from our diet once and for all. "I can serve Chilean sea bass any day," one southern chef told me. "But if I serve largemouth bass from a local lake, the health department could shut me down." In fact, most restaurants in the country can't serve game legally unless it's raised on a farm, and fewer and fewer people prepare it at home. In 1997, when the *Joy of Cooking* was overhauled, the squirrel section was quietly deleted.

"I watched my grandmother eat squirrel, and my mother eat squirrel, and I eat squirrel," Rector says. "But my son, he won't touch it. 'Daddy,' he says, 'that looks too much like a rat to me.'" Like everyone else around here, he's a deer hunter now. "There was a time, back in the sixties, when Kentucky didn't have any deer, and you could hunt squirrel just about anywhere," Rector says. But the coal company stripped everything out that squirrels would eat—sixty thousand acres of black oak and black walnut, mulberry, dogwood, and hickory in this area alone. The first thing that grew back was honeysuckle and saw brier: perfect browse for deer.

When Steve and Jimmy Vincent were kids, it seemed as though the land had no limits, and its rhythms were the only clock they followed. They'd drive anywhere they wanted, split up for a few hours, and meet back at the truck when the katydids hollered. But when the deer came in, local farmers got smart. "First they started charging deer hunters a dollar an acre. Then the next year it was two, then three, then eight. Pretty soon, the deer hunters were kickin' me off the land, when I was just tryin' to shoot squirrels." Nowadays Steve has only four places left to hunt—one of them next to the power plant where he works, shoveling coal ashes with a front-end loader. "I'm a dinosaur," he says. "Nobody hunts squirrel anymore." But he still manages to put a hundred squirrels in the freezer every fall.

It's been six hours since we last ate, I'm reminded, and for the past half hour we've been enveloped by the smell of frying meat. Perhaps that explains why I'm suddenly more open to the thought of consuming rodent. "I was watchin' the Discovery Channel the other day, and it was sayin' rat is a delicacy in some places," Rector says, emptying his pressure cooker onto a plate. "It's just a different concept. It's like we look at a cow and think that's somethin' you eat, and we look at a horse and say that's somethin' you ride. But a horse probably tastes even better than a cow."

I hesitate for a second, staring at the creamy mass of jumbled limbs. But when I take my first bite, the meat is tender and its taste straightforward—sweeter and richer than rabbit, I think, though it's hard to tell through the Kitchen Bouquet. By the time Rector reaches for the only head, I almost envy him.

"Here's how you eat one of these," he says, lifting up the skull with his fingertips. Seen in profile, it looks like the head of a monstrous ant: streamlined and mechanical, with buck teeth in front and incisors curving down the sides like whiskers. First Rector nibbles off the neck meat, then the cheeks, then he pulls off the lower jaw and plucks out the grayish blue tongue. When all that's left is the braincase, he picks up a teaspoon and smacks it down smartly on top.

Inside, beneath the eggshell-thin surface, lies a pink organ about as large as the first joint of my thumb, stained inky black between its lobes. If some infectious agent lurks there, no pressure cooker could have killed it: brain tissue from a mad cow can pass on the disease even after baking in a seven-hundred-degree oven. "Ya want some?" Rector asks, holding the glistening brain toward me. Before I can answer, he pops it into his mouth. "Too late," he says.

Late one morning, after another few hours of hunting, I head for Louisville and Lexington, leaving western Kentucky behind. "There's more difference between your life and mine than there is between mine and Jesus'," an opossum hunter once told me, and today I have to agree with him. The clock jumps forward an hour as I drive east, but as small town gives way to cityscape, it feels like a millennium or two have passed. Along the highway, at first, there seem to be more pedestrians than drivers: broken-down old men waving flags around concrete barriers; women with bad backs and distended bellies, holding up signs that say "SLOW." But the construction clears eventually, and the faces give way to gleaming headlights, hurtling headlong for modernity.

"Let me give you a sense of the culture shock," Joseph Berger tells me later, reclining in his office high above the campus in Lexington. "When we first moved here from Miami, my wife went to our little grocery store one time and asked the proprietor if he had any Danishes. 'Ma'am,' he told her, 'we don't have Finnish, we don't have Swedish, we don't have Norwegian, and we *certainly* don't have Danish. But if you'd like a Twinkie, it's over there.'" He points toward an imaginary counter and bursts into an infectious giggle, his small round face and dark brown eyes turning even more impish than usual.

Born and raised outside of Harrisburg, Pennsylvania, Berger spent most of his adult life on the East Coast, first in Philadelphia for medical school, then in Florida for seventeen years. When he got the offer from Kentucky, he says, he first had to find it on a map, but the chairmanship of a department was too much to turn down. Sure, it took a while to get used to the place. "When we first moved here, I was having my bread baked and half-frozen and brought in from Chicago. My meat was all imported, and I had those French cookies that I particularly liked—Petit Beurres—shipped in from friends in France." But there's been a sea change in the past four and a half years, he says, a "tremendous maturation" in the city: "There's no fine French restaurant yet, but we do have some decent nouvelle cuisine, as well as Mexican and Japanese restaurants." A few stores have even started carrying Petit Beurres.

The squirrel-brain letter was just an accident of circumstance, it seems, a spin-off from old interests colliding with new surroundings. Berger had seen more than twenty cases of CJD in Florida—a surprising number, given its rarity—and become the medical director of the Creutzfeldt-Jakob Foundation, but he'd never known so many to have so odd a common trait. "In putting this letter together for the *Lancet*, I did it almost tongue-in-cheek," he says. "Had I known how prevalent squirrel consumption was, and how volatile the issue would be, I probably wouldn't have bothered to report it." On further consideration, he says, the risk of getting CJD from squirrel brains is "vanishingly small." If he were offered a squirrel brain he'd probably decline. "But if you feel funny refusing it, go ahead and eat the damn thing."

Berger's ambivalence is understandable, if a bit convenient. Since his letter was published, only one other squirrel-brain eater in Kentucky has been found to carry CJD. In 1998, at Berger's request, the state department of wildlife killed fifty squirrels in western Kentucky. By then, however, fears of CJD infection were so widespread that lab technicians in Kentucky refused to autopsy them. (More recently, in Louisville, a man suspected of having died of CJD was hastily buried, only to be exhumed at a senator's insistence, autopsied, and declared free of the disease.) Frank Bastian eventually agreed to examine the squirrels at his lab in Mobile. But he found no evidence of disease in their brains: no spongelike holes, no profusion of glial cells, no signs of any infection at all.

Fifty squirrels are hardly a representative sample, Weisman is quick to point out. "Even if you are looking at the right squirrels, you might still miss it," he says. "What are you supposed to look for? No one has ever seen mad squirrel disease before." Bastian agrees. Until he searches the brains for prions and spiroplasma, he says, the negative autopsies "don't mean anything at all."

But when I quoted Bastian to Ermias Belay, the epidemiologist in charge of CJD studies at the Centers for Disease Control in Atlanta, he let out a long, low chuckle. "Well, it means something to me," he said, then chuckled some more. After the *Lancet* letter appeared, Belay called the Kentucky Department of Health to check the state's CJD rate. "It wasn't a hell of a lot different from other states'," he says. "That doesn't rule it out, but you would expect it to be higher." Next he called a squirrel expert, who told him that squirrels live less than five years on average, making them poor candidates for a slow-incubating disease like CJD. Finally he took a closer look at Berger's and Weisman's material.

Cause and coincidence are hard enough to tease apart for

most disease clusters, Belay says. But for CJD it's almost impossible. "What does it matter if you have two cases in the same neighborhood, when you know that they probably contracted the disease twenty or thirty years ago, when they lived in different states?" The *Lancet* letter blundered blithely into such statistical pitfalls. Berger and Weisman hardly examined the countless other common traits that surely connected their five CJD patients. Squirrel-brain eating seemed so exotic, so reminiscent of what caused mad cow disease, that they felt compelled to single it out. Yet if their surveys were representative, more than a million Kentuckians have eaten squirrel brains at some point in their lives. Fewer than that, Belay points out, have green eyes. "If those same CJD cases all had green eyes, would you then say that green eyes are associated with CJD?"

Truth be told, Belay's office is less concerned about CJD from squirrels than CJD from deer (though even that doesn't worry him much). In southeastern Wyoming and north-central Colorado, deer and elk have been found to carry a form of the disease known as "chronic wasting disease," and many more Americans eat venison than squirrel brains. But though a few deer hunters have contracted CJD, and though the *New York Times* ran a story on the topic similar to the one on squirrel brains, Letterman and Leno never quite got around to working mad deer into their monologues. Chances are they'd eaten some venison lately. And deadly diseases are never quite as funny when you might get them yourself.

•   •   •

These days the epidemic of epidemic stories seems to be dying down at last. Reporters have moved on to newer, fresher fears, and even mad cow disease seems to be petering out: only ten new human victims were reported in 1999, and only 1,600 cows caught the disease—down from around 6,000 in 1997. The *Lancet,* for its part, is unlikely to publish a follow-up letter about squirrel brains—much less a retraction. "It's very hard, in science, to prove that something never existed," Belay says. "And when you do, people are not usually interested."

Kentuckians, in any case, have long since made up their own minds. Only a year after the controversy erupted, Rector gave a squirrel-cooking demonstration at the Kentucky Folklife Festival in Frankfort. When he was done, he says, a local health inspector had to shoo people away to keep them from having a taste. "One elderly lady came up to me afterward," Rector remembers. " 'If I can't eat this squirrel,' she said, 'can I just take this biscuit and dip it in the gravy?' "

A year later, at the same festival, I wait under an open tent for Rector to give another demonstration—this time of guitar playing. Up and down the mall of the state capital, quilt makers, basket weavers, and wood whittlers are earnestly expounding their craft. Coal miners, at the "Narrative Stage," are telling stories from underground, while cooks, in the "Foodways Area," stir an enormous kettle of burgoo. The whole scene is both authentic and deeply contrived, edifying and dispiritingly predictable. But for a day, at least, it turns the tables on popular culture: tradition matters more here than the marketplace, and a good story has more authority than any scientific study.

When Rector shambles on stage for the day's last session, he hardly seems to notice that the tent is almost empty. Though the festival guide calls him "a key figure in the music of his region," Rector knows by now that his style is too eclectic for the average folk fan. Settling gingerly into a small folding chair, like a walrus balancing on a rubber ball, he lays his acoustic guitar on his knee and silently fingers the fret board. He talks awhile about his teacher, Mose Rager, who invented the thumb-picking style, and about his idols, Merle Travis and Chet Atkins, who perfected it. Then he feathers a few harmonics to verify his tuning, plucks a chord or two, and he's off: "Bed-Bug Blues" at full throttle.

In the latter stages of mad cow disease, patients may twitch so badly that they can barely hold a coffee cup. But Rector seems to be doing all right. Though his fingers are stubby and thick-knuckled, with nails so ragged that he has to wear paste-ons for concerts, they look as nimble as acrobats dancing on steel tightropes. While his thumb snaps the bass line and the heel of his hand thumps and dampens the soundboard, the other fingers play the melody and ornaments. They contort themselves into odd chord positions, then skitter down the strings for solos; they swing wide for bent notes, then hop up the fret board again side by side. During one particularly tortured run, a nail pops off and flies into the crowd. But Rector doesn't miss a lick.

For the next forty-five minutes his set follows an ascending curve of virtuosity. He plays a few more blues tunes for the traditionalists in the crowd, then gradually chucks in the rest of popular music: "The Shadow of Your Smile" and the theme from "Popeye," Duke Ellington, Elvis Presley, and John Philip Sousa, with his pinkie playing the piccolo part. Though his eyes stay glued to the fret board—out of shyness rather than necessity—a look of rising delight plays across his clenched features. "I haven't practiced this one in a while," he mumbles, and promptly seems to make a series of mistakes. Then I realize that he's really playing two songs at once: "Yankee Doodle" in the bass and "Dixie" in the treble—the perfect anthem for Kentucky, whose soldiers fought for both sides in the Civil War.

Watching Rector's fingers travel up the guitar neck, seeming to grow more confident the more difficult their position, I remember riding in his truck after our last hunt together. He'd shown me most of his childhood hangouts and hunting spots by then, but before I left he wanted me to see the Rochester Dam, the one John Prine sings about in the last stanza of "Paradise":

> *When I die, let my ashes float down the Green River*
> *Let my soul roll on up to the Rochester Dam*
> *I'll be halfway to heaven with Paradise waiting*
> *Just five miles away from wherever I am.*

Those words always reminded him of his cousin, he said. Jimmy never could get used to losing his old hunting grounds. Without a guitar or children to distract him, he couldn't stand to keep going to the same small patches of forest every week, where once he'd had the whole countryside. "You know that Indian?" he once told Rector. "The one in the pollution commercials that's always cryin'? I feel just like that Indian."

After his wife left him, Jimmy twice tried to kill himself, but both times he was too drunk to succeed. He used a long-barreled shotgun the first time and blew out part of his jaw. He aimed at his heart the next time and blasted off a piece of his shoulder. The third time he finally got it right.

One by one, Rector said, his heroes had died around him: Jimmy and Merle, Mose and Chickenhawk Murphy. "Chet's had cancer five times," he said, "and the last time they took a tumor the size of a hot dog out of his brain." Now, as we drove within sight of the river, he admitted that he was worried for himself—and mad squirrel disease had nothing to do with it. "My doctor tells me I've got the heart of an old man," he said, "and I've been passin' a lot of blood. They want me to get a colonoscopy, but I know how that works: You get all cut up, and then you still die."

We parked on the shore and looked out at the drought-stricken river, its sandstone ledges and muddy shallows, dark bluffs and sunken caverns exposed to the sun. And I thought about how rarely we face the true topography of our fears. Though death winds its way through every living moment—in the cars careening past us and the chemicals coursing through us, in the thickening of our arteries, the withering of our cells, and the uncertain courage of our hearts—we submerge its traces almost completely, letting our hopes and routines wash over its implacable shores. Each generation has more time to confront its mortality, and each generation concocts more outlandish threats— whether from Alar or aliens, fluoride, power lines, or mad squirrels—to defer the confrontation, to preserve the delusion that death can still be defeated.

Rector said that he might not live through the year, and his pale, possessed features showed that he meant it. But then, too, I could tell he was still riding his luck, hoping that colon cancer was just another death threat he could escape through inattention. "You know, I never did understand that line about his soul rollin' up to the Rochester Dam," he said, pointing at the gray green waterfall below us. "To do that, it would have to float *upstream*." Then he gunned the engine and turned his truck toward home.

The Mall of the Wild

⌒

KEN HOLYOAK's fish hatchery, frog farm, and wild hog preserve sits on a small gravel drive guarded by a very large fish. Eight feet long and six feet high, bristling with exotic fins and fluorescent purple-and-yellow scales, the fish looks like a cross between a bluegill and a beetle—a Volkswagen Beetle, that is, circa 1969—and hovers above passing cars as if scanning for minnows. Even Holyoak doesn't recognize its species. "I just asked this feller that goes to my church to make me a feesh," he says, "and that's what he come up with."

Such a fish might make a splash in any setting, but in Holyoak's part of the country it has the quality of a vision. On every side, Georgia's coastal plain stretches to the horizon in a weary ostinato, its peanut fields and forests repeating endlessly from the swamps of Florida to the hills of Alabama. Twisted oaks and linear pines sit so far back from the highway that the sky seems to engulf them, and the locals have little interest in raising the skyline. Alapaha, the closest town, has no visible sign of industry and only one restaurant—one so secretive that I drove past it three times without seeing it, though I was famished at the

133

time. But then there is Holyoak's fish: a thing both of the landscape and monstrously out of place; a blazing seraph, come to warn you of man's indignities to nature. Or maybe just to sell you a few hybrid bass.

One day, while researching the country's ballooning aquaculture industry, I came upon a press release from a group called the Future Frog Farmers of America (FFFA). "Move Over Chickens!" it declared. "Here Come the Bud Boys!" After thirty-five years and a million dollars of investment, Ken Holyoak had finally grasped the slipperiest of holy grails: a way to mass-produce frogs. "Anyone who is remotely familiar with bullfrogs realizes immediately that frogs are discriminate feeders," the release said. But Holyoak had taught his frogs to eat food that didn't move, and he had a patented system for growing them with little or no manual labor. Thanks to his techniques, frog farms might soon spread across the country like the poultry industry. "Ken still has to pinch himself to make sure he is not dreaming . . . "No! He is not dreaming anymore! It is Bullfrog Reality!"

This was news to me. I knew that frog gigging is an old southern tradition, and I'd grown up with kids who still caught their family dinner, on occasion, with a flashlight and a forked stick. But I also knew that frog legs have never quite made the leap into mainstream American cooking. As a chef I know put it: "A frog is either lowbrow or highbrow. If you catch it, it's low. If you order it in a French restaurant, it's high."

The FFFA promised to change all that. Frog demand,

they insisted, is a function of frog supply. The United States imports 3,800 tons of frog meat a year—more than any other country—and schools take another two million live frogs, at $20 apiece, for class dissections. But with a good domestic supply, the FFFA believed, the total market might be worth more than a billion dollars. Add the profits from tanned frog skins, frog intestines as surgical supplies, and frog-oil cosmetics, and you had a gold mine in the making.

As novel as it seemed, the pitch had a familiar ring to it. I knew that aquaculture and game farms were changing the face of the southern landscape, and with them the economies of several states. But I also knew that such farms are a natural breeding ground for fraud. For every one hundred legitimate catfish or wild-game farms, there are two or three Ponzi schemes—breeding animals for a nonexistent market, making money only so long as there are new suckers to lure in.

On my way to Holyoak's hatchery, I stopped off to talk to Jeff Jackson, a professor of wildlife management at the University of Georgia. Over the years Jackson had made something of a hobby of busting quacks. He had exposed crooked worm farmers, kept a sharp eye on emu and ostrich suppliers, and pulled the rug out from under a beaver ranch. When I told him where I was going, his eyes lit up like Pat Garrett's at rumors of Billy the Kid. Holyoak was a special case, he said. He'd been selling fish for decades and had trademarked a popular hybrid sunfish called the Georgia Giant. "But when he talks about frog farms . . ." Jackson looked away wistfully. "I wish I could go with you and ask a few questions. But he'd be on to me right away."

Holyoak's office was a plain, cement-block structure with windows on four sides. Inside, stuffed bass floated along every wall, mounted on plaques inscribed by friends and happy customers. Holyoak, flanked by four local secretaries and ranks of untidy cabinets, spieled away on the phone, reclining so far that his chair back was nearly horizontal. As much as anything else here, his body was the product of selective breeding: 245 pounds of Georgia good ol' boy, hybridized from local and Utah Mormon stock, born and raised on the swamp. "I've got somethin' I got to show you," he murmured into the mouthpiece, his consonants muffled yet gravelly, like the sound of a country road heard from inside a car. "I've got to show it to you *real* bad." Along the walls, the fish rose toward their imaginary lures, mouths gaping, eyes mesmerized.

After brief introductions to his staff, I settled down to talk frog, but just then the door burst open. In walked a meaty, impatient little man dressed in a striped knit shirt. "My name is J. C. Bell," he said, "and I'm looking for some advice on fish." It seemed he owned an experimental farm about twenty-five miles away. Poultry, cattle, sheep, and goats grew there, all grazing the same pasture in strict rotation. Cows mowed the grass, then laying hens scratched through the cow patties for bugs. The scattered dung encouraged weeds, which the sheep and goats liked to eat, and pecan trees turned their dung into nuts. It was a three-hundred-acre farm, Bell concluded, making $1,000 profit an acre, and the products were all natural. "If I can just find a fish that'll eat the animal by-products, I can close the loop."

Holyoak nodded his head and peered at Bell for a long moment, from above his black reading glasses. "Try piranha," he said.

Like most of his jokes, this one had a kernel of sense. Two years ago Holyoak had spent a month on the Amazon, living on a raft with native fishermen, scouting for new ideas. "We spoke hand language mostly," he said. "But they knew what I wanted. Got up every mornin' at four o'clock, jumped in a dugout canoe, and went six miles down the river to fish in a dead lake. Monkeys and fish, that's all they ate. I took the fish." He lost fifty pounds, he added, but he developed an appreciation for piranha.

Bell was unconvinced. "I was hoping some catfish might do the trick," he said. But he agreed to come back with some water samples from his pond. "Maybe tilapia will work," Holyoak called out as Bell left, "or African catfish!"

In the lull that followed, I tried to steer the discussion back to frogs. Once again, though, we were interrupted— this time by a family of nineteenth-century farmers, or so they seemed. The women were in bonnets and gingham dresses, the patriarch in black slacks, black suspenders, and a white straw hat. Though they looked Amish to me, they soon revealed themselves to be Lubavitcher jews, returning home to Kentucky by minivan after a Florida vacation.

While the secretaries watched, fascinated, the old man shuffled forward with his cane, aimed his bony, bearded chin at Holyoak, and assessed him with squinting eyes. "Have you got any night crawlers?" he asked in a faintly eastern European accent.

Holyoak looked him in the eyes and smiled. "No," he said. "But I've got something even better." He reached under his chair and pulled out a Tupperware bin the size of two shoeboxes. Inside, corkscrewed through a thick bedding of oat bran, lay hundreds of centipede-like creatures, faintly venomous looking, with tan and gold stripes—another of Holyoak's Amazon discoveries. "I call 'em super wiggle worms," he said, reaching a hand into the bin. "They'll keep in here for a year; all you have to do is add a slice of potato every now and then." One of the centipedes clasped on to his forefinger with its two front legs, then writhed around to find purchase for the others. "They wiggle better than anything I've ever seen," Holyoak said. "People are goin' crazy over 'em. They're gonna replace the cricket. They're gonna replace the worm."

The patriarch stared at him, befuddled. He shifted from foot to foot. He glanced at his son. Nope, I thought, he isn't biting. The centipedes were just too strange and, at $68 for two thousand, too steep an investment.

Ten minutes later he walked out with a bin under his arm and a new fishing pole besides.

Around here, Holyoak is fond of saying, you can get up at sunup and shoot a hog, bag a frog, catch a fish, and trap a turtle by sundown. Sometimes it seems that what he's running is less a hatchery than an amusement park—one that grows larger and more bewildering with each new enterprise. When his fish business needed boosting, Holyoak stuffed his catalogs with snake guards, pond aerators, and "Bug-O-Matic" feeders. When a herd of wild hogs invaded his land, he started a hog-hunting business. (He keeps them fat by dumping fifty-five-gallon drums of peanut butter in the woods.) When turtles started eating too many of his fish, he invented a "solar turtle trap" and sold his catch to a supplier in Florida.

The result, unlikely as it sounds, is a kind of microcosm of America's increasingly privatized wilderness. Over the past twenty years, as annual sales of hunting licenses have dropped from seventeen million to fourteen million, operations like Holyoak's have rushed in to fill the vacuum. Catfish were once considered fit only for other bottom feeders; now U.S. farms grow more than half a billion pounds every year; crawfish gross $45 million annually in Louisiana alone; and other animals are making the same transition. Bison ranches, deer ranches, pigeon, alligator, and turtle farms have sprung up across the South, and their meat is being served in the finest restaurants. In Boston, at Savenor's market, kangaroo meat sells for $14.99 a pound, camel for $34.99, lion for $21.99, and zebra for $39.99. All of it is raised on game farms in the United States.

Biologists worry that game farms incubate diseases and can water down the gene pool for some species. But for other species, living on a game ranch may be the only way to avoid extinction. More Indian black bucks live on game ranches in Texas, with its vast grasslands, than in their native land, and bison have made a similar comeback across the country. In 1972 there were fewer than 30,000 bison nationwide, relegated to a few paltry preserves. By 1992 there were 110,000 bison, and by 1999 there were 300,000. "The more people eat buffalo," one rancher told me, "the more buffalo there will be."

Holyoak made a similar argument. "Silent Spring is now here for the bullfrog," one of his leaflets declared. "Pollution, destruction of habitat and overharvesting" are decimating frog populations worldwide. Frog farms may be their only hope, Holyoak suggested, yet glancing around his office I still heard Jackson's words in my ears. What if all this bustle and earnest business was just an elaborate ruse—a setup like the fake bookie's office in *The Sting*? As soon as I left, I imagined, the secretaries would stand up, take off their glasses, stop typing nonsense, and collect their checks from Holyoak. The computers and file cabinets would get trundled off, the stuffed fish would come down from the walls, and Holyoak would drive off in search of another small town, another scam.

I was wrong, of course. Those ponds out back, stretching to the horizon in rectilinear formation, were no painted backdrop, and those were real people calling in their orders. Though his claims were probably inflated and some of his products a bit strange, one thing was certain: Holyoak knew fish.

The question was, did he know frogs?

•   •   •

"During the millennia that frogs and men have lived in the same world," John Steinbeck writes in *Cannery Row*, "a pattern of hunt and parry has developed. . . . The rules of the game require the frog to wait until the final flicker of a second, when the net is descending, when the lance is in the air, when the finger squeezes the trigger, then the frog jumps, plops into the water, swims to the bottom and waits until the man goes away."

Trying to get a grip on Holyoak's life feels a little bit like that. Most self-made men spend half their time composing their autobiographies, editing out the failures and eliding the equivocations until their lives sound as propulsive and single-minded as Horatio Alger stories. Not Holyoak. Ask him when he started his hatchery or where he found his super wiggle worms, and his answers will trail off into misty generalizations: "It's been years and years" or "I've been just about everywhere." At first you think he's being evasive, but little by little you realize he just doesn't remember. "I've got too much to do *today*," he says, "to worry about yesterday."

The beginning, at least, is clear. He was born, appropriately enough, in Enigma, Georgia, six miles from Alapaha. (When I asked where the name comes from, he glanced over as if embarrassed for me. "Enigma means puzzle," he explained.) His father was a Mormon missionary, sent to Georgia from Geronimo, Arizona. He had a genius for numbers and a "photogenic memory," Holyoak remembers. "I wish I had half the mind he had. He could quote the Bible word for word, and he could do numbers in his head faster than any calculator I've ever seen." By the time he died he had grown his farm to six hundred acres and developed special systems for raising hogs and cows. Unfortunately for him, his son's talents lay elsewhere.

"When I told him I wanted to grow nothin' but fish, he about died," Holyoak remembers. "'Bout had a heart attack right there." But he might have seen it coming. From the age of five Holyoak would stand by the door and bawl until someone let him hold a fishing rod. By the age of eight he was scratching out pools in his backyard and dropping in his live catch. By the time he was a teenager he was providing most of the protein for his family.

It wasn't just that Holyoak liked fish, it was that he had a psychic connection to them. "I just understand what they're doin'," he says. "I can walk out by a pond and tell you where they are." Even today, when he drives around his grounds, his eyes constantly scan his ponds' surfaces for signs of trouble. That one is too acidic, this one is over-populated, that one is infected by bacteria and needs to be drained. "Some of these things," he says, "I don't hardly know why I know 'em."

At the University of Georgia he discovered a second skill: making money. While other students relied on their parents for their allowances, Holyoak operated three or four ventures from the house he rented. First he sold sandwiches to other students, eventually hiring twelve salesmen to run orders for him. Then he started a side business in hypnosis for students who wanted to quit smoking. "I would just talk to 'em and they'd go under. Had this fellow from New York show me how." When the air force drafted him after graduation, he still managed to make some spending money selling pictures of other airmen to their girlfriends. "You could drop me in the middle of a desert," Holyoak said, "and I guarantee I'll have a business started within an hour."

After that, the details start to get fuzzy. He went to work for U.S. Steel at some point and won an award for "100 percent sales performance," whatever that means. He built a sprawling ranch house of white brick with Greco-Roman columns in front, buried both parents, and somehow found time to visit thirty-three countries to look at frogs. There was a first wife in there somewhere, and the birth of his son Hugh, and then another marriage and another boy, Jason. But the exact sequence is known to no one—least of all Holyoak.

"Go ahead! Guess how old Jason is!" his second wife, Judye, asked him one day while Holyoak and I were eating lunch at her kitchen counter. Holyoak cut a thick wedge from a raw Vidalia onion and put it in his mouth.

"Twenty-seven?"

"Thirty-one! *Ken!* How about Hugh?"

"Thirty-five?"

"Thirty-six!"

She put her hands on her hips and shook her head. The two of them were about as different as could be, she said. Take the food we were eating: pulled pork and butter beans, stewed cabbage, cornbread, and tomatoes and rice. She wouldn't eat it for the world, but he wouldn't let her serve anything else. While she had branched out into Victoriana and interior decorating, pant suits and fancy pastas, he was still doing the same things he'd always done and tuning out the world around him. "I'll bet you he doesn't even remember when we were married or how old I am," she said. "The only reason he knows my birthday is because it's a holiday."

Holyoak looked up, a gleam of genuine hope in his eyes. "Christmas?"

Judye stared hard at him for a moment, then smiled despite herself. "You can't believe anything he tells you," she said. "He's teasin' all the time." Holyoak jabbed his thumb in my direction and told her, "He doesn't know when I'm teasin' and when I'm tellin' the truth."

Only this much is certain: at some point Holyoak managed to bring his two gifts together. He started out small, growing run-of-the-mill bluegills on his daddy's land. But he soon became impatient. "Here we had hybrid strawberries and dogs and cats and seed corn, but we were growing the same fish that Columbus had," he says. "It just didn't add up to me." And so, for the next ten years, he dedicated his life to breeding the world's biggest bream.

"I made him from scratch," Holyoak said. "Built ten or twelve ponds, brought in fish from all over, the biggest I could find, and bred 'em together." For ten years, he invested everything he made—around $10,000 a year—until he had ten or twelve hybrids. "I called the best one the Georgia Giant," he says. "He grows 300 percent faster and 300 percent bigger and bites 300 percent better."

It's easy to question Holyoak's claims. His numbers have a suspicious consistency—ten or twelve fish, ten or twelve ponds, 300, 300, 300 percent—and Jeff Jackson is quick to point out that Holyoak didn't really invent the Georgia Giant: large hybrid bream occur naturally. Then, too, some of Holyoak's stories are simply outlandish. He insists, for instance, that Cubans and Haitians buy most of his turtles for use in voodoo and fertility rituals: "The Haitians, they put the turtle on a pedestal and worship him, and when they're done, they chop off his head and drink his blood. The Cubans tie him to their stomach and dance around. When he urinates, it means they'll be fertile. . . . 'Course you can't do that with a snappin' turtle."

Still, Holyoak's success is indisputable. His operation has grown from one pond on two hundred acres to seventy-nine ponds on fifteen hundred acres, and now hatches forty-four million fish eggs a year. Even when he's giving you the runaround, it's hard not to admire his work ethic. From four in the morning until eleven at night, with two late-night patrols thrown in, he inspects ponds and makes sales pitches, invents gadgets, shoots hogs, and breeds fish. "I just keep lookin' for ways to make 'em better and bigger and faster growing," he says.

Without hindsight to hinder you, the future is a realm of perfect possibility.

"Make your hand into a fist, or it might get bit," Kevin, one of the hatchery workers, told me. "Then reach around inside until you feel somethin' strange." We were standing knee-deep in one of Holyoak's artificial ponds, pulling up one of the buoys deployed along its shores. Attached to the buoy was a thick nylon rope; attached to the rope was an army surplus fuel drum, banged up and perforated with rust: the preferred nesting hole for Holyoak's channel catfish.

Inside the black mouth of the drum, my knuckles scraped tentatively against a rough, flaking surface. I'd done my share of hand grabbing by now, but this time we weren't after fish. Halfway down the side I felt it: soft and spongy, with loose, flowing tatters like boiled egg white. Slowly uncurling my fingers, I felt along the thing's edges and delicately peeled them loose from the wall. Then I reached under the quivering mass, pulled it free, and floated it to the water's surface. There, glistening like living amber in the midday sun, were some twenty-five thousand catfish eggs: Holyoak's next generation.

Just why I was doing this wasn't clear, but I suspected it was a diversionary tactic. Over the past couple of days Holyoak had been feeding me frog information at about the pace of a Bug-O-Matic—that is, just slowly and regularly enough to keep me famished. I now knew how long his bullfrogs take to grow to full size (180 days) and how much feed they consume in that time (a pound and a half—about a dollar's worth—per pound of meat). I knew that a seminar in frog raising costs $1,000, that a complete system costs around $25,000, and that such a system should be able to churn out twenty-five thousand pounds of frog legs every year at a wholesale price of $6 a pound.

After some prodding I'd even been shown Holyoak's top-secret "North American Raniculture Research Center": a domed, corrugated hangar where the frogs are raised.

"We can't stay long," Holyoak said, half blocking the door. "Those frogs spook easy." But I squeezed through anyway. Inside, a heavy vegetal smell hung in the air and a watery silence reigned. The room was filled with rank upon rank of algae-covered tubs, each about the size of a large kitchen sink, stacked five high and fifteen deep. Every stack had a pipe above it that sent water cascading down to the tubs below, and every tub was covered in black mesh to keep the frogs from hopping away. Just a few months ago, Holyoak said, there were 150,000 croakers in here—nearly 250 per tub—but they'd been selling so fast lately, there were hardly any left. I looked in on a couple of the survivors: wide-eyed and mute, their bodies like pools of green-and-yellow wax, they listened like Zen adepts to the sound of water falling. "They won't eat for strangers," Holyoak said when I asked why they weren't touching their food. "It upsets them. I don't know if they'll even eat for a camera."

Who was buying these frogs? When would their products reach the market? How much "perfecting" did his system still need? Holyoak's answer had been to dump me off here to collect fish eggs. "It takes about three days of this job before the snakes get ya," he said, deadpan, as I climbed out of his pickup. "So we take all the New York journalists we can get."

Working my way along the shore, feeling pale and

ridiculous in my swimming trunks (the others were wearing T-shirts and hip waders), I passed the time compiling a list in my head:

TEN SIGNS THAT KEN HOLYOAK IS PARANOID

1. He won't let me see the frog hatchery.
2. He won't let me talk to his frog biologist.
3. He won't let me see his top-secret super wiggle worm breeding laboratory.
4. He says he "can't remember" what kind of worm the super wiggle worm is, and he won't let me ask his worm biologist.
5. He suspects that the Chinese sold him sterile frogs.
6. His office is surveyed by videocameras.
7. His land is posted with signs that say "Warning: This Area Is Patrolled by Trained Attack Dogs."
8. Twice a night, between midnight and four, he drives around his grounds looking for fish thieves.
9. He says he can't offer me a room in his house because it's full. Yet his house is enormous and he has no guests.
10. He suggests I spend my nights in the motor home where his father died, deep in the countryside. "Just don't walk out at night. My trained attack dog will kill ya."

Still, I had to admit: Holyoak's paranoia was not entirely misplaced. According to the journal *World Aquaculture,* frog farming was a field so starved for good ideas that "successful frog farmers often guard their technology closely." Later in the same issue, a graph showed how little aquatic species had been improved by breeders over the past sixty years—especially compared to other species. Up at the top, shooting across the grid like a Patriot missile, were chickens: between 1940 and 1990 they nearly tripled the speed at which they grew. Just below them were cattle, rising in an equally vertiginous line; then came pigs, which merely doubled their productivity. Since the 1970s Norwegian salmon had begun their own rapid ascent. But frogs were still scurrying well below the page somewhere, with emu and ostrich to keep them company.

After all those years of running a hatchery, of designing bigger and better fish and schooling them from embryo to adulthood, Holyoak must have been tempted to think that nature was his to control. But a frog is not so easily broken. Nothing else seems so docile yet so hard to domesticate, so vulnerable—like an exposed organ, pulsing in the open air—yet so suicidally stubborn. As a result, most frogs eaten today are caught in the wild, largely in Bangladesh and Southeast Asia. They are gigged or caught in nets, gutted and stripped clean, and then shipped around the world frozen: a tasty, if inconsistent, variety of meat. In Brazil frogs are grown in outdoor vats. In China they're grown in concrete tanks with perforated floors. But those operations turn a profit by hiring cheap labor and catering to the frog's way of life, not by domesticating it.

"These things are just not very tough," says C. Greg

Lutz, an associate specialist in aquaculture at Louisiana State University (LSU). "They're very aggressive, but also very fragile, and they tend to succumb to all sorts of bacterial infections. If you grow them inside, you've got to wash down their whole habitat with chlorinated water every day, give 'em a light dose of bleach every day, and even then you run into disease problems."

In 1981, when Lutz first came to LSU, he joined ranks with the country's one true frog-farming expert: Dudley "Bud" Culley. By then Culley had spent twenty-five years trying to perfect an indoor frog-raising system, but year after year his food and labor costs were higher than the costs of frog legs from Asia. According to Lutz, Culley's frogs were reluctant to eat processed food—a crucial step in bringing down costs—and even when they did reach marketable size, they tended to cannibalize one another. By the time Lutz arrived, Culley was ready to clean out his lab and retire. "I helped in the grand slaughter," Lutz remembers. "Then we had a big frog fry."

At the end of another long day, I climbed on the back of a truck and headed toward the main hatchery building, an open-ended hangar of steel and concrete. There the gelatinous masses of eggs we'd collected would be dropped into one of two hundred metal troughs, bathed in a steady current of water, and gently jostled by paddle wheels. (In the wild, fish continually fan their eggs with their tails to oxygenate them.) At any given moment there could be bream, bass, crappie, catfish, grass carp, trout, or even Japanese koi growing in there, all at different stages of development. In some troughs the eggs were still quiescent; in others you could see a coiled twitching within them; in still others the fry had broken free and were beating futilely against the current. Snub-nosed and jet black, their tails whipping back and forth, they looked like little hair follicles in search of a scalp—a wig on the run.

The light was slowly fading, and I was weary and sunburned and crusted in slime. But while the others took a break when we arrived, scratching the mud from their boots with sticks, I decided to give it one last try. Turning to one of the older hatchery workers, a former manager at a Winn-Dixie, I asked if he knew how many frogs Holyoak sold every year. "I don't have any idea," he said. "I've never worked with those things." He was about to go on when one of the others signaled for him to shush. Grinning strangely, he walked over to a wooden post beside me and pointed at the intercom hanging there. Up in its left-hand corner, a small red light was burning. "Somebody over there," he said, nodding toward the office, "is listenin' in on us."

We glanced at each other in silence. Each of us, I imagined, was doing the same thing: madly rewinding the last minute's conversation, scanning for any self-incriminating quotes. Finally one of the younger guys broke in. "There's the man you need to talk to," he said, pointing through the hangar door. Out in the parking lot, a tall, angular figure shambled past, shoulders hunched and hands in his pockets.

His name was John Joyce. He had a master's degree in aquaculture and divided his time between the hatchery and the University of Georgia, where he was a research technician. He had short gray hair, protruding ears, and eyes that peered at you intensely for a moment, only to skitter off when you tried to meet them. He'd been with Holyoak off and on for twenty years, he said, mostly breeding fish and tending to their health troubles. But when I asked about the frogs, he started to fidget like a subpoenaed witness. "I don't know," he said. "They've had some problems lately."

For years, he explained, Holyoak simply collected frogs from his ponds and sold them to farmers a few dozen at a time. Then, five or six years before, he began to grow them in vats at the main hatchery building. "We fed 'em larvae and pellets at first," Joyce said. "After a couple of years we had a good breeding stock of frogs, eatin' just pellets."

It was a promising start. But though the frogs had learned to settle for fast food, their wild instincts were only napping: the minute Holyoak moved them to an open pond, they staged a mass escape.

"So that was two years down the drain," Joyce said. To make up for lost time, Holyoak flew to China to buy some domesticated breeders. But then the eggs they laid weren't fertile. In the end they had no choice but to collect thousands of bullfrogs from the wild again and to teach them to eat pellets.

Then the disease struck.

Holyoak's stacked trays were natural breeding grounds

for bacteria, Joyce said, especially if the frogs were over-crowded. Once a frog got sick in one tray, his infection drained down to any neighbors beneath him. "Two summers ago, that building was full of frogs," he said. "But bacteria about wiped 'em out. They're down to less than twenty thousand now. And he hasn't sold *that* many of 'em."

Holyoak later denied this version of events, but Joyce had no reason to bad-mouth the operation—quite the opposite. Listening to him, I realized that Holyoak's frog farm hadn't cracked the amphibian code after all, but neither was it a Ponzi scheme. It was something altogether sadder and more grand: a failed dream. Holyoak had done his homework. His tray system showed Chinese and Brazilian influences; his indoor operation was similar to Culley's. Yet after thirty-five years of catching frogs and feeding them pellets, tinkering with automatic feeders and inventing vaccinators, the Future Frog Farmers of America were no closer to dropping their first name. "I've been watchin' him work on this thing for a long time, and he's never quite gotten it," Joyce said. "I don't know if he ever will."

Many days later, at the Horseradish Grill in Atlanta, I sat at a gleaming oak bar and awaited my dinner. Behind me, the sun-baked evening crowd lounged about in summer dresses and linen suits, under the heavy beams of the vaulted ceiling, as a fire blazed in the corner. "Let me suggest a Sancerre," the sommelier murmured as soft jazz wafted down from hidden speakers above him. "It's a great summer wine from the Loire valley, with a bit of a tang to stand up to what you'll be eating." Then he laughed despite himself and leaned in closer. "The truth is I have no idea what to suggest. About the only thing I've ever done with frogs is flatten 'em with a post."

Earlier that day I had dropped off a pair of bullfrog legs at the Grill's kitchen. I had been told, on good authority, that this was the finest authentic southern restaurant in the country and that the chef, David Berry, was a big fan of farm-raised game. When I had called to ask if he would prepare one of Holyoak's frogs for me, he had agreed immediately.

There was only one problem: The frog I brought wasn't raised by Holyoak.

Holyoak had promised to give me a frog before I left the hatchery, but when the time came, he said the North American Raniculture Research Center was locked. Instead he drove me out to a pond and pointed a high-powered rifle out the truck window. In the evening's whiskey-colored light, I could see a bullfrog's eyes floating on the surface like soap bubbles, mesmerized by passing clouds. Then suddenly he was cartwheeling across the water, belly flashing like a green-and-yellow whirligig, trailing a ragged red streamer as if in an excess of joy. "D'ya see how far that bullet blowed 'im?" Holyoak chuckled beside me. "I ain't got nothin' but hollow-points in here for shootin' hogs."

Now, as Berry set my dinner before me, it was hard to connect that memory with the thing on the plate. On the one hand, no meat is quite so recognizable—so luridly anatomical—as a pair of frog legs. Stripped of its slinky tights, each ligament, tendon, muscle, and articulated joint looked ready to leap across the room. But then the taste was worlds away from the swamp. Tender and buttery, with a subtle, amphibian chew, it was so mild that the Sancerre almost overwhelmed it. "I sautéed it for three or four minutes and then drizzled it with a lemon-caper sauce," Berry explained, settling in next to me. "Frog doesn't need a lot more than that."

I had thought that the moral of Holyoak's story was clear: Some things just aren't meant to be domesticated. But here, in the elegant finish of this dish, in its seamless transformation from bullet kill to haute cuisine, lay another story. All nature's stubbornness, I thought, is no match for a good imagination. We've taught pigs to find mushrooms and dogs to lead the blind, corn to manufacture its own pesticide and watermelons to grow without seeds. Why shouldn't the Holyoaks of the world one day domesticate anything on legs, turning frog farmers into princes of industry? For an ever more ravenous, ever more ingenious society, wild game is just another work in progress.

Not long after that meal I finally managed to track down Bud Culley, the grand old man of frog farming. He lives in Liberty, Mississippi, now, far from the scene of his final frog fry. But rather than stewing in bittersweet memories, he's already in the throes of a new venture. "We've got the only frogs we know in the world that are entirely on pelleted food!" he said over a crackling phone line. "They're on pellets from metamorphosis on up!" When I pressed him for details, though, he cut me short: "I make my living off this consulting, so I'm not going to give you a lot of information to spread around." Then he hung up.

Is he dreaming? you ask. Call it Bullfrog Reality.

Send in the Hounds

We will, fair queen, up to the mountain's top, and mark
the musical confusion of hounds and echo in conjunction.
—*A Midsummer Night's Dream*, Act IV, scene i

A DARK FOREST, far from any porch light or murmuring
highway. A gang of hard-bitten men, silent and single-
minded. A pack of howling dogs, circling restlessly. These
are things most women try to avoid. Sondra Beck, though,
has a curious habit of seeking them out. "There ain't no
natural reason to like it," she admits. "Stumbling out there
in the night just to listen to a dog howl—it doesn't make
any sense." Yet ever since the age of six, Beck has been a
coon-hunting fanatic. In the foothills of Oklahoma's
Kiamichi Mountains, where she has lived all her life, the
raccoons are in a constant state of alert: Beck hunts them
more than 340 nights a year.

Tonight was the first round of the Oklahoma State Professional Coon Hunters Kennel Club hunt in McAlester.
Throughout the low-lying hills around us, "casts" of four
dogs—one per coon hunter—were competing to see how

many raccoons they could run up trees. (Raccoons are nocturnal, so they're always hunted at night.) A few minutes before, our judge had punched his stopwatch and the dogs had been released. Now, the first to strike a trail would win a hundred points, the second would get seventy-five, the third fifty, and the fourth twenty-five. The first dog to tree a coon would win a hundred points, the next one seventy-five, and so on. The dog who racked up the most points by the end of the night would win the cast.

Somewhere out there, in other words, a raccoon was running for its life, scrambling over branches and paddling across streams, trying to stay ahead of the gnashing teeth at its heels. As the dogs lost its scent and circled to rediscover it, their voices laced together and unraveled, climbing and falling through the stunted hardwood forest. I knew that coonhounds change voices as they hunt—bawling as they search, yelping when they strike a trail, and when the coon is finally treed, switching to a choppy bark that can carry for miles. But in that midnight dark their sounds were like radio signals from another galaxy. I heard a bark out there, a yip and a grunt or two, and what sounded like a ray gun. Then, abruptly, the noises faded, leaving us stranded in those strange woods.

"Which way did he go, George?"

"I can hear the blue bitch, but I think they're all lost."

"They'd get found if they'd come back this way."

With our headlamps off I could just make out five human shapes, their outlines faintly phosphorescent with starlight. Though I couldn't see their faces, I could imagine their expressions: a smirk here, a squint of concentration there, nowhere a hint of fear. Most of them knew this forest in the dark better than I knew my own neighborhood by day. Every passing scent belonged to a plant they could name and describe; every change in terrain fit the contours of some mental map. They knew where the wild persimmons and hackberries grew and whether they had ripened yet, and what they didn't know their dogs could tell them.

Beck's sinewy shape hunched over a cigarette ember, drawing in a long breath before exhaling. "I don't know what I'm doing with Sandy out here," she said. "She just had a litter seven weeks ago." Most hunters prefer larger, more aggressive males, but Beck has never had anything but females. "They may be in heat twice a year," she says, "but males are in it all year round." If she felt any sympathy for Sandy tonight, it was only because she had been in the same situation herself: two months after giving birth to her daughter, Beck was out in the woods again, hunting raccoons while her husband took care of the baby.

Suddenly a sharp, squeaky bark rifled through the woods, like the sound of an ax biting into hickory.

"Tree, K.C.!"

One by one the hounds' voices lifted from the same direction, sounding as hungry, if not quite as harmonious, as wolves. I waited for a long moment, but no one moved. "Can I turn on my headlamp now?" I whispered finally.

"Yeah," Beck said. "Go ahead."

But when the blinding light surrounded us again, I

could understand her reluctance: in a forest at night, only those in the dark can truly see.

Beck's sixty-acre farm lies down a long dirt road in southeastern Oklahoma's Pushmataha County—"twenty miles from the nearest loaf a' bread," as she likes to say. The farm consists of a double-wide mobile home with a satellite dish, a dilapidated barn, two rectangular paddocks, and the Clear Creek Kennel, where she breeds perhaps the finest English coonhounds in the country. Pastureland lies all around and beyond it a circle of forest that drops, on one side, toward Clear Creek and some of the last virgin bottomland in Oklahoma.

For now it's still wild country—just driving to Beck's house, I passed snapping turtle, muskrat, skunk, armadillo, hawk, and raccoon lying along the roadside. But within a generation, she knows, much of the wilderness may be cut over as the last of the big landowners dies. (People here are sometimes poor and sometimes only posing as such: when one local farmer died not long ago, his relatives discovered that he owned fourteen blocks of downtown Oklahoma City.) "This is probably the last place around here like this," Beck says. "We can hunt for three days and nights without ever hitting the highway."

When I first came to Beck's farm, I'd recently become the proud but somewhat befuddled owner of a redbone coonhound—a dog bred, over the course of centuries, for the sole purpose of tracking and treeing raccoons. I knew that I would probably never hunt Hattie—I lived in Cambridge then—but I wanted to get a better sense of her heritage and what drove coon hunters into the woods night after night. The previous year, at another coon-hunting championship, Beck had been pointed out to me in the crowd. "That's our champion from the last two years," Bill Cavner, the secretary-treasurer of the Oklahoma Federation of Coon Hunters, told me. "Most of these guys are scared to death they'll draw her cast tonight." Afterward I'd called Beck a few times to talk about coon hunting, but this was my first time meeting her in the flesh.

Ambling out to greet me, she seemed to blend into the landscape as well as any coyote. At fifty-three Beck was tall and rangy, with bristly, sandy blond hair, stone gray eyes, and weathered skin. Her voice was as hoarse and raucous as a raven's, but with a sweetness that kept it from being intimidating. Around those parts, I'd heard, Beck was famous for taking in strays—not just cats and dogs, but deer, goats, and pigs, too. "The game warden brings by any wild animals or orphans he finds, even though keeping them is illegal," she told me later, in her kitchen.

While I watched, she poured warm milk into two nipple-topped baby bottles and brought them out to her two orphan calves, Midnight and Curly Sue. In the neighboring paddock, a bunch of goats clanked around among the lawn detritus, their eyes maniacal above their bony bodies, while a pony and a potbellied pig named Louise looked on. "Over at McAlester prison, they train some mean dogs to walk between the fences, to prevent escapes," Beck said. "I have a friend who works over there who brought me a dog once that was just too mean for them. Well, I kept it chained up in our barn and fed it from a stick for a week. In the end that dog loved me. Always made my husband, Brent, nervous, but it would have done anything for me."

Some people might see a contradiction between caring for orphaned animals and chasing raccoons around every night. My mother, for instance, finds raccoons every bit as exotic and adorable as koalas. A native of Germany, she calls them "bears that wash themselves" and tends to sigh at their mention. When she and my father drove me to my first coon hunt, she suddenly turned and pleaded: "You aren't going to shoot any yourself, are you?" Later, when we passed a simple church entitled House of Prayer, my father looked over and grunted: "That's where you'll find all the raccoons right about now."

When I mentioned these qualms to Beck, she just shrugged: "This is bad country for animal rights activists." Back in the 1970s, when coon hides sold for $30 or $40 apiece, Beck used to earn her Christmas money coon hunting. (Winter, when raccoon pelts are thickest, is official coon-hunting season.) Some of her poorer neighbors went further, all but making their living from hides. "You couldn't really blame them," Beck said. "A man could work all week for $100, but he could make as much in two hours in the woods." Still, today, with raccoon coats out of fashion, pelts bring as little as seventy-five cents and most hunters have put away their guns, leaving only sportsmen behind. While the number of commercial coon hunters has plummeted, the number of coonhound events has nearly doubled in the past ten years. These days, at Christmas-time, Beck puts out feeders for the raccoons rather than selling their hides.

This was a tale to gladden my mother's heart. But wildlife biologists, I later learned, are less than pleased by it. Raccoons and coonhounds, it seems, have spent most of American history locked in furious evolutionary competi-tion, an arms race of sorts to see which side can outwit or outsmell the other. Like the cold war, the battle hasn't always been good for its participants, but it's been good for the world at large, giving the dogs something to chase and keeping the raccoons from eating everything in sight. Only lately, when coon hunters have declared détente, has all hell broken loose.

The story began some five centuries ago, when the first boatload of Spaniards arrived on the shores of the New World. American dogs were a motley crew back then. From the long-haired pueblo to the Mexican hairless to the Peruvian pug-nosed, there were seventeen types in total, all of them descended from wolves, coyotes, din-goes, and the Siberian dogs that followed the first Asian trekkers across the Bering Strait. "Surly and snappish . . . snarlish and intractable," in the words of one settler, they were used by native people to stampede bison over cliffs, to herd llama and alpaca, and to find the breathing holes of seals. But no historical account, no early Indian account, recalls dogs hunting down raccoons—much less chasing them up trees and barking like maniacs.

Then came the Spanish and their dogs of war. "They have eyes which shoot out fire, throw out sparks," wrote a Franciscan friar named Fray Bernardino Sahagún. "They are very stout and strong; they are not peaceful, they go panting, they go with their tongues hanging out. They are marked the color of tigers, with many colored spots." In 1495 Christopher Columbus's twenty hounds ripped through ranks of Indian warriors at the battle of Vega Real in Hispaniola, a spectacle so terrifying that many tribes later surrendered without a fight. "Within a few years," anthropologist Marion Schwartz writes in *A History of Dogs in the Early Americas,* "public markets sold human body parts for training Spanish dogs to develop a taste for people, and these dogs were pitted against Native Americans for sport."

Once the Indians got over the shock of facing such animals, Schwartz goes on to say, "they were eager to get their hands on this new 'technology.'" Soon European dogs were interbreeding with local mutts, adapting effortlessly to climates from the arctic to the tropical, bearing offspring that would almost completely replace the native varieties. Just as the Spanish brought their dogs of war, the French, English, and Germans brought their own breeds, carefully tailored for other tasks. There were slender, sharp-sighted whippets and greyhounds, so fleet they could outrun a deer; dachshunds for digging out badgers; Airedales so strong they could stand up to a wolf. But the true triumphs of the breeders' art were the scent hounds.

In August of 1785 seven such beasts arrived at George

Washington's home in Mount Vernon, a gift from his friend the marquis de Lafayette. Known as Grand Bleu de Gascogne hounds, they were first bred in 1360 by Gaston Phoebus, comte de Foix. The Grand Bleus' noses were said to be the keenest of any breed, and their voices, Washington noted in his diary, rang across the Virginia forest like the bells of Moscow. Yet even they still needed some fine-tuning. For centuries, blue Gascon hounds had mostly hunted things that stayed on the ground: wolf, hare, deer, red fox, wild boar. Once in Virginia, however, they had to go after game with a penchant for heights: bobcats, American gray fox, mountain lions, raccoons. Dogs without a good treeing instinct were likely to charge right past their quarry or else abandon it before the owner caught up. Four months after receiving his French hounds, Washington complained that he was still "plagued with the Dogs running Hogs."

In time Washington would come to be called the father of coon hunting as well as the father of his country. But the truth is that creating coonhounds was a group effort. Content with any dog that exhibited the right instincts, other settlers threw English foxhounds, Cuban bloodhounds, Hanoverian schweisshunds, and red Irish hounds into the canine melting pot. By the 1800s new American breeds began to emerge, all with strong noses, floppy ears (for stirring up scents), insensitive coats (for tearing through brambles), and a peculiar passion for chasing things up trees. The United Kennel Club now registers six of them— English, Plott, bluetick, redbone, black and tan, and treeing Walker—but the elite American Kennel Club fully recognizes only black and tans. As one bluetick owner told me, "The AKC would rather register some strange, furry little animal in China than the dogs that helped build this country."

Sandy, the dog Beck would be hunting at the state competition, was the latest model in coonhound breeding and training. Trim and light on her feet—more foxhound than bloodhound—Sandy didn't waste time worrying out cold trails inch by inch, as a "cold-nosed" dog would. She skimmed over the terrain to home in on the freshest, "hottest" scent and ran it down as quickly as possible. Some hunters missed the behemoths they grew up with and the epic hunts those dogs used to lead, but Beck had no regrets. "In my opinion, the dogs have gotten better and better," she said. "Those old black and tans and blueticks, they might pick a trail three days old and howl and boo-hoo over it for hours and hours. I don't have any time for that. I need my dog to move that track."

Raccoons, meanwhile, have done some evolving of their own—thanks no less to European settlers. First hunters wiped out wolves, bears, mountain lions, and the raccoon's other natural enemies. Then settlers came in and created ideal raccoon habitats: successional forests grizzled with fruit bushes, villages free from predators, and cornfields laden with food. Finally, as a kind of bonus, we gave them garbage dumps to get them through the lean times. Two centuries ago no raccoon could get far from a forest or swamp without starving or being eaten. Now they're happily ensconced even in the prairie states.

Growing up in Oklahoma, reading *Where the Red Fern Grows*, I always thought of raccoons as underdogs. In that book a young boy kills enough of them, with the help of his two redbones, to lift his homesteading parents out of poverty. True, much is made of raccoons' wiles: Doubling back on their own tracks, swimming down rivers to erase their trails, leaping from treetop to treetop, they constantly pit their wits against overwhelming odds—small, furry Steve McQueens hoping for a Great Escape. But their struggle is clearly doomed: inevitably the dogs chase them up a tree and the kid shoots them down.

It was only later that I began to hear the other side of the story, the one where the raccoons got away. In the early 1940s, for instance, hunters in north-central Arkansas had a hard time treeing any coons at all for a while. The reason, they found, was a conveyor belt, built to carry rocks from a quarry to the nearby Bull Shoals dam. "Coons learned they could get on that conveyor belt to get away from the dogs," Forrest Wood, a resident of nearby Flippin, Arkansas, told a reporter. The tactic, he added, nearly drove local hounds crazy. "Several dogs had to be locked up. They just couldn't stand it."

So it went: raccoons ever scrambling into new environmental niches; coonhounds ever evolving to flush them out. For two centuries the race was a dead heat, with raccoons expanding their range yet supplying skins for countless coats and hats. Then, in the 1980s, when raccoons became too worthless to kill, the balance of power abruptly, disastrously, shifted. With the last of their predators gone, raccoon populations began to swell drastically.

Ecologist Justin Congdon remembers the change more vividly than most. For the past twenty-five years Congdon has followed the nesting habits of turtles living in a single 1,500-acre preserve in southeastern Michigan. Raccoons always ate their share of turtle eggs, Congdon says, but the turtles were prolific enough to cope: from 1976 to 1980, 40 percent of the nests survived. Once fur prices plummeted, though, raccoon populations reached "plague proportions": for most of the 1980s only 4 percent of the nests survived. "Some years," Congdon says, "out of 150 nests, 150 were destroyed." On Florida's Canaveral Peninsula, in the same period, a study found that 397 out of 400 loggerhead sea turtles' nests had been destroyed. More recently, in northern Louisiana, raccoons have destroyed nearly all the turtle nests in a number of study sites.

Like most animal researchers, Congdon has a grudging respect for raccoons. Over the years lab studies have demonstrated the animal's intelligence—"Discrimination of the Number Three by a Raccoon," a typical paper is titled—and field studies have confirmed it. "They work an area just the way I do," Congdon says, "except they're not doing it for science, they're doing it for dinner." First the coons case the most popular nesting spots—road banks, fire lanes, dams. Then, when egg-laying season is at its peak, they converge. "I've seen a raccoon take the eggs from a female snapping turtle as they're being laid," Congdon says. "He just stood behind her, where she couldn't bite him, and caught the eggs in his hands." If the turtle is small enough—like a painted turtle—the raccoon will just bite its head off, eviscerate it from the esophagus down, and pluck the eggs from its oviduct.

The same sorts of stories are told by people who study neotropical birds and wild turkeys, whose eggs are also eaten by raccoons. Right now, they say, only diseases like rabies, distemper, and parvovirus are keeping coon populations in check. (After an epidemic, young raccoons sometimes have to learn to find their prey's nests again, since their mothers weren't around to teach them.) But the violent booms and busts are hard on a habitat. Much better, everyone agrees, would be to control the raccoons more consistently—for example, by hunting them. As one wildlife manager put it: "I wish the coon hunters would just go ahead and kill them."

Walking around the parking lot in McAlester, on the evening of the coon hunt, felt a bit like visiting an American military base: all that sleek, high-tech weaponry for what amounted to war games. Though the hunters looked as ragged as sharecroppers, few of them had spent less than $10,000 on coon hunting. Their hounds, though tied to tailgates with frayed lengths of rope, could fetch up to $20,000 from a breeder. Their beat-up trucks were crammed with electronic gear: radio-tracking systems, lamps with interchangeable lenses, and collars that could shock a dog's vocal cords if it barked up the wrong tree. When these men weren't demonstrating such gizmos, they were usually discussing their dogs' sperm count. Many of them regularly sent their champion studs to places like Galaxy Genetics Reproductive Center in Ohio. There, employees collect semen in a plastic vagina, package it in "straws" chilled by liquid nitrogen, and send it off by courier for next-day insemination.

Beck, as usual, was the only woman in hunting gear. "Some women, they try to love coon hunting 'cause that's what their husbands do," she said. But a coon hunter is born, not made. "I was a tomboy, of course. Now I'm an old woman and I'm still a tomboy," she said. "Now, my sister, she was different. She was all, you know, feminine and things. She was the type, you'd say 'spider' and she'd run a mile."

Another female coon hunter I'd spoken with, Vickie Lamb Deal from southern Georgia, had complained that it took her years to get the other hunters' respect. They held barbed-wire fences open for her, stuffed phone numbers in her pocket, and their wives grew so jealous that they sent her an anonymous letter. "They told me that I had no business hunting with men, that I should form my own club with other women," Deal said. "If they had just stopped to think about it, they would have realized that out in the swamp—with the mud and the bugs and the snakes—is not a particularly good place to flirt with someone's husband."

Beck hadn't had that kind of trouble. "I really don't think

that they think of me as a woman hunter out there," she said. "There's no holding the fence for me, and that's the way I like it. If you put yourself in a man's place, you ought to be able to carry your weight." By now she'd hunted for so long and in so many places that everyone in the coon-hunting world knew her by name. But even when she drew a cast full of strangers, she never had a problem. "'Course, I never encourage nothin'," she said. "But I just think coon hunters are awful nice people. At least they are to me."

Three hours later, as we drove toward our third hunting site of the night, I could only envy her insouciance. As the roads grew thinner and more twisted, branches squeaked and scraped against the outside of the windows, and I could see our driver's face glistening with tension as he worked the wheel. "I don't whip my dogs much," he said, "but when I do I keep it up until they've got blood on their backs. That way they know they've been whipped."

We were having a tough night. A couple of hours before, we had hoped to surprise a few raccoons munching on ripe mulberries, but the dogs led us to huge, crooked post oaks instead. We probed the trees' branches with the beams of our headlamps and blasted on whistles designed to sound like an injured animal—raccoons are incurable rubberneckers—but our lamplights caught no glimmering, inquisitive eyes. For a while one of the hunters swore that he could see a dark shape in the upper branches, but the others ignored him. "He didn't see no coon," Beck muttered. "When another guy's light shines up on the other side of the tree, it can fool you sometimes. But it ain't a coon until three people see it."

Now there was less than half an hour left on the judge's stopwatch and we still hadn't seen any raccoons. Slogging through a marshy meadow ahead of me, the dogs and their owners looked equally abashed, their shapes stooped and spectral in the light of my headlamp. "Well, Katie, I don't know what the hell you're doin'," one hunter told his bluetick. "But it's about time you treed a damn coon."

Beck grinned next to me. She didn't usually talk to her dogs much on a hunt, she said. "But I like 'em to talk to me a little bit more than Sandy's been doin'." At such moments hunters used to comfort themselves with tales of raccoon subterfuge—of animals running on fences or down gravel roads to hide their scent—but competitive hunts, with their quick-treeing dogs, have changed the character of coon legends. Hunters now talk about how tough coons can be in a fight, how they can whip almost any dog one on one. The week before, Beck had been at a hunt in Paris, Texas, where four dogs had chased a raccoon into a lake. While the raccoon was in its element, the dogs were clumsy in the water and had to content themselves with circling and barking. The coon bided its time. When it noticed that one of the females was tiring, it calmly crawled on the dog's head and drowned her.

The hunters found the other three dogs an hour later, still swimming around the raccoon.

Tonight, halfway back to the trucks, our dogs flared another trail. As the minutes ticked off on the judge's stopwatch, we listened to the dogs toiling in the eaves of the mulberry grove, their voices insistent, exaggerated, as if trying to convince themselves as well as their owners. Fireflies drifted above the marsh grasses, like torches carried by a distant search party. Then a blaring squall erupted from far to our left, well away from the other dogs.

"Tree, Sandy!"

While the other dogs were wasting time on cold trails, Beck's dog seemed to have peeled off and found a coon on her own. If so, this was a "split tree" in coon hunter parlance: the crowning skill of a well-trained coonhound. But Beck was suspicious. Her dog Alf would bark 135 times a minute when he treed a raccoon. And though Sandy wasn't quite so loquacious usually—she averaged 80 or 90 barks a minute—tonight she was downright taciturn. We tried to follow the sound of her voice, but minutes went by without a bark. When Sandy started up again, her voice had a hesitant, faltering quality, like a child who knew that she was lying but couldn't seem to remember the truth.

"Please, y'all, don't judge her by tonight," Beck said, gripping the top strands of a barbed-wire fence and scissoring her legs across. Sandy wasn't the quickest dog in her kennel, but she was usually a "classy" tree dog: up on her hind legs, propped stiffly against the trunk, head thrown back as she barked. By the time we reached her, however, she was cowering against the base of the trunk with the rest of the dogs. She looked up at Beck, clearly disconcerted, her only consolation being that the other dogs didn't know what to make of the situation, either.

We strafed the branches with our headlamps, still hoping for a glimpse of flashing eyes. Like Sandy before us, we whooped just once at the sight of scuttling forms, then realized our mistake. These creatures were too small, too indifferent to our lights and noise, to be raccoons. The fringe of folded white fur along their sides eventually gave them away: flying squirrels.

In a night of misdirection and disappearing coons, this was the forest's final practical joke. Few in the cast had ever seen a flying squirrel before, though they had thousands of hunting hours between them. "I know my dog didn't tree those things," Beck said. "They don't hardly touch the ground to leave a scent."

John Dennis, the lowest-scoring hunter among us, reached down to leash his bluetick. When he stood up he was holding something he'd found in the leaves: a dirty Coke bottle with a scroll of paper wound up inside. Given how the night had gone, he probably expected the message to read, "Nyah, nyah, nyah." Instead it just said, "Hi, Fred." Dennis wadded up the note—"My name isn't Fred," he said—and threw it into the blackberry bushes.

Later, as we headed back to our trucks, the dogs were still straining at their leashes, eyes rolling back in their heads, desperate for more. What do they get out of all this? I wondered. Their days were spent in a cage or in training (some owners took them running down country roads, tied to a pickup driving at a steady clip), their nights in a forest hunting for something they'd never kill. What kept them going?

The answer wasn't clear. But I thought a clue to it might lie in a lecture I'd heard a year before, at a meeting of the American Association for the Advancement of Science. Two animal behaviorists from Hampshire College in Massachusetts had compared the sounds dogs make to those made by wolves. Genetically, for all intents and purposes, dogs *are* wolves: they share all but 0.2 percent of their mitochondrial DNA (wolves and coyotes are twenty times as genetically distinct). Beyond their appearance, the sole thing separating them is behavior. Although wolf pups whine just as dog pups do, wolves eventually graduate to growls and howls, while dogs never get past barking. A dog's bark, the scientists had said, was midway between a whine and a growl—a confused, "ComeHereGoAway!" sound indicative of arrested adolescence.

Dependent, petulant, overly excitable, most dogs are easy to imagine as terminal teenagers. But these coonhounds were different: though loyal beyond reason, they had careers of their own, in a sense. I remembered going to buy Hattie at a breeder's house, expecting to be chased by a pack of bloodthirsty dogs as I came up the driveway. But they barely turned their heads at my arrival: "Go on," their eyes seemed to say. "You aren't what we're after." On this night, listening to the dogs howling down the trail, so nearly like a pack of wolves, I couldn't help but wonder if they hadn't managed, against all odds, to break free of their adolescence, to transcend their domesticity by returning to the hunt.

The more elusive question was what kept the owners out

here. A competitive hunt was exciting, sure, but what about all those other nights, alone in the woods without a trophy to win? "It's a simple deduction," one coon hunter told me. "You love it or you hate it. And even if you hate it, you can't quit it. It's as bad as bein' a damn dope addict." No coon hunter really expects to make his investment back with breeding and prize money, Beck admitted. Yet pleasure wasn't really the point, either. "There are some nights, before I go on a hunt, when it's kind of cold outside and I'd rather stay home and watch TV," she said. "But I don't think of it like that. When it's dark, I just go hunting."

Both Beck and her husband, Brent, had been married before, and they seemed to keep a certain teasing distance from each other. Although they were often in the woods together, they always trained and hunted with their own dogs—Brent mostly with males, Beck always with females. During the week Brent worked full-time at an ammunition depot in McAlester, but he still managed to match Beck's training regimen. He'd take two young dogs with him on Monday, spend three nights training them after work, and then come home for the last four nights of the week.

"Yeah, I kind of believe there might be some competition there," Beck told me. "A lot of times, even when we're just pleasure hunting, we'll go by competition rules to practice." In 1991, Brent and Beck both advanced to the quarterfinals of the UKC world coon-hunting championships, only to draw each other in a cast. "They changed the rules after that so that two dogs from the same owners can't ever be in the same cast together," Beck said. "Why would you want to pay a $500 entrance fee just to be eliminated on the first night by your own dog?" As it turned out, she won the cast.

By the time we made it back to Beck's farm, the pastures were glowing grayly in the false dawn, and I would have been more than happy to sleep in the kennel. Moving at half speed, Beck led me to her mobile home, but she seemed reluctant to open the door. "We're a different breed out here," she said, glancing in at the flimsy gold paneling and faux wrought-iron latches, the worn shag carpeting and plywood cabinets. "Beyond civilization." She made up a pallet of quilts for me on the floor, in front of the console television, then sat on the arm of the couch, her face half in shadow. There was a house here once, she said, but it burned down because of a faulty hot-water heater, and they spent the insurance money on their trailer and kennels. "There're a lot of things I would change if I could."

Though Beck still lived in her hometown, and though she'd married twice and had five grandchildren, her dogs were her true legacy. Her own children had only confirmed her belief that a love of coon hunting can't be taught. "I tried to get my kids interested," she said, "but it never did seem to stick. They're town kids by nature—town kids who just happened to be raised in the country. I remember one time, we took 'em out to the woods and my husband was shining a light on a coon to show my daughter, to get her interested. Well, I suddenly noticed my son was missing. I called around, but I couldn't find him, and I was starting to get real worried. When I finally found him, you know where he was? Sittin' in the grass, using a penlight to read a Hardy Boys novel." He is a computer programmer in Dallas now.

All around us, in the dingy light, trophies lined the walls in triple ranks, their golden figurines and silver hounds gathered in a great circle around me, like miniature gods awaiting a coon hunt on Mt. Olympus. Over the past ten years Beck and Brent had won the Oklahoma State Coon-hunting Championship twice and the Oklahoma State Nite Champion hunt four times; they'd placed second in the Texas State Coon-hunting Championship and in the prestigious UKC American Heritage hunt, qualified more than fifteen dogs for the UKC World Championships (five in a single year), and won countless smaller hunts. Over in the corner, a gigantic, four-tiered purple trophy commemorated a hunt that their dog Cadillac had won in 1994, in what was then the largest open event in history. "I need to get rid of a bunch of those," Beck said, following my gaze. "I have boxes and boxes of plaques in storage."

Brent nodded on his way to the bedroom. "You can't eat trophies," he said. "You can boil 'em three days and the soup's still bad."

Beck and I sat quietly for a moment then, listening to the night sounds outside. And I wondered how it changes a person to know the sleeping world as well as the waking one. I got up each day to the relentless immediacy of the world at work—the clamor for attention, for conversation, for instant gratification. But Beck had spent half her waking life watching the world at rest. Driving home after a long hunt, she could probably picture her grandfather still alive within one of those darkened farmhouses, her husband a dreaming child, her children asleep with families of their own. In the half-light between dark night and morning it was easy to confuse the future and the past, the hills an empty stage for your imagining.

After a while Beck groaned to her feet and cast a last look around—a look that seemed to encompass all the profit and loss, the mortgages and divorce and missed opportunities embodied by those gilt statuettes. Then she turned to me with a tired smile. "Have you ever tasted a dewberry?" she said. "They're like blackberries, only bigger. Oh man, they're delicious." On fall days like this, she said, when she took her puppies into the woods for a run, the pig and the goats sometimes tagged along. If she wanted to, she said, she could sustain herself on wild fruit as she went—on dewberries and muscadine grapes, sand plums, hog plums, and wild persimmons—following the seasons as they wheeled through the last of the old bottomlands. "This is still big country," she said. "We can just ride and ride and never get out of the woods."

I think about her out there sometimes, when I'm home at night in my brownstone, and wonder what I might be willing to trade for such a life, as Beck traded in her house and first marriage and more besides. I live in Brooklyn now, where the lights burn even brighter than in Cambridge, with a coonhound at the foot of my bed who may never know what she's missing. It's too late to teach Hattie about raccoons, and I wouldn't have the patience for it anyway. But I like to think that if I had she might have done her bloodline proud. A good coonhound is born, not made, Beck says. And it's hard not to imagine what Hattie could have been, when her ears prick up and her nose traces crazy patterns through the autumn leaves. At night, when friends see her twitching her paws in her sleep, they tell me that she's chasing rabbits in her dreams. But I know better.

Low on the Hog

What a group of people we were, I thought. Why, you could cause us the greatest humiliation simply by confronting us with something we liked. Not *all* of us, but so many. Simply by walking up and shaking a set of chitterlings or a well-boiled hog maw at them during the clear light of day!

—RALPH ELLISON, *Invisible Man*

TIM PATRIDGE was seventeen years old and hungry for the wide world beyond Atlanta, when he first learned that you can make a silk purse out of a sow's ear. He was working at the Hyatt Regency at the time, in the kitchen of a German chef named Walter Staib. As *chef tournant*, Patridge filled in wherever he was needed—trussing a pheasant here, carving a prime rib there—leaving the delicate touches to his boss. Then one night an order arrived that reversed their roles, if only for a moment.

Sammy Davis Jr. was staying at the hotel, a waiter announced, and he wasn't interested in the regular menu. He wanted pig's ears and pig's feet for dinner, and he wanted them served on silver chafing dishes, with the Hyatt's full "celebrity service."

"Staib, he just turned to me and another black guy and said, 'You handle this one,'" Patridge remembers. "Wasn't no big deal about it: just put 'em in a pot with some onions and green peppers and boil 'em down. But that was a significant point in my life. I mean, these days I can make you a galantine of duck or a *navarin* of lamb, I can make you a *poitrine de veau* or a French peasant pâté. But I've never been ashamed of southern food since then."

Patridge tells me this story over a plate of steaming chitlins at Scholars, the restaurant—or "laboratory," as he prefers to call it—that he founded at Morris Brown College in Atlanta. It's late in the morning, and the room around us hums with expectation, a vacuum soon to be filled with the lunch rush. Waiters in tuxedo shirts, bow ties, and paisley vests move soundlessly across deep burgundy carpets, hooking table skirts onto curved buffet tables. Fresh-cut flowers and old books decorate the tables, and a grand piano, standing in the corner, awaits some student musician's limber fingers. All along the walls, above the dark oak wainscoting, Langston Hughes and Zora Neale Hurston, Louise Jones and Dizzy Gillespie, look out from faux naïf portraits, reminding students how much has changed since 1881, when Morris Brown became the first American college to be founded by blacks for blacks.

It's Friday, so the waiters are setting out a full silver fish service and wheeling in Patridge's ice sculpture of a tugboat. But chitlins are emphatically not of the sea. To make them,

Patridge took the large and small intestines of a hog, painstakingly scrubbed them and stripped them of their fatty inner membrane, then cooked them down with onions and garlic. Stretched out on my plate next to a hill of coleslaw, they look like pieces of old lasagna (some people call them "wrinkle steak") and give off a smell that shoulders roughly through the dining room's faint floral perfume. It's an aroma not so much of meat or excrement as of pig itself—the live animal, unwashed and uncut, charging bodily off the plate and into my nostrils. Yet the taste is surprisingly subtle: tender, musty, and slightly gummy, but inoffensive on the whole. If I pinch my nose, the pig disappears.

"Your new generation of southerners, they don't want to be seen eatin' that," Patridge says. "But it's just like anything else: you get past the smell, it's all right." I nod noncommittally, but he doesn't need encouragement. "I don't believe in soul food being particular to one race or culture," he says. "I mean, you can get *high class* and talk about 'sweetbreads' and 'organ meats' and stuff, but they're all down there with the chitlins anyway. They're all cleanin' and digestin' and filterin', too."

He's finding his groove now, voice rising and falling like a country preacher, body rolling and bobbing in his chair like a balloon on an updraft. At six feet and 225 pounds, Patridge looks less fat than well inflated, with taut cheeks, bulging eyes, and a gleaming bald pate, like a miniature version of his gut. He turned forty-eight this year but looks and acts at least five years younger than that, despite his grizzled beard. "Old folks say chitlins raise your blood pressure," he says, lowering his voice and leaning in closer, thick glasses widening his already wide eyes. Then he jerks back with a shout, chopping the air with his out- stretched finger. "But you're talkin' about pure *protein* there! That's very low in fat! You put in a little bit of the *maw* to give it some body, you get a little bit of that natural *gelatin* goin', and you've got a dish that satisfies the human *soul*."

The world is full of people who define themselves by what they won't eat: macrobiotics, vegetarians, weight watch- ers, and weight lifters. But sometimes the more difficult, more audacious act is to define yourself by what you *will* eat—especially if it turns everyone else's stomach. So it is that Scandinavians eat lutefisk, Germans eat Limburger, Scots eat haggis, and little boys eat chocolate-covered ants. As a Chinese cop put it in a recent movie, chewing on sea cucumbers while talking to his white partner: "You want to be Chinese? You got to learn to eat nasty stuff."

Soul food is the epitome of this phenomenon. Not so long ago chitlins and pig's feet were slave rations—the parts the master threw away while he ate the cuts "high on the hog." Though most blacks and poor whites kept a taste for such food long after the Civil War, others came to see it as a kind of self-abasement. Then in the 1960s black activists briefly, thrillingly, turned history's tables. What were once the master's leftovers, they declared, were now soul food: dishes so earthy, so rich in shared suffering and redemption, that only blacks could truly appreciate them.

Soul food was a form of culinary alchemy, transmuting humiliation into self-respect, exile into ethnic pride. But its magic was unstable at best. First there were the practical drawbacks of eating the fatty pork dishes that increasingly dominated soul food: a third of all blacks suffer from high blood pressure, and they have a 50 percent greater chance of dying from heart disease than whites do. Then there were changes in taste: as blacks joined the middle class, they wanted to live high on the hog as well. Then, finally, culinary scholars began to redefine African American cooking itself.

By now soul food has been knocked about for so long by separatists and assimilationists, pummeled by so many qualifiers and redefinitions, that it sometimes seems out for the count. Most soul food restaurants have gone the way of the Afro, and many blacks never refer to soul food anymore, much less eat it. Yet today the odor of these chitlins does more than cut through the room's cloying perfume; it revives the old arguments like a bottle of smelling salts. Does soul food honor slave history or just trivialize it? Does it enrich black culture or misrepresent it? The further the tradition fades, the more urgent those questions become.

Even in Patridge's laboratory, there are no easy answers. While he raves about pig's ears and wrinkle steak until they seem fit for the menu on the space shuttle, the other black cooks on staff have kept their distance this morning. Earlier I walked in on Michael Chaires, the dreadlocked young executive chef, sneaking some chitlins from the pot.

"You got to be in the mood for it," he mumbled, shooting me a guilty look. Then he took a bite anyway. "Oh, *man!*" he said. "I guess I'm not in the mood for it today."

As I write, three African American cookbooks are sitting on the desk beside me. *What Mrs. Fisher Knows About Old Southern Cooking* is the first African American cookbook ever published: a collection of household recipes, published in 1881, by a former slave from South Carolina. *The Welcome Table,* published in 1995, is a nostalgic gathering of traditional recipes by Jessica Harris, the country's foremost scholar of African American cooking. *A Taste of Heritage,* published in 1998, contains nouvelle soul food recipes from twelve of the country's leading black chefs. Though they cover the same field, the three books don't have much in common. From fried grits to terrapin stew, peanut soup to venison patties with wild mushroom sauce, they wind their way from country cooking to haute cuisine with only a few shared landmarks. What, then, is authentic soul food?

Thirty-five years ago the answer seemed obvious. "In the Confederate states, three cultural and gastronomic styles blended," *The American Heritage Cookbook* declared in 1964. "Latin, Anglo-Saxon, and Negro—romance, tradition, and primitive strength." But that simple outline now seems simple-minded, or worse. Nearly every bit of conventional wisdom about slave food is wrong, it turns out, beginning with what the first slaves brought from Africa.

The people whom Europeans met in West Africa were accomplished farmers, scholars have shown. They had fields of millet, sorghum, rice, and yams, patches of pumpkins, turnips, cabbage, and eggplant. For meat they had wild game and the inexhaustible sea; for dessert, wild lemons, oranges, dates, figs, and palm wine. On occasion they even found truffles—bigger than rabbits, according to one source—and carefully roasted them or cooked them in broth.

Once in the Americas, the slaves added more than "primitive strength" to southern cooking, they helped invent it from the ground up. Okra, sorghum, sesame, and watermelon all came to the Americas with the slaves (it was a two-way street: the Americas gave Africa potatoes, peanuts, chilies, corn, and tomatoes), and only slaves had the expertise to grow and prepare them. The same was true of rice, which Africans had cultivated for three thousand years. By the eighteenth century plantation owners were deliberately buying slaves from rice-growing parts of Africa, and rice was the backbone of Carolina cooking. In the nineteenth century, a rice grower named Elizabeth Allston Pringle acknowledged that "only the African race could have made it possible or profitable to clear the dense cypress swamps and cultivate rice in them by a system of flooding the fields from the river by canals, ditches, or floodgates."

As in cultivation so in preparation, slaves were the guiding intelligence behind Southern food, waging their campaign on two fronts: the slave cabin and the big house. At home they struggled to make decent dishes from meager monthly rations—"eight pounds of pickled pork . . . often tainted," as Frederick Douglass wrote, and "one bushel of Indian meal, unbolted, of which quite fifteen percent was more fit for pigs than for men." After a grueling day's work, a slave might plant greens in a communal garden or hunt for opossums, raccoons, and other nocturnal animals. These could then be thrown into the stewpot, as part of African recipes adapted to American ingredients: sweet potatoes substituted for African yams, chilies for melegueta peppers, cornmeal for millet and sorghum.

At the big house, meanwhile, slaves invariably prepared the master's meals. Though the mistress often supervised the baking and preserving, she rarely cooked a dish herself. "Those African-American women left their thumbprint on every dish they cooked," historian Karen Hess writes in the afterword to *What Mrs. Fisher Knows About Old Southern Cooking.* "They did the cooking; it's as simple as that." A black cook, instinctively following African recipes, might add a little okra to chicken soup to thicken it, some black-eyed peas and bacon to rice to give it more taste and body, or cayenne pepper to almost anything to give it some zing. "The Negroes are born cooks, as other less favored beings are born poets," a gourmet named Charles Gayarré mused back in the 1880s, in *Harper's New Monthly Magazine.* "The African [has] gradually evolved into an artist of the highest degree of excellence, and [has] created an art of cooking for which he should deserve to be immortalized."

All southern cooking, one could almost say, is largely

African American cooking. But soul food is something more specific, more self-conscious. Leafing through the three cookbooks beside me, I can see a pattern gather and then unravel, like the stitching on an old sampler. When Abby Fisher wrote her cookbook, soul food didn't exist yet. Though Fisher was an ex-slave, what she knew about old southern cooking was what any good southern cook knew: fried chicken, oyster croquettes, and Maryland beat biscuits; chow-chow, custard pie, and sweet pickle peaches. (Fisher won two medals at the 1880 San Francisco Mechanics' Institute Fair, her book proudly notes, for her pickles, sauces, jellies, and preserves.)

A century later *The Welcome Table* winnows out those dishes in favor of ones that smack more pungently of slavery. Jessica Harris doesn't like the term *soul food*, but her cookbook could well be its bible: chitlins, okra fritters, cornmeal mush, and gospel bird are all here. "Our way with food," she writes, "combines the improvisational impulses that gave the world jazz with the culinary techniques of the African continent. It combines the African taste for the piquant with the American leftovers from sorrow's kitchens." But though Harris explores the full breadth of African American cooking elsewhere, this menu is mostly low on the hog. The French, Spanish, and English dishes that slaves adapted, as Louis Armstrong did Bach fugues, find little welcome here.

A Taste of Heritage tries to redress the balance, to reclaim some of the old plantation elegance. "We have a mission, however paradoxical, to make the established 'soul food' more respectable," the authors write. "Let's face it, some African-Americans are no longer eating chitterlings and other pig's offal because of painful memories. . . . They appreciate their culinary heritage, but they refuse to be defined by it." Though *A Taste of Heritage* has its share of down-home recipes, it also reaches for dishes no slave ever cooked—in the big house or elsewhere: "Chilled Georgia Peach and Sun-Dried Cherry Soup," for instance, or "Grilled Salmon Fillets with Cilantro Vinaigrette." It's the end of a cycle, you might say, from southern food to soul food and back again—from slaves inventing dishes for their masters to blacks reclaiming and reinventing those dishes for themselves. But surely something is being lost.

Ten years ago, when Harris published her first book on African American cooking, she wrote that she hoped it might "fix the taste of cornbread, beans, collard greens, okra, chiles, molasses, and rum on our tongues for generations to come." But these days she eats such things only on New Year's Eve. The rest of the year she prefers salads. Dishes like chitlins have become more "totemic" than dietary, she says. "We keep them for the memory as much as anything else. It's like the lamb shank at a Jewish Seder: everybody doesn't eat it, but it's there."

On a breezy April evening, with the day's embers still glowing in the city's sidewalks and buildings, Patridge trudges down a concrete staircase, leaving the hushed confines of Scholars for the Morris Brown Football Stadium. He'll make this quarter-mile trip ten times in the next two hours, always on foot, as he directs simultaneous dinners at both locations. "When I was the director of operations at Epcot Center, I put a pedometer on one time," he says, wiping the sweat from his eyes. "By the end of the day, I'd done nine miles." He stops and leans against a wall, chest heaving. "I'm doin' my jogging here, then later I'll do my weight training in the kitchen."

Tonight's events typify Patridge's two worlds. Over at the stadium, built for the 1996 Olympics, 150 athletes are attending an awards dinner ("The football team was three and eight," Patridge quips, "so this ought to be short"). At Scholars, meanwhile, Sigma Pi Phi, one of the city's most distinguished black fraternal organizations, is having their monthly meeting. At the stadium, the menu is pulled pork, baked beans, and coleslaw; at Scholars it's seared salmon with caper sauce and wild rice. Soul food over here, plantation finery over there: the path between them is steep and circuitous, but Patridge doesn't mind the trip. You might say he's been preparing for it all his life.

His father was a country boy from Fayetteville, raised by sharecroppers. His mother was a city girl from Covington, a professional cook who had traveled to thirty-three states. On his father's side every food was tied to some person, season, or life event: there was reunion chicken (crispy and tender, because all the wives were competing) and funeral chicken (soggy and burnt, because the cooks were too sad to care). There were Aunt Lily's preserves and Aunt Cora's cakes and Aunt Ethel's chitlins, a week in the

cleaning. On his mother's side, dinner was more unpre-
dictable. "She was good at inventing dishes," Patridge says.
"She used to make this thing called heavenly rice; it had
rice, crushed pineapple, whipped cream, and sugar. . . .
Oh, man!"

For most of Tim's life his mother worked for the
Atlanta school cafeterias. Then, when he was in junior
high, she opened Patridge's Dinette, on Bankhead Highway. Between there and the farm, her son learned an equal
love for home and commercial cooking, plain food and its
transformation. When he turned twelve his father handed
him a knife and told him to go kill a hog. When he was
fourteen his mother handed him a spatula and told him to
make country-fried steak for her customers.

By the late 1960s, when Patridge went to Morris Brown,
Atlanta was full of soul brothers and soul sisters, wearing
soul combs and doing soul handshakes. "Everything was
getting souled," as Harris puts it, "sometimes by African
Americans, sometimes not." Whether the fashion called
for Technicolor dashikis or denim jackets and work boots,
Patridge fit right in. But his goals were hardly trendy. He
wanted to be a doctor, he says, though anything ambitious
might have done. So he found work at a veterans' hospital.
"I started out as a dishwasher and pretty soon moved up to
pot washer. Then I started delivering patient trays, and I
saw those guys comin' back from Vietnam. It was like,
'Oh no, I can't do this.'" Soon after that he took a job as a
cook at an airport restaurant and never looked back.

On paper, at least, the career that followed rose as unerringly as a guided missile: from the airport to the Hyatt to the Ritz, from line cook to sous chef to program director. Patridge was the first black executive chef at Callaway Gardens, a resort in Pine Mountain, Georgia; the first black *garde-manger* at the Ritz; and the first black president of the Atlanta chapter of the American Culinary Federation. He became a certified executive chef and a member of the American Academy of Chefs, always putting CEC and AAC after his name, even on a pamphlet on barbecue.

But Patridge was bent on more than exploding racial barriers. He was after a "global concept of food," he says, one that could reconcile the disparate elements of his culinary education. After so many years of separating soul food from haute cuisine, spoonbread from soufflé, he wanted to find their common denominators. Rather than settle in at a single restaurant, therefore, he began to travel. He went on cultural exchanges to Russia, eastern Europe, and the Caribbean, where he met his future wife. He took jobs with the Atlanta Olympics and the Smithsonian, studied the historical connections between jambalaya and cassoulet. Finally, in 1997 he landed near the shores of the Magic Kingdom itself, as one of the first black executives at Epcot Center.

It seemed a fitting climax to his career, an almost eerie amalgamation of his interests. Where better to demonstrate culinary affinities than at Epcot's international pavilions? Yet at Epcot something in him splintered. Finding cultural common ground had seemed a noble idea, until he was surrounded by puppets singing "It's a Small World."

With his family still in Atlanta, and Disney leaving little room for improvisation, he began to yearn for his old double life again. "If I'd been a little younger, they could have robotized me," Patridge says, "turned me into a Stepford wife." Instead, six weeks after arriving, he resigned. Then, like an escape pod jettisoned from a flaming rocket, he tumbled home to his family again—back in the arms of sweet Georgia.

He lives on a small farm now, seventeen miles from downtown Atlanta. His children all bear Yoruba names—Devika, Adisa, Ajani—and the two eldest go to Morris Brown, as he did. On weekdays he still hosts cooking shows on TV, prepares continental cuisine at Scholars, and proudly lists the honorifics after his name. But on weekends, when he cooks for his family, he leaves his ego—and haute cuisine—in the cupboard. "I know my daughter doesn't eat carrots, my son doesn't like okra, and my wife likes her chicken fried, not boiled," he says. "That's what southern cooking is all about—traditions and family—not someone tryin' to be the number one biscuit maker."

Tonight, lurching into the Scholars kitchen after his climb from the stadium, Patridge looks winded and sweaty, but at ease with his contradictions. "Mr. Chaires!" he shouts between gasps. "How's that dinner coming?" Then he walks over and shows the cooks how to arrange it: a scoop of wild rice to one side, a broiled tomato with Parmesan to the other, a broiled salmon fillet to complete the triangle. "You got to lay these with the tail inside,"

Low on the Hog • 195

Patridge says, placing an asparagus spear across the plate with his big paws. Then he spoons capers over the fish and crowns it with half a lemon wrapped in lace.

Out in the dining room the Sigma Pi Phi men are having cocktails, discussing politics and art with the easy refinement of diplomats. Their suits are finely tailored and cut from exquisite cloth, their hair swept back and shot through with silver, their eyeglasses held loosely in their hands. "I knew all about these guys when I was growing up," Patridge whispers, watching them through a small window in the kitchen door. "They've got a couple of college presidents out there, a state senator, and a former superintendent of schools."

Yet even here, at the apex of the black elite, the menu can't shrug off the old ambivalence. Patridge's dinners are all on their plates and ready to be served when Chaires staggers over, carrying a tray piled high with fried chicken. "What do you want me to do with this?" he says. Patridge just stares at him: he forgot about the chicken. Glancing over at me, he slowly shakes his head. "I told them it didn't go with the salmon," he says. "But they got to have it anyway. Fried chicken every time."

Through the window, under the soft lights and softer music, the men are taking their seats, shaking out their linen napkins and looking about expectantly. Do I see a glint of defiance in their eyes? Maybe they're reluctant to give up on soul food, having worked so hard to reclaim it in the sixties. Or maybe, after so long in the minefields of race, where every symbol can explode in your face and every misstep draws friendly fire, they just want to eat their favorite dish in peace. "Just pile the chicken up in big bowls and put it in the middle of the table, Mr. Chaires," Patridge says, laughing despite himself. "That's the way they'll want it."

Late one night, after another twelve-hour day at Scholars, Patridge takes me on a ride through Atlanta's old black districts. "When I was a kid, all these places had special names," he says, surveying the sagging storefronts next to his old street, their boarded windows flickered by neon and tattered posters. "There was Lightnin' and Beaver Slide, Mechanicsville and Vine City." His father drove an Ace cab, he says, and on Saturdays he'd take Tim along to help the ladies with their groceries. Tim got to know the whole city that way, and to like most of it. But his favorite place—the true heart of black Atlanta—was Sweet Auburn.

Just a few blocks from the center of town, Auburn Avenue was lined with restaurants, barbershops, private clubs, and funeral homes. During the day people walked the streets in their Sunday best, stopping to gossip at the Silver Moon barbershop or to eat at B. B. Beamon's and Henry's Grill. By night Jackie Wilson, James Brown, Major Lance, and Little Richard were on stage at clubs like Zanzibar and the Royal Peacock. "I saw Bobby Blue Bland at the Peacock when I was just sixteen," Patridge remembers. "But don't ever let my mom know that."

It was on Auburn Avenue that Martin Luther King

spent his childhood, playing pickup games at the YMCA and checking out stacks of books every Saturday from the public library. And it was here that he returned in 1960 to be pastor of Ebenezer Baptist Church, as his father and maternal grandfather had been before him. These streets, where all of black society gathered on the same sidewalks to reach for the same elusive prize, were the true inspiration for King's dream.

But tonight, cruising down Auburn Avenue, it's hard to recognize his vision in these ruins. B. B. Beamon's has long since gone dark, its windows painted with a mural of the neighborhood's history, and where Henry's Grill used to be, there is a nameless Caribbean restaurant. The Royal Peacock is a rap club now, and the Masonic lodge and Odd Fellows hall lean like pallbearers along the street. "*That's* the only thing keeping this place alive," Patridge says, pointing to a dim white shape lit by spotlights off the side of the road. "Martin's coffin." In 1980 then-president Jimmy Carter signed a law declaring the neighborhood a national historic site. In the years since, the National Park Service has bought twelve acres and twenty-four homes here, including King's neighbors' houses, and a new church has risen along the avenue, angled toward King's shining tomb like a shepherd toward a star, attracting some twelve hundred tourists and pilgrims every day.

If Auburn Avenue survives, it does so in the shadow of a double irony: for if King's death keeps the neighborhood alive, it was his life's work that nearly finished it off. Before the civil rights movement, nearly every city had an all-black business district, built and maintained by its captive audience: the south side of Chicago, the north side of Milwaukee, Beale Street in Memphis, Farish Street in Jackson, Greenwood in Tulsa. As soon as white businesses opened their doors to blacks, however, black businesses began to shut theirs for good. Affluent blacks fled for the suburbs, leaving only the poor and working class behind. Black shopkeepers began to look for newer digs, and "urban renewal" leveled what they left behind. (A highway now crosses Auburn Avenue, and desolate apartments stand where a square mile of houses used to be.) "Desegregation deconstructed the African American community," says Sterling Plumpp, professor of African American studies at the University of Illinois at Chicago. "It used to be, if I owned a soul food place, I could expect the crème de la crème of black society to come through—you'd get the mayor and the aldermen and celebrities like Lou Brock. But now, in the inner cities, everyone is basically poor. That whole cross section—doctor, lawyer, opera star, blues singer—it's gone."

Like the black community itself, soul food never left Sweet Auburn. Ace Barbecue Barn still sits near the avenue, and dozens of places like it dot the city, offering the same black-eyed peas, the same peach pie. But theirs is a degraded form of the art—soul food without the soul. It substitutes fatback and boiling grease for the roots, greens, and fragrant stews that slaves once favored at home. It's a product of lengthening workdays and two-income families rather than loving hours in the kitchen, of a society ever more addicted to speed, the great homogenizer. "At one time, I don't care how poor you were, you gathered them around the dinner table," says Leah Chase, chef and owner of Dooky Chase, a fixture of Creole cooking in New Orleans since 1939. "Now they get a leg and a thigh and a biscuit and sit around the TV."

Well past midnight, Patridge and I pull up at one of the birthplaces of fast food in America—and the graveyard, perhaps, of soul food. Founded in 1928, the Varsity now cranks out 6,500 hamburgers and more than two miles of hot dogs a day. On a typical football Saturday it serves forty-five thousand customers. Until 1964 blacks weren't allowed inside, except as fry cooks, but now they're close to a majority. Some come for the retro decor—the neon lights, streamlined steel counters, and red-and-yellow walls—or to watch the workers peel potatoes from fifty-pound boxes. Others like the gift shop and the autographed pictures of celebrities like Nipsy Russell, who was a "curb boy" here in the fifties. Still others come for something more basic: sitting on cheap patio furniture, watching TVs suspended from the ceiling, you can almost feel as if you're eating at home—as long as you can ignore the food.

"Tim," I say, choking down a mouthful of grainy chili and mealy meat, "this . . . is not a good hot dog." He chuckles nervously, glancing around to see if anybody heard me. He knows I'm right, of course—as a friend of his puts it: "Every time I drive by the Varsity I order two hot dogs, an order of onion rings, and a bottle of barbiturates"—but that doesn't mean he likes to hear it said out loud. When a cop walks by a little later to lock the doors, Patridge takes the opportunity to hustle me outside.

Back in the car, he shudders theatrically. "I had to get you out of there *fast*," he says. "I was afraid the earth was going to open under us: *blasphemer!*"

Two miles from the Varsity, on a patch of land that was once a residential area, Atlanta's other great attraction rises like a rose-colored memory—like a promise that history's messy subdivisions will one day be razed clean, replaced with a brighter, shinier past. When it was built in 1993 and 1994, to house the Olympics and then the Atlanta Braves, Turner Field was designed to look old-fashioned. But beneath its brick walls and outsize colonial fixtures there beats a modern heart. Under the bleachers and quaint concession stands, delivery trucks barrel down an interior road and electronic gates snap open and shut, forklifts whir from crate to crate, and beer is pumped, by the thousands of gallons, to spigots secreted in the concrete above.

It's here, on a fever-hot Sunday morning, on my last day in Atlanta, that the future of American food will be on display—or at least one version of it, courtesy of *Cooking Light* magazine. Ten white tents have been set up for cooking demonstrations, and sales booths entice the health conscious—thirty thousand of them, the promoters predict. There are booths where you can measure your body fat and booths where you can book "healthy vacations"; a tent devoted to giving away granola bars; and an artificial cliff face for rock climbing. "That's Graham Kerr over there," Patridge says, pointing to the "Healthy Choices" pavilion. "He used to be the Galloping Gourmet, but he got too *fat* to gallop—had to slow down to a *trot*. So now he's cooking light."

Patridge has been asked to give a fifteen-minute presentation on light southern cooking, though he says, "In the South, 'light' just means a little less *lard*." So he's brought the ingredients for some salmon cakes. All around us the other presentations are in full swing. Skinny white audience members head off to hear skinny white cooks bemoan the evils of heart disease, the pleasures of arugula. When Patridge barrels through them, streaming with sweat and lugging a battered ice chest, they scatter like gazelles before a rhinoceros. "You'll notice," he says, grinning, "that I'm the only African American out here."

If the Varsity is the Scylla of soul food, surely this is its Charybdis. Racial politics will cycle and change; black families will grow tired of takeout and return to the kitchen; but the slow corruption of recipes can take decades to undo. Oleo for butter here, turkey bones for ham hocks there, a teaspoon of salt where the taste used to be: substitute or skimp on enough ingredients, and people will forget why they ever ate such things. It's hard to believe in the richness of African American cooking while eating a plate of boiled collards and cottage cheese.

Patridge, luckily, is an old hand at navigating such straits. Ten minutes after we arrive, he rises up on stage in his white, double-breasted chef's jacket: a god of plenty, come to lead us from this blistering desert. "Good afternoon, ladies and gentlemen, on this *hot* day," he begins. "We'll all be lighter when we leave." While the audience titters, he looks around at the bare counter and meager implements, the chunk of cold salmon and handful of eggs. "I knew that there'd be nothing but light cooking here today," he says. "So I went down to the Varsity last night and got loaded *up*—you know, so it wouldn't be too much of a *shock* to my system. I even brought some canola oil." He turns his lips down at the corners as if vastly impressed with himself. "But I had to go out and *buy* it."

Beside me, a middle-aged woman in jogging shorts and a platinum blond wig sits upright and peers at the stage, not sure if she's hearing right. But Patridge is already off on another riff. He talks about salmon and how southerners first tasted it in a can—"ain't no salmon swimmin' up the Chattahoochee." He says he's all for light cooking, as long as you can eat twice as much of it. And he points out that southerners are no strangers to haute cuisine. "Look here," he says, pointing to the lone black man in the audience. "If I showed a southerner some polenta made with Parmesan, what would he call it?"

The man frowns for a second and then breaks into a grin: "Cheese grits!"

Then Patridge points to a white woman in the front row. "And if I mix this grape jelly with some ketchup and apple-cider vinegar, what would you call it?"

She looks at him quizzically. "Sweet-and-sour sauce?"

"*That's right!*"

By now there's a crowd inside the tent. Stragglers come

in from the sidewalk to see what all the commotion is about, and defectors are arriving from the lecture next door. The old lady beside me is having a hard time breathing, she's laughing so hard, and I can feel a giddy, subversive spirit building around me. "Let me show you the *professional* way to separate this," Patridge says, holding up an egg. He smacks it against the counter and cracks it open into his hand, letting the white stream through his fingers. When all that's left is the yolk, he throws it over his shoulder into the trash. "That's the cookin' light part," he says. Next he mashes the egg white into the salmon, adds some flour and seasonings, and forms four little cakes. "You know sometimes when you go to a restaurant and you see egg whites on the menu?" he asks, placing the cakes on a griddle. "Anyone here ever eat those egg whites?" Not a hand is raised. "I knew it," Patridge says, his sermon complete. "We're at the *wrong* show."

Watching him up there on stage, so alone and yet so fully in command, so out of place and yet so eager to connect, I can't help but think how far we've come—both forward and back. Not so long ago Patridge's grandfather was a sharecropper, devoted to making the best from the least, whether turning a sow's ear into a silken dish or a slave's life into something more human. But history and hard-won prosperity have contrived to turn that gift upon itself. These days the older our country grows, the weaker our traditions seem to become; the more varied our food, the more predictable our cooking. It's a hall of mirrors we've wandered into, where hog maws are a rare delicacy

204 • Noodling for Flatheads

and the world's richest people eat the world's blandest food. Any eighteenth-century time traveler, transported here in search of wonders, might well react as Patridge did, looking out across this sea of dissatisfied faces: "We're at the *wrong* show."

After Patridge's talk, the crowd drifts away—some to other talks, others to the "Free Stuff" tent for more granola bars. But an elderly woman, pale and pinched by one too many diets, stays behind. "Can I ask you a question?" she says when the others have cleared out. "Are you from around here?"

Patridge looks down into her glimmering little face and chuckles. "Born and raised, ma'am, born and *raised.*"

She squints at him a moment longer, as if still unsure, and then curls her mouth into a smile. "I knew it," she says, sidling up to him like a bookie with a hot tip. "I'll tell you one thing, though: Most of these other folks around here are *Yankees.*"

Patridge shakes his head as she wanders toward the exit. "I wish you were right," his eyes seem to say. "I wish you were right."

The Rolley Holers

LIKE MOST MEN who aren't much good at sports, I spent a good deal of my childhood making up Olympic events, just to have something to be best at. Mine weren't the usual obstacle courses, bicycle jumps, or beanbag tosses. They were cryptic and personal and hard to re-create—more gestures, really, than games. I might cross my fingers in a certain pattern, say, and use them to flick a penny across the room, or shoot a rubber band over my shoulder with my toes—it didn't matter, as long as I could do it and no one else I knew had ever tried. After an hour or so of dedicated practice, having achieved a kind of cockeyed perfection, I'd stop and pat myself on the back. "Right now," I'd tell myself, "you're better at this than anyone else in the world."

I was probably wrong. Every backyard Ping-Pong player thinks he's the king of the world, until he plays a Chinese exchange student. Every family Scrabble champ believes the game can be played no better, until he hears that the world champion scored seven hundred points in a round, closing out with "qi." There are five billion people living on the planet, most of them with some idle time on their hands. Somewhere, in an alleyway in Calcutta or a forest clearing in Papua New Guinea, some boy has probably discovered my weird little gestures, practiced them assiduously, and beaten every one of my records. To me they were just a way to pass the time. But to him they were a way of life.

I thought about that not long ago, standing under a hickory tree in the hills of northern Tennessee. It was a cool September evening, with the darkness just beginning to well up out of the hollows, and the crowd I'd joined was so hushed and watchful that I could hear the forest chitter and chime with katydids and field crickets. We were gathered around a rectangular court of fine umber dust, sheltered by a pavilion and illuminated by spotlights. Four men in jeans and T-shirts were on the court, slouched with hands in pockets or sitting on their heels. If not for the crowd, you might have taken them for roadies waiting to set up equipment on an empty dance floor. But then one of them knelt down and reached his right arm out in front of him. For just a second I could see a pale gray marble, held loose and precarious in his curled, upturned fingers. Then it was gone, flying twenty feet or so across the yard, hitting another marble dead-on and spinning to a stop in its target's place.

It was an impossible shot—one I could never reliably make—but no big deal to the shooter. He shuffled over, picked up his marble, and flicked it toward a shallow, marble-size depression in the dust two feet away. This was more of a putt than a drive, and the marble rolled rather than flew. Still, it headed straight for its nesting place, skidding on backspin until it settled in with a final fidget, like a fat man getting ready for a double feature.

The shooter's name was Jack Tinsley, and he'd been sinking shots like these all day. Like all the other players here at the fifteenth annual Standing Stone Marbles Tournament, he was a local boy, born and raised not twenty miles from here. A plumber, builder, and some-time tobacco farmer, Jack had the furtive, half-wild look of a mountain man—bony shoulders, unkempt hair, Rip Van Winkle beard—and he seemed uncomfortable in bright light. Between shots he held his elbow and avoided people's eyes, as liable to trip over his own feet as over his words if you asked him a question. It was only when he crouched down to shoot that his body seemed to untangle, to move with the fluid, unconscious grace of a profes-sional athlete.

Jack was a fanatic rolley holer. This is not to say that he belonged to some odd evangelical sect, but simply that he loved to play a game called rolley hole. Rolley holers play in teams of two, sinking their marbles in holes and trying to prevent their opponents from doing the same. There are three holes in all, one at either end of the court and one in the middle. The first team to work its way down the court and back three times, sinking its marbles in each hole in succession, wins the game. You might say rolley hole is a combination of marbles, croquet, and golf, but that does it little justice. It's a game that demands dexterity, an intu-itive grasp of spatial relations, and a subtle command of field strategy. It's a game that rewards fanaticism. As one molecular-biologist-turned-rolley-hole-aficionado put it, "Rolley hole is to other marble games as chess is to checkers."

By those terms Jack was a grand master, yet he had never won this tournament. Anywhere else he might have been a local legend by now, but on the upper Cumberland, marble virtuosos are as common as raccoons. For generations those hills have been swept by rolley hole fevers as intense as religious revivals. They've seen players murdered by their rivals and border wars break out between factions from Kentucky and Tennessee. They've seen people hike miles in search of the hardest flint and craftsmen spend hours grinding it down in pursuit of the perfect marble.

This is the story of how the rolley holers came down from the mountains one day to challenge the best marble players in the world. It's a story about a gonzo folklorist who helped keep a tradition alive when the whole notion of tradition was starting to ring hollow. But mostly it's about an old and oddly entrancing game—one that has earned its players' consuming devotion, though it's as peculiar, in its way, as shooting rubber bands over your shoulders with your toes.

The upper Cumberland River flows from northern Tennessee into southern Kentucky, dipping and rolling through narrow bottomlands and high beechwood forests, across the limestone highlands that encircle Nashville like a great amphitheater, stopping just shy of bluegrass and coal country. The land here is as stingy with resources as it is profligate with beauty, and making a living from it has never been easy. After more than two centuries the towns still look makeshift—the houses lean along the roadsides as if dropped there by a passing tornado—and folks can be so understated, they hardly talk at all. Even the local barbecue joints don't fool around. Not for them the dry rub and pit roast, tenderloin and sweet sauce. They prefer their pork sliced thin, with the bone still in it, then grilled tough as shoe leather. A swab of acrid orange grease, a piece of white bread, and voilà! Though no one here would ever say that word.

People with tastes like these don't seem the types for a kids' game. Then again, maybe that's why they're better at it than anyone else. In most places people have lost patience with low-tech toys. Basketball players wear advanced polymers; Frisbees are tested in NASA wind tunnels; Rollerbladers streak past on titanium bearings, their bodies armored like tech warriors. But a marble is hard to accessorize. Its geometry is pure as Euclid, its physics merciless. It takes a mind of flint, Wallace Stevens might have written, to master rolley hole.

Once upon a time, the country was full of people with such minds, and most of them played with marbles. The Zuñi hid them in wooden tubes and made people guess where they were; the Shoshoni juggled them; the Tewa threw them at targets; and most other Native Americans used them as dice. Even the ancient mound builders found time for simple games. Beneath most of their massive funerary earthworks, they buried at least one "chunkee stone": a chiseled disk of quartz, four to six inches wide and slightly concave on both faces. Not yet a marble, perhaps, but well on its way.

One November morning, just outside of Little Kansas, Oklahoma, I watched twenty or thirty Cherokees play a game called Cherokee marbles. They were full-bloods, for the most part, with jet black hair, squat bodies, and flat, chiseled features, and it wasn't hard to imagine them back a thousand years, playing with chunkee stones. More than anything, though, their game reminded me of rolley hole.

Like rolley holers, Cherokee players split up into teams of two and try to sink marbles on a yard with shallow holes (a Cherokee yard has five holes instead of three). And in both games players can knock each other's marbles out of position only once at each hole. The differences are mostly a matter of scale: instead of a carefully tended, twenty-by-forty-foot court, the Cherokee play on a huge, scraggly meadow surrounded by old tires; instead of real marbles, they use pool balls. "We used to make 'em ourselves," one of the players told me, "but they broke too easy."

I could see the problem. Everywhere I looked players were rearing back like demented shot-putters, hurling their balls around hard enough to crack skulls. At the far end of the field, a player named Isaac Youngbird was balanced on one leg like an ungainly pelican, his Fu Manchu mustache whipping in the wind, waiting to see if his shot hit home. When it missed, he jumped up and down and screamed, "Shit!" The effect was both playful and deadly serious, like the lacrosse matches that Creek and Choctaw warriors once staged as substitutes for war. This was marbles, against all odds, made visceral.

Both rolley holers and Cherokee marblers like to say the Native American version came first—if only to give their games a more ancient pedigree. But it's easier to imagine it the other way around. Before the Trail of Tears, the Cherokee lived in eastern Tennessee and the Carolinas and were famous for adopting European ways: they wore trousers and built frame houses, invented an alphabet and published their own newspapers. Perhaps, moved by some ancestral memory of chunkee stones, they adopted rolley hole as well. Then they put it on steroids.

Of course, that still begs the question: Where did rolley hole come from? Marble games have been played in Europe since before the Romans. But though games similar to rolley hole, known as three holes, are still played in Australia and England, rolley hole seems to be a purely American invention. Like gospel or gumbo, it's a compound of memory and necessity. Somewhere in the Appalachians, it's tempting to think, a frontiersman must have woken up one morning with a hankering for golf. Putters, drivers, and immaculate lawns being hard to come by, he made do with the next best thing: marbles.

Marble maker Randall Dulworth is close to eighty now—he still takes his first car, a 1929 Model A, out for the occasional putt around Livingston, Tennessee—but he remembers when marbles were a countywide obsession. When I visited his garage, he held up two creamy specimens from the twenties: dented, fissured, but patinaed by generations of hands. "I made 'em when I was yea high," he said, stretching out a hand at waist level. "They've seen many a battle."

Like pneumonia, marble fever was always a passing state, a seasonal disease. In late summer, when the crops were laid by and the weeds beaten back, locals were granted a rare gift of absolute leisure, their days long and honey golden, the tobacco reaching lazily toward the sun. It was then, with the earth stuck in idle and the hours coasting from August to Indian summer, that players dusted off their old shooters and wandered back to the marble yards. After months of grim purpose and hard labor, the game's pointlessness must have been a kind of balm, its circularity the ideal relief from all that earnest forward motion.

In Dulworth's day half a dozen games were played on the upper Cumberland—games like euchre, ringer, and Tennessee square. Most were equal parts skill and luck, and people never took them too seriously. If a kid ran out of marbles, he might use acorns instead. If that wasn't good enough, he'd find some other cheap replacement. One folklorist showed me a picture of two stolid German craftsmen, lying on their stomachs in bib overalls, carefully touching marbles to a grinding wheel. "Now, the hillbillies, they didn't have time for this," he said, grinning. "They'd just go out to a stream somewhere, drill a hole in a rock, drop a stone in it, and wait about six months. When they came back, the river would have rolled it round."

The rolley holers didn't have it that easy. Only flint could withstand their crack shooting, and no stream could shape a flint marble fast enough. For generations, therefore, rolley holers kept the locations of good flint outcroppings as secret as gold strikes. (There's no shortage of flint in the upper Cumberland—deposits of it gird the hills like a rib cage—but most of it is thin, crumbly stuff.) Once they found a good, hefty nodule, they would rough out a blank and grind it down with a bow drill, specially adapted from the ones Indians used to start fires.

Nowadays technology can speed things up, but only to a point. Dulworth still starts with pieces of local flint, in colors from alabaster to bloodred, and good rock gets scarcer every year. Yellow flint is the toughest, rolley holers say, but brown makes a harder target against the dirt of a marble yard. Red is beautiful but brittle; gray and black, sturdy but unattractive. When Dulworth has chosen his rock and struck a few sparks from it, just to make sure it's genuine, he rounds it off roughly with a chisel. Then he takes a grinding stone embedded with diamond fragments—one in which he's drilled a hemispheric hole—sets the piece of flint in the hole, and holds it up to a sander, letting the marble jiggle and spin like a ball bearing in its casing. "It'll roll about a thousand miles an hour," he says. "But when it's smooth it stops rolling: the centrifugal force needs a rough spot to grab on to."

Back when Dulworth was really cranking, he could make three marbles a day and sell every one. But little by little demand began to drop off. Beginning in the 1950s, as television and organized sports began to take the American childhood in hand, marbles passed out of players' pockets and into those of decorators and nostalgia buffs. At a collectors' show you can now sell a vintage Cracker Jack marble for $300 or a rare sulfide for $5,000 or more. But kids who can talk of "mibs" and "downsies," "aggies," "alley-taws," "biffs," and "bonces," are an even rarer commodity.

Rolley holers, being adults in a region long sheltered from popular culture, held on longer than most. "There was a kind of Darwinian thing going on up there," says Robert Cogswell, a folklorist with the Tennessee Arts Commission. "In other areas your kids play football or basketball. But up in those counties, the really great natural athletes, a lot of them were marble shooters." Well into the fifties there were tournaments throughout Kentucky, and on summer nights the private marble yards still twinkled from hilltops and valleys. But the game was too sophisticated, too hard to learn and maintain, to thrive on shortening attention spans. Year by year the armies of Little Leaguers and midget football players, satellite dishes and video arcades, marched deeper into the upper Cumberland, and year by year fewer fathers taught their boys to play. For a while, in the 1960s, a man by the name of Dumas Walker kept rolley hole alive by sheer force of personality. But when Dumas quit, the game nearly died. By the late 1970s only a handful of players was left, and all of them lived in two adjacent counties—one in Kentucky and one in Tennessee.

Like some rare animal that dines only on an equally

rare shrub, rolley hole had nearly evolved itself out of existence.

"The part I remember," Bob Fulcher says, "the part that's
burned into my brain, is comin' up on those lights behind
the trees."

It was a moonless night in early June, with summer's sul-
try breath already rising off the highlands, and Fulcher was
miles from any street lamps or houselights. He'd parked his
Mazda hatchback on the shoulder of the road, as instructed,
walked past the ditch and the long line of pickups, crossed
the sagging barbed-wire gate, and followed the trail into the
trees. It was then, knee-deep in weeds, encircled by cicadas
and fluttered by moths, that he noticed it. "There was this
glow," he says, "this tungsten glow coming out of the forest.
And you could see men moving around in it."

Fulcher had heard about these gatherings before—as
director of the Tennessee State Parks Folklife Project he
heard no end of strange stories—but he'd never managed
to see one. Stumbling toward the light, he remembered the
first time he'd been told about rolley hole. He was at a
music festival in Nashville when he came across an old
rhythm-and-blues player named Bud Garrett, hunched
over a weird contraption. In the 1950s Garrett had cut
some records for the Excello label, but nowadays he ran a
junkyard in an old black community called Free Hill, spik-
ing his income with moonshine and other ventures. The
contraption, it turned out, was a marble-making machine.

"Bud was a champion talker," Fulcher recalls. "Just unbelievable. So he very quickly evoked the name of Dumas Walker. Now Dumas had been going around for a few years saying he was the world champion of rolley hole, and Bud was a great supporter of that claim. He'd repeat it at the drop of the hat. Evidently he'd beaten Dumas one time, so by supporting the claim, he elevated himself." Unfortunately, when Fulcher sent a folklorist to check out Bud's stories, both Garrett and Walker begged off. "It was: 'Oh no, I can't play. But I'm the greatest there ever was.'" A rolley hole exhibition was organized anyhow, and Garrett managed to scratch out a marble yard for it. But on the day of the event a downpour washed everything out. Though a few players showed up, they soon faded back into the forest.

Now, two years later, emerging into the clearing at last, Fulcher had to laugh: all that mystery for so harmless a thing. "Here was this strange, manicured little space in the center of the woods," he says. "There were wood shavings and old bucket seats and ranks of chairs around it, but the yard itself was an amazing sight." The owners, Russell Collins and his brother Herman, had cleared the yard with a bulldozer, brought up a generator, and strung it with electric lights. With white oak and red maple clustered all around, shielding out the night wind and gathering in the light, the place felt faintly ceremonial, like the scene of a harvest dance or a solstice ritual. "And then here were these men shooting marbles," Fulcher says, pausing at the memory. "And they could really shoot."

Like most small-town boys, Fulcher had played a few rounds of ringer as a kid, shooting marbles from a small circle. This was nothing like that. Rolley holers regularly had to make shots four times as long as those in ringer, and their marbles, like pool balls, had to ricochet to just the right position afterward. This was like a game of basketball with baskets thirty feet high. The locals dribbled, dunked, sank fadeaways from midcourt, then shrugged as if to say "Doesn't everyone do it like that?"

While the men played, one of them pulled out a fiddle and dug into some old-time tunes—"New Five Cents," perhaps, or "Weepin' Willow Tree." Soon the men had settled into an easy, bantering rhythm, their clicking marbles keeping time. A frog hopped across the yard, Fulcher remembers, and moths fell from the lamps in clusters. As the men moved around the court, they'd crush them casually with their heels. At one point Fulcher tried to join in the game, but he fared no better than the moths. "There was just this enormous gulf," he says, "between what a person like me could do with a marble and what they could do."

Fulcher had seen his share of dying traditions. He'd seen them bandaged and mummified, sent lurching around festivals and then stuffed back into the crypt. And he'd seen them heartbreakingly vital, pumping life into a community until a cultural vacuum bled them dry. Compared to those, rolley hole was alive and well. But for how long? These guys were the last active players in the country, and they were hardly cut out to be cultural ambassadors. Like most people on the upper Cumberland, they were shy, secretive, allergic to hype. It was no surprise that they'd kept Fulcher waiting all these years; it was a surprise they'd invited him at all.

Still, something about seeing them play set Fulcher's mind spinning like a roulette wheel. A good game, he knew, is a universal language. It's a distillate of pleasure, an elegant algorithm for squeezing the most fun from the shortest period. Once explained, it makes as much sense to an Aborigine as to a hillbilly, to an ancient Babylonian as to a modern New Yorker. "This marble thing," Fulcher began to realize, "was like a boulder sitting on top of a cliff. All it needed was a little shove, just a tiny bit of momentum, and it would be off and rolling again."

The first thing the rolley holers needed, Fulcher decided, was a public marble yard. But not just any old piece of dirt. "Those Tennessee farmers," Fulcher says, "they look at dirt the way other people look at fine wine." For years the best yards in Tennessee had been made with spongy loam from a farm owned by Ralph Roberts, a player whose cantankerousness was rivaled only by his skill. The soil there, in the floodplain of the Cumberland River, had a peculiar toffee color and a texture, when pounded and dusted, almost like powdered skin. In time Fulcher would cap his yard with Roberts's soil. But because he built it at Standing Stone State Park, he first used loam from the bottomland around Mill Creek—the creek that had been dammed to form Standing Stone Lake. "The park maintenance guys just put down some clay at first," he says. "But one of the rangers was kin to some players, so he knew a lot about dirt." Once the yard was roughly level, Fulcher had it groomed with a tire iron weighted by cinder blocks and fluffed up with a straw brush, just as Russell Collins used to do.

So far so good. Fulcher could probably flush twenty or thirty rolley holers out of the woods on the strength of their curiosity alone. Then again, the Monroe County Fair, just across the border in Kentucky, had been staging a rolley hole tournament every Labor Day for fifty years running, and that hadn't kept the game from nearly dying.

Fulcher needed something more than a passing novelty. He needed "to get the fever going." And for that there was only one thing: "I think it was the $400 that really jolted them awake," he says. "Over at Monroe County, they were giving away the smallest trophies I've ever seen—they probably cost them 50¢. But the $400 kind of made them sit up and take notice."

That first year the Standing Stone Marbles Tournament drew fifteen teams, with Bud Garrett playing rolley-hole blues on his beat-up Fender electric. Fulcher, on the strength of a phone call, managed to convince the *NBC Nightly News* to cover the final. But that feat of persuasion was easily outdone by Travis Cherry, a mild-mannered foreman at the local Hevi-Duty factory. In the weeks before the tournament, Cherry convinced his bosses to build three marble yards next to the factory. With the $400 dangling in front of them, the men were soon playing during coffee breaks, lunch breaks, nights, and weekends. They played so much that when players at the

Honest Abe lumberyard asked to build a yard, too, the owner refused. With rolley hole around, he said, no one would get any work done.

The fever, it seemed, was taking hold. By 1982 there were twenty-five teams playing at Standing Stone; by 1987 there were thirty-two, and the final was played, with fingers numbed by cold, at three in the morning. Where hog lots and potato patches once were, marble yards began to appear, and a kind of rolley-hole grand slam circuit developed: the Dumas Walker Memorial in early August, then the Monroe County Fair, the Watermelon Festival, and finally Standing Stone on the second weekend after Labor Day. At Amos McLerran's marble yard, in a tobacco field southeast of Moss, Tennessee, parents would gather on makeshift bleachers, collect some change in a hat, and then watch their kids play like fire to win it. Even the Army Corps of Engineers joined in, building a yard in Clay County, next to an old jogging track. "They used the wrong kind of dirt," Fulcher told me when we visited it, "so this was where the outlaw, heathen element would play. They'd sit here and shoot and make rude comments about the ladies hurrying by."

Another folklorist might have stopped then, with kids shooting marbles at school again and going back to their fathers' secret stashes of flint. But Fulcher is hardly your standard-issue folklorist. With his liquid blue eyes and pale, scraggy face, thick aviator glasses and lopsided grin, he seems too offbeat and easygoing to worry much about

dying traditions. His voice has a kind of stoned-out genial-
ity—one part southern drawl, one part hippie slang—and
when he talks about some old-fashioned thing, he seems to
both inflate it with wonder and deflate it with the gentlest
prick of irony. "Boy, that is some cool stuff," he'll say.
"That is really low-down."

Yet behind Fulcher's oddball manner lies a mind of
quicksilver creativity and natural daring. As a young man
fresh from the University of Tennessee, he first fell in love
with old-time traditions through music. On weeknights he
played banjo in bands with names like the Mango Boys,
the New Rock Creek Ramblers, and Dr. Scantlin's Red
Hot Peppers. But on weekends he headed into the hills,
hungry for new material.

Guided by legends, liner notes, and half-forgotten
memories, Fulcher would start by knocking on doors and
bothering people in cafés. If he could scare up a banjo
picker or a fiddle player, he'd convince him to lay down a
few tunes then and there, on a reel-to-reel Fulcher had on
loan from the Library of Congress. After two summers of
this, Fulcher put together five albums' worth of traditional
recordings for County Records, most of them classics: fiddle tunes by Clyde Davenport; ballads by Dee Hicks and
his wife, Delta; banjo work by Virgil Anderson.

It was the mid-1970s then, and the southern string
band revival was winding through the South from North
Carolina, trailing fiddle bands behind it like tin cans
behind a wedding car. There were folk conferences and
chautauquas, music festivals and vast fieldwork projects

sponsored by the Smithsonian. And everywhere a kind of earnest optimism reigned: the mantra was that these traditions just needed a little hand-holding—a new suit and a hot meal and a chuck under the chin—and they would be back on their feet again.

But though Davenport would go on to win a National Heritage Fellowship and Anderson would play Carnegie Hall, Fulcher began to feel as if his records had missed the point. The real treasures were scattered like gold dust among the recording reels he had collected, in ragged voices and often clumsy fingers, in songs that distilled countless lazy afternoons and evenings, on front porches and at kitchen tables: a living sound track of Tennessee. It was the texture of that world, more than just its best musicians, that he wanted to help preserve.

In the fall of 1977 Fulcher moved to Nashville and took a job with the Tennessee Bureau of State Parks—the same one he has today. A year later he applied to the National Endowment for the Arts and won a grant to document folklife in Tennessee. If the "tradition bearers" needed anything, he decided, it was a good promoter. So he developed a kind of souped-up revivalism—Appalachian agitprop— yoking bedrock tradition to pure showmanship. He put together cross-cultural banjo festivals, staged an exhibition of "Dixie wrestling," booked unemplyed preachers to proselytize to festival audiences ("That turned out strange"), and hired folklorists to head into the hills as he had done. "We call him the Colonel Tom Parker of folklife programming," Robert Cogswell says. "Bobby's always got some grandiose scheme cooking that he hasn't quite revealed to the world yet."

As Fulcher worked his way deeper into the marble world, his mind began to percolate. He read up on traditions in surrounding counties and worldwide, started attending marble conventions and subscribing to marble newsletters. He consulted archaeologists and hung out with marble-playing immigrants. The rolley holers, he was convinced, were the greatest players in the world. What they needed were some worthy rivals to help them prove it.

One day, leafing through a book on marbles, Fulcher came upon a picture of an old man with a long white beard, shooting marbles from a sand-covered concrete circle. For more than four centuries, the caption said, the finest shooters in England had come to Tinsley Green for the championship of British marbles. Like rolley hole, British marbles was played mostly in two counties—Sussex and Surrey—and like rolley hole, it had a history rife with legend. There was Jim "Atomic Thumb" Longhurst, who could smash a beer mug with a single shot, and Wee Willie Wright, who was five foot two and won the championship five times. Most important, the British claimed to be the world's best players: in four hundred years no outsider had ever beaten them at their game. "When I told that to the rolley holers," Fulcher says, "it kind of got 'em fired up."

The first clash of American and British sharpshooters took place in the hills of the upper Cumberland in 1991. It was convened, through a joint resolution, by Fulcher and

Sam McCarthy, secretary of the British Marbles Board of Control. The British, it was agreed, would send their two greatest champions to Standing Stone to compete in the tournament and an exhibition match of British marbles. The following year the Americans would return fire, sending their six finest to England for the World Marble Championship.

Fulcher was not one to let such historical echoes go unamplified. As soon as the date was set, he scribbled out some lyrics, took a bluegrass band to a studio in Jamestown, and sent tapes to all the local radio stations. In the days before the tournament you could hear his rolley hole anthem blaring from every pickup truck and construction site, to the tune of Jimmy Driftwood's "Battle of New Orleans":

In 1991 when the British came across
The great Atlantic Ocean
Just to see who was the boss
With a pocket full of marbles and a little bit of luck
They said they'd whup old Tennessee
And tailor old Kentuck

We fired our flints and the British fired their tollies
But we hit them before they hit us
We fired once more and
We give 'em such a volley
Then we busted all their marbles
And we left them in the dust

For B.S. and for Ingrid

ME AND JAMES HAD BEEN DEFYING LIFE FOR NEAR FIVE YEARS when we decided to try our hand at defying death.

Defying life as one knows it is a full-time job. But it was in the midst of this worthy vocation that we found the other. We simply went to sleep one rank, muggy night in June and then found our new venture at dawn, sprouted up as though one of God's own proliferating creatures, upon our very doorstep. It boasted a crop of gaudy tents and midway rides, and the swath of lights spattered across it twinkled, even in the first wet breath of day. The fact that we couldn't have *missed* it unless we were struck blind in the night was the drawback. Upon that date in 1966, me and James were spending our nights in a car parked in an empty lot in north Toronto. We weren't making too much money those days, see. As I believe I've mentioned: we already had a full-time job. The following evening, when me and James went out to visit the fairgrounds, we barely even had the dough to get through the gates.

"We could do that," he announced out of the blue as we picked our way back in the dark, at the end of the night.

"Do what?" I wasn't paying much attention to James. I was too busy trying to scope out the car in the dark lot beyond the grounds. Trying to remember where in hell we'd left it. "Where's the car, James? You remember where we parked?"

"*That*," James said. "The sideshow. Those stunts."

He fingered a cigarette butt he'd found lying in the gravel a ways back, and now, impossibly, he'd also managed to produce a working matchbook. For a guy so lucky as to find that kind of complementary shit just lying out on the ground, it was profoundly irritating how we always lost the car. After walking back to it in the dead of night with my feet hurting like they were, in fact, it was galactically irritating.

"Man, I hate when this happens," I bitched.

James breathed in, his lips pursed around who-knows-whose cigarette stub: disgusting.

"You're disgusting," I said. And then: *Pick it up before ten seconds and it's not dirty!* I thought. *Who taught James THAT one, Tev?* "Give it here," I said.

James passed the butt over grudgingly and watched me inhale. "I didn't think any of the stunts were *scary*, though," he said. "Did you, Tev?"

"Not scary." I passed it back to him. The cherry was so low I nearly lit my fingernail on fire, a thing my God-loving Pentecostal mother would identify as divine reprisal for the habit itself. "Supposed to be, I guess, but no."

James nodded and returned the cigarette to his teeth. He sucked away, his eyes slit into a posture of deep, careful concentration: the eyes of a gymnast teetering on a balance beam. A moment or two passed before he spoke.

"What we do looks sort of scary."

I looked at him. "No it doesn't," I said. In the back of my mind, I knew it was a little telling that I didn't have to ask what he was talking about.

"Yes it does," James countered.

"No it doesn't."

"Yes it does."

I looked at him firmly: firmly between tired and irritated. "Shut the hell up, James," I said. I turned my head and spit. "What do you know anyway, huh, James? Dumb nit."

James, James-like, did not dissent. Instead he spun the cigarette butt out behind him—he'd smoked it until it was a black eyeball, its scope siphoned almost entirely away—and as I watched the fading red pupil upon it fly, I spotted the car. A big '55 Chevy shouldn't be hard to spot on a lot. You had to wonder how we could park the thing specifically in one corner, out of the way, and then fail to remember where we'd put it. Sometimes I speculated if James's dumb-nitness was catching.

James followed a few steps behind me. "You wouldn't know," he murmured from back there, as though confident I couldn't hear him.

I spun around and eyed him. "What'd you say?" Because I *couldn't* quite hear, though I knew he'd said something. I was beginning to get a little unreasonable in the way I was thinking, and I was wondering if that was catching too. "What'd you say, huh?" I asked.

James hesitated. He drew back, as though I might reach out and nab him around the buttons of his shirt and shake him. "I don't know," he began, which is the phrase that prefaces nearly every one of James's thoughts, a dummy's idiosyncrasy. "Said you wouldn't know, Tevan," he said, finally wagering he had nothing to fear—and in being twice the size of me, he didn't. "You never see what it looks like."

He didn't tell me what *it* was, no, and again I didn't have to ask him. Instead I stopped beside the car and studied him. James looked gaunt, typically gaunt; but tired and spent and all-around unhealthy, which for us wavered between typical and not, depending on the time of year and the resources at hand. I'd noticed this earlier in the day once already, when I'd taken him for his visit to the downtown courthouse. Paul and Paula had been playing on the radio, the smarmiest of tunes to hit the airwaves since Pat Boone:

True love means planning a life for twoooooo—

I'd cranked it up, James beside me riding shotgun, and I'd lit off on Paula's solo in a high, wheedling falsetto. It was during the second verse that I thought I heard him laugh. My eyes skirted curiously over at the sound of it, and I saw the way his upper lip was curled, the swift upward rise of his cheek. "Hey, Paul," I said aloud, impromptu and solely for James's benefit during the musical bridge, "I really love you in those pants. Come to think of it, Paul, I think I'd like you better *out* of those pants. Hey, Paul, why don't you come over here and show me what love *reeeeeally* means."

James had laughed even harder. He actually had to cover his nose with his hand to keep from snorting.

"Come on," I'd said then. "Give me a break. Look at their names, James: Paul and Paula? That'd be like you, James, falling for a chick named Jamie or . . . Jamesette or something. Me, I'd have to hook up with a girl with a name like—like . . . Oh, never mind, there's no hope for me." I'd turned my head: and that's when I'd caught him. Laughing or not, you could not help but see it in him. James looked terrible. I noticed this now, the second time in a day, and it struck me like a needle of sympathy for him. I decided that maybe that was enough for now.

"You think it's scary?" I said. "Hey, James?" In years of knowing James, I've come to understand that he generally responds best when addressed by name. Tricks of the trade.

A tentative smile spread onto his face. "Yeah," he tried. "Sure I do." And in that moment we consolidated into a working party again.

I unlocked my door first, then walked around to his. I looked up at him. "You think people would pay money to see that, James?" I asked.

"Yeah," he agreed, though now I couldn't be sure if he really meant it. James did that sometimes, like a kid who concurs because he wants to remain part of the team. Kids like James are what made Hitler's army; kids like James were advancing enthusiastically toward Vietnam as we spoke. It got hard to tell what he thought, and in the moment I found his tendency to agree— usually an underground, useful sort of privilege to me—to be a nuisance.

We got in the car, dark even with the doors open because the interior bulb had been spent for months. You couldn't read past dark. It was a condition that drove me wild with boredom, and likely why we found ourselves hanging around a carnival midway, monetary resources or not, in the post-twilight of a summer day. A car is pretty dark past sundown. That doesn't leave a lot to do for a person who doesn't sleep before the stroke of midnight. Man, I wished we'd fixed that light. How much could one of those things cost anyway? Ten cents? Jesus.

James settled into the passenger seat beside me. His jacket was unzipped and he stretched his long legs into the footwell as he stared at the windshield. You'd think we were about to drive cross-country by moonlight like a pair of loose convicts or something, sitting there in the dark like we were. But the fact is, we just really didn't have anyplace to go.

A few minutes passed.

"James," I said. "James, you going to sleep right away?"

He shuffled his neck against the headrest. His tangled hair bunched up like a Brillo pad. "Nup," he said. Then he gave a small giggle, like I'd caught him thinking something evil. "Keep thinking of those girls in the tent."

I smiled. "Girls in the tent." Then I added wryly, "Who we never got to *see*."

"We *saw* them," James insisted. "Saw that one in the pink anyways. You know, before she went in."

I smiled again. Girl in pink. She was sitting out back smoking a cigarette in her bathrobe when we caught a glimpse of her, lingering in her imperfect privacy. Before she headed inside and hauled it all off for fifty cents a head and a dozen gawking, hard-up eyes.

"Hmmmm," James murmured. "I think pink's my favorite color."

I laughed. I don't know if he was serious or what, but I couldn't help it.

"You ever been with a girl wearing pink, Tev?" he asked suddenly. "Ever have a girl in pink let you get . . ."

I answered him because he was asking, but also because I can commiserate with James's need to live vicariously through me sometimes. Pentecostal mother notwithstanding. On, you know, certain subjects. When the girls let you get funny with them they usually end up not wearing much at all, but I respect James's innocence, so I didn't say that. "Naw, I don't think so,"

I began. There's a fine line between satiating a curious mind and encouraging it to covet. "Oh, wait," I said. "Wait. Well, this one time—"

But already it was too much. He'd been thinking too long, which goes to show what happens when James gets to thinking. "Aw, you been with 'em all, Tev," he said, turning his eyes. "It's not fair. I don't get it, Tev. You've known all those girls and I— and really, I—"

I didn't say anything—it's not like I can apologize for it; shit, it's not like I can even *congratulate* myself for it—until James continued under his breath, but meaning for me to hear: "You got it worse than me."

I flicked him a look. "I didn't get it worse than you."

"Yes you did."

"No I didn't." *Here we go,* I thought.

"Yes—"

I cut him off. I turned right around in the seat to look at him. I don't see the point in talking in circles. And plus, it was obvious he needed to hear it again. James was doing what he did best, which is remembering.

"There is no worse, hear me, James?" I said. "There's no worse. Ain't no difference between yours or mine. It happened, is all." *Which,* I could've added, *is what we already spend enough time knowing.* But I never say stuff like that to James. It isn't good for him. "You got that, James? You got that?"

He didn't reply.

Didn't make a sound for a long time, actually. I hadn't meant to, but it'd come out a little heated, and now as I peeked over to assess the silence, I could see him beginning to crumple. Bigger than me, but Jesus, the biggest suck you ever met in your life. I wanted to roll my eyes, but I never do stuff like that to James.

"Hey," I said to his bowing shoulders. "Hey, James. Come on. You're okay." Already I could hear him breathing, tortured and snotty-sounding. "Hey. Hey, friend." I was doing what I did best, which is talking, and James was doing what he did best.

"James," I whispered, putting my hand on his arm. "James? James, you want me to—I mean, you want to—"

(Remembering)

His eyes came up then, fast. Fierce and determined. I would have been scared if I didn't know him as well as I do. *But we're never doing that again!* something shrill inside of me said—a reminder like a string wrapped round your index finger. *You said we're never doing that again!* But I knew too well what *it* was, and we'd said this a hundred times before (and likely would a hundred times again, I wagered in my weakness, so what the hell difference did it make?), and I deftly closed my eyes to it all over again.

"Yes." His voice came low and gnashing. "Yes."

I let my head back against the seat. "Come on, then," I said.

I hadn't even reclined the seat back when he moved his hands up quick and close to my face. But not quite. He seemed to catch himself. He breathed a little, watching my face for any sign that he had gotten carried away.

"Don't be scared," James said in a soft voice. "I would never hurt you, Tev."

I hadn't begun to be. But with this admonition, I admit he cast one brief quiver across my throat and mouth. For in it I understood that even dumb nit James saw the seam between one place and the other, one time and another.

Perhaps saw, even, one set of hands working, hurting, evaporating over time, and reintegrating somehow as his own.

"I'm not scared," I returned.

And I never was.

My mother was superstitious as well as Pentecostal. When the carnival arrived in Hamilton, Ontario, each first of July, she would take my brother Kenny and me to watch the parade. *Never look back upon a circus parade*, she'd say, holding our hands to her sides. *It brings the bad fortune of the past back upon you.* My father died when I was less than two years old; Kenny was eight, and my mother just thirty. She wasn't willing to chance a glance backward in that direction. No matter how firm she held her eyes to the ground as each carnival thrummed by, Kenny still died a short twelve years later. And so maybe I can be forgiven for taking no heed of her caveat. The day following our night in the parking lot, I turned James and me around and headed straight back to the carnival.

As for James, he opened his eyes that morning as though God's conferred light of day was the searchlights of a UFO. I brought him with me anyway. He didn't say a word, which happens on occasion, and stared straight through me while I gesticulated and pointed and bawled at him to change his shirt. The sun had already burned the dew off the grass, and it began working hard on our backs as we set out walking. I had to stop to make sure James was keeping up. We walked the whole way in silence, one trailing the other, like strangers who just happen to be following the same route. And if you want to know the truth of that as well, I suppose I can allow that that's been known to happen between us in history too.

I stopped a final time when the fairground came into view. The midway itself was a dusty field of color and steel rods. A breeze across it brought a breath of processed sweetness to my nose and a continuous, quivering flap to the sidelong tents. The tents were lined up in rickety rows, their canvas skin heavy and hot. The alien metal arms of rides shot out and upward from the far end of the mix. I pulled my gaze to the fringes of the set-up and spied what I was looking for.

To the left and strategically placed under a row of somber, swaying poplars stood a wide Winnebago. The walls were yellow and cracked in places, and the awning fluttered upward in silky hanks like a shirt that has been through the wash too many times. I cast a glance back at James: he looked like he could've slept in its undercarriage that night.

"Come here," I said.

He shuffled before me.

"Come *here*," I said again. He bent his face in diligently.

He continued to stare at me, tepid and empty, while I swished his hair around trying to make a part. His eyes were listless despite their color. Between my fingers the strands felt heavy and dank, like a baby's with a fever. He didn't say anything.

"That's a little better, huh, James?" He looked back at me and didn't answer. "It's going to be like an interview," I said as I took some of the worse-looking hanks and hooked them behind his ears. "Who knows what will come of it. All goes well, we'll have a room someplace tonight. Hey, James?"

It came out like I was saying it for him, as though I believed this information would please him. In truth, James and me both know it's me who goes flaky without sleep and falls ill easily, growing urinary tract infections and cold sores and fevers like weeds sprouting up in an untended lot. I caught myself turning my head at all angles, as though I could peer through James's forehead and catch sight of what lay on the other side.

"If you're lucky," I said, "you'll even get your own bunk instead of having to put up with me."

The suggestion rolled through him like a small earthquake: his eyes slid forward—a slip, a crack in the glass that was, on a good day, my simply simple friend James—and then away from mine. If I had been in a better mood (*and he*, I told myself, *a better goddamn conversationalist this morning*), I might have been disgusted with myself for bothering him. Instead, I found I was just getting my engines rolling.

"Hey," I said. In a hard voice this time, a voice that meant business. "When we get in there, James, I don't want you to say one fucking word." This instruction jarred him less than the one directly before, which did not surprise me. For a stupid guy, sometimes he isn't so stupid. "You understand, James?"

I watched the vacant stare. I nodded for both of us: "Good."

We marched up the grass, then took the rickety stairs. We entered the camper without knocking, and as we breached the doorway, one after the other, the heat hit us like a wall. It was a veritable greenhouse in there. Slouched behind a desk and reading a magazine sat a young man. He had one of those haircuts that only hoods wear: short around the ears but grown out too long in back, like an outdated, unkempt version of Elvis. It looked like he'd tried to neaten it up by tying it back. Red swatches sprouted across his forehead, and his shirt looked well worn. It occurred to me that maybe I hadn't needed to bother with James's hair. And as though he could feel my gaze like a heat on his skin, the guy suddenly looked up.

He jumped at the sight of us. In fact, right then he stood.

"We're hoping to see someone from the management," I said quickly. "Is this you?"

The guy took a step toward us. His eyes looked me over, at once cagey and questioning. I noted he looked a little older than James, and he had an awkward comeliness to him, tanned like a triathlete. He came up in height someplace between us. I thought that all this information might come in handy later.

The guy seemed to be sizing us up the same way. Now his gaze traded between James and me. He looked at James. He looked at me. He drew back to James again, this time taking in his full height and the on-vacation look of him that a person couldn't help but catch. He averted his eyes—as if James might be a loose cannon, and he didn't want to be the proverbial detonator. Finally he spoke:

"There a problem?" he asked. His eyes flicked over me: up, down, up, down.

"No," I said carefully. "Well, yes. I guess—I guess I'm asking about employment."

A relieved, baffled expression overtook his face. Then a look to James, one more time—quick as water bouncing off a hot skillet—for good measure. "Hang on," he said. "I'll see what I can do."

He came around the desk, passed us, and put his head through a door into another room; there, he offered up some low murmurings beyond my range. My eyes traipsed the room, waiting, taking in the rickety table and chair, the cabinet in one corner, and the avalanche of paper spilling across it.

"*Why was the door unlocked?*" a voice boomed from the adjoining room.

When the guy came back a moment later, his brow had furrowed into a wounded, furious little snit. He motioned for us. I followed his signal and James followed me, and then the two of us were in the next room. And there, sitting behind a monstrosity of a desk, was a guy similar to the one we'd just left, only all of him twofold. Twice the amount of sweat, hair, and weight; twice the look of dubious exasperation on his face. You could spot the resemblance at once. I would've laid a bet it was the younger guy's father.

"Tevan George," I said, putting my hand out.

The man before us didn't get out of his seat. He took my hand as though accepting a flyer or Book of Mormon handed out on a street corner. *Book of Mormon,* his indifferent expression read. *I'll throw this out when I see a trash bin.*

"This is James."

James didn't offer his hand. James isn't one to remember small tokens of hospitality.

"Buddy Merit," the man said.

When I'd stood long enough to understand that he might share James's perspective on hospitality, I gestured to James and we sat down. The man watched us from behind the desk, his eyes trained on us like a sniper's scope. It was really hot in there, hot as blazes. I decided it was high time to get to the point.

"You've got a sideshow, I noticed," I began. "We been last night, though it's not much to spit at. Says Ten in One on your sign out front, but we had to pay separate for each show." Then, to pique his interest: "Plus you've just got nine acts. And you must've had ten before. And so I got to thinking—"

The man—Buddy—stirred in his seat. The bolts beneath him gave a rusty squawk. "Nine," he cut in. "*Nine.* The sign is old, Tevan George. We have a lot of working acts this route, so we've changed them all to Single O's. Costs more to run, of course." He spread his hands. "Then it costs more to watch. But more value for your money." He smiled. "Suppose I really ought to change that sign, though, don't you think?" Merit watched us, waiting, then smiled again. "And we've got a kootch show and a card reader. Not acts, no—but that makes *over* ten, technically, in case you need me to add it up for you boys."

I didn't say anything. Me and James had arrived late the previous night expecting to pay one fee for ten exhibits, as the sign indicated, but when it turned out this wasn't the case, I admit we went ahead and shelled out again anyhow. I got Merit's point immediately: the "old" sign had been left out strategically, and I, like every other schmuck with fifty cents jingling in his pocket, fell for it. In fact, me and James plain ran out of money before we even *got* to the kootch show, which is why we had to be content with the girl in the pink nightie instead. That was a real disappointment and a bitch, having to tell James, *No, we're not seeing the girlie show after all, sorry.* The guy doesn't see much action with a gourd like that. Even I have to admit it.

As if to press the point, Buddy looked at James and spoke so loud you'd think he took James for some old fart with a hearing problem. "Don't you talk, son? *You born without a tongue or something?*"

"Do you want a tenth act?" I said. "That's what we're here for. Do you want a real tenth?"

Buddy's gaze ran in my direction. Now he looked at once amused and dubious. "That depends," he said. "I'm a showman. What do you do? You're obviously not human oddities, which is generally what one finds on a freak show." He barked a laugh. "Unless you count this one here. Shit, you planning on having your friend here pull a brain out of his ass? Is that where it is, son?" Loud again, to James: *"Is that where you've lost all your smarts?"*

I don't sweat to stand up for James. I was about to tell this guy that if James had his brain up his ass, then at least he *had* one, better than some. But I needed the job. "You said you have working acts," I said.

Buddy nodded at me, then shrugged, noncommittal. "I do.

Plenty of them. What kind of working act might we be talking about?"

"Near-death," I said.

There was one horrible moment where I thought he might laugh out loud on what had been planned as a very serious note. This moment passed gracefully.

I motioned to James. "He puts me unconscious. I stop breathing. Then he brings me back."

Merit frowned. "Well. Now how would he do that?"

I hesitated, my eyes pulled toward James. I considered using a literal term. I thought about what the cops, or a court, or even a doctor, might call it. I decided I didn't like any of these. Finally I just went with my instincts.

"He chokes me until I drop," I said.

Buddy's eyes drifted to James, packed and unreadable in the little office chair. He looked down at James's wide hands and then up at his brow, furrowed above his eyes like an angry watchtower. I saw Buddy's pupils rise, taking in James's full height, and then sink down to his big, black engineer's boots. I have to tell you I'd thought twice about it all: but now it occurred to me how wise it was to bring James in there with me.

"Until you drop," Merit repeated. "Until you *drop*. What a feat." He paused. "Well, of course you would—*look at him!*" he exploded. "And then what? Your friend here sues me for a million bucks? Sure! You'd be *dead*, for Christ's sake! If he chokes your breath, *damn right you'll drop!* Getting up again would be impossible! Even for me, it'd be impossible!"

I began to shake my head. "No," I said. "No, please, it's not *impossible*. Hey, no, I can really do it—" But I understood that Merit was right, to some extent: stopping breathing generally means you're dead. So I added, for good measure: "Please, there won't be any accidents. No accidents or—funny business, or anything, if that's what you're suggesting. I mean, there hasn't *ever* been any—"

Buddy's hairline climbed his head. "No funny business." His tone touched on disdain. "Is it fake?"

"It's not *fake*," I said. "I mean, you can't fake it. I would never—"

And Merit caught my statement for more than I'd meant it. "You ever done this before for show?"

I slid my eyes to James, caught myself doing it, and grew thankful that he wasn't lively enough to have exchanged me a look. "Yes," I said slowly. Because Buddy hadn't specified side-show, just show, and heaven forbid we discount the time when some punks paid James fifty dollars to knock out that pretty boy sitting at the bar and he'd actually taken the money and done it. *If I came and warned you, they'd a known we were friends*, he'd told me days later. I was still rubbing my throat even then, my chin feeling like a caustic lump and my glands beneath, a row of hot marbles. *I'll give you the money, Tev. Here. I did it to give you the money. Take it, please, take it*. He kept saying it until I did. I took it and we walked into another bar the very next night (we weren't allowed back into the first one) and spent it on . . .

Well, I don't recall, exactly. Who cares anyway? I do recall getting sick to my stomach later that night, but that's about as far as my wits will take me.

"Yes." I watched Merit hopefully. "Yes, I—"

"You're saying," he cut in, "that it's been done before, then."

My eyes bounced to James again. "Yes," I said. "Yeah, loads. I mean, tons of times."

"And so how long have you been doing this"—Merit spun a hand through the air—"particular stunt?"

Nobody had ever asked me such a question. So I raised my eyes to the ceiling. *Well, let's see now, then*, I thought. *Hooked up with James in 1961. Then there was '62. '63, '64, '65 . . .* Merit's eyebrows lifted as he watched me. And what came out next was a lie that I never intended:

"Five years," I announced. "I'd say it's been five years now."

"Five years," Merit remarked, impressed. "With who?"

I blinked, bewildered. For a moment I had no idea what he meant. In the next, I understood what he was asking for—a verbal curriculum vitae. I didn't have one. I didn't even know any shows circulating the province. But as luck would have it, all of a sudden I didn't have to. In that moment, Merit the Younger burst in.

"He's here!" he yelled. Buddy popped from his seat, flying out from behind the desk. I turned left and then right; then I jumped from my chair to press my face against the window. It all happened so fast that if James, deaf-mute to the world, had blinked at precisely the right moment, he might have opened his eyes an instant later and wondered where everyone had gone.

A loud ruckus had erupted outside the wall of the trailer. Outside stood a man, bald and hefty in appearance, banging his fists into the front door.

"Open up in there, Merit, you goddamn con sack of shit!" he screamed.

My eyes stuck upon him through the screened window with a horrified attraction. The fellow's colorful address emitted from a mouth that was a near-empty socket—three or four yellowy and tenuous remainders clung to his top gum line like spare parts, but this was all. The visual effect was of a man with fangs. Jesus, no wonder Merit wanted the door locked.

"Give me my goddamn money or else I'm gonna—"

Merit, purported con sack of shit, did not wait to hear the rest. The door unlatched with a thick snap, and he released his progeny into the wild.

The Younger stepped out of the office, and his voice boomed above that of the fanged man: *He,* the fanged man, had nothing on them, the Younger professed at high volume; *he* was full of it. *He* could go tell his problems to Jesus if the need should take him, but *he* wasn't getting a cent more than he'd already been awarded.

A crowd of young men had slunk out from all directions to watch. Now they collected at the foot of the Winnebago. As this goon squad closed in, the fanged man backed up. He was smart to do so. He shrank into the parched grass with Merit's son on his heels, and the band of cronies, on the heels of this. I watched in awe.

Buddy Merit reappeared in the inner office a moment later, smiling broadly.

"Sorry, boys," he offered, as if returning from the call of nature. He spread his hands. "Okay then. How does this work?"

I was momentarily tongue-tied.

"This giant chokes you, you said," Merit put in, his finger toward James. "You 'go unconscious.'" His round eyes narrowed as he grew speculative. He raised them to the ceiling, nodding.

"Yes," I put in quickly. "Near-dead."

"*How* near?"

"Well . . ." I made a face. "Not breathing. I mean, people will pay money to see that."

"Maybe. But how do we know it's not gaffed?"

A pause.

"Gaffed?" I said.

"*Gaffed,* son! *Fake*! How do I know you're not shamming me, breathing through your nose or your ass, say, while I'm standing there in the front row?"

I looked at Merit. "There's no trick. You'll be able to tell I'm not breathing," I said, "because I'm not."

Merit shifted in his seat. "You're able to show this? Then how does he bring you back?"

"A.R.," I said.

Merit leaned in. "What's that?" The incident with the fanged man had left him not only unscathed but focused, and now he was genuinely curious. Propitiously, the only thing that he seemed to have forgotten was the issue of references from my previous employers. I was only too happy to forget them along with him. And I guess I forgot all about the way he'd treated the fanged man, too—because the next part came out without a moment's hesitation, and I almost cost us the whole deal.

"Mouth-to-mouth," I said.

A long silence stretched out between Merit and me. Suddenly

his eyes swelled in their sockets. His forehead crept into a sky-scraping posture. And then his mouth opened into a snarl that I never expected.

"*What is this, some kind of a homo thing?*" he roared. "*What are you guys, a couple of homos? One cute boy and one bull, you think I can't figure you two out! What kind of a show do ya think I'm running here, kootch or not—*"

"He can really do it, you know," a voice said.

Buddy Merit heaved in his seat. The sound seemed to catch him off guard.

It came again: "He can really do it."

I turned my head toward James. I'd told him not to open his mouth; in fact, I'd told him not to open his *fucking* mouth. Buddy stared too. He blinked—one slow-motion, staggered signal. And then, for some reason, he paid James a little courtesy. He kept watching James; we both did. And in the humid, shocked silence, James continued to speak.

"I drop him and he goes out. He lies there for a while looking like he's dead. Then I bring him back."

"You bring him back. How do you do that?" Buddy asked.

"Like he said. A.R."

Buddy's expression contorted. He spoke as though he were chewing glass: "You put your mouth on his."

James looked momentarily confused, then broke to complete honesty. "Yes. Yeah, I guess I do. I breathe for him and that's how I bring him back."

"How long's he out for?"

James's chin fell into his hand. He leaned back and gazed at me for a long while. I gazed back, uncertain. I couldn't answer the question. If Buddy was asking how long I go down for, personally I'm never around to time it.

"Two minutes," James said finally. "The longest I'd say is maybe two minutes."

Two minutes? Man, even I was impressed.

"But I start breathing for him before that," James went on.

"If I wait too long, he throws up. And it's not good to go long without breathing."

Merit's mouth bowed into a frown. "Two minutes isn't very long."

"Yes, sir, Buddy Merit," James said, "it *is* a long time. When I drop him I have to count, and it's a long time." He paused. And then as if no one had heard him the first time: "It's not good to go long without breathing."

"You drop him," Merit repeated. "How exactly do you do that?"

James turned in his seat again and fixed his eyes on me. I watched him back without moving. It reminded me of a bad experience I'd had at the barber's once. The perilous moment when I was in the chair, committed, and hair began to fall about me in suspicious, unconsented-to quantities: *Oh Gawd, where is this going?* I recall thinking in frozen alarm.

I kept sitting there watching James, James watching me. And then, just as I began to think that James wasn't going to do anything at all, that he'd turned hollow and glassed-off again right before our eyes, that I'd get the chance to pick up the reins and recover us, James moved. Like a hunter striking with his bare hands—casting his shadow across the pool, waiting long enough to allow the fish to skitter, linger, and then grow lazily unconcerned with his presence—he snapped his hands outward.

His right hand landed at the base of my skull; the angle between thumb and pointer met the soft spot under my chin. I didn't even get a chance to draw a breath. I managed one startled declaration before I lost my air completely.

My eyes went wide, popped outward like kernels fired in a pan. They fixed upon James, but in the periphery all I could see was Buddy Merit. He began to rise from his chair like a child leaning in to watch the first pitch of the baseball season, or to see polar bears swimming in the aquarium at the zoo. His jaw unhinged and his eyes went wide. And in this instant, even though me and James had done this countless times before, I believe I saw for the first time what it was that we were doing.

I saw how James was twice as big as me and twice as ugly. I saw his hands, sprung and loaded, with me caught inside them like an animal in a trap. I saw how the determination in his eyes could look like something else, something less benign. I saw this all in Buddy Merit's face.

I looked at James and he looked back at me. My back straightened and my nails began to claw at the crummy varnish on Buddy's chair. Me and James knew each other very well by then. But now, just like that time in the bar worth fifty dollars, a prize so intoxicating I don't even remember it, I was startled by the dive inward. I became aware of a temperature change in the seam of my pants. If James didn't let up soon, Buddy wasn't going to be the only one rising to the call of the wild.

This all passed in seconds. Before such events could evolve, James released his hand from my chin. "Like that," he said. "Only longer."

My lungs reached hysterically and I flopped forward onto the desk. My shoulders heaved up and down.

"Do it now!" Buddy shrieked. "Can you do it right now?"

James drew his gaze to me. He watched for a long moment, taking in my tearing eyes and my mouth, frosted with spit and gasping for air. His eyes held a strange combination of malice and apology. And just as I started clenching up for round two, James spoke.

"No," he said. "I'm not going to do it now."

"Do it now!" Merit cried.

"*I'm not going to do it now*," James said, getting loud. "He's tired. He's tired and he hasn't eaten in almost—"

I put my hand out and clapped it across James's wrist. "Talk fast," I said at Merit. "And soon enough you'll see the whole thing."

Merit turned to survey me. It was the first look I'd gotten from him since James opened his fat mouth. He looked me up and down, his slow, even respiration a terrible contrast with my own. He cut me an equally terrible grin. And in it, I understood that he and I both knew there was little room for bargaining. Between Buddy's enthusiasm and James's and my dire straits, whatever came next would be mostly lip service.

"I just lost my geek," he announced. "On account of that, you see where this places me." His eyes panned thoughtfully over us. He paused at James, raised one contemplative finger. "I do have a little test I give my employees. A few skill-testing questions, let's say. Are you up for that just now?"

James'll never make it through this, I thought, pained. And just as though he'd heard me, Merit flashed his grin.

"Oh, it's not hard, don't worry. You can answer together. Do you have social insurance numbers for me?"

"No," James said with an immediacy that I couldn't have competed with. That was *my* answer; but like I told Merit, James had been with me for five years. He knows the rules. For a stupid guy, sometimes he ain't so stupid.

Merit's grin bloomed. "Good. Then we're off to a good start. And do you know who's the boss around here?"

James frowned. "You?" he offered.

"Right again!" Merit clapped his hands. Then he sobered. "But if you break your neck or kill yourself, or your little ditty here fails to do its job one day on my stage, who's your boss then?"

Nobody answered as me and James exchanged glances.

Merit's tone grew strident. "*Who?*"

"Not you," I said.

Merit's eyes switched between us. "That's right. *Not* me. And what with my offering you the kind favor of your entire gross pay—not a penny for this fine government of ours, that is—we'll have the paperless kind of arrangement that, if you should change your mind, you'll find confirms this. Yes?"

"Yes," I said.

Merit nodded. "And finally, boys, while I'm on the subject—do you have any idea how much minimum wage is in this country of ours?"

"Yes," I said, and witnessed the slow rise of Merit's eyes upon me. "No?" I revised.

"That's right." He flourished a hand. "You don't! Forget you know a thing about it. We pay a flat-rate weekly round here, the specs to be worked out between you and my own kith and kin."

"What do you mean?" I said quickly. "Is that more or less?"

Merit smiled. "Well, that depends on the worth of your trick, son. Your following, how well you can gut the marks. Like I said, Single O's cost me more to run. But if you play your cards right on stage, I wager you'll work strong. Am I talking too fast for you, son? I said we'll take you on." He tapped the desk as though to signal the end of the discussion. "Any questions?"

"What's a geek?" That was James, and so my fingers tightened across his wrist in a silent, preemptive wring of forewarning.

"Geek's a sideshow performer," Buddy said. "A loser. Nobody. A person no one will miss. Someone whose ass I just fired." He looked at us meaningfully and I thought I understood. James had been destitutely underemployed the first summer that we lived together, and the only work he'd been able to find was at a campground, shoveling shit into the honeydew wagon. *Don't ask, James,* I thought, looking at Merit and remembering this indignity. *God, don't ask. Probably the crummiest job on the whole damn fairgrounds, by the looks of the guy. And the sound of it.*

Merit's brow danced upon his forehead. "Anything else?"

"Yeah," I said. "You got anyplace for us to stay?"

Merit bared his teeth. "Sure do." He shuffled a hand through his pockets to produce a set of keys. "You can stay at the geek's, if you two don't mind sharing. He was renting from me." He slid the keys across the desk. "He certainly won't be staying there anymore." The message here—as with that buried within his game of Twenty Questions—was somewhat ominous, but I admit it wasn't one that I cared to wrap my head around. I snapped the fob up as if Buddy had just handed me the key to the city: no reclined car seat tonight for me, no siree Bob.

"Come round the sideshow tent tomorrow morning so we can stake out your routine," Buddy said. "Practices are free, boys. You should know you won't see a cent until after your first performance. Again, my son will see to all that." He nodded toward my hand upon the keys. "And don't get to thinking those come for free."

"I can't pay you," I told him. He answered me just the same.

"You will." He stood then, and as he did I was reminded of his son's sudden pose when he believed that me and James had arrived to stir trouble. "Any questions?"

I shook my head. James and me stood. Buddy waited until we were nearly out the door, his eyes on our backs, before he let fly with one last proclamation: "Hey, I have one."

I turned back, meeting his gaze.

Buddy smirked. "I just can't help but ask," he said. "How in hell'd you boys figger out you could do this trick, anyway?"

In the moment Buddy put voice to the puzzle, I saw James rising to the challenge. His lips parted with impossible confidence. After all these years of studying James, I was glad I'd made that investment.

"*James*," I charged, swinging my head in his direction. "I thought I told you to *shut it.*"

I witnessed a certain bewilderment cross Buddy's face. It was as if, among those rusty cogs turning in his head, he considered for the first time that he'd read the two of us all wrong. His look was one of combined apprehension and confusion, and it left me feeling pleasurably self-righteous. This time it was me who grinned.

And then I gave him the line.

As truthful as James's would have been, but a little less detail-oriented. After all, me and James had been running through the part for almost as long as we'd known each other. Or—let's not argue semantics here, my friend—maybe even before that, if we count the time at Mount Rosa's.

"Lots of practice," I said. "I guess."

THE FIRST TIME I CAME TO MOUNT ROSA HOSPITAL, I ARRIVED by bus. I was fourteen years old, and I traveled the entire route from Hamilton to Toronto by myself. I'd been advised I was contagious, but with my brother Kenny out of commission, slated to join me at the hospital within the month, and my mother never having gotten a driver's license herself, it was the only way to get there.

It was 1957, and I didn't know a lot about tuberculosis. Soon, gratuities to Mount Rosa's, I'd come to know it resided most often in the lungs. I'd know that it got around in close quarters, sharing personal effects and passing the bottle. I'd even come to understand that this was probably why my brother Kenny had come down with it three times in his last five years. And likely how I got it from him.

Just before I left for Mount Rosa's, my mother put herself through two transfer points and a good amount of change in order to reach the downtown Hamilton bus terminal on my behalf. She went all the way there to buy my Toronto-bound ticket; then she came all the way back home and handed it to me. When I was finally on my way a few days later, ticket in hand, a girl took the aisle seat beside me at the Burlington terminal. Remembering my mother and her acute toiling to respect the contagion, I did what I thought she'd want from me: I got up and moved.

Instead of decency, however, what I felt was a dose of heartache. She was a nice-looking girl. It would've been nice to sit next to some cute thing on my last day on the outside for nine long months. I thought of her a lot on the inside, actually. Inside Mount Rosa's, quarantined with ten other adolescent boys and no female body around for miles—save the old biddy nurses, and whatever fantasy women we might have within our psyches. I was fourteen then, so without much experience on the subject of women, though I was awakening every day to things I'd never known before. I awoke one morning to find pimples lining my shoulder blades; on another, to hair running the length of my thighs. And so my eyes and my body were open. Whatever I knew of girls was gleaned from issues of *Sheena, Queen of the Jungle, Romantic Love,* or *Betty and Veronica.* What I knew of sex was a conglomerate of my mother's admonitions about dating, my brother's terminology for body parts, and a few books I happened upon. Once, for instance, I was crouched on my hands and knees in Kenny's bedroom in search of an underarm deodorant, and I met a half-nude lady. The booklet she frontiered was stamped long before I'd started reading comics, likely at a time when I never dreamed women could look that way. But there she was, nonetheless: in my brother's sock drawer, her long hair spinning about her, her eyes welcoming. *Go on, sweetheart, take a closer look.*

So I did, of course. I took that book from Kenny's drawer and I brought it with me to Mount Rosa's.

The comic was titled *The Phantom Lady.* I opened that comic book up a thousand times over, as if, in doing so, I could inject myself inside it. I read with my head bent into the drawings and my prick hidden beneath. For the first time in my life, the prospect of the body in the book brought more than just pictures or parts to mind. She made me think of undertakings, activities—the things that people *did* with such parts. Finding *The Phantom Lady* was like coming upon a fossil in the ground, in my brother's room. It was like tunneling into a sandy beach as a child and coming across a silver dollar—an adult currency, but one that would eventually prove as applicable to me as it did to the guy who dropped it there.

I came to Mount Rosa Hospital in 1957, awakening.

I left Mount Rosa Hospital for the last time at eighteen, awake but anesthetized.

The years that came after this with James, I can only mark as something in between. Like the right word that gets caught in your throat—not spoken, but not exactly contained anymore. I couldn't take it in, but I couldn't forget it either.

It got caught there. Somewhere in between.

Somewhere in between, all I could do was choke.

As I said, the first time I walked into Mount Rosa Hospital, I was fourteen years old and alone. But the last time I walked in I was high on a spliff; and when I came out again, there I was with James. Let that be a lesson to all of those who feel that substance expands the mind.

I pulled the spliff out of my pocket, leveled it between my teeth, and lit the match just moments before I went inside that final time. Mount Rosa's is a giant brick building, and so I hid around the corner in order to do it, where the delivery trucks drive in and nurses come out for cigarette breaks.

It sparked up on the first haul. "*Hooo,*" I managed, out loud and squinting, because that stuff hits you in the throat like hot needles. Either that or I'm just a pussy. I probably am. It's not my fault. With the history I have with those lungs, I'll be damned if I inhale much other than basic air these days. Or so I've been told. My mother would kill me, I mused, studying the cherry on the end. Then it occurred to me that I didn't give a hang what my mother thought either way. And *then* I leaned in quick and took another haul: clearly, the thing was working.

It was her fault I was there anyway. Her fault that they found me and signed me up after all this time. I'd plucked the note from my door a few weeks before—the one reading *Your mother called looking for you*—and hadn't hesitated to march out to the phone booth on the corner and return the call. If I had known what it was about, I never would've been so enthusiastic.

"The sanitarium called," she told me. "You're supposed to go back there this month."

"Aw, Ma!" I exploded. "No! God, I don't want to go back there! Man, I hate that place. I'm through with them. I'm done with all their Christly medication and—"

"It's a test, Tevan. A follow-up." She paused. "Don't let me hear you using that kind of terminology. It's uncouth for a young man."

I huffed into the mouthpiece. "It's been *four years*, Ma. Four years! I don't want to. I don't have to. I don't see why in hell—"

She cut me off: "Tevan." *You got a tongue like a snake when you're hot*, my brother Kenny used to say. And he was older than me, working with guys who were miners and drivers and others of foul-mouthed repute, so that's saying a lot. "Tevan, you'll be going whether you want to or not," she said. "You know that."

And I did know. Because whether one wanted to or not, not going is known as noncompliance to the Ministry of Health. They were particular about you, even after four years. If you showed up, that was good. If you didn't, that was like going AWOL on a tour of duty. It was like a Pentecostal breaking all Ten Commandments in one fell swoop. My mother's a Pentecostal.

"And Kenny would be going too," she said to me.

I nodded, not saying anything this time.

"There's a date set already, Tevan," she said. "You don't get to choose. I told the nurse that you were in school and so you might have to miss some class."

More silence from me. I was in school, yes, but only in a theoretical sense. I'd made out pretty well in high school, but once attendance wasn't recorded on paper I just couldn't keep myself in line. Half the problem was that classes began at an unfathomable nine in the morning, and I'd started to work a casual nightshift for cash during the week. The truth was that while I'd paid my first year's tuition, I was barely a student anymore. Just her mentioning class was enough to ignite my stomach in a blaze of guilt.

"I'm going to give you the number now," she told me.

"Okay," I said. Then I added, in my defense, "I hate that place."

"You got *no reason* to hate that place." Her words were fierce this time. They were also, incidentally, grammatically incorrect—a failing she never hesitated to point out in others when she was touting higher education. My mother never had any higher education herself. And so I didn't say anything to that either.

I was standing right there in the booth and I didn't see any point to beating around the bush. I called up the nurse at the sanitarium right away. It actually isn't a sanitarium anymore. Now it's just a hospital.

"Tevan George. You spoke with my mother?"

"That's right," the nurse said. "Tuberculosis screening, isn't it?"

"Yes."

She paused with me on the line. I could hear her shuffling papers around. "How old are you now, Tevan?"

"Eighteen, ma'am."

"Mmm-hmm. That would put you here at Mount Rosa in . . . 1957, correct?"

"I was admitted in 1957, ma'am," I told her. "For nine months, and then I was an outpatient until 1959."

"Mmm-hmm." She sounded pleased. "My, my, you boys have all grown up. If this x-ray is clear, then this is the last we'll see of you, Tevan."

That's when she gave me the date. The date looked fine at face value—hell, *all* dates look good when you're an unofficial school dropout doing part-time night work on the side. You have all the time—all the days—in the world. But when I heard it, something important occurred to me for the first time.

"Hold on a second," I said. "Why is it that I have to come on that one day?"

The nurse rustled her papers again. "Because that's the day we're holding the reassessment x-rays. The TB clinic is limited."

"Limited," I said.

"Yes," she agreed.

I waited in silence. "That's the only day," I said.

"That's right," she said, pleased again. But *I* wasn't feeling pleased. I felt sick all of a sudden. My stomach had wadded itself up so that it almost hit my throat. I forgot all about the *ma'am* crap.

"Well . . ." I started. "Well, how many people did you *call*?"

"Oh, you won't have to wait long," she assured me. "Only those up for a four-year reassessment will be in on that day. And you'll remember that when you were with us it was a rather small group, Tevan." Shuffling of papers again and I knew that what came next would be a number—a number that would be stamped upon my brain like a hot, prickly brand for the next three weeks. I suddenly wasn't certain I should hear it. I got the thought in mind to pull my ear away from the phone, but then I hesitated and it was too late:

"Eight," she said.

Eight. *Eight!*

"There were eight pediatrics admitted in 1957, which is hardly a high number at all." She paused, then returned happily: "Tuberculosis surveying isn't as necessary in 1961 as it used to be. We're not a sanitarium anymore, you know, Tevan."

I know that! I thought hotly, though that's not what I wanted to say. I wanted to say *Who?* And *Which eight?* And *What names, can't you tell me? Please, other than Tevan George, can you tell me please, for the love of God Almighty! I need to know, which names?*

In the wake of my silence she took me for either surprised or impressed with the scope of medical technology, of which I had been an obvious beneficiary. "I imagine the clinic could be a little reunion of sorts, Tevan," she said. "Perhaps you'll see someone there you know."

It took all that was in me not to slam the phone down and yell some profanity at the top of my lungs. In its place, I took a deep breath.

"Perhaps," I agreed. Then I hung up and walked slowly back to my room.

I can't think of many times in my life where I faced something that I was this scared about, and I'm almost positive that every one of those times had something to do with Mount Rosa's, which means I had no choice in the matter anyhow. My visits to the old hospital had been mandatory unless I wanted to relapse and die like they told me I would, or be hunted down by the Ministry of Health, whichever occurred first. But now it had been four years. Four years and plenty of time to feel safe. Plenty of time to feel I didn't need the place to keep me alive anymore.

I thrashed in my bed for weeks, thinking about it. I missed more school. I worked more nightshifts. *You'll be going whether you want to or not.* And it was on the fourth out of five nightshifts of the second week that the idea came to me.

I was chewing a piece of gum at three in the morning on the assembly line when it happened. It's easier to stay awake when you're sipping a cup of coffee or eating a doughnut or otherwise noshing on something. I'd wound the chewing gum three times through a little gap I have between my incisor and second molar when the wheels inside my head shifted to high gear. Actually it was the tooth that had been replaced by the aforementioned little gap that did it.

I was seventeen when I'd had that tooth extracted from my lower left jaw. The tooth had been a squashed, sunken, and almost concave mess, and I spent years telling myself that it simply had character. Really it was an artifact from my childhood— a primary that missed its rite of passage and just never fell out, as my dentist put it—with a major fleapit right down the middle of it. Inevitably, one day it didn't just have character: it started to hurt like a bitch.

I don't like the idea of a professional extracting pieces of my anatomy that I'd spent years refusing to part with. Worse, I hate needles. I'd had enough streptomycin needles during my months back at the san to last a lifetime. "Don't stick me with any needles," I said to the dentist the day I went in to deal with the tooth. "I don't want any. I'll be fine on my own."

"It's going to hurt, Tevan," he told me. "It's a baby tooth.

I'm going to have to break it in half to get it out. Trust me. You don't want to do this dry."

Strep shots go straight into the muscles, a part of the body that never forgets. "Oh yes I do," I said. "I don't give a hang. I hate needles." And so, as a compromise, he offered to set me up with an assistant of his called nitrous oxide.

"It doesn't go in through a needle," he assured me. "It's a gas. You ever heard of laughing gas?" When I told him no, I never had, he grinned. "Makes you feel like you've had a few highballs before lunch! Oh, wait. You wouldn't know about that yet. You're underage."

Underage. Yes. And then he hooked me up.

I sipped the first few breaths tentatively, unable to stop myself from thinking of aerosolization and bacilli and lung cavities. I wondered, worriedly, if I should've reminded the dentist of my medical history, but I felt like a malicious liar mentioning it at this late hour. Such concerns didn't last long. In minutes I was high as a kite.

And within a few weeks, I scarcely noticed the vacated space anymore either. I never did get it filled properly, so now I tell myself that the gap has character. Either way, I believe that tooth stayed in there for a reason. For I was chewing a piece of gum at three in the morning, winding it through the gap . . . when all of a sudden the answer struck me.

What I was going to do when I went for my TB reassessment was smoke a spliff.

Yeah. A fucking spliff. A *good* one. A fine one. A big, fat, noisy one. *That's* what I was going to do. I didn't have any laughing gas, but I could get a spliff, no problem! I knew this guy at work, a guy who knew a guy—it was 1961, after all: everybody knew a guy who knew a guy—who could get the ball rolling. The guy's name was Steve, Steve Orono. He didn't bring it until the night before my date with Mount Rosa's, but I made my request that very day.

"Thought you didn't smoke junk, man," he said in response.

I shrugged. "I don't really."

He shrugged back. "You want something to warm up with too, then? Scotch?" he suggested. "A big'un too. I can do it. You don't want any piddly little jug if you're going to go spending your dough."

"Yeah, okay," I said. "Whatever. Hit me up."

Steve slid me a grin. "You planning something special, good-lookin'?"

I smiled. "Let's just say it's a special occasion."

And it was. I started in on the scotch the morning of my trip to Mount Rosa's. Its warmth fell over me like a soft blanket as I sat on the bus. In fact, at a stoplight near Yonge and Queen, I bounced my head off the grab pole before I even saw myself inclining toward it. Once in the back alley at Mount Rosa's, I was ready for round two. I found the spliff, alongside a lighter and a pack of gum, buried in the bottom of my backpack. I smoked the joint all the way down, with the roach held firm between my fingers like my brother had shown me years ago. By the time I chucked the butt to the ground, my face had bloomed into a smile. I don't even remember if I crushed the ash out, making sure it didn't flutter off and burn the whole bloody place down. It didn't, of course.

I'd remember if Mount Rosa's burnt down.

And to this day, it's still there.

I made it up to the outpatient counter, grinning all the way. I put a stick of gum in my mouth. "Hi," I said, pulling my fingers through my bangs.

The nurse at the desk smiled. "Hello there. Name please?"

"Tevan George."

"Year of birth?"

"1943." I produced my social insurance card, and waffled my hand through my hair again. I couldn't seem to stop doing it.

The nurse pointed down the hall. "Waiting room," she indicated, then told me a room number.

A bartender told me once that you can tell who's reached their limit at the barstools by their body language: men always laugh and women always touch their hair. I took the ends of my bangs into my fingers and tugged at them. Then I told myself to knock it off. "Thanks."

Now it crossed my mind to pass by this waiting room once or twice—a dry run, a practice, a go-round just to be safe—maybe even catch a glimpse of who could be inside before I stepped in. But by then I was long past fooling myself: I didn't want to know, and I never would. What I felt instead, ever since the nurse spoke to me over the telephone weeks before, really, was a squelched, bottled sort of fear. A spliff and a few shots of scotch had got me this close; but even fifty spliffs, swigs, and practice rounds combined couldn't have lent me acceptance of what I feared might be sitting in that room, waiting for me. It's like slipping into Georgian Bay in your swim trunks in spring: the chill is inevitable. It's more painful to inch in bit by bit. And anyway, you know what they say: Once you get in past your crotch, the worst is over, right? I paused for one second outside the door, turned—

And there was no one there I knew. Not a one.

Or at least that's what I thought at first. I swung my head back and forth, looking. I didn't bother to count, and probably didn't have much of a head for numbers just then anyhow, but it looked like we were all there. We, being myself and a bunch of guys I'd never seen before in my life and—say, what the hell had I been so worried about? The seats made two rows in total, one against each wall, and facing one another. Within them sat a collection of kids waiting for chest x-rays and, as in the pediatric ward of 1957 where I spent my time convalescing, reading comics and playing poker, all boys. I sat down on the end, next to two boys who looked remarkably alike to me.

(You're on DRUGS, Tevan)

Something glimmered in my memory, soft and barely there, like a hair tickling the flesh behind your knee. I took a seat to their left, but I couldn't draw my gaze away from them for a moment. A long moment, I guess. One of them nudged the other and then they were both looking back at me.

We stared at one another. They had different hair, as though one had pledged himself to a commune while the other had his sights set on the military. But their faces and posture were identical: Boy 1 and Boy 2.

Boy 2's face narrowed, starting from the eyebrows and folding swiftly down. "What are you staring at?"

I didn't realize I had been. I couldn't help but laugh. "Nothing," I said, showing my teeth. "Nothing."

I leaned back in my seat, averting my eyes. The leer was still pasted to my face, and I pulled my feet onto the chair. I put my fingers into my mouth and pulled the chewing gum out in one long strand. Snapped it loose. Pulled it out. Snapped it.

The kid to my side sighed, annoyed. I smiled and kept doing it. They whispered to each other and my eyes grew busy skirting the room. Here's a guy with long hair. Fat kid in a dress suit (his mother probably made him wear it), and a guy with more freckles than Einstein could count. A guy in denim here, and a guy—

(Hey. Wait a second)

There came another flicker of recognition as I passed this last fellow. More than a flicker, really; more than just the old tickle-behind-the-knee. I did know this guy. And more than that, I realized, it didn't bother me. In fact, if I weren't as stoned as a groupie right then, I could've sworn that I was actually *glad* to see him after all this time. I snapped the gum back into my mouth and returned my feet to the floor.

"Hey," I said, out loud but not meaning to.

The guy didn't budge. His hair was black and ragamuffin. He looked as though he hadn't had a shower in days. His eyes were a dim green, giving him a slightly creepy, paranormal look. And it wasn't only that: they were staring off into nothing. Staring but not seeing, or staring and seeing it all, heaven knows which. I almost turned my head around to check out the wall above me, just to make sure there wasn't something of interest up there that I had missed. Finally I turned back.

"Hey," I said again, louder this time. "Hey, I know you." I did, but *man* the guy had gotten big. He was thin but huge—imposing. He was folded in the chair like a fat letter crumpled into a too-small envelope. I knew if he stood he'd be well over six feet tall.

In any case, he didn't respond. His eyes remained upon the spot above my head. I thought maybe he hadn't heard me. Or perhaps he had no idea who I was. So I leaned in.

"Hey buddy," I said. "Hey, you know me. You know me, man. It's Tevan."

Boys 1 and 2 tittered beside me and I shrugged one shoulder, trying to wave them off.

"You know me, hey, buddy? Come on," I said. I sat back against my chair, trying to access my memory banks. After four years of dust and three weeks of anticipatory doom, with a screen of weed on top, it took a little while. Finally I grinned: "Hey, buddy. *James.*"

It was like a charm dangled inside a spell: the guy moved. His eyes unhinged slowly from their center and slid in my direction.

I grinned wider. "James, that's you. You remember me? Huh? You remember me? *Tev-an.*"

The gaze was dry and unintelligent. His hair hung almost to his eyes.

"Hey, James," I said. "Yeah, you know me. You know—"

There came a sudden flurry of activity from beside me. Boy 2 jumped forward in his seat. Then he spoke so loud you'd think he took me as some encroaching menace that the guy needed protection from. "Hey," he said. "Look here instead. Hey, James!"

I turned, but Boy 2 didn't meet my gaze.

"You don't have to talk to him, James," he said.

I opened my mouth with indignation; the lump of gum nearly rolled right down my tongue and onto his arm. But Boy 2 didn't flinch. He continued to lean over his knees, call out to James, and ignore me. "You don't have to talk to him," he hissed to the mannequin across from us both. "I think he's mistaken you for his boyfriend, but he's wrong. His boyfriend isn't here. And I hope his boyfriend's dead."

I stared. The words registered a dimwitted five seconds later. What he'd *said;* what it was he'd just *said* in front of a whole room, guys with freckles and guys with long hair and fat kids in suits—as my mother liked to say, "before God and everyone." I stared at him with a mixture of confusion and hatred. The thought of my mother notwithstanding, I was suddenly an inch from saying something terribly uncouth. In fact, I was already opening my mouth to let it fly:

"Hey, fu—"

But in the instant that I started to launch off with my tongue, my eyes came to rest upon the stiff across the room. I couldn't help it; he was right there, directly in my field of vision. Now I noticed him a second time. He had shifted, silently, from blank, dead air to tempest. I saw him sitting, his eyes still fixed upon me but his hands gripping the arms of the chair like white-hot claws. I saw his eyebrows cave in on his face to leave a loathing, determined expression. I saw him unfolding like a large caged animal emerging from its confinement. Then I saw him rising up taller, and taller and taller and—

"Jesus," I breathed, my spine hitting the chair like I'd been slammed against it. Because I saw he was coming right for me. "Jesus," I said again, wishing I could close my eyes, but he was looking right at me, and I was much more afraid of what might happen next in the dark than I was knowing it in the light of day. The guy was huge.

He was coming right for me, coming closer and closer—and then his arm shot out and rocked Boy 2's head against the wall so fast that the kid didn't even have a chance to make a sound. It was done fiercely and with great agility. A second later the kid crumpled into his own hands, and his double literally had to catch him before he slid from his seat.

"Jesus," I whispered.

The stiff's eyes came to rest upon me. He arrived at my feet, practically on his knees from the force of the blow. He wasn't even close to stiff anymore. It had been a full-body swing.

"What's your name?" he said, like I hadn't said it before, like he hadn't just punched some dipshit kid's head sitting so close to my own that I'd actually felt the current of wind lift my hair from my eyebrows.

I stared, my eyes wide. Afraid to speak, afraid not to. "Tevan," I whispered.

"That's right," he said. "I keep wanting to call you Pretty."

Something passed on my face—something strong enough to negate my state of shock in that moment. It was the fear I'd known hanging up the phone on the nurse nearly a month back, the panic I'd felt thrashing in my bed for weeks straight, the trepidation I'd held right up until I breathed in the spliff and floated off. I'd worked hard all those weeks trying to keep that information off my face. But it reached an apex of concentrated strength when he said this to me. And for a moment we both saw it all.

"Tevan," he repeated. "Tevan."

He stayed on the ground, crouched in front of my knees. My hands were fixed to the arms of the chair like they were superglued. Beside me, Boy 2 still reeled with his head over his knees and his brother at his shoulders. There was an awful noise coming from him too: a wet, moaning kind of noise, the sound of a plugged-up spigot. I flicked my eyes to watch. I couldn't help it.

"Tevan," James said again. "My memory's not so good these days." His tone held that vague unintelligence that his expression had betrayed, yet here it took on a strange, astute confidence. "I don't remember things so well, Tevan," he said. "But I always remembered you."

Buddy Merit gave us a home on wheels. It was far superior to my 1955 Chevy.

The camper was merely a square box with a double bunk on each end wing. We had no table, although a high-backed armchair sat close to the screen door. A row of cupboards marched above a modest countertop and wash station. The cupboards came stocked—cans, saltines, and a small store of dry goods, that was all. But after three days of cheap coffee, doughnuts, and cigarette butts picked up off the ground, we had no complaint.

Outside, the sky grew dark, and the midway cranked up brilliantly against it. James and me heated a can of soup over a hotplate, watching this. We had time to trek out to the car and haul back our worldly possessions; we had the luxury of visiting the carnival's shows if we wanted to. But James and me found we weren't interested in doing either. Once we stepped inside our humble ramshackle of a space, we didn't want to leave. I sat down on the front step outside and gazed out into the sawdust tracks and lights a while. James settled into the door-side armchair like a sentry guarding his keep. Only he could not keep himself from nodding off. It wasn't late, but with the shuteye I hadn't got the night before, and now something warm in my stomach, my body, too, was insisting it was much later. "James," I said. "Go to bed. Go on. I'll see you later."

I watched with one eye as James crawled up into the bunk furthest from the door. He watched me with one eye right back. It was he who surrendered first. Soon enough, his breath yielded to a soft, easy rhythm. It was only then that I stole onto the mattress at the opposite end.

I didn't sleep right away. I lay with my eyes on the opposite bunk, thinking. I didn't think of the sideshow in the direct way you might expect a fellow to the night before his first-time contribution. Instead I thought of Mount Rosa's.

James and me left the TB clinic—and Mount Rosa's—for good after his altercation with my seatmate. "Where you going tonight?" I asked him later that night, my eyes heavy from Steve Orono's straight scotch. "Where you staying?" I didn't know until then that James had been staying at a residence for guys who had a history of trouble keeping out of trouble. As for me, my apartment was just one rented bedroom and washroom in the basement of a house. James may not have been the sharpest tack in the box, but he wasn't brainless: me and him both knew that he had broken enough of his boys' residence rules—knocking some kid's nose into his head, for instance, not to mention failing to proceed with a mandatory medical test and drinking to excess—to know that there was little point to his returning there.

When James pulled his shirt off some time later in the dark, the dim, meandering glow from the streetlamp across the road streaked across his bare back. It looked fearsome, exotic, like inverted tiger stripes.

"You can stay," I told him. "So long as you don't have any bad habits or anything. Do you?"

James turned and watched me. "Like what?"

"Like I don't know. Jesus, like snoring or pissing the bed or anything." I closed my eyes, curled up on the bed, and laughed. I had a king-sized mattress then. It had been Kenny's until 1957, one of the few things that I inherited from him, other than the car. I eventually sold the mattress trying to get James and me some cash, which is why I feel compelled to mention it. It was a good call on my part, though: you can't drive a mattress, but you can always sleep in a car. "Anything like that," I said, James watching me.

"No, Tev," he said. "No, that wouldn't be me."

I slipped between the covers on the outside that night, with James a mile away at the wall. He did not speak or move. The way I saw it, it was like being there by myself, but James didn't share this illusion. I wouldn't understand this until much later. If he'd believed he was alone he would've placed himself on the floor, concrete basement and all.

My body loosened into the mattress as I drifted off. Then James was a voice in the dark.

"Tev," he said. "Tevan."

I shuffled my head against the pillow.

"You wet the bed once, Tevan," James said to me. "Remember?"

My eyes opened and I stared into the light-and-dark pattern of the room. I thought very carefully. It took a minute to find my voice. "Yes," I said when it finally came. "I remember that too."

Inside Buddy Merit's camper, just like that night five years before, sleep found me in seconds. In motels over the last few months, I would wake wondering where I was. In the car I would wake, roused by strangers walking through the lot in the dead of night, to the cold seeping in the cracked window. This night offered none of these. I wager I slept damn near straight through the whole thing.

I did wake once in the early morning. The sky had turned a less serious shade of black. The walls were long with shadows, and the angles of the room seemed elegantly sketchy. Across from me, the opposite bunk was empty.

This did not alarm me. I knew James was there. I turned my gaze downward and found him as expected.

I let my eyes rest upon him, there on the cold, filthy floor where he'd chosen to arrange himself at some hour in the night. Eventually I slipped from my blankets. I shook him and he stood at my command, then followed me back up into the bunk. He closed his eyes; soon his face softened. And then he offered me a sort of apology, or a sort of excuse. I'm not sure which to call it. It doesn't matter. I've heard it a hundred times by now.

"Bern was after me," he said. "So I started getting out of bed. Bern was after me. I don't know why, Tev."

I passed my gaze over him. "No," I said. "I been here the whole while. It's just you and me. You just didn't know where you were, is all."

I kept my eyes upon him until I could keep them open no longer. In that time, I could not help but wonder what James might have been had he never come to Mount Rosa's in 1957.

I've wondered that a lot over the years, actually.

But just as a bally facilitates a good sideshow, Mount Rosa's set the stage for James and me both. For everything that came after.

3

THEY CALLED IT CONVALESCENCE WHEN ANYBODY ENTERED the sanitarium with TB, because before the 1960s, when it became possible to treat people as outpatients, it took a person a long time to chase the cure. The tuberculosis I'd read about in *The Stone Angel* was much different from what it felt like in person: self-evident, gory, victims who coughed and hacked away, consumed from the inside out until the lungs literally drowned in their own blood.

Maybe in the 1800s that was accurate. But in the 1950s, when it found its way into my family, what was known as "the little bean-shaped germ"—tuberculosis—rarely had the chance to progress to such extremes. Ever since the Great War, the Lung Association, at one time called the Tuberculosis Association, instituted government-run facilities for those afflicted and contagious. The good news was that this slowed the curse so it rarely had the opportunity to kill anyone anymore. The bad news was that tuberculosis was soon able to get around under a cloak of invisibility. In place of identifying very sick people, the Lung Association now had to identify guys like me—*obscurely* sick people, walking around the neighborhood, working, hanging out, going to school—unwittingly doling out their little bean-shaped germs everyplace they went.

I had no idea I was sick. My clothes started to fit funny, I sported a low-grade fever, and I began waking up in the night with a case of night sweats. But at fourteen I could exhibit the same symptoms after reading a good *Sheena, Queen of the Jungle*. When mail from the Association arrived, Kenny snapped it out of the mailbox, certain it was for him. He sat down at the kitchen table, his brow bent in wary confusion. Then he looked at me, looked to my mother—and fanned out the envelope in his fingers. "Look, Ma," he said. "Another summons to the Hall of Lame for the George family." Slowly, the paper multiplied in his hand: "Presto!" he announced. "This time there's two." I remember he started to laugh, though there was nothing funny about it.

Convalescence means "period of recovery," which suggests that recovering is a thing you do the entire time you're at the san. At the san, recovery entailed plenty of bed rest. It involved twice-a-week injections that left you feeling like you'd played rugby with the steelworkers' union, and liquid meds that made your stomach clench as though you'd just downed a big green chili pepper. More than anything, it meant a long stay—awakening each night, sweating, to find yourself in a strange place that never closed its windows instead of in your own bed at home.

Of course it didn't take long for the inside to become friendly. After the first six weeks, one graduated from complete bed rest to total boredom. As the days spread out before us we began to spend our time on the inside doing stuff that made us think of our lives on the outside. So there was the guy who wanted to teach you to play bloody knuckles, and a weird kid who wanted to show you how to perform all different sorts of first aid from a collection of sensationally morbid books. There was a guy trying to create a Chinese checkers dynasty among us, and a kid who peddled a bunch of games to play with dice.

There was also one of two lookalike brothers who loved to demonstrate *Mad Magazine*'s front-page metamorphosis. Jesus, this kid thought it was a neat trick. You'd think he'd *invented* it the way he went about folding Alfred E. Neuman.

"Come on. *Everybody* knows how to do that," I said, rolling my eyes.

The kid's double watched from his bed, smirking. The two boys—Peter and Jonathan—might've looked alike, but they differed in temperament as much as Betty and Veronica in the comics we read at night by flashlight. It's probably how one of the older Mount Rosa inmates came to dub the timid brother "Betty" in the first place. They knew it too—or at least "Veronica" did.

"Yeah, dickhead," he scoffed at his brother. "Some trick. Hey," he said, looking at me. "You wanna play Asshole?"

I was new around there, and no matter how long I stayed, I was always the youngest of the bunch. To the old nurses I was the baby of the ward, and to the young interns, "the young one with the pretty eyes." Still, I was fourteen: pretty eyes or not, those eyes had vision enough to know the score.

"What'd you call me?" I said.

The kid grinned. "Sheesh, I didn't call you anything. *Ass*hole. That's a card game. It's a good time."

I'd already handed down my own repertoire of card games from home, most of which I'd learned from Kenny. "This is my brother's favorite, five-card draw," I'd said to them a week earlier. "When he comes, we can all play." And then, in addendum, just as Kenny had shown me: "Don't worry—it's really easy on beginners." I walked away from the game with a respectable two bucks in my pocket. When Kenny did show, I'd thought, grinning, boy, would he be impressed.

Now Veronica spread the deck out before him. I moved over to watch, deciding to give him the benefit of the doubt. Anyway, anything with the name "Asshole" sounded like my kind of game. "How do you play?" I asked.

Betty joined us on the bed. We sat cross-legged around the cards. "Well," Veronica began. "There's three face-down each. Then three face-up on top. Jokers are wild, twos start over, and tens clear the stack." They played a mock round to demonstrate. It went pretty quick, but I caught the gist. They dealt again, this time for three players.

"The guy who clears his hand last is the asshole," Veronica said.

I gave him an eye, as if to demonstrate that I was wise if he was in any way trying to pull my leg.

"There's benefits to clearing first," he insisted. "That's why there's titles."

"Then what're the other titles?" I said.

"Well, if you clear first then you're the president. Second and you're the vice-president. Last holder is always the asshole."

Catching on to the pattern, I began to empty my hand.

"You see," he continued, "next round, the president starts off by passing his worst two cards to the asshole—and the asshole gives his *best* two cards to the president." He grinned and raised his eyebrows.

"Piss up a rope," Betty said, last man standing with cards in hand.

"My brother's always the asshole," Veronica mentioned, and I grinned.

We played another few rounds, growing quicker, more strategically defensive, and more insulting as the game wore on. He was right—it was a good time. And he was right about his brother always being the asshole. I, on the other hand, achieved promoted status within the first few rounds.

"You're the president," Veronica praised.

"President," I said. "Who wants to be the president?" This was par for the course, with Eisenhower having to worry about all those encroaching Communists abroad. "I think I'll be prime minister. No, wait, I'll be Lester B. Pearson." He was up for the Nobel Peace Prize and all.

"Nuts," Betty grumbled. I laughed out loud, insanely this time, and Veronica couldn't help but grin conspiratorially across at me. "This sucks," Betty bitched. "If I don't move up soon, I'm folding!"

"Pussy," I said under my breath. And didn't he look like I'd just swatted him with his stupid *Mad Magazine*?

"I'm folding," he announced, indignant.

Having an older brother usually puts hair on your chest. I was used to Kenny telling it like it was. But I guess these brothers didn't operate that way. To my surprise, the older, gutsier one became the pussy's ally in the blink of a defecting eye. "Hey, don't be a jerk," he barked at me. Then, to his sulking brother: "Come on, he was just fooling around. Come on. We can't play with just two guys." With this he shot me a *see-what-you-did-now* look.

I looked away from the brothers and down at my cards. "Sorry." I fluttered my eyelashes—the ones the nurses found so endearing—and said it genuinely this time: "*Sorry*, Betty, okay?" We resumed the game and I turned over in my head what Veronica had said.

"Hey, why don't we ask some other guys to play?" I suggested. I thought it would be in our best interests to recruit fallbacks in case I inadvertently caused Betty to go wigsville again. "We could have some neutrals."

Both brothers looked over their shoulders. "Like who?" the older one asked.

I looked left and right. The first person I spied, with the foot of his bed facing the foot of mine, was Bern. Bern's full name was Bernard Charles, but he had earned his nickname. He was known as the guy with all the burns, which meant he always had a remark on hand to provoke you with. He tended to elicit a cross between awe and fear in the rest of the group. He was twenty years old, the same age as my Kenny, making him more of a young man than a candidate for the pediatric ward. Bern had been in and out of the san repeatedly over the last few years: checking out and relapsing and being assessed, then getting hauled right back in again like he was some type of germ loose on a Kleenex. The nurses had a nickname for him too—guys who came back over and over again like Bern were called "old-timers."

The trouble with old-timers was that they kept trying to avoid missing work by lessening their time in treatment, when success only occurred the whole other way around. Kenny, for instance, was always telling my mother that he wasn't going to spend another goddamn year in a sanitarium. He wasn't going to chase a cure when, for some reason or other, the goddamn illness seemed to be chasing *him* instead. And he sure as hell wasn't going to spend months lying around in bed, he said, while Ma and Tevan went on welfare.

But the truth was that people relapsed because they didn't lie around and complete their treatment. *The fundamental reason for treatment failure and subsequent development of drug resistance is noncompliance,* they told us again and again at Mount Rosa's. It was almost the first thing they told us when we walked in the doors, like the first of the Consumptive's Ten Commandments. In those days, they had a term for breaking the commandment, too—"discharge against medical advice."

Bern was like Kenny—he didn't like it on the inside. Depending on his mood, he could have the cleverest mouth (it was he who had started calling the lookalike brothers Betty and Veronica in the first place) or the meanest. I liked Bern for all these reasons. But in the moment, I also considered the fact that Bern might skyrocket to president status in no time, quashing my own winning streak. I shuffled my cards around in my hands and decided to pass him up for now.

Instead I chose the kid on the bunk beside us—a tall, gangly guy, the one with the gloomy reading collection, incidentally—and pointed him out: "Well, how about that guy?"

This kid was only about a year older than I was, yet he didn't take class with the rest of us. I came to understand that he was a kind of "When God was handing out brains, he thought He said 'trains' and asked for a slow one" type, and on account of this, we didn't talk to him much. I wasn't even sure I knew his name. "Hey, Jimmy, Slim Jim," Bern would sometimes yell across the room at him. "Hey, Jimmy Lowe, *what's goin' on behind the Green Door!*" Jim Lowe's "The Green Door" spent about three measly weeks at Billboard's number one in '56, but Bern thought it was the greatest fucking song on earth.

"Naw," Betty said, a smirk on his lips. "That one's probably too stupid to pick up Go Fish." His brother mirrored the expression and for a moment they looked utterly indistinguishable. "He gets homesick," Betty went on in a low voice, still eyeing the gangly kid. "Used to lie there crying like a girl. You ever hear him at night, getting up all the time?"

I glanced at the kid lying on his bed and reading. Although I'd had similar suspicions myself on the matter, I was in no way interested in indicating I knew anything about homesickness. In the san, home was so far away. My mother felt equally remote. And my brother? Well, that was something I was trying hard not to think about at all. "Piss on that," I said. "I don't fuckin' miss anything at home."

Betty looked up at me, his expression partway between disgusted and astonished. "Geez, you got a foul mouth," he managed.

"Yeah," his brother agreed, although he looked more impressed than anything. "Ugly."

Across the room, Bern stirred on his bunk. "Ugly?" He made a *tsk* noise between his teeth as he gazed over at us. "That's not what the nurses call him. Is it?"

I smiled, and when he saw me shake my head he grinned too.

"Come on," he said. And then, even though he surely already knew: "What do they call you?"

"Pretty," I said.

Bern grinned, a sort of discerning *aha!* look upon his face. "Pretty," he repeated. "For sure." It was a jab at me, at the nurses' estimation of me—like teasing a classmate for his status as the teacher's pet. It sounded different coming from Bern, though, the oldest and undoubtedly most worldly inmate of all of us. It was like receiving a distinguishing title: a mark amid the otherwise monochromatic, disenfranchised population of Mount Rosa's. It was, I thought, like playing your cards right and being dubbed the president as reward.

I shook my head and laughed. "Sure."

There came a sudden flurry of activity from Betty and Veronica. "Lookit, Tevan," Veronica said. "Let me show you how to play this other neat game! It's called twenty-one. When your brother comes, you can show it to him too."

And out of nowhere a terrible fury spilled over me. I reeled

46 | Nicole Pietsch

my head around and glared at him. "Why don't you shut up about my brother?" I spat.

The two boys blinked.

"He already knows how to play it. *I* already know how to play it! For starters, it's not called twenty-one. It's called blackjack, at least if you're over eight years old it is!"

They stared back at me, startled. Bern raised an eyebrow.

"I think maybe what Pretty here is saying," Bern began slowly, "is that your game just isn't doing it for him, kids. At least a worthy opponent like his brother would know to call a game by its proper name. Isn't that right?"

And it was. For when what you've been waiting for fails to appear, nothing can fill the gap. If I'd had any choice in the matter, I'd have had Kenny right there beside me. Even a card game with Jesus Christ himself at the san wouldn't have been good enough for me.

Veronica took my rebuff in stride. For a moment he looked hurt; next he was unimpressed. "Suits you," he offered, gathering up the cards. "We'll play without you."

Maybe there's a lesson to be learned here. Years later, I would be paid a respectable wage for defying death. But accepting death hurts. It exacts a price.

I talked about Kenny so much during my first two weeks in the san that when things went bad, the nurses actually had to go around and encourage the other boys to hush up about him. I had told them everything about him by then, you see—everything except for details of the illness that chased him till the end.

I didn't tell them how Kenny opted for a procedure called a lung resection. Surgery wasn't in vogue like it might've been before the stiff drugs came along in the later '50s, but it was still an option for those who fit the bill. It seemed fitting for Kenny, a guy who had lung cavities from prior TB infections that continued to promote reinfection. It was also fitting for a guy who consistently turned up tubercular and was inconsistent with taking his meds. Last but not least, it suggested a shorter term at the san, which fit Kenny more than anything else.

He'd have to come to the san all right, they told him. If you were tubercular and catching, there was no getting out of that. But with his lung resection the doctors could tackle Kenny's bacilli—germs—at the source. Surgery was a little riskier—hell, for a guy with failing health, an unspoken affair with the bottle, and a body a decade older than it looked on account of the physical labor he did, what wasn't? But Kenny didn't care. He was too busy dwelling on the diagnosis of a lower lung cavity that had been with him for as long as he'd had pubic hair. Theoretically, he could have it removed in one fell swoop. Theoretically, his term at the sanitarium would be less. And it was less.

In the end, my Kenny never turned up at Mount Rosa's at all. By the time I was three weeks into my convalescence, Kenny was just a pair of lungs scaled down to one in Hamilton Mountain's intensive care unit.

After my loud, buoyant anticipation of him, this news brought me to a sudden silence on the matter. The news of his passing (my mother called me, I remember; I had to leave a game of cribbage and the horrified, knowing looks of my comrades to respond to it) that followed this silence was almost a gift.

I didn't go to his wake. I was both contagious and on a firm order of complete bed rest. They would've let me all the same, I know, but it costs money to tool back and forth between Toronto and Hamilton. But really, mostly I didn't go because I didn't want to. I was scared that if I went to see him off, I might be driven insane with loneliness at the prospect of having to turn right around and go back to Mount Rosa's.

So, on the night of the wake I stayed. We all continued our silence on the issue and, alongside the rest of the boys, I played cards and read comics like normal. I ate mashed potatoes and swallowed my para-aminosalicylic acid dose too, and I got into bed at the stringent, unbudging lights-out hour of ten o'clock. Mattresses creaked, flashlights flickered. And then I lay there alone in the dark beside the beds of two boys, Betty and Veronica, who made a beautiful, heartbreakingly matched pair.

My eyes rested upon one particular boy as I held my water. I couldn't help it. It was the one that Betty had pointed out to me, the homesick one he'd vetoed as a participant in our game of cards. "If your lungs stop working, somebody can start them up again for you, you know," that particular kid had told me once. He'd gone on to show me this very procedure in a book. It was an expensive, high-and-mighty book in those days: Dr. Peter Safar's ABC version of artificial respiration and other strange first-aid techniques. "It doesn't matter if your lungs get sick. I read it in this book," he'd gone on, his eyes large and hopeful. "I think it means I'll go home soon."

I didn't bother to correct him, tell him that he'd likely be here a long, long time. Tell him that what he had read in his books was first aid, not a cure. The cure was the san—and we were already in it.

Watching that kid and thinking of his words, the reality of Kenny felt magnified, crushing. I became too full in a room that was already packed. I didn't want to be the next fellow who Betty whispered about. I slipped out of my sheets in silence.

I made it to the boys' lavatory. It was the only place I could think of to go. It held three shower stalls at one end, and a large basin for brushing your teeth and hand-washing (*Wash hands often!*—another of the Consumptive's Commandments) at the other. I crouched down where the lip of the shower stalls rose up from the floor. And sitting with my head in my hands, I thought of Kenny.

Kenny alive and Kenny now dead; Kenny here at Mount Rosa's, Kenny there in Hamilton, and now Kenny in the ground. Kenny never warned me; I never said good-bye. There were endless possibilities to think on. If you've ever had anyone you love die on the sly, you understand how it makes time branch out into a thousand strands of *shoulda*, *coulda*, and *woulda*. By the time Bern wandered into the lavatory, my eyes were bloodshot and I felt beat.

He paused and put his hands in the pockets of his pajamas. "Say, I wondered where you went." When I did not reply, he gazed at me for a long moment. "I also wondered"—he pursed his lips, smiled gently—"who got it first, you or him?"

Silence ran between us. Both of us knowing, even without Bern's saying it aloud, that he meant Kenny and this damn, relentless illness.

"Him," I said finally. "Three times."

"Ah." Bern nodded. "Lucky guy. Just like me."

I didn't respond. Everything had made me think of Kenny those past few weeks. I didn't need anybody doing it for me.

"Sorry," he said. "I'm sorry, Pretty." Bern sat down on the shower lip beside me. "We have Betty and Veronica. And here's Lucky and Pretty. Please. Tell me about him."

And so, tentatively at first, I did. I told him about how Kenny said you always had to walk in there with a bit of the old attitude, and about the hockey games Kenny had always been so crazy about. I told him about how Kenny had babysat me for years while my mother worked weekends, yet he'd never treated me like some irritating kid brother. I told him about Elvis Presley tunes playing constantly (*It's like a nightmare you can't wake up from!* my mother used to say), and about the scholarship Kenny was awarded upon his high school graduation. I told him how instead of taking his university midterms, Kenny used that scholarship to sign the ownership papers to a '55 Chevy Nomad. I went forward and backward in time, telling him about the time when I was ten years old, and Kenny and his friends lit off cherry bombs behind Sak's Convenience, and the manager ran out the back door. We'd ducked behind a dumpster and I'd busted up laughing. Kenny had to turn around and knock me in the family jewels—*Tevan, shhh!*—to keep me from giving us away. I even told him about the time I put a nail through my foot and Kenny had to slap me back into composure. I told Bern all of it.

After some time I was bawling, but I hardly noticed. What I did notice was that Bern listened and nodded like he got me, got me one hundred percent. He even laughed at all the right parts.

"You thought he was coming, didn't you," he said finally.

"Yeah," I said. I breathed deeply and gazed about the tiled, sterile walls of the boys' washroom. "Now I guess I'll just, I don't know—convalesce alone."

Bern gave me a doubtful look.

"And I'm never going to get free of this thing either," I said. "Just like my brother."

To which Bern shrugged. "That's not necessarily true. You take your meds; you get your weight checked like the rest of us. You follow the routine and you'll get better." He waved a hand. "It's all the same around here."

I believed him—felt thankful, *relieved* to believe him. Bern, after all, was like my Kenny. He knew the score.

"For instance, the nurse checks in every night at twelve and again at about three. You'll get up around nine. Tomorrow is Sunday." Bern raised his eyes to the ceiling, counted the days upon his fingers. "Which means you'll have French toast for breakfast." He even had the menu memorized. He laughed at that and so did I. "It's all the same around here. You're in, so what? We're all in along with you. Well . . ." He paused, raised an eyebrow. "At least *I* am."

I'd been playing board games, rummy, and cribbage with my fellow inmates for weeks, yet this marked the first time I felt I had somebody on my team. Somebody who understood the hand I'd been dealt. I nodded my agreement to Bern. I still felt angry, but at least I could distinguish this from feeling cheated. Which is a thing—I'll give him that—I don't believe my Kenny ever meant to do to me.

We returned to our quarters. And after this I did not go to bed wrapped in the icy chill of loneliness, which had perhaps been the worst part of it all, the magnifier overtop all those other shit musings.

After this, in fact, I really did begin to convalesce.

4

ME AND JAMES STRUCK OUT BEFORE THE DEW LIFTED FROM the grass the next morning. We passed empty concession stands and deserted tents as we walked the length of the lot. The midway, with its spindly arms and colorful tubs, stood stop-motioned in time. It looked like me and James were the only live things about.

We weren't the first to arrive at the sideshow tent, however. I slipped through the curtained entranceway with James behind me, to find a makeshift room murmuring with activity. The enclosure itself was just four walls and a roof. The floor was a square of lawn upon which the tent had been erected, and it held a damp, cool scent. Although there were no lights on, the canvas ceiling was lit up in a bright, hot orange. Within hours that ceiling would act as a magnifying glass against the noonday sun, and everything below it would sweat as though incubating in a greenhouse.

On the far right side of the tent, three men stood talking among themselves. In the center, a young fellow walked a slow, lazy circle. He held a burlap bag in one hand and bent periodically to snare a wrapper or cigarette butt out of the matted clumps of grass. Just as often, it seemed, he paused to shoo a mangy dog from his feet. At the back of the tent, spanning perhaps twenty feet in length, stood a low wooden platform.

I looked at the platform for a long moment. This was the stage, and even upon this first glimpse of it, my head ran wild with speculation. I glanced to James and caught him staring in the same direction. His eyes were large and unblinking as he turned to me.

"That there's a magician," he said. He grinned, gleeful, waiting for confirmation.

I looked toward the stage platform a second time. Indeed, a young man sat upon its edge. I hadn't paid him any mind the first time. His bent neck aimed his gaze downward, although his eyes were hidden from me behind a wild puff of hair. His hands, working steadfastly in his lap at a row of handkerchiefs, were black, like the rest of him. To the fellow's left sat a collection of sparkling implements: a baton, a set of gold rings, and some other gadgets that I didn't recognize (*whangdoodles,* my mother would have called them, as she did any device that she had no real word for: "Tevan, hand me some of them whangdoodles over there by the counter, will you," she'd say). And on the fellow's right, propped against the platform itself, was a broom.

So fuck it, I'll be honest: between his skin color and his proximity to the broom, I'd assumed he was just the help. I felt a twinge of disgust for myself and an odd humility beside James. "Yeah," I agreed, not letting on. "Yeah, I think maybe he could be a magician."

On the other side of the room, one of the men raised his hand to us and waved. I recognized him from the day before: he had a deep tan and hair grown a little too long, and when he started over to us, his gait was quick, unwieldy—the pace of a man worried that hundreds of eyes are upon him.

He stuck out his hand. "Damon Merit," he said. "This is Rajid," he said, pointing to a short, brown-skinned man behind him. "John and Sandy over there." He indicated two others. Both of these I recognized as members of yesterday's goon squad.

"Tevan George," I said. "This is James Rowley."

Damon nodded. "I'm the talker on the show. I'm going to be talking up your act when you're on, so I wanted to look over the particulars. What say we run through it once or twice?" I nodded and he turned. "So—" He gestured toward the platform. "There it is."

A strange moment elapsed as we stood there together. Merit the Younger surveyed the stage with some semblance of informed pride, but out of the corner of my eye I witnessed James's increasingly crinkled brow. All of a sudden I understood that Damon was waiting for me to do something. And I had no idea what.

"Talker?" I managed, feigning nonchalance.

"Yeah, talker. You know, ballyhoo? Talking up the stunt?" He walked up to the platform. "It's also stage direction. You know how every good show's based on even better bullshit. I heard about your act from my dad, and—" He paused, looking at us. He watched me specifically for a moment. A funny expression crossed his face. "Well, maybe you can help me out. What kinda talk do you guys usually get?"

Blank expressions from James and me. I was beginning to worry that Damon might be reading the facts right off my face.

"You've never had a ballyhoo?" In fact, his expression was metamorphosing from keen interest to amusement as he spoke. "Don't tell me—" he started, pointing a finger. And just as I was expecting him to say *You're new!* or *You don't know your head from your ass*, or just plain *You lied*, his lips spread into a smile. "Don't tell me you performed this act in a Ten in One show. Did you?"

He didn't wait for me to answer. "What a rip!" he cried. "Hey, Ray!" he called across the room. "These two patsies here ran a working act inside a Ten in One!"

"Green help!" Rajid yelled back.

"Wet behind the ears, he means." Damon turned back to me, grinning. "What did you get for that, huh? Pennies?"

I stared at Damon. "The pay was all right," I offered finally. Which was true, and even James nodded. The money that came our way following our only, albeit inadvertent, public performance thus far had been the biggest one-shot payment I'd ever received in my life.

"You got jacked," Damon informed me, unapologetic. He grinned, pleased to finger James and me for a pair of pushovers. *Takes one to know one*, I thought to myself.

But to Damon, I only shrugged. "Maybe we could set the, ah, talk up right now," I offered. "Me and James don't care what you say. You could say whatever you want."

The look on Damon's face read that he was already thinking on it. "Oh, don't worry, that'll be easy." He nodded as though he was going to enjoy the challenge. "From what you showed my father the other day, I'd say you've got a lot to work with. Man, he was crazy about it! It's me who usually scripts out the talk. So let me give you an idea about how it works. Seeing you're green"—he grinned up and down at us—"we'll start at the beginning."

Damon approached the stage platform. He took the steps in two long strides. From there, he pointed to Rajid.

"That's the sword swallower," Damon indicated. He tilted his chin. "But that's not all. That's Rajid, the Iron-Stomached Man. Ray is from Ghana, where the indigenous people eat the skins of poisonous snakes and come of age by swallowing strychnine-tipped daggers." He paused and James stepped back, his eyebrows knit in consternation. "*Whole*," Damon added. "*If* they survive." He turned, noted James; and when he did, he suddenly laughed out loud. "Look at this one. Taking the talk just like the marks!" He shook his head, then yelled across the room, "Hey, Ray! Where you from?"

Rajid, the purportedly iron-stomached man, looked up and grinned. "Montreal. But my parents are Somalian."

Damon gave us a knowing look. Then he kept right on going. "And that there's Shawn." He indicated the man with the whangdoodles. "Round here we call him Schroeder. Schroeder the Magician and Mentalist. Schroeder made the mistake of sleeping under Stonehenge some years ago on Halloween. Schroeder was just a wee British lad in 1945—" Damon tilted his head toward us with a meaningful expression. "That's a year when England got a major Leonid meteor shower. It didn't pass on Halloween, though. It passes annually in November, actually"—here Damon looked at James—"but most fools don't know that. Hey, Shawn." He gave the black fellow a nudge with his foot. "Where you hail from again?"

The guy looked up from his seat on the stage. "Ooh?" he said, producing a terrible British accent. "*Me?*" Then he abandoned it, and gave way to a grin. "Well, Maine first, but that don't count. I'm from right here in Toronto," he said. "The Annex. Truth, I never been to England at all."

Damon turned back to me, satisfied. "You see? The talk. It's half the show."

"I see," I told him. James looked as though he still thought Rajid had snakes crawling around in his belly.

The magician smiled at us both anyhow. "The object of the ruse is that seeing is believing." He nodded at the stage. "Now you boys want to decide what it is you're going to show."

"You," Damon said, on cue, aiming a finger at James. "Come on up."

James had slithered away during Damon's performance. Now he took a slow step forward.

"It's my understanding that this one carries out most of the action," Damon said as James arrived at his side. "So he'll probably come out on the stage first. Do you agree?"

I nodded and Damon pointed to a gap in the canvas tent, just behind the stage. It hadn't been there before, but now with the sun in the sky and a low ebb of traffic flowing in and out of the tent, I saw that it appeared to be a concealed side entrance.

Damon pointed and spoke to James: "See that, you?"

The memory of the girl James and I had seen a night ago, the girl in the pink bathrobe, ran through my mind. She'd been sitting outside the tent, outside that very entrance, when we'd spotted her. I wondered to myself if that's how Damon stage-directed her. I had my doubts.

"You'll come out a little later," Damon said to me. Then back to James: "And this one will meet you in the middle."

"His name's James," I said. Damon was beginning to sound like a five-year-old counting out his dominoes: *this one* goes here, and *that one* goes there. And *that one's* probably too stupid to pick up Go Fish.

"Sure." Damon backed off and left the experts to their work. I mean, if you could even call it that. He walked back down to the lawn and I joined James on the stage.

"Where do you want to do this?" I asked. James swung his head around until he spied a long post running vertically up the back of the tent. It was a support beam, part of the tent's skeleton. The canvas skin ran overtop.

"Here?" he asked when he arrived at it.

I knew right away what he was getting at. I put my back experimentally against the beam. "Yeah," I said. "Okay."

James put his hands out. He watched me from under his eyelids. "He keeps staring at you," he managed under his breath.

I would've asked who if I didn't already know. I gazed past James to Damon. I shrugged. "So let him."

My eyes came to rest upon James and the back of my head came up against the beam. I breathed in the scent of canvas, damp and tempered with cut grass, and held it. Then I felt James on me, and my throat tighten. It took a minute—a minute of this tightness with no breath in or out. The room slowed. Then suddenly, beyond James's shoulder, no one was moving. Instead, all of them were watching. Waiting. All of them—except Damon Merit.

"Hold up!" he hollered. "Hold it! Hey, are you some kind of an idiot? What are you doing it *way back there* for?"

James's hold stiffened and then fell away. My upper body, in response, fell forward into a crouch. In the moment that I assumed this position, James's face—incensed, prickly, crumpled—was a sliding portrait in my field of vision. And then I was half standing, my hands on my knees, breathing again. I put a hand against James and moved to the center of the platform. The eyes of every man in the tent followed me. Their collective expression was one of combined amazement and disgust.

"Man," the young man with the dog at his feet breathed. He stood at the base of the stage, where he eyed James and me as though we were a pair of rumble fish in an aquarium. "That looked awful real." He watched me rub at my neck before looking to James. "Hey, buddy. Were you really doing it?"

James turned to show a face twisted into a glare and the kid stepped back. "I was doing it," James said.

"Sure," Damon put in. "You were doing it *ten feet back*, practically outside the tent!" He looked to me pointedly. "All I could see was your lug's back. Do you get me? Are you going to show us a show, or—"

"*I can do it*," James said, getting loud. "Only the last time I gave it to him standing up like that, what *happened* was that—"

Damon looked bewildered. "What do you mean?"

"What James is saying," I cut in quickly, "is that there's a design flaw in the set-up."

My voice sounded like gravel poured from a bucket, but James was right, and it was important. Unless we constructed another support beam closer up, impaled and centered down the middle of the tent, my head was going to free-fall like a sack of shit splattered five feet eight inches to the ground. And James was right on something else too: the last time he'd come at me while I was standing up, he almost killed me.

I coughed and spit on the floor. "The problem is that when he attacks me, I hit the deck."

Now Damon's brow cinched in the middle. "So?"

"What do you mean, *so*?" I said, impatient. "I thought your father told you all about the business. I'm going to pass out! And when I do"—I rotated on one heel and pointed to the back of the stage—"if I don't have my head against *that*, I'm going to drop and break my neck!"

Damon looked suddenly uncertain. Perhaps he didn't expect the behavior inside such an act to be at all enlightened. "Oh, great. Is this going to be expensive? I mean, I suppose in your previous experience," he said, tetchy, "you've had—what? A prop? A pole or something?"

No, I thought. *In my previous experience, I lie down in bed for this.* "Something like that," I managed.

All about him, Damon's men stood watching. They were waiting for him to let us get on with the show. Damon looked from me to them, then back to me again. Finally he huffed a breath. "Well," he said. "Come on, then. What would you all suggest?" And suddenly the place was full of experts.

"You could use the hootchy-kootchy trailer," John said, smirking. "Those girls got a pole they dance around."

"Maybe you could do it closer to the ground," the magician offered. Alongside Damon and the others, he stood at the base of the stage studying us as though we were the Ringling Brothers. "Or maybe you should grab him from behind. Let him fall *onto* you when he goes down, like."

Damon nodded. "Laws of gravity," he muttered. "Fuckin' laws of gravity." He wagered to himself that perhaps I could do without the tent pole if James came at me while I was on my knees. So Damon positioned us: James standing at full height, me on my knees. James's crotch was at my eye level.

I looked at the crowd and they looked back at me. Then we all busted up laughing.

"Trade places with him, Merit," John said, enjoying the irritation on Damon's face. "Come on and see for yourselves."

But Damon didn't want to see; he wanted to *show*. And so when it came to stage direction, what Damon wanted was not just a close-up. He also wanted a profile and a specific order as to who entered the stage, when, and from where. Me and James, who had never done this for a paying audience, shuffled clumsily around the platform. "Jesus," I muttered. "What a pain in the ass." We turned left, we turned right; we stood in front of one another and facing, our sides to the lawn and two contours to the wind.

"Now that's more like it," Damon said, his head cocked to one side. "So. What now?"

"Well," I said. "Now he attacks me. And then I'll be lying on the ground."

Damon waited. "Well, then?"

The object of the ruse, as the magician had said, is that seeing is believing. The spectators had paid me the favor of believing thus far. I knew what Damon was getting at: he, Rajid, Sandy, and the magician sat avidly watching to see the finale of the trick. Gawkers, rubberneckers—Jesus, even the fucking *dog* was watching.

"James resuscitates," I said at the ground. "And then that's it."

Damon looked to the left and right. He spread his hands, expectant.

"Look, that's it. That's *it*," I said again. "You said yourself your father told you all about it. You got the gist. That's it."

Damon studied me. He leaned against the stage. "Maybe *you* know the gist," he offered slowly, "but *I* don't." Then he gave me a zinger: "You're the gasper after all, Tevan. Not me." *He's staring at you*, James had warned me—and now I knew why: Damon's term marked the first time anybody said outright that me and James's act was preoccupied not with breathing but with some covert, breathless desire.

James looked up. "What's a gasper?"

"Nothing," I answered. "It's something rude." My eyes narrowed at Damon, and my voice was filled with venom. "But I'll tell you what a voyeur is, James. It's a fellow who's so hard up that he wants to see two guys going at it. Isn't that right, Damon?"

His entire crew turned their gaze upon him. Damon, sanctimonious a moment before, saw his jaw drop in horror. Sometime later, when I was broke and tired and feeling like a loser in life, I would replay this moment in my head at night for the sake of my own amusement. But instead of a laugh at Damon's expense, what I always wound up with was a heavy sort of regret in its place. It was a mean trick, and I told myself he deserved it. I'm not so sure anymore. As for Damon, he recovered himself by saving me:

"I wouldn't know," he said through gritted teeth. "But if my father's seen you run through it, then sure, that's good enough for me. Personally, I think I've seen enough canned fruit for one day."

"Suits you," I said. I got to my feet. As I did, I saw the faces of the assembled gawkers drop in collective disappointment.

We broke up and sat along the edge of the stage. James hunched over his long legs; Damon put his hands in his pockets. The magician went back to his whangdoodles. John and Sandy wandered outside. I tried to think of some questions to ask, questions that might have been quelled by my wet enthusiasm the day before.

"So when do we start?" I asked.

Damon deliberated. "How about Friday?" he said. "Friday night always draws a crowd worth tipping. Plus I still need to sort out your intro." He gazed up into the ceiling. "I'm thinking something like 'Death-Defying, the Struggle Between Good and Evil.' Something like that. What do you think?"

Friday! Man, that was ages away! "I think that's an awful long time from now. Shoot." I heaved a sigh. "Anything else need doing around here?"

Damon chanced a look over at me. "Keen to get at it, are you?"

"Keen to get paid, maybe."

"The rides further down the grounds always need help," Damon said. "You can head down there if you want. But don't worry. After your first night on the show, you'll have run enough acts to earn a coupla rocks for the both of you."

Enough acts. James suddenly looked up from his knees. "How many times do we go on in a night?"

This was, in fact, a very good question. "Yeah," I echoed. "How many times?"

Damon shrugged. "Well, we used to run a grind show. But this season we only been having about five or six times a night, seeing's we got so many working acts. Guys like Rajid can't swallow swords continuously. Same with the geek. You can't expect a guy to—"

But already I wasn't paying attention. It entered my mind that James and me had a real problem on our hands. "Six times," James interrupted, giving voice to it. "Tevan, six times?" he said across to me. "Can you *do* that?"

Of course I can do it, I thought, dismayed. I already *told* them all I'd been in a grind show, a Ten in One act that repeated its chintzy tricks all day without pause. How on earth could I dissent now?

"I can do it," I lied, but I was beginning to stare around wildly despite myself. I caught Schroeder the Magician gazing back at me. "I can do it, don't worry," I said. "How about those rides, Damon?"

Damon glanced over. "Right. You want to ask for Keith. Keith Cruikshane. He's an Irish fellow. Said last week he needed some work on his Roundup. He's got a few machines out on the lot."

I nodded and looked to James. We both stood. "We ought to head out," I said. "Guess we'll see you around." And then, figuring it polite to include a footnote, though not really wanting to think much on the subject, I added: "Lemme know how that—ah—talk shapes up." Already I could feel myself starting to sweat.

"Sure," Damon said. "Tomorrow I'll see you back here for another run. If it turns out to be a real gut-turner maybe we'll get you guys a banner." He put his fingertips before him, outlining a rectangle in the air. "I can see it now: Death-Defying!"

A banner, I thought. *Death-defying. I'm going to choke six times a night. Shit, I might not even be around to see any fucking banner.* I couldn't wait to get the hell out of there. And yet just as we hit the exit he called out to us again.

"Hey!" Damon said to James. "Hey, buddy, I wanted to ask you something! You ever been in the cooler for anything you got a record for?"

Damon stared at us, waiting. James stared back. "You mean have I been arrested?" James said.

Damon nodded and suddenly my head screamed inwardly: *No, James, don't say it! Oh shit, James, no! Wait just a second, don't—*

"Yes," James said. For a guy who doesn't say shit nine times out of ten, you sure had to watch James's mouth a lot. "Hey, Tev." He turned to me. "What's that thing I got in trouble for again? You know. Those four times. The thing to do with the airplanes?"

It was something I did not intend to let on to upon our first employed day in weeks. But James had already said it aloud. Was there any use saving face now? "It has nothing to do with airplanes, stupid," I said to James. "I've told you that."

Damon looked completely bewildered. "Airplanes?"

"Aw, he's thinking of reports from Vietnam." I waved a hand and threw James a heated look. "Assaults, air assaults, like they're always talking about on the news."

Damon blinked. "I'm sorry?"

The Americans had been in Vietnam since the middle of March, and in full combat action as July approached. You couldn't pick up a paper without reading about it. And so we simply looked at one another for a long moment, until Damon connected James's words with mine and comprehension dawned upon his face. And that's when I understood something too: Damon's confusion had nothing to do with current events. I was the one who actually said the word. It was me who gave James away.

"Assault," Damon repeated back to me. "Four."

"Yes," I said carefully.

"Four," Damon said, incredulous. "*Four*?" And this time I said nothing at all.

Four was right: twice before me and James met, and then two times after. Five, actually, if you count that last time where the guy he'd knocked out refused to talk. The guy who'd shook his head and offered, *Nah, he didn't know what he was doing, he musta got mixed up! Look at him, look at him, sorry, stupid dipshit, I think he's retarded! Come on, let it rest, please, he didn't mean it*—the lousy guy in the bar, who lay unconscious long enough for the girl behind the counter to become hysterical and call the ambulance, who in turn called the cops, who in turn laid a charge whether the guy wanted them to or not.

Five, if you count that last time, for which James still visited the downtown courthouse once a month as required.

"Four," I said. Five, actually. That comes to about one time for every year I've known James.

Damon put both hands in the air. "Well. It's not like nobody else here's never been in the can. I'm not going to spread it around or anything. I was just trying to get an idea. I mean, if you had a court paper. It's the only reason I asked. For instance, we could've used his real name, shown the paper outside the tent at the ballyhoo. It would draw more marks in, I'll swear to it. Pump things up like he was a real live crimin—"

"No," I said, fast, and so firm that Damon drew his head back.

"Sorry," he began. "No problem. I just thought you might want to sell it. The idea, that is. He'll go over well with the whole good-versus-evil bit—"

"Ask me if I give a hang," I cut in. I gestured to James. "He cares even less." That part, at least, was true. And it was a subject that I clearly needed to go over with him again, too.

I didn't say anything as we made our way out of the tent. When we got out into the sunshine, James already looked like a puppy who'd just wet the carpet. "Why'd you go and tell him that, James," I said under my breath.

"I don't know," he bleated. "You said it too!"

I turned and pointed at him. "Hey, I only said what *you'd* already blabbed. It was a lost cause. *You're* a lost cause. You want to tell the whole fuckin' universe that you got strung? Like that dick in there was saying, that you're a real live—" And then, over James's shoulder, something caught my eye. A billow of black, fluffy hair bobbing its way toward us.

It was the magician.

I huffed, rolling my eyes. As he closed the distance, I put my arms over my chest. "Now what do *you* want?" I said as he came up behind James's back.

James turned. The guy's hands came up in defense. "What?" he tried. "Why, I'm just—doing a little follow-up, that's all."

I huffed again. "He doesn't need any follow-up."

The magician looked at me. He looked at James. He blinked, puzzled. Finally his lips curled into a smile. "Oh, I'm not talkin' about *that*." He waved a hand at James. "I'ma talking about you. You looked a little worried back there. And besides, I'm not too convinced about your trick." He paused, smiled gently. "I mean, no offense."

"Offense taken," I said. "No offense to you on that."

The magician smiled again, unruffled. "I just think you may still have a little work to do on your act. In fact, I got the sense maybe you guys could use"—his fingers leapt up and down before him, exaggerated, as if to convey quotations—"a little magic." He shrugged again. "That's all."

I waited, weighing this. "What do you mean?" I asked finally. "Are you talking about—faking it?"

"*I'm* talking about sleight of hand," he said. He put a hand to his head and tipped an imaginary hat. "Come now, my friend. Sideshows are never faked."

Six times. Of course not. I'm going to choke six times a night straight. "No sir," I said.

"Smart kid," the magician said, then looked to James. "And your buddy here I'm sure's just as smart." James beamed, and the magician's smile took on a scheming appearance. "Look, I think I might be of some assistance. I got a lot of resources, me, and some tricks up my sleeve if you're open. I'll need to know a little more about your act, of course."

There was nothing fake about it, I thought dismally. How did he figure on sleighting *that*? "You can't expect us to go giving away all our surprises," I said.

And this time the magician laughed. "This one's big on secrets, ain't he?" he said to James. Then he turned to me, paused, and managed a softer expression. "It's okay," he said. "I understand. It's personal, isn't it?"

Somewhere low inside of me, for the first time in years, I felt a breath of alliance between myself and someone else other than

James. Instead of the wild, hammering heartbeat that I usually fingered it for, the part of me that was big on secrets dwindled to a low pulse. Having no clue as to what he might be intimating— or scared that I actually might, after all—I made no comment.

"You think on it," the magician said. "I'll see you in a few days, some time before the show. I'm sure we'll be able to work something out. Don't you?" He grinned one last time. It was a grin like the one Damon had had earlier—the one that said he might enjoy the challenge.

5

DOWN THE HALL FROM OUR COMMON QUARTERS AT MOUNT Rosa's, past the nurses' station and hidden in an alcove, was the boys' lavatory and shower room. The room itself was a monochromatic gray like you'd find in a high school phys ed changing room. The shower lips and the floor were tiled, and I remember how the ceramic would echo hysterically when crossed by feet clad in anything at all. Each morning following breakfast, that floor was busier—noisier—than an expressway at rush hour. Other times, it was empty—nothing in there but you, humidity, and a grim sterility that was evocative of the mandate of the hospital itself.

In April of '57, when I arrived at the sanitarium, I was—as they say on the carnival—"as green as they come," but by June my arrival felt like an event already a thousand years gone. Once you got on the inside, life on the outside appeared to take place on an entirely different planet. We took lessons from a tutor each day, and our medication—shots, mostly—like men. The lights went out at ten o'clock every night. If you were surreptitious enough (and had—thanks to those at home who loved you—a good book on hand, a penlight, or some confection or other that you'd been smart enough to hide away), you might be able to stretch your bedtime out to eleven. If you were clever and had a trusted associate in the joint, however, you might succeed in doing so indefinitely. It was Bern who told me it was best to head down to the shower room with bare feet, no slippers, and to keep my yap shut on the matter if I wanted to join the club.

This turned out to be just him and me. But I didn't mind. With my mother moonlighting as an au pair most weekends, unavailable for visiting day, and Kenny, dead and out of the running altogether, it was nice to have somebody all to myself again.

And I told Bern that, though not in so many words—told him how my family was faring now that Kenny was out of the picture.

"Are you worried about her?" he asked me of my mother, one night when summer was just beginning to breathe its warmth into Mount Rosa's windows.

"I don't know. She's worried about *me*," I told him.

"Not my mother," Bern said, snorting. "Boy, she was *pissed* that I had to come back again! Never free, just like you put it. Wasn't your mother mad when you got the notice?"

"Mad?" I made a face. "No. She just sounded disappointed. It was a pain to have to come." I recalled Kenny offering the notice up to our mother, apologetic, as though it were a scandal or court summons. I laughed then, out loud, and it echoed across the tiles. "You know, my brother, he looked so sorry. For a second there, I thought he'd knocked someone up or—"

"*Shhh!*" Bern held a finger to his lips and we both froze. According to Bern's classified information, the nurses checked the pediatric room once at midnight and again at three, giving us plenty of time to disappear and return at our leisure. Still, everybody knew it was wayward to be found out of your bed after lights-out. We paused, eyes and ears straining, the rest of our bodies motionless, before he continued in a low voice. "For real? You thought your brother knocked someone up?"

"Yeah. For real."

Bern flexed his toes up and down. He set his chin in his hand and thought to himself for a while. He even picked a comic book up off the floor—a resource gathered and pooled between the two of us for such sitting-up-late occasions—and appeared to peruse it with interest. Finally he spoke, this time without looking at me.

"He have any girlfriends?" he asked.

"Nothing serious," I said. I hadn't been especially interested in girls before that year, so I hadn't really paid attention. Kenny told me I'd grow out of that. "But yeah, he did."

"But I bet he had *a lot* of girlfriends," Bern put in. "Didn't he tell you about them?"

I shrugged. "Sure."

"Did he tell you what kind of stuff he did with them?"

I considered. "Sure," I said again. "My mother goaded him for every detail. Like where they were going. What show they were seeing. Had her parents met him, the whole drill." I smiled. "He liked Roger Corman flicks. You know, *The Haunted Palace* and all the rest? But he said that didn't go over too well with girls, so mostly he let them choose the movie. Yeah." I nodded. "That's the kind of stuff he did."

Bern smiled down into the floor. "Right, chump." He turned to me and rolled his eyes. "*That*'s not how I meant it. I meant, did he tell you *what kind of stuff* he did with them."

The term *stuff*, when it arrived at my ears, sounded stiff, loaded—too many syllables stretched out of one thin word. I frowned, uncertain. I had no idea what he was talking about.

"I mean," Bern amended, his tone slow and lofty, "did he tell you about *fucking*?"

Kenny had taught me how to shoot hockey; he'd explained how to do long division. He'd even taught me Tag-in-the-Bag, an affectionately named game one conducted when halfway soused. He'd plied me with Jim Beam the day I'd joined him and his friends at it, and I'd been the frontrunner too, before I'd shot full-speed into the summit of the playground slide. My forehead hit the metal with a crunch, a momentarily blinding flash of white, and then a gracious sense of soaring away.

He didn't tell me about fucking, though, that I recall. Or at least if he did, he hadn't gone around calling it *that*.

"No." I laughed a little in spite of myself.

Bern did too. "What do you know of it, Pretty?" he said to me, and I noticed from his intonation that it was more of a statement than a question.

So I weighed my reply carefully. During Tag-in-the-Bag I'd lain there for about five seconds before awakening—bewildered, horizontal, Kenny and all his friends staring down at me. "What are you, dead, boy?" Kenny had cried, his face a full moon rising over my own. "Don't you use those eyes that God put in your head?" I hadn't wanted to admit that yes, I'd lost my bearings and had stupidly run myself aground. I hadn't wanted to admit that I was a *kid* and inexperienced with alcohol. I'd jumped to my feet despite the stars before my eyes.

In the same way I looked at Bern self-importantly. "I know enough," I said.

"No, you don't," he said, laughing. "I bet you have *plenty* to find out. Take your *Betty and Veronica*s here." He pointed to the comic books laid out on the tiles by our feet. "Tell me which one."

"Which one"—I frowned—"what?"

"Which one you'd fuck." Bern rolled his eyes again. It was the second time he'd said that particular word to me in private. And although he was certainly not the first adult to say it unself-consciously, I knew I had never heard it used exactly this way before. Bern was uttering a verb—an undertaking, an activity, a thing people *did*—instead of simply a common swear. The terminology gave me a prickly feeling; the look on his face lent a measure of condescension. The cumulative effect of this was some impression of delicious endangerment. Delicious, on account of the subject at hand. And danger, in finding myself at the brink of self-disclosure. Because Kenny—and now Bern—was right: I grew out of my lack of interest in girls. Who didn't? Yet in the moment, I didn't understand this as a universal proclivity. I simply believed Bern was either smarter or more intuitive than anyone else I'd ever known.

I thought he could see right through my head.

I looked at him warily. "I'll tell you," I said, "but you have to *swear* you won't tell anybody." I paused, thought carefully, then went on, in a rush, "Or I'll never hang with you again."

"I swear," Bern said, neither of us bothering to mention that at that time I scarcely hung with anyone besides him anyway. "I won't. Then you won't tell anyone about what goes on here either."

And then I told him a truth that I would hold myself to for an impossible four years: "*I'm* not going to tell anyone."

He smiled. "Fine, then. Me neither."

"Fine."

I'll tell you, but you have to swear. It wasn't about *Betty and Veronica*, and I didn't have to pause to collect the actual document: I had the cover of *The Phantom Lady*, the comic I'd filched from my brother, memorized. I told Bern the general outline of where I'd found her. Then I started with her hair and went on to her outfit. I ended with the look in her eyes—smoldering, beckoning—hovering overtop those exotic, immense breasts.

My lips shaped the words describing each part of her. I'd never told anyone those kinds of things before in my life. I never thought I ever would. To be fair, I didn't know that anyone else thought them but me. Yet when I was finished I could hear Bern's even breathing close to me.

"A girl sat down beside me while I was reading it on the way here," I added. "Brother, I had to get up and move seats." There were other reasons I'd switched seats on the bus, plenty more that merited mention. Reasons like I had a contagious illness, and my brother had it too, and we were up shit creek in its midst, he more than I, and I didn't really want to talk about it, even to a cute girl. But I had waited weeks to tell anyone *any* of that story.

The one safe person I'd wanted to tell had never shown up.

Bern nodded. "Keep going," he said.

A perplexity prickled at me then. We were aiming full-tilt at delicious endangerment, endangerment giving delicious a run for its money at about seventy to thirty now. I suddenly wasn't sure what Bern wanted me to tell him. A small part of me even had the chutzpah to wonder *why* he wanted me to tell him. And thinking of reading, it occurred to me out of the blue that while the Chinese checkers champ of the sanitarium had had my latest issue of *G.I. Tales* for nearly a week, he hadn't given me his collateral.

"Shit," I said out loud. There wasn't a lot of reading material on the inside until the Women's Auxiliary turned up on the first of each month. "Is David in occupational tomorrow, do you know? He's got some stuff he's supposed to lend me." David was eighteen, which meant he had occupational therapy once a week, which meant he had better things to do than forking over his comic books like he ought to have. But Bern looked at me unblinking. His expression never shifted.

"Keep going," he said. "You wanted to tell me. You were telling me about this girl."

A third time, wishy-washy deliberation. I paused, and then I just started telling him. As I had in the case of the "phantom lady," I told him what the girl on the bus had looked like. I told him what she had smelled like. I told him which parts of her had looked particularly fascinating to me and, with some coaxing, went on to tell him what I would have liked to have done with those parts. If she had offered. Bern was my stand-in older brother, and also my friend. The one that I could disclose such things to, who would not only get me, but get me one hundred percent. I guess I did it because—well, now that some years have passed, I understand that I couldn't exactly identify any reason *not* to.

Years later, within the same year that I reunited with James, in fact, I would make an acquaintance at a college party on a similar premise. A girl came over to show me this interesting glass of something—a drink of cherry red, thick, with all these nice little grapes and orange slices floating on top.

"I can't finish this," she said, thrusting the concoction toward me. "Here."

It wouldn't have been my first drink of the night. In fact, I'd had so many already that parts of me were beginning to turn off, like a fuse blowing in self-preservation when there's too many extensions plugged in. So I looked at her apologetically. "I really don't think I should."

The girl swished the contents in the bottom of the glass

seductively. "But there's hardly any left. It's called *san-gree-ah.*" She leaned in. "I don't really like fruity crapola? But the girl who rooms next to me mixed it and I don't want to offend her." She swished the glass again—you know, with all those nice little grapes and things floating on top.

I looked at the glass in her hand. I looked at her. She was cute, a fact that is a relevant footnote to the tale. And as I looked at her, a very convincing thought entered my mind: *Oh well, why not. It's not like it's going to hurt.*

"Fine, fine. Okay." I batted my eyelashes. "I'll finish it up." Just one glass. But you know where this story's going.

Next thing I know, I'm turning my guts inside out on the way back to her dormitory. Then I'm hurling up my lunch (with all these nice little grapes and orange slices floating on top) inside the men's room. And moments after that, I'm heaving into a wastebasket at the foot of her bed. "It's your fucking sangria, Catharine," I managed between pitches. "I *knew* I never should've drunk it."

In the boys' room with Bern, a similar opportunity for evaluation arose.

"Shush," Bern said suddenly.

My eyes came up and my ears perked, listening for any outside movement: polished shoes marching down the hall, slippered feet around the corner, the rustle of bedclothes at the door. For a moment we sat in silence, and all I heard was the staccato *drip-drip-drip* of water hitting the basin across the room. Some hours after this, I would thrash in my bed for the first time in my life, reviewing the instant where one moment in the boys' shower room inexplicably passed into the next. The splinter of an instant where something in the room shifted from the banality of a faucet dripping and Bern's calm, speaking voice to something completely different. When I could not identify the shift precisely, I would come to believe that I must have imagined the whole thing.

The next sound I heard was the muted yelp of my own voice as something came down in my lap. Not painful or offensive, but solid and there nonetheless. I almost laughed out loud, thinking Bern was landing me in the balls like Kenny had that time years ago outside the convenience store. "Shush," he said to me. Yet a moment later I looked and saw that it was still there.

I looked, I saw it, and then I looked away. I couldn't look there and I couldn't look at Bern—Jesus, I didn't know where to look. And so in the end he decided that for me too.

His other hand came to the back of my neck and gripped it—again, not painful or offensive, yet firm and directing nonetheless. His hand pressed inward until I found myself staring down again, into our laps, side by side. I saw something that I hadn't the first time. I don't really want to say what it was. But I can allow this: it was on his side, above his flexing toes yet below the waist, and it was saying how Bern knew he wanted it.

Over the next many years I would awaken countless times, sweating and shaking, from a dream in which I looked down and saw that thing attached to my body in the place where my own honest prick should have been. But in the moment I grew confused and horrified and aroused all at once, and this congealed sensation brought no words—only tears to my eyes and acid into my throat.

I sat not breathing, his hands upon me. They remained there as a moment passed.

"Keep going," he said. "You were telling me about the girl."

My mouth filled with spit, my torso with heat—but mostly my mind was filled with questions. So I wagered and I assessed, and again I simply believed him. Thinking back on this moment today brings a little song to my mind. The line in the song that sticks with me most goes like this: *It smelled like turpentine and looked like India ink. I held my nose, I closed my eyes, I took a drink.*

I found my tongue inside my mouth, and even then I spoke words that were there merely by the faculty of suggestion.

Amazingly, I continued to speak about the girl.

It's okay, I told myself as I did. *He knows what he's doing.*

He knows better than me anyhow. And when that left me with some lingering shard of doubt: *He wouldn't do anything that was bad for me.* And finally, when the unease still wouldn't subside and yet time had passed now, had in fact spun out into a long, habituating moment so that it felt either discourteous or naïve to say something now: *Jesus, Tevan, relax. Why not. It's not like it hurts.*

Like the time with Catharine's sangria, it wasn't until later, some time after I'd ingested the

(Just one glass of India ink)

notion did I know for certain. I swallowed it all down, the pitch and the sickness it brought with it, and so, as in the dormitory, Catharine sitting beside me at the foot of her bed, soon enough, on the rising grit of my own assessment, I began to choke.

6

BY THE TIME ME AND JAMES REACHED THE MIDWAY, THE LOT was coming alive for the day. The grounds were filled with the scent of grass, diesel fuel, and sweet stuff spun inside of confectionary booths. James and me had walked through the pavilion just a day before, our stomachs rumbling, our eyes and bodies hungry, and our pockets a comparable blank. Now I combed the clutter of midway rides with my eyes, hoping to spy the redemption that Damon had promised within it.

The fellow we were looking for stood out from the fray almost immediately. We found him towering over a little kid. The pair—father and son, clearly—boasted identical crests of curly hair and they stood between two hunks of metal thumped down in the grass. The man was yelling at his boy in the ginchiest accent I'd ever heard. "Do ya calla poor job a finish job, heh?" he screeched.

The kid bowed his head. "No, sir."

"Whuh happens when ya do a job poorly the firs' time round?"

The kid, who looked to be about eleven years old, said nothing.

"I *sid* whuh happens when ya don't understand the lesson the firs' time?"

"You do it again, sir?" the kid offered.

"Tha's right. Ya go and do it agin."

The boy nodded and ran off toward the first of two contraptions. I noted that one was a maze of rods sprouting seats at each arm; the other appeared to be nothing but a giant round bin. I'd never ridden either.

I grinned as James and me walked over. "Tough love for the kid, no?"

The fellow returned my smile. "I s'pose. But we're not raising kids, are we? In the end we're raising adults. Keith Cruikshane." He put out a hand and I took it.

"We're from the show," I said. "Damon Merit gave us your name. He said you were looking for help."

The man looked both me and James over. "The *show*, eh?" He showed off a huge set of teeth. "Then I 'ave to ask—which did yare mama raise you two as, then?"

"Adults, sir," I said. I stuck a finger at James. "He's not my brother."

"Ya ever work with rides before?" When James and I both shook our heads, Keith was unconcerned. Instead he looked around to the contraptions behind him. "That"—he pointed to the giant bowl—"is called the Roundup. Straightforward maintenance—my boy'll show ya how it's done. Cleanin' and oilin' before afternoon." He pointed to the gangling machine to his left. "And this here's the Scrambler"—*Scramblah,* in his lingo. "A bit more heavy liftin' today. Needs some attention to detail round the cogs." He eyed us meaningfully. "There's *lotsa* cogs, son. Take your pick."

I looked from one piece to the next. "James." I pointed to the round bin. "Go on over there."

"Ya sure?" Keith cut in. "My Scramblah here aren't like liftin' hay, now!"

I knew what he was intimating—James was bigger than me. But the spindly thing looked complicated. Most days, long-winded instructions passed through James's head like sand in a sieve. So I nodded to James a second time. "I'm going to stay here with Keith," I said. "You're going to go over there and have his boy show you how it's done. Right?"

James hesitated. "I don't know . . ." he began, his voice a plummeting whisper.

I took him by the sleeve and leaned in close. "Well, what do you know, James?" I hissed, giving him a shake. "Huh? What do you know? Do you know anything, James?" I let go and James tottered a moment on his feet. "Come on, friend. Go on over."

When James turned toward the Roundup, I brought my eyes back to Keith. "My friend. He's—ah, not one for complex machinery," I offered.

Keith and I tightened bolts, set seating tubs, and realigned chains for what felt like a day. After a while Keith mentioned that he did in fact need a hand running the rides during the day—that is, if I was interested in *larning to tairn her* and *larning to slough*. I didn't know what sloughing a ride meant, and I'd never operated so much as a pickup truck before this. Sure, I said.

By the end of it—three hours, a dollar and a quarter for myself, and a dollar for James—I looked like a cat who'd just slept on the cooling parts of a carburetor. "Thet's a job done," Keith said. He wiped his fingers onto a rag, then tossed it over so that I could do the same. I rubbed it over my hands and arms. Then, hardly able to contain myself, I passed it over my face and hair too. The rag came away gray, gritty, and soaked with perspiration. *Cleanliness is next to godliness*, my mother used to say. Here on the carnival, where a good wash came scarcer than a damn flush toilet, cleanliness already appeared next to impossible.

"Don't git too vain now," Keith said, watching me.

The comment was well timed. For right when I lifted my sweaty head looking like a man who'd just run the four-forty through a screen of diesel fuel, I laid eyes on the most beautiful girl I'd ever seen. I spied her walking the causeway, approaching Keith and me. Her hair was long and brown, hanging right to the small of her back. A pink gauzy skirt swung to the ground. Beneath it, her feet were bare. As she passed I heard the tinkling of her belt bouncing against her hip, as though it were fastened with tiny bells. Like the sound of cowboy spurs, I thought. *Giddyap.*

"Hello," I said under my breath—to myself, to her, though not meaning for anyone to hear. She continued down the midway looking neither left nor right. Which I guess, in my state, I was thankful for. She made off in the direction of the sideshow tents.

"Ya like seein' the fewchah?" Keith, beside me, grinned wide. It took me a second to understand him, seeing as my mind was heading south with the girl.

"The future?" I said. "Man, if *she's* in it I do." I laughed, my cheeks flushed. "*Do* I."

Keith laughed too. "She's the card reader. Reads the tarot on tha *show*." It occurred to me that he always referred to the sideshow in the same damn way: "tha *show*"—evocative, intimating, wink-wink-nudge-nudge—as though he believed there was far more to it than the word could ever suggest. "Lotsa girls over there on tha *show*," he said, drawing out the word again. "In various states of undress too, yah." He folded the grease rag into his hands. "Got a sharp eye, you. Seein' past all them hotsie-totsies to an Annie like that." He paused then, his expression momentarily grim. "Watch out a that'un, though. Medicated, she is."

I had no idea what he meant. I had no mind to care. "Uh-huh," I said. "I think pink's my favorite color." I curled my lips over clenched teeth. "*Rrrrrr.*"

Keith laughed again. "What's the diff'rence between the circus and the midway?"

I shook my head, the grin still on my face.

"On a circus they keep the animals locked in cages. On a midway they let 'em run the rides."

The summer was proving sweltering by day and racked by humid thunderstorms by night. Under such conditions, you could either wash your Christly undershirts every few days, or stink to high heaven as payment for your lassitude, or maybe your poverty. Me and James picked through our belongings—underwear, socks, T-shirts, denim—and chose from this a careful load of crucial items. Thanks to our newfound pocket of change from Keith, we headed out that evening to find a Laundromat.

We were five minutes on our way, just coming upon a small highway town, when I spied a guy walking the asphalt with his thumb out. It had begun to drizzle as we drove off the midway; now it was raining like a pissing beast.

"What do you think, James?" I said aloud, eyeing the hitchhiker.

James, who often didn't think very much at all, offered nothing. We were heading downtown anyhow. I slowed the car.

I leaned across James in the passenger seat, nudged him with my elbow, and cracked the door open on his side. The door swung open to reveal the guy: soaking wet, grinning, and looking like he'd been out there for a good long while. You didn't really have to wonder why—the second he turned his bloodshot eyes to us, I knew he was shitfaced. And so what took place next all happened very fast.

"Hello!" he said, like me and James were a prize and a half. He tipped his head in at us. "Heading downtown?"

I paused, deliberating. We were there in the car; he was outside. Me and James still had the luxury to renege, and I began to understand that this might be in our better interests. And on account of the delay, and perhaps the driving rain or the substance riddling his brain, the guy grew impatient. He didn't give me a chance to make a decision. Suddenly he wasn't outside the car anymore, he was *inside*, or at least partially anyway, his hands wedging the passenger side further than I'd meant to allow. I wasn't particularly scared. I was surprised—and incensed.

I let out a yell—"Hey!"—although I was powerless to do much more from my side of the car.

James was closer. He heard my voice, and something in him hardened. He turned with a whip, and popped the door outward hard enough to knock the guy right on his ass.

Actually he did it hard enough to show that he'd meant to hurt him. I saw the look on James's face—pinched, inflamed— as if he could've just as easily torn the fellow's hands off at the wrists and tossed them out onto the concrete beside him. A split second later he hauled the door inwards. It closed with a mighty slam and the window roller connected with his ribcage. He actually split himself open—the knob had fallen off years before and we'd never bothered to replace it. I saw the misery upon his face just before I punched the accelerator.

"Jesus," I breathed, a moment later. "You okay?"

James nodded—a suck in his head, maybe, but a warrior in the body—and rubbed his side. Keith's remark about animals on midways darted through my mind.

"Ungrateful bastard," I muttered.

James stared out into the driving rain. After a long moment, he spoke: "What's an ungrateful bastard?"

"It's an asshole," I said. "An asshole who doesn't know how to say thank you."

Later that night, inside our camper, James took his shirt off to get a look at his collateral damage. It took the shape of a half-moon below his ribs. Blood Moon, I thought to myself, noting its color. That's what you call a full moon under eclipse. Of course that refers to a *full* red moon and, like everything else of James's, it seemed, his was flying half-mast.

James sat on an overturned washbasin, surveying the wound. "Geez, Tevan, don't you hate that guy?"

I turned to see James, seated, pointing, his face twisted with indignation.

"Hate him?" I frowned. "No, I was just annoyed, James. I might've let him hitch, but it turned out he had some nerve."

"Well, *I* hate him, Tevan. He scared you! And now look what he did."

I paused, deliberating. I thought of how pissed James could get in an instant, his face growing tense, the tendons in his arms standing out, his senses seeming to cut out completely. I thought of all the trouble that had caused him. "You don't hate him, James," I said slowly. "You don't even know him." Instructing though not patronizing, I hoped. "And I wasn't scared. The guy wasn't all there, James, that's all. You get me?" I put a finger to my ear and spun it in a circle, demonstrating the universal ding-a-ling sign. After delivering my ten-second sermon on tolerance and self-control, I remembered that James liked to smoke various things. For James's sake, I try to make a habit of articulating the evils of illegal substances, just as I do the wrong of violent solutions. So I added, "He was loopy, that's all. Probably LSD. Or something."

James nodded, putting his hand over the cut. His voice was small, tentative. "Tevan," he said, "do you hate Bern?"

I turned and eyed him sitting on the washbasin. I never lie when he asks me, and I never tell him to leave the subject alone.

"Yes," I said simply. It was for James's benefit that I lectured about LSD and explained that you don't pound guys when you're mad, but I couldn't be certain that these were things that sank in. Giving my word and letting him talk when he brought up Mount Rosa's were things that did. James had enough of lies and silence before he met me, you see. That, after all, is what taught him how to kick ass.

James looked to the floor, processing, and seemed to agree. He asked the next question gently. "Tevan, was Bern—your friend?"

I watched him a little longer. It wasn't the first time we had had this conversation, no; yet every time, it seemed, I needed to consider the question carefully. Look myself over, and James and Bern and whoever else was there, and try to draw a line from each of us, to the other, to the other. Understand it, I think, from so many different angles.

I weighed what I knew, and again I answered him honestly. "Yes."

James frowned. "That's what I thought." A long pause. "*They* didn't think so." He bobbed his head. "You know. All the other boys. I mean, that's not what *they* said." He paused again, maybe waiting for me to ask *What did they say?*, maybe just taking a breath, I don't know. I had no intention of asking. I'd heard plenty when I was there. And if I hadn't known that decreeing such things wasn't good for James, I would've told him to shut up right then. But I let him continue. "They said you were just like him."

In the moment I heard his words, a different, years-ago remembering arrived at me—the boys' washroom at Mount Rosa's and Bern's toes upon its floor.

For the second time in an hour, I recalled Keith's comment about animals. I looked up. James sat with his shirt in his hand, staring at me.

"I know," I whispered. "Don't you think I know that, James?"

"My brother has this car," I'd said aloud one night in the boys' washroom in summertime. "It's a '55 Nomad."

Bern whistled through his teeth. "One tough set of wheels." His feet were bare as usual, his blond hair sticking up. He'd crawled from his bed an hour or so before, me at his heels. "Not anymore, though. Who do you think has it now?"

I thought for a minute. "*Me?*" I said incredulously. I'd never considered such an idea before. The car was Kenny's and he'd paid a whole holy buck for it. Then again, my mother didn't even have a license and . . .

"Geez, you think it's mine now?"

Bern smiled, rubbing his hair. "Unless your old lady sells it. Why not?"

Oh, she wouldn't sell it, I thought at once. The moment Bern put the idea in my head, I wanted the car to be all mine. Kenny had saved up years for that Chevy, and even with the help of his ill-fated scholarship, he still had one motherfuck of a loan on it. I wanted it because it had been Kenny's dream. Even if it were a *bicycle*, I'd have wanted it.

"I'm not old enough to drive, though," I mused. "Shit, that's nearly two years from now."

"Yeah, that's right. You're only fourteen. Just a little thing." Bern laughed, at my expense, but I joined him. I was two years away from becoming a licensed driver, he was right. In my mind, I was nonetheless conjuring up the moment in the future in which I, authorized by the Province of Ontario as road-worthy, would sit down in that Chevy. I'd sit down in the wide, waffle seats, I imagined, and rest my hand on the knob of the shifter, and it would be beautiful.

As I sat on the shower lip, my mind forecasting this portrait, Bern made an eerily similar motion. I didn't think about it, which is not to say I didn't notice. Only that the noticing, by now, manifested itself as some incomprehensible combination of awful yet weirdly unremarkable. Years later my workplace friend Steve Orono, the person who would sell me the spliff and jug of booze to facilitate my return to Mount Rosa's, planted trees up north over a summer. He described a similar response to foul elements: "At first you want to kill 'em," he told me of the incessant mosquitoes he'd lived with on the job. They'd stung his neck so bad that he came home with weepy scabs that would probably scar for life. "But then you get so accustomed to them, Tev, that after a while you don't even bother swatting the fuckers away."

In the late '60s I read a tagline on some hippie's flyer. The tract was meant to encourage social activism, but instead I thought of Steve's remark. Next I thought of Bern. *If you think you're too small to make any difference in the world,* the tract read, *then you've obviously never been in bed with a mosquito.*

"I want to show you something," Bern said to me.

"What?" I looked up, distracted, my mind still on the car.

"Do you really want me to show you?"

"Okay. What?"

He smiled. "Say it."

I rolled my eyes. "I *reeeeeally* want you to show me," I repeated in a bored sing-song.

Bern gazed at his feet. He got up off the shower lip. Then he turned three-quarters of a circle and seated himself on the floor before me. He looked up at me, his gaze querying mine, asking me if I understood. It was a pose similar to the one that Damon Merit would configure James and me into nine years later. Only this time I found nothing funny about it. I was totally confused.

"Pretty," he said, "I'll show you. But you ought to be quiet about it."

I'd heard such instructions before. When I was small, my mother had a never-ending habit of yelling it through the house. And once when I was twelve, me and Kenny were walking through a car lot and I stepped on a two-by-four, putting a nail through my foot. I screamed so long and loud that Kenny had to slap me. "Sorry, kid," he said to me. "You were wigging so bad I couldn't even get a look at it! You ought to be quiet now. Get yourself composed." Calm Kenny, who once, upon putting a fishing knife through his hand (he'd gotten overexcited talking about Bill Barilko while filleting), had simply looked at me coolly and said, "Oh boy. I'm going to scream now."

With Bern watching me, I held my breath.

"I'll show you," he said. "You can think about the girl on the bus. You can think of whoever you want." Bern nodded as he spoke. "But first," he said, "I want you to say it."

This time, however, I made no reply. I told myself I didn't know what he was referring to; I told myself I had no response. Above this, my chest pistoned in and out in terror. *Say what?* I might have tried, but I knew. I knew. And so for one thin, wild moment I actually almost just said it: *I really want you to show me.* Deeming, perhaps, that in saying so aloud, I might come to believe it. Instead, I chose some shade of gray in between. I managed what might've been the last noncompliant words of my life for the next nine months.

"Wait," I said, my voice a whisper. "Wait, I don't think this is a good idea."

Bern paused. His brow vibrated upon his forehead and his lips drew themselves into a line. I didn't have to ask if he was pissed at me for that. I knew him well enough. After all, we were friends. When he finally pronounced the word it came out hard and put out and genuine—

"Why?"

—yet impatient and somehow *persuasive* so that a thousand voices in my head mutinied and turned upon me all at once. *Yeah, why? Why, Tevan?* And *It's not like it hurts, Tevan.* And *He knows better than you anyhow.* And *He wouldn't do anything that would hurt you!* And again, *Jesus, Tevan! Why?*

"Why?" Bern said again. "I don't understand. You told me all those things. I know you want to." He tilted his head to one side. "You know, know what it's like."

I breathed in, and in this slow, stretched moment I progressed from wondering how he'd come to believe this, to believing I had actually, inadvertently *caused* such an event, to believing that in some sense maybe it was even *true*. Because, well—shit!—I *did* want to know what it was like; of course I did! Though there were some split hairs mixed in there somewhere.

Weren't there?

"Are you scared?" Bern asked, and I could not discount the smile I saw playing at the corner of his lips.

"I'm not scared of anything." Yet like his smile, the hesitation squirming inside me like a can of worms could not be ignored. "I just—I don't think I'd call it a good idea, is all."

He watched me, considering. "No," he said, after some time. "It's called experience. Or at least if you're over eight years old it is."

Now, I've already said that Bern had a mouth on him and that he could use it for good or for evil. I can't remember what I thought it was when he said that to me, but today I categorize it as unequivocally evil. Hurtful and mean, a strategic stab. Today I recognize that sentence for what it really was—the same damn thing I'd said to the twins when they asked me to join in their little game and I wanted to convey that they weren't good enough for my precious time. It was a statement seated in disappointment and yet lined with the ominous threat of desertion. No wonder I understood him so unwaveringly:

He took the words right out of my own mouth.

"So what do you want to do?" he said.

Some moments passed. My mind, churning all over the

place; my breath, a live thing that seemed to fill the room. Bern was presenting me with an argument of semantics, but I wasn't in any position to understand this. Not until years later would the logic of our disagreement become clear to me: we weren't disagreeing at all. For all intents and purposes, when you don't want to take part in something, "I don't think this is a good idea" and "It's called experience" are technically the same thing. But I was too busy crossing my eyes, trying to pinpoint where I'd gone wrong. When I couldn't, I raised my gaze and saw the reasons for indignation spelled out upon Bern's face. And so yet again, I swallowed back the hesitation in my guts and simply believed him.

"Okay," I whispered, though my voice sounded rusty and my breath shuddery—like it does before you begin to cry; yeah, like that. But he went ahead and gave it to me anyway. But who could blame him—after all, I didn't cry, not quite; not this time, anyway. I didn't think of the girl, though. I couldn't think of *anything* as I tried to categorize exactly what was going on between us. And when I knew what was going on, I couldn't believe it, or wait, I could—I did a lot of reading, you'll recall, some seedy stuff if I could get my hands on it, I admit, so I did believe it— but I didn't *want* to, and again I wondered how it was that such a shifty feeling could come from someone who was your friend, someone who wasn't shifty at all.

And so I pointed my thoughts elsewhere. And so I put my body I don't know where. It felt as though a part of me—my mind, or my back, or my breath maybe—was floating away from the scene. And I put my head to another universe. I thought of Betty and Veronica, and I thought of Elvis Presley, and I thought of Kenny telling me to get myself composed. I thought of four-card draw and how you weren't very good at it until you gained a little experience and how I had taught the other kids using a little cheat sheet describing the coveted hands, which Bern wasn't exactly doing, but I suppose it was close, wasn't it? Because it *was* a demonstrative kind of thing, at least he *said* it was, just an example passed down from one person to another. I think. And it didn't hurt—or wait, maybe it did. I couldn't tell. Because the thing is, if it hurts, you say, *Oh boy, I'm going to scream now,* and I never screamed.

I never screamed anything.

I only said, "Bern," in a whisper. "Please—"

And time passed, quickly, blurrily, and it occurred to me that it might be fitting to think of this one time at Christmas, when I was ten and Kenny was a teenager. We'd been goofing around after opening up all our presents. Kenny, always bigger than me, pinned me down and tickled me, and I laughed and screamed until I cried. Until I started yelling that I'd drunk too many virgin apple ciders and if he didn't let up I was going to spray my goddamn shorts. But Kenny had had a few (non-virgin, I presume) ciders himself and he just kept saying: *What? Let up? But you're laughing, Tevan, you're laughing. You look like you're having a good old time! You tell me with a straight face, boy, you tell me—* And I did, I tried, but I was laughing whether I liked it or not by then: *I'm gonna pee, Kenny! I'm gonna hose myself! You have to believe me, Kenny, you have to—*

"Bern," I said. "Please—"

(STOP)

but I couldn't say it aloud. Even if I'd had the guts to say it. Every time I opened my mouth or moved a muscle or inhaled to breathe, he took his thumb and finger to the underneath of my knee, like a father pinching his boy's ear in church if he wriggled around during the hymns.

(Shush)

"Bern," I tried, a plea, a question.

Then a heaving feeling, the next moment a feeling of abdominals shuddering—like a rope towing an anchor line, taut, from a harbor. The sensation of a million synapses firing below the belt all at once; like tasting something sweet with the knowing, gentle skin of your privates; like being struck by an interior bolt of lightning.

I didn't mean for it.

But if you've ever had the backdoor trots, or thrown up in school, or even passed gas out loud in a silent room of strangers, you know how it is that sometimes your body takes off running, organically speaking, whether you've complied wholeheartedly or not.

And all of a sudden James is looking at me, looking and nodding very seriously.

His shirt is off, and I'm not sure where I am at first. It's only that little blood moon—the today's-special event of the hitch-hiker, like a date stamped onto today's newspaper—that brings me back.

"They said you wanted to, Tev," he says.

I look at him, bewildered, until I understand: and in understanding I suddenly wish to be dead—or at least very, very drunk.

"They thought you went along because you wanted to."

"I didn't mean for it," I say, though I've already said this a hundred times before. There's a lesson in there somewhere, I believe, but like the platitudes on drug use and brawling, it doesn't seem to be sinking in. James and I stare at one another. I want to take it all back, the whatever *I didn't mean* and the narcotics lecture, I do, and in its place I want to say to James: *Go on and kick some ass, James. Go on and smoke that shit then, go on, James. If that's what makes you feel better, then go ahead and I won't bitch about it anymore. Go on then, friend.*

"I know, Tevan." James shakes his head. "I know. I tried to get away from him too, but Bern was after me."

I hear his child's description of an adult event, the only words he has for it. I feel sorry for him, but also suddenly and profoundly hurt. Alongside this, a mean, prickly anger aimed squarely at James. For there's something else here. It's the worst feeling, too.

It reignites in me, springing from James's use of the word "too."

It's not news to me. It's the reason we're here, after all, James and me, together on Merit's sideshow and in this camper—and before that in the car, and before that all those wayward, shitty little apartments or rooming houses—linked together by some unspoken commonality. But still it gets to me every time, the worst part.

So I shake my head. It's the one thing I never say aloud to James, the part I hate the most.

"He used to get me in my bed," James says, oblivious to it. "And he used to get me in that little—that little room down the hall there, that little—you know—"

"Yes, James," I interrupt. *Shut up,* I mean to say, more than ever now, but I don't. I finish for him: "Don't worry. I know the one."

A slow nod from James. Sitting on the washbasin, he slouches inward. His hair falls over his eyes. "He used to get me in my bed and so I started getting out of it at night." He peers at me. "That stopped when you came, Tevan. When he was your friend? Because then he was after you. You got it the worst, you know."

My eyes smart and my lips purse. I can't silence him on this; I don't even want to. But still, that feeling!—the worst part. I can't admit to it because a hand is no worse than a tongue, or a pinch no worse than a slap. *There is no worst,* I tell James every time. I tell him that sometimes Bern tricked me to shut me up, and sometimes he pinched me to shut me up, and later he slapped me to shut me up. I tell him that later still Bern put his hands around my throat to shut me up.

"He only told me nobody would believe me," James tells me in reply. "Because I'm stupid, you know? He never hit me, though. Boy, you got it the worst."

"There's no worst, James," I tell him again. For I see no difference between the pinch behind the knee and the hands around my throat. Bern progressed from one to another to another, yet I see them as expressively equal. I was just as scared of his hands connecting with my neck, his fingers to my knee, and his lousy, prying want upon the rest of me. There's *reasons* I shut up, and the worst is that I remember how mostly they had to do with keeping someone you love close rather than with pushing him away. They're all the same—*shut up, say nothing, hush, Pretty, Stupid, be quiet.* It holds you down all the same. There's lots of ways to get held down.

I never screamed.

He progressed from one to another, yes: but the truth is that Bern shut me up well before he even touched me.

"Ungrateful bastards!" James bursts out.

"James," I manage, blinking. I make a mental note to watch my mouth a little more around him.

"It's true," he seethes. His breath is coming hard, and I know that soon he'll be crying. "The things they *said.*" His words are coming strong and I know that if he had any of the Mount Rosa boys before him now he'd probably kill them. "I'm not the smartest guy, Tevan. Nobody would believe me! But at least I know that once you were there, Bern didn't bug any of us anymore. They knew that, Tevan." He bows his head. "You got it the worst. Of all of us."

And I contradict him again, just one more for the record, don't you know, telling him once more *There is no worst, James, there is no worst.* The worst is that I'm miserly, jealous, the part I can't put words to, the part that knows that Bern was my two-timing, traitorous friend. His hands were at my throat the whole time. There and now, his hands are there. He choked me with my own desire. With want. Stuffed it down my throat. And it's still down there

(Say *I really want you to show me*)

suffocating me.

In front of James, I hold my breath and my tongue.

I never tell him about the worst part.

"You knew about me?" I say. I already know the answer. For there was once, I remember, when the boys' shower room deviated from its mandated quiet. An interruption! And so I put my foot out, my heel against the door. There was nothing either of us could do about the rest of the show, though. I was on my knees.

The intruder saw it, I suspected. He saw it, today I know.

The tall guy, the skinny, black-haired, couple-crayons-short-of-a-box guy. Thank God, just him. He was bigger than me but not as smart as the other boys. He was bigger than me, but that was no matter: you always want to come off like you knew the score: *Get lost*, I said. *I'm busy.*

Now James nods, his slow and nonchalant admission. "Yes," he agrees. "Everybody knew about you and Bern, Tev. Betty, Veronica. Me. Everybody." He waits. "Did you—know about me?"

I look at James. I remember how Bern had smiled at the intruder. *Hi, Jimmy*, he had said. And the words—the worst ones, that clarified everything to me and yet the same ones I never admit aloud: *Miss me? You want to come in now too?*

I shake my head.

"No," I say to James, a lie. "I didn't know at all."

I turn to him, the crimson semicircle again the only stamp of the present, glowing like a burn in his side, and offer nothing more. He's been quiet a while and I know that he's crying, working to hide it the best he can beneath his long, straggling hair. *At least he's learned some things since he was sixteen*, I think. *At least he's learned some things.*

"James," I say, quietly this time. "Come on, then."

And we get up into the bunk.

And I don't fight him for my own this time around. Instead, hands at my throat and a rope pulling upward. Soon enough, *yeah, like that.* Yeah, just like that. *Quiet now, you Pretty.* Sometimes you just keep learning your lessons over and over again.

7

I worked on Keith's ride over the next three days. He was right: the Scrambler was more work than the Roundup. Stationary, the Scrambler was a loping silver nightmare with a thousand metal arms to clean and just as many sweeps to grease. But in action, that same metal became an awesome, rotating web. Once Keith allowed me to man the controls, I loved how its motion lifted my hair off my forehead and put a rhythm into my hands.

James worked alongside me, just one piece of machinery over, and reaping a wage slightly less than mine. He managed to knock off work before me without fail. I returned to the trailer on the day of our first show to find him asleep.

"James," I called. James was in his place by the door—he always fell asleep in that same goddamn chair. He looked like a cat now, just opening its eyes to the light of day in midafternoon. "*Blechh.*" I wheeled my head around the place. "Something smells like puke in here."

I crossed over to the basin under the window. Dishes and a spreading orange mess stretched out from the counter to the basin. A soaked towel lay splayed across it like some orange-blooded creature had impaled himself, oozed all over, and then run off someplace to die.

"It's tomato soup," James offered. "I made it."

"I see," I agreed. The sun was heating the place like a furnace. "There's only two types of people in this world, James." I lifted the towel, two fingers held out like tweezers. "People who make tomato soup, and people who think tomato soup smells like puke."

"Well, I made it," James affirmed, seeming to think I was asking a question.

"Yes, I see." I put my finger out and touched the surface next to the element. "And you've also left the gas on. No wonder it's so fucking hot in here." Not to mention that the place could've burned right to the ground. "Don't do that, James." *And don't think that comes for free!* Buddy's voice echoed in my head. I'd already learned that on a carnival this type of proxy expense—gas, electricity, water—was called a ding. "Next time just use the hotplate outside, okay?" I didn't want to think about dings, with only the few dollars we currently had between us.

"Okay." James watched me for a moment. "We going to see Schroeder?"

"Soon." We'd run into Schroeder on the lot the day before, and had taken a moment to plot out a meeting time for the magician's promised follow-up concerning our act. Still, I'd been putting so much of my attention on other things—rationing our money, developing some finesse on the Scrambler so that the tubs rounded each curve without bouncing, maybe even considering the barefoot card reader in some private corner of my mind—I'd scarcely had time to worry about the upcoming show.

Now that it had again entered my mind, I wasn't in any mood to wash dishes, tomato soup or otherwise. I put my hand in my pocket, jingling my change. Fuck dings, I decided. "Hey James, I was just thinking," I said. "We should go and get some ice cream."

We met Schroeder on our way over to the midway concessions. Once inside the pavilion, we stopped at a little kiosk on wheels. In exchange for three vanilla cones, I parted ways with the change that had found its way into my pocket just that afternoon. The three of us sat outside the kiosk, our backsides parked on a bench and our sneakers sinking into the surrounding tract of sawdust.

Finally Schroeder tossed the last sticky inch of his ice cream cone into the sawdust and checked his wrist. "What say we get to business. You guys are on in a couple of hours and I have a feeling you might need some props." He turned to me. "You talk to Damon today?"

"Yes," I said.

Schroeder raised his eyebrows. "And?"

"And we got new names."

His lips spread out into a wide smile. "Names, huh? Names like 'Schroeder'?"

I grinned. "Sort of. I'm Seraphim and he's Faustus—or the other way around, I can't remember which. Though don't ask me what in hell that means."

Schroeder nodded. "Means Damon's got something cooking. He's good at that. He tell you what the talk's all about?"

"Yeah." I looked to James. "Told James to wear black and me to wear white. He sort of explained the gist."

Schroeder nodded again. "His daddy may be a sponge, but Damon's a good talker, you can rest assured. Anyway, just call me Shawn." He looked from me to James, then back to me again. Finally he stood. "Come on," he said. "Let's take a walk. The deal is this: you tell me all about your game"—his eyebrows bounced up on his forehead—"and I'ma show you a nice place to watch the sunset."

Shawn walked us across the lot, then into the grassy lawn beyond. He strolled right along beside me while James went ahead.

"You nervous?" he asked after a while.

I shook my head. James, walking with his head up and wiping the ice cream's stickiness across his jeans, looked unconcerned as ever. But I could feel myself sweating, a little behind the neck and on my brow, and it wasn't just the heat. James and I had been performing our trick for years. But we'd never told anyone a thing about it.

"Cause you seem like you're freaking out a little, man." Shawn pushed my shoulder. "Relax. It's just a show."

We stopped a ways out in the grass. You could just barely spy the midway rides, tiny at this distance. There was nothing out there but bush and grass for miles. Shawn sat down cross-legged on the ground and facing away from the carnival. He breathed in, eyes closed. Years later, I'd think upon this portrait of Shawn and muse that he had looked a little like Jimi. In the year 1966, though, nobody knew Jimi. Jimi Hendrix was just arriving back in America, discharged from military service due to an ostensible injury. It's certainly lucky that he got whatever injury he did, because things were heating up in a little peninsula country half-way across the world. And in any case, Tom Jones and frigging Elvis were still hitting number one, one after the other after the other, like a nightmare that you can't wake up from.

"You got a bit of an accent," I said. "Where you from again?"

"Maine." Shawn smiled. He put a finger to his lips. "We mum's the word on that, though."

I made a face. "What do you mean, mum's the word?"

Shawn held a sly grin, as though he had just divulged ascription to communism in the year that McCarthy sicced his army upon it. "I'm an American. And actually, I'm not supposed to be here."

I looked around. "Where you supposed to be?"

"In the bush," he said. "In the green."

I furrowed my brow. "You mean to say—I mean, you're *not* saying—" I broke off. Suddenly it occurred to me that perhaps Shawn the magician had pulled a little disappearing act. Perhaps not even a *little* one. "Are you in the service?" I offered.

"Not exactly."

"But you got called up to go to Vietnam," I tried again.

"Yeah." He smiled.

"Did you just leave?" I exploded. "You got called to go, and you just *left*?" The idea presented itself as so incredible that when it flew out of my mouth it almost sounded silly. "Holy shit, Shawn! I bet that's against the law!" My mind shot out a mean and traitorous sidelong thought at this: *Four times?* it said, in the same wary tone that Damon had used in repeating James's conviction record: *Five, actually.*

"No," Shawn said to me. "It's not against the law, Tevan,

no. There's no draft in Canada, which means here there's no law against fudging it."

"Geez," I said. "I didn't know you could get drafted that quick."

"Of course you didn't." Shawn looked me over before giving into his smile again. "You're Canadian. You're also a white guy."

I was going to get defensive. Then I remembered the broom. So I didn't.

"I'm actually not part of the service. Halfway, maybe," Shawn said. "Which means I had my physical, but I took off before my attestation. Sittin' there before my pre-induction physical, though?" He cast me a wry look. "I never seen so many black guys in the man's office before."

I struggled to say the right thing. "So you decided not to do it?" I put in.

"No." Shawn waved a hand. "No, no. I did it. Me and all them guys. Guys saying 'Hot diggity dog, this'll be the first time I ever got boots that didn't have holes in 'em' or 'I never flown in any air-o-plane before, fightin' in Nam'll be my first time.'" He laughed. "It was after *that* that I left." He turned his head and studied me. "Your daddy a professional, Tevan?"

"I don't have a dad," I said. "He died when I was little. I just got my mom."

"I see, then." Shawn folded his hands behind his head, lay back, and looked upward. "Then you're lucky to be Canadian too. One-A status, my man. No student deferment? Working on a line someplace, probably? You, Tevan George, would've been the first to go to the front, just like little ole me."

Some moments passed. Nobody said anything. I caught myself starting to think of Kenny again. The Chevrolet Nomad bought on the premise of appearance. The job Kenny picked up in place of college because, after all, college don't pay you to go. Kenny and his lung resection because he wasn't going to spend months lying around while Ma and Tevan went on welfare.

"What's going to happen?" I asked. "Won't anybody . . . you know, come after you or anything?"

"You mean is the FBI gonna hunt me down?" Shawn shrugged. "Dunno. I don't think I'm technically AWOL. I'm not gonna try to cross the border anytime soon, though, if that's whatcha mean." He turned his head in the grass. "I came here, just me. My mother gave me a hundred and twenty dollars before I lit out." He offered me a wry, disenchanted look. "That's what she gave me—a hundred and twenty dollars. No health insurance, near to no dough, no job, and no social insurance number." His shoulders lifted up and down. "Some things not so different than home. But the social insurance number, man. That I could really use. It's tough finding work without one, see—"

I opened my mouth and Shawn continued, and we spoke the same words in the exact same moment:

"Merit never asked me for my social insurance number."

An instant later, we were staring at each other. "Yeah," I said.

"Yeah," Shawn repeated. His eyes drifted over to James, then back to me with interest. For while I doubt that Buddy Merit was the only man in the country to pay his employees under the table, fellows like Shawn and me were of the select few who appreciated that wayward sort of policy. A long silence ran out between us.

"Ah, me and James disappeared on the Ministry of Health," I began finally. I waited, but Shawn didn't reply. "We were supposed to go to this—ah—tuberculosis reassessment and we never turned up. I don't know what that means or anything," I went on. "I mean, I don't know if anyone *cares*. But TB is monitored. We had to get reassessed. Public Health has to keep this record of you, it's the rules and all of that." During my intake at Mount Rosa's, I filled up a form recording my addresses, memberships in any clubs, and aliases. *Aliases?* I recall thinking. I was fourteen years old; it seemed laughable at the time. But in the medical field this process is called tracking, and by the time I left Mount

Rosa's I didn't see it as laughable. I didn't want Mount Rosa's to track me. I didn't want them to call me. It began to weigh on my mind as the single worst measure of TB compliance I'd ever participated in. Once me and James cut out on the reassessment clinic, I'd covered my tracks—*our* tracks—ever since.

"So they lost track of us. It's why neither of us use our social insurance, or see a doctor now," I said to Shawn, and witnessed the sharp climb of his eyebrows upon his forehead.

"You saying you got TB?" he asked suspiciously.

"No!" I was indignant. "Jesus, not anymore! I'm clean. So's James. I'm *saying* that we punked out on a medical test, that's all. A 'reassessment.' And because of that, there's probably people wondering where we went."

Shawn weighed this information carefully. His response was tentative. "Does *anyone* know where you are?"

"Yes," I said, and thought, *My mother.* But then I realized that she didn't. "Well—I don't know," I amended. There *was* no address at times and I never wanted to admit this to her. Even when there had been, I hadn't given it. *There's no phone here, Ma,* I'd told her more than once from some seedy phone booth, often adjacent to some even seedier rooming house. *Listen, I'll call you. Don't worry, I'll call.*

"Oh." Shawn pursed his lips. "So," he began a moment later, "does it hurt?"

"What?" I said, bewildered. "Oh no, not really. Having TB's a little like having the flu. Only for a really long time, and—"

"No," Shawn interrupted. "The test. This—whatever you guys gotta do. This *sessment*, you called it. Is it, you know, like shock therapy or something?"

I stared at him a moment. Then I erupted in laughter. "No," I said, not getting him at all. "What in hell do you mean?"

Shawn frowned. "Well, if you're okay," he began, "I guess I'm wondering why don't you just go back and get the test done."

The words were polite, spoken with the apprehension of the sincerely diplomatic. But in my head I practically exploded.

Because I'm never fucking going back there! I nearly shrieked aloud. *Do you hear? Never!* But I didn't. I looked down at the grass, steeling myself. "I don't have to, Shawn," I managed. "James and me neither. *That's* why."

Shawn smiled. "Listen, man. I got to tell you, Tevan. I'm not too sure some days if I made a mistake or what. Because if I could go back to the States, clean like you and James, I would. I ain't no conscientious objector or—whatever they all calling it these days. 'Less you consider being poor and without obligation at the same time a particularly conscientious idea. Which I don't figger my good friend LBJ does. I don't have the option." He fluttered a hand through the air. "If I were you, I'd just go, easy-breezy, and take my test. Get it over and done with."

I looked over at James and saw him looking back at me. *You never have to go back there, James,* I'd told him countless times. While he talked nonsense on the floor, yelling that Bern was after him in his sleep, and while he was awake and crumpled in tears like a kid in the corner. I'd told it to him while he was remembering. *You never have to go back there, James, hear me? Never. I promise you. And I promise you this too, it's not true whatever they told you. Your memory's fine, James. You remember it the same as me.* I suddenly felt the wild, misplaced urge to protect him like I have all those times guys have called him stupid and retarded and full of shit. "We're fine," I said to Shawn. "It's fine this way."

"As it is?" Shawn said. "Then tell me why you're not using your social insurance number." He looked at me, expressionless. But he knew too much to argue with me further. He knew what it was like: true threat or not, when a fellow believes that life itself is on the line, he doesn't take his chances. Finally, Shawn gave a small, commiserating laugh. "Hey, if you don't want your social insurance, give it to me," he said. "Boy, I could use a steady job. I ain't got plans to be a magician the rest of my life."

"Magician," a voice piped up. Stretched out in the grass, James looked like he was suntanning, on vacation. "You're going to teach us how to do magic," he said.

Shawn nodded, wiggled his fingertips in the air. "That's right, friend. More specifically, James, I'm going to teach *you*."

"What about me?" I asked.

Shawn rolled his eyes. "As I understand it, you're the one passed out for most of this. That right? If that's the case, then you ain't gonna do magic *nothing*."

"Magic nothing," James repeated, sitting up. "Tevan goes out, that's right. I'm the one who has to bring him back."

"That's right," Shawn agreed.

"Yeah, Tevan goes out when I drop him." James nodded. "He doesn't have to go back to the san. He got it the worst."

In all my years I never denied the connection between what me and James knew in the dark and what we had known at Mount Rosa's. As for James, some days I believed he scarcely understood the link at all. And some days, like this one, I believed he knew it all. I sat bolt upright.

"James," I said at once. "Watch your mouth, James."

James looked at me and waited. I turned to Shawn.

"Okay," I began, and then I paused.

I thought of what I'd told Buddy Merit the day we'd met him (*Lots of practice, I guess*) and I thought about denying the connection. I thought about incentives and restraint and performing. I thought about how we didn't have to go back there, and I glanced at James. This is the story I told to Shawn, but bear in mind:

I didn't tell him all of it.

I didn't tell him where the idea came from

(You wet the bed once, Tev. Remember?)

and I didn't tell him about the expression on James's face when he takes his part. I certainly didn't tell him about *my* part, the part that's like a rope towing an anchor line from a harbor, or a million synapses firing below the belt all at once—God no, certainly not that. I explained to him how we do this trick, but I could not explain why.

I told it to Shawn not two minutes after I'd said that James and I were never going back there again, and knowing full well, somewhere inside my bitter, nattering brain, that we return to that damn place every single time James's hands land upon my throat.

Who the hell did I think I was?

"Okay," I began. "This is how it's done."

8

I REMEMBER ME AND JAMES WERE BOTH A LITTLE SOUSED ON the night we first tried our trick.

It was late as hell, and I could see that James was about to fall over sideways. I told him to go on and lie down, but I didn't have the intention of doing so myself right away. My stomach has a tendency of awakening with a vengeance if I get horizontal when I've been drinking. Also, I was still pissing every bloody ten minutes. I hear that's good for your urinary tract. Then again, I hear alcohol isn't. I'm never certain which of those I'm supposed to believe. In that year—1961, the year James moved into my apartment alongside me—I thought about that a lot. Which is to say, during the first year me and James lived together, we drank a whole lot.

James rolled onto the king-sized mattress and looked up at the ceiling. "Did Jonathan make fun of you at Mount Rosa's?" he asked.

"Me?" I shrugged, slipping out of my T-shirt. "Naw. His brother, maybe. The one with the chutzpah, old—ah—what's-his-name? But Jon, he was a rubber chicken. Sincerely."

James nodded. "Peter," he supplied, reminding me (*Veronica,* I translated on the side). "His brother. The both of them used to say mean stuff about me. But Jonathan was the *worst.*"

It often seemed that James was obsessed with worsts. In all fairness, though, he had every right to rank such experiences. James had been slow to the starter's pistol, intellectually, from the day he was born. And so, he had a lot of experiences to rank. James had guys making fun of him his entire life.

"If it makes you feel better," I told him, "I made fun of both Betty and Veronica." It made *me* feel better to call them by their deprecating, Bern-attributed names; that much was true. "Man, I hated how those two used to team up on everybody."

"Hmmmmm," James said. I saw a smile playing at his lips and gathered that *had* wrought a little redemption. So I continued.

"So did Bern. Did you know that, James? Bern razzed Betty more than anybody else." I thought to myself, *At least the guy was good for something.*

"Yeah?" James asked.

"Yeah."

I stopped there, waiting to see if James was prepared to go there. "What'd Bern say?" he asked. And so I knew he was.

"Jon was a liar," I told him. "You remember how he fibbed about his grades, how good he was doing in class? Bern got in on that. 'Watch it, Betty,' he used to say to Jon—" I stuck a finger out at James, swooped my hair back, and feigned a look of utter malice. "'You better hand over Alfred E. Neuman before Pete and I tell your mother the truth about that math test last week.'"

Oh yes, Bern knew right where to burn you. I laughed, a big one, at the thought of it, *Ha ha ha ha ha*, like Jonathan the Lying Sack of Shit was the funniest thing in the goddamn world. Or like pretending to be Bern was the funniest thing. But James laughed too. You know how funny things get when you're in the bag.

"Usually his brother stuck up for him," James said. He turned his head, looking very serious. "They fought him off by being together. That's how he was able to keep Bern from"—a pause as he deliberated over the correct wording, made a face, then simply gave up—"like, you know."

"I know," I said, the smile still on my face, insanely, although it wasn't funny at all.

"Bern was after me," James said, as he had a million times before and would a million times after. "I don't know why."

"I know," I said again. "You told me."

James nodded, his chin bobbing against his chest. "They fought him off and I started getting out of bed at night. That's what happened."

"I have to pee," I said. I went into the john, a dingy corner space in our basement apartment with an overhanging light bulb on a chain, unzipped my trousers, and urinated *again*, long and hard. When I came back into the room I found James upon the mattress, his hands folded. I sat down gingerly, then decided to give my stomach the benefit of the doubt, and lay down beside him.

"Tev?" he said.

"Huh, James."

James turned his head and frowned. "What did *you* do, Tevan?"

I looked back at him. I was loaded with three pitchers of brew, my head was spinning, and the time was well past midnight. *What are you talking about?* I could have said. But James had just offered up a concise recap: *They fought him off and I started getting out of bed at night*, he had said. I knew exactly what James was talking about. And so I considered my own moment within this story: *Okay*, I'd said to Bern when he had asked for me. *Okay*, I had said, which sounds like an agreement—though my voice had sounded rusty and my breath shuddery, like it does before you begin to cry. In the moment here with James now, I considered and reconsidered: I could tell James what I'd said to Bern, yes. But he was asking what I had *done*—and this, too, I knew, was much different.

I thought then, randomly, of Catharine, the young woman I'd spent my time with in college. Calm, strong Catharine with her sangria. Her pinup of Dylan and a print of multicolored, curvy figures, swimming with their hands upraised, tacked to her wall. "Women," she told me once of these. "It symbolizes a universal sisterhood."

I recalled lying in her little dormitory bed beneath these, morning after morning, pleading with her, *Please, Cath*, whenever she made to leave for class. Undoing my belt and putting her hand under my shirt, as though I were offering up a trade: *Please stay, Cath. Look, I'll do anything—*

Just the memory of this made a knot rise in my throat.

"I complied, James," I said finally.

James grinned a stupid drunk's grin. "What's 'complied'?"

"It means," I began, "well, I *guess* it means I just did what he said." I made a face, placed my arms over my head against the mattress. "It means I knew what he wanted and I did what he said. Because I had the impression that those were the rules."

James turned on his side. His lips were pursed. "Were you scared, Tev?"

Scared? Confused, maybe. Horrified. Embarrassed, the unrelenting pride of a teenager, yes, but back then I had thought—

"Look, I'm not scared of anything," I said. "You know that." But all of a sudden I wasn't certain I believed myself. James didn't look so certain either.

"Then how did you get—that impression?" he asked. "The impression about the rules?"

I looked back at James. A second time, I wasn't sure how to respond. And my voice had taken on a thick quality, that old rusty one, the one that was like a fourteen-year-old far from home. "I did what he said, James." I shook my head, tried again. "Then I just sort of floated away."

James frowned. "Floated?" he said. "You mean like on an airplane?"

Was that the word for what I did? Was there a word for what Bern did? If James had asked me the same question five years later, after we joined Merit's troupe and after we'd run through our trick—after I'd seen the way people's eyes swelled and their jaws dropped open and they covered their mouths with their hands when they saw what we did to each other within it—I think I would have known it without pause. Maybe I would even have said it aloud:

Assault, James, I would have said. *And it has nothing to do with airplanes.*

And so I cleared my throat and tried again.

◆ ◆ ◆

Now I've already explained how the layout was at Mount Rosa's. It was a hospital, an institution, and so we slept, eight to a room, in a large ward. Nobody had his own lavatory, either. There were just two washrooms that we boys used: one adjacent to the bedroom itself, and another located within the shower room down the hall.

I suppose we could've used another privy if we'd really put our minds to it. I imagine there was another *further* down the hall, and then plenty more beyond this. But the truth is, the thought of seeking them out never crossed anybody's mind. Part of chasing the cure was adhering to a specific, strategic lifestyle: we held to a routine that you could literally set your watch by. We slept and studied and ate our meals like preset machines. Even the music we heard through our bedside headphones (*like a nightmare that you can't wake up from!*) was assigned by the staff. We were busy complying. And so that is how it was: David only had occupational therapy on Tuesday, the new crosswords only came on the first of the month, and you only used the shitter on your own damn ward.

Come summertime at Mount Rosa's, the prestige of me and Bern's two-man faction—the one that I had loved, had even felt privileged to be a party to in previous months—became a curse. The most cursed places were in your bed after lights-out, and the aforementioned washrooms. The former, your bed, proved the most problematic of all and was entirely unavoidable.

But the latter, one could strategize around. And so when it came to avoiding Bern during the day, I was successful: I simply stopped going to the washroom.

By October I was holding it so long that whenever I did relieve myself it felt as though I had turned into a sort of human welding torch. Whatever was in there was searing hot and felt twice as agonizing on the way out. It was like pissing fire. I didn't tell anybody, of course. For starters, I didn't have anyone to tell. I didn't have any friends other than Bern; I didn't have any visitors, what with my mother keeping her nose to the grindstone all by her lonesome at home. And last, I didn't know what the problem was. Yes, I figured my dick had some kind of sickness, but this certainly was not the type of thing that you went around conversing about. Dick-situated sickness, I weighed at the time, might very well have something in common with going blind, getting pimples, or losing your marbles—you know, all those horrors that Catholics warn their children about regarding touching yourself, reading skin mags, and what you could expect if you dared fist your way down that sordid path. Which is to say, I suppose, that by then I knew that I was involved in something sexual. And I knew, by then, that I was involved in something iniquitous.

The obvious never occurred to me: When you're purposely avoiding urinating, your urine is apt to find itself some ulterior purposes. And so while my mind was absorbed with evading the washroom at all costs, my body got busy cultivating the worst bladder infection it would ever know.

In the dark and after midnight, the hour of night when—as mothers and fathers warned their children—monsters had free range of the earth, I would writhe in my sheets, as if infested with sandflies.

Come on, Pretty, Bern would say across to me. *Come and meet me.*

Oh go on, I'd tell myself, with some vague mixture of irritation and weariness, *it's not like it hurts.* But even this was a lie, even this an inculcated persuasion, because by then sometimes it *did* hurt. By then I knew that Bern could give it to me here or there; and better there in privacy than here before my schoolmates, my fellow inmates, my *room*mates—before, that is, God and everyone. And so, aided by my growing talent for cheap rationalization, I complied.

My pelvis ached like a ton of concrete. My back was sore up and around my hips.

"Man, I'm not feeling so hot, Bern," I said; although on the contrary, I was feeling hot as hell. Perspiring, burning, even. "Please, Bern," I said genuinely. "I can't do this."

Bern didn't say anything in reply. By then he didn't have to say much at all.

James shifted in the bed. "Tell me," he said.

Me and James, living in that apartment during that first year reunited, we were like soldiers after years of combat and a purportedly normal peaceful life afterward, meeting up at the summer Veterans' Third Battalion Annual Picnic. We saw it in each other, what we'd seen in some ditch somewhere.

"Tell me how he told you about the rules, Tev."

I always tell James the truth. Lying on my back, my face aimed at the ceiling. Breathing, just breathing; I said nothing for a moment or two. Then I reached my hands out into the dark and found his folded upon his chest.

I took them up in my own. We both watched—my hands upon his, and floating in the air. Then I turned them, palms down, and guided them like a mother would to an infant, placing them strategically, encouraging, to demonstrate the softness of a cat's fur or the smoothness of a pacifier.

I took his fingers. I placed them on my neck.

"Like this, James," I said into the dark. "Like this."

Bern held my neck and I held my breath and when the end finally came, this time, drained and feverish and flush out of good manners, I choked. I gagged into the dim echo chamber of a room, and he moved quickly to close me up with one hand. He slapped me with the other.

"*Shut up.* Okay? You've got to shut up."

It happened so fast that my head nearly spun. His hand landed on my skin, and I took in one sharp, countering breath. A thousand associations came with that breath. Things I'd read about in seamy, stirring magazines, for instance. Things I'd thought about while peering at the drawings in *The Phantom Lady*. And then the other side of it. Things that were sickening and tedious. Things I didn't *like* to think about, no matter how stirring. Breathing in, I experienced a bizarre moment of seeming to know everything in the world and yet being totally confused.

This time I did start crying. My eyes and face muscles caved in as I struggled not to make a sound. As James would have put it, the *Shut up* was the worst part. It banged inside my head, sinister, dangerously double-crossing. Once I got started crying, it seemed I couldn't stop. I stared at my knees and I fell to pieces. And then, impossibly, insanely, I offered:

"I'm sorry." Then in my own defense: "I *told* you I didn't want to."

Bern's eyes shifted. "Excuse me?" he said, though he did not wait for me to answer. "If I recall, Pretty, you said you *couldn't*— but then you went ahead and did it anyway, didn't you?" He pressed at my neck, the tendons standing out like damp veins in a leaf after a rain. "So don't tell me now that you didn't want to."

I stared back at him, dismayed by the truth of this, stunned by its moot technicality, saying nothing.

"I think, Pretty, you'd better just shut up now."

So I did. I could feel his fingerprints soldering into my chin. His fingers were shaking against me. I wasn't afraid, necessarily, that if I spoke another word he might contract them and kill me. I was never scared of that back then. Instead, the impact of those fingers was more psychologically comparable to having hand-cuffs clapped to your wrists or a rope cinched about your ankles.

In the silence something came into my head. *He's right, you know,* a traitorous little voice said. *You did say you didn't want to. But then you did it. No wonder he's mad at you. You're not making any sense.*

Sobbing. Reaching to breathe. In the moment I was nearly driven mad with the incongruities between the way a body could both feel and not be felt. The way a body could be forced to perform, yet still be forbidden to act. And so I only continued to cry—sobbing, heaving, a blubbering pile of shit. If James were ever to ask *(What's an ungrateful bastard, Tev? What's "com- plied"?)* what the word "hysterical" meant, I would draw on this moment and derive for him a concise, flawless definition. When I lost my job in the spring of 1966, just before me and James came upon the sideshow, I sat in my car and wept in panic-stricken, soundless desperation. Yet when I went to Catharine's bed during my stint at college, the response from within me was often so vociferous that the girl rooming next door to her would bang on the wall and yell for us to shut up.

There are only two modes of expression now. And that's either silent as death, or begging for my life.

I cried hysterically, I cried gutted. And then Bern's hand was upon me again. Touching down at my neck. Yet instead of resting where the flesh still beat a wild pulse at the front, it came to rest at the back.

"Hey," he whispered. "Come on. Come on, quiet now. It's okay. Is it really that bad? It's okay," he said again. "Come on, come, Pretty." Bern got to his feet, tucked in his shirt. I watched and did the same—mechanically, and rather like a cowed, brainless machine. "Come on."

He brought me over to the sink basin and stepped on the pedal below it. Water sprung outward *(Wash hands often!)* and onto his hands. His fingers left the nape of my neck to catch the spray. "Wash up," he instructed. "Come on, me too." He splashed the stream demonstratively against his face before doing the same to mine. He did this repeatedly, watching my expression, waiting for the heaving and hiccuping to subside. Our hair snared in the stream. Our chins, dripping, wet through.

"How's that, huh? How's that?"

Breathing slow and jagged. Bern's hand on my shoulder, his blond hair dripping, the water in rivers upon his features.

And then something really terrible happened.

Watching his calm, concerned expression, I was suddenly beset with the wild urge to kiss him. At fourteen and with nary a history of physical intimacy, the drive felt at once foreign yet organically instinctive. I don't know what I was thinking. Perhaps I believed Bern was apologizing; perhaps, incredibly, it seemed to me that he was my friend. And in the moment—the one post-horror, pre-composure, yet currently weirdly mid-benevolence—I got it all mixed up in my head. I was reciprocating the only way I knew how.

I interchanged my feelings

(Please stay, Cath. Look, I'll do anything)

with fucking.

For the first time in my life, I thought they were the same thing.

"Hey," he said, pulling back. "What in hell do you think you're doing?" He stared at me, a cross between bewildered and alarmed. I often think back upon this expression on his face. Pondering it conjures up an odd sense of smugness in me. The truth is, I can't help but wonder if Bern might have known for just one honest moment to what extent he ruined me. Though I don't know if that really makes me feel so smug in the end.

After all, I'm the one that's stuck with it. Aren't I?

He wiped my face dry and combed my hair off my forehead. Then he took me by the arm and led me from the room.

Now, typically Bern and I left that washroom in a discreet fashion. You weren't supposed to be out of your bed after lights-out. We'd worked out a one-at-a-time routine that had saved us from any earlier speculation. Years later, Catharine and I implemented a similar routine at her dormitory. And years after that, Damon Merit did too, at a highway diner just south of Midland. "Now I'm going out to the parking lot to start the truck," he said under his breath when the bill arrived. "One by one, you guys all start heading for the bathroom." We went along with the plan (although I'd been pretty worried, I admit; with his record, James didn't look too reputable in the cop's books). By some grace of God, we never got caught. Neither, come to think of it, did me and Cath. Neither, in the end, did Bern.

He led me out of the washroom with no furtiveness at all. We walked out into the hallway, looking neither left nor right, and headed straight for the nurses' station.

"Hi," he said to the lady behind the desk. Real friendly-like, that was Bern—eyes shining, teeth flashing. He nodded at me. "Tevan's not looking so good." This marks the first time—the *only* time in person—that Bern called me by my real name. In 1959, following my discharge from Mount Rosa's, he wrote long letters to my home in Hamilton: *Dear Tevan*, he began each time in his slanted script, then went on to write about the ordinary life back in the san. He complained about the food and the incessant schedule. He apologized for bossing me around more than he ought to have when I was there. He hoped I wasn't angry with him.

I don't recall writing back. I read them, every one. I hardly thought a thing about them. In fact, I saved them for years, like you would the tokens of a pen pal from summer camp. The only thing I ever balked at on them was my name. I wished he had never used it. Until he put it on paper, just as when he said it aloud to the nurse, I might have had the luxury to believe it wasn't really me in there all along.

The woman came out from behind the desk in a hurry. "What's the matter, sweetheart?" she asked, putting a hand to my cheek. "My, you *are* warm." Warm was an understatement. By the next morning the bladder infection would reach my kidneys and I'd have a temperature registering an impressive one hundred and six. "What do you feel like?"

I looked at Bern and he looked at me. A weird, expectant silence ran between us. I don't know what the fuck I was waiting for. No, actually I do. I was waiting for him to answer her, to speak on my behalf. The truth is I had no sense of how I felt. I'd just had a lesson specifying that either end of the spectrum—doing and not doing, saying and not saying—were simply not allowed. The result was feeling as though someone had come along and yanked the plug connecting my body to my brain.

"It burns when I pee," I said.

The nurse sent Bern to bed. Then she turned me around and marched me right back into the shower room. She stood me in the stall where, not ten minutes before, I had sat on the tiled lip and crumpled into a blubbering mess. She turned on the faucet and ran cold water over me. I bawled all over again, of course. She apologized, telling me it was necessary to reduce the fever, that the reason I felt so cold was actually because I was burning right up. I wasn't crying because I felt cold, though. There was nothing cold about it. I'd never felt so gutted in my life.

She installed a pitcher of water at my bedside and gave me instructions to drain it before sun-up, then took my temperature and recorded it on a chart. The next morning another nurse would stand me on a scale and note to everybody's serious dismay that I had lost weight. Losing weight in the san was the mark of an invalid. On the adult ward, guys used to stuff their pockets with oranges, drink buckets of water, layer on extra clothes— anything to keep from going down on the scale. Any decrease was an indicator of something noncompliant going down in the old anatomy. Worse than anything, losing weight meant gaining more time in the san.

If anyone had warned me that little germs could crawl up to construct a furry, heat-seeking nest inside your guts, I wouldn't have believed them. At fourteen I hadn't the faintest idea that urine had the capacity to make your furnace turn on full blast and that your penis could make your back ache like sauna rocks were sewn inside. Shit, I always thought it was the other way around. Years later I learned that streptomycin, one of the various ingredients in the TB-fighting cocktail of the 1950s, is expelled through urine. I probably had bigger problems than a bladder infection that night in the san. If inadequately voided, streptomycin can build to toxic levels inside the body.

In trying to get free of the place, I could have killed myself.

I fell into my bed, and by then I did feel cold. It was a brutal, bone-deep chill. *It's getting worse*, I contemplated saying to the nurse, but didn't. I didn't say anything. I was scared that she might read that particular statement for more than I meant it for. And Bern, he was thinking the same thing.

When the nurse departed, he tiptoed the distance between our beds and sat down on the edge of my mattress. He looked me over, my wet hair especially, with something that at the time I deemed as altruistic concern, but now understand as more of a self-interested kind of worry. In all my life, I'll never forget what he asked me.

"Pretty," he said. "You didn't tell her, did you?"

The object of the ruse, Shawn would advise me years later, *is that seeing is believing. Now you boys want to decide what it is you're going to show.* It occurred to me that, in this circumstance, the wrong answer was coincidentally the right one.

"Tell her what?" I said.

"Nothing," he said. "Nothing, Pretty." The reward for my obedience was quick: he put a hand to my shoulder and smiled. Today I can't stop myself from speculating that this benevolence was just as damaging as the rest of it. For in this moment, it was as though my short-term memory was wiped entirely clean.

"Do you want me to stay here?" he asked.

Fear of him became squelched inside me, crushed beneath the hope that things were okay between us. It became squashed like a paperback under too many stacked hardcovers—an important paperback, the one you'll need in order to write that thesis in the end, perhaps the most profound research of them all, under other palpable weights.

And I let it be squashed.

I told myself that if I was careful not to piss him off anymore, everything would be okay.

"Yes," I said. "Stay."

"Why did he do that, Tev?"

James's hands were still in position, splayed but neutral upon my neck, as he asked me the question he'd by now asked a thousand times, and would come to ask a thousand times again. He studied them as one would a sudden, interesting find. "But why?"

"I don't know." I put my fingers on James's and pressed them inward. My throat tightened beneath them and a pleasant, quiet breeze of excitement fluttered inside me. It was a combination of fear and enthusiasm, the kind of shiver of doom you might get as the roller coaster reaches the top of the hill and you sit, quaking, in the front car. It took me by surprise and so I laughed—still loaded with the alcohol (though not so much as before) and still wondering the very same thing as James. "Why don't you tell me," I said.

So James contracted his fingers a second time, this time on his own. He peered down at me as he did so—whether because he's smart or because he's dumb, I'm not sure—as though watching for something.

Press and release. Press and release. The eye contact between us, like the hypnotic swirl inside a crystal ball.

At first it was as though we were having a competition, a game of chicken. Perhaps I was waiting for James to be impressed with my resiliency. Press and release, press and release. But the more I waited, the more I knew it wasn't like a game of chicken at all. It wasn't *scary*, for starters. And it didn't hurt the way a game of bloody knuckles does, for instance, when you're waiting for your partner to cave and scream Uncle. Worse than any of these, the more I looked at James, the more I became convinced that what we were doing felt kind of exciting.

My brother shoplifted an entire grocery list out of a convenience store once when I was twelve, right before my disbelieving eyes. He was talking the whole time he did it. Talking about the weather, talking about hockey. Talking and talking, *blah de blah blah*, until it occurred to me that if I had a dollar for every word that left his lips I could've *bought* the whole store out of my own pocket. I understood what was going on, too. The words were the only barricade between me, him, and what he was doing.

So to James I said, "Uck. You smell like beer."

And James said, "So hold your breath."

"What do you think I'm *doing*?" I asked him, laughing.

Was this what I looked like when Bern was choking me? I wondered. Press. Wait. Release. The release beginning to come only after a brief delay now. On the heels of this, I wondered how long I could go at a stretch. I held my breath and giggled. I couldn't contain myself. Ha ha ha.

"What's it feel like?" I whispered.

"Like I could kill you," James said. "If I wanted."

I nodded, my brow folded. My breath stalled between my chest and my throat; again I got the riotous, uncontrollable urge to laugh out loud, and again I wasn't sure why.

Today I know that as a person's air supply declines, he becomes affected by a condition called hypoxia. Hypoxia is problematic for professional skydivers and high-elevation pilots: it means your organs aren't getting enough oxygen. Military pilots are trained to identify the biological symptoms of hypoxia as a life-saving preventive. I've heard they participate in simulator exercises as green cadets, affixing gas masks to their faces and allowing their oxygen intake to dwindle to nothing, as they're made to answer drill questions and draw pictures. The object of the exercise is simple—to learn. For in real, biology-based time, the signs of hypoxia are not easily identifiable once they're taking place.

James looked sharply to my eyes. "What's it feel like to you?"

Like I could die. But I didn't say that. I didn't say anything. I only stared, grinning, blinking, and feeling weirdly awestruck. In real, biology-based experience, the signs of hypoxia make a person feel like he's going to heaven.

My eyelids began to flutter. A second later I opened them to see James looking down suspiciously. I opened my mouth and the rush of air came with relief. And the feeling of hilarious, wild pleasure departed with dismaying speed.

"Hey," I said. But what I was thinking was *Hey, come on* with an impatience that was as perverse as it was compulsive. Someday soon I would say these words to James aloud.

Shoplifting. Stuff nabbed and shoved under a sweatshirt. Hidden away. Cloak and dagger. Yeah, like that. Secret. Shut up, you. *Shut up.*

"You still drunk?" I whispered.

James shook his head. Slow, deliberate, considering. His eyes were beginning to widen as though he were beginning to understand something either truly forbidden or exhilarating. "Nup," he said. Or maybe even both. Shining, intoxicated—though not with the booze, I don't think. Whatever it was, was his alone. James sat squeezing, staring; a man with a butterfly net, scoping the landscape with his eyes. For a stupid guy, sometimes he ain't so stupid.

I coughed.

"Tevan?" he said, as though snapping out of a trance. "Does this hurt?"

I shook my head, straining to keep my eyes open. It was like driving your car through the night after twenty cups of coffee and little sleep, at the point where the road signs and little yellow lines begin to appear less and less significant, even though you know that the Ministry of Transportation doesn't shift its rules after the stroke of midnight. I'd done it a hundred times, staring into the taillights of the trucks on the highway. *Don't fall asleep, Tev,* a voice whispered to me during such times (most often while James slept, oblivious, beside me). It was a voice that sounded like Kenny's darkness-has-fallen, perpetually twenty-year-old voice. *Keep your fuckin' eyes open, man.* A voice from the dead, steering me through a fog of otherwise driving biological release. *But,* I thought each time my bottom eyelid bounced off the top, lending me a stolen, dangerous instant of darkness, *but it feels so good . . .*

"Had enough, Tev?" James said. "Tell me when you've had enough. I'll stop whenever you say. Tev. Hey. Does it hurt?" He shook me, his wrists bouncing against my collarbone. As the air in my chest rebounded and found no place to go, my chest bounced, the way a hiccup bounces around inside you when you hold your breath.

"Mmmmm," as I managed to shake my head no.

In the 1980s, a sudden influx of new-age weirdos would claim to have experienced "near-death" or "out-of-body" experiences. They said they'd "seen the light" or "crossed the threshold to another place" during anesthesia mishaps, car accidents, or childbirth. Those people wrote narrative accounts of their encounters, describing a world beyond God's proverbial green earth. Within the decade, researchers would compare notes with those working with the military cadets I previously mentioned, the ones drawing pictures and undergoing the third degree under the influence of oxygen-deprivation training. What they would find is that the Age of Me transcendants were full of shit. They hadn't undergone any religious or out-of-body experience at all. Over half of all military volunteers reported that, within their hypoxia training sessions, they too mistakenly believed that they had actually physically entered another universe.

By the year 1961, on the night that James first held me down by my neck, I had already experimented with alcohol. I had already experienced weed and, thanks to my dentist, nitrous oxide. I'd had my turn with drugs and booze, had even had a lengthy TB-fighting regimen of para-aminosalicylic acid, and streptomycin. But I'd never entered another universe on account of any of these.

My eyes gave in to the force of gravity. My limbs buzzed as though hundreds of tiny vibrating insects had come to roost. As campy as it may sound, the closest description I can find is to say I felt as though I'd been injected with peace, love, happiness, and all the other shit that the hippies and Catharines of the world profess. If I had been asked to die at that very moment, I would have done so willingly. And lo and behold, in a location still inside my current universe yet outside of simple hands and feet, another extremity began to awaken.

I picked one hand up from where it lay upon the mattress and I had to place it below my navel.

James's brow climbed his forehead, watching. At that

moment, James was a nineteen-year-old virgin. Still, the man has all the same plumbing as me. So let's not be coy here—for a stupid guy, sometimes he ain't so stupid. "Want me to stop?" he said, surprised.

When my hand touched down, I felt at once plugged in to some visceral, intimate part of me—and yet compelled to distance myself from it all in the same moment. I was hard, ready; unapologetically turned on. But in front of James, I closed my eyes and ignored his question, instead hoping to convey that he had imagined this, that me and my dick weren't in the same room. That, at the very least, if we were, we weren't doing anything of any significance.

"Tell me, Tev. Stop?" he said again.

Keep those eyes open, a bodyless voice spoke inside my head, and again the driveling reply: *But it feels so good.* And for the second time in my life, it occurred to me that, within these circumstances, the wrong answer was coincidentally the right one. *Stop what?* the part of me feigning innocence aimed to say, but my lungs were bursting and my teeth clenched. My cheeks felt like two burning red stoplights.

James shook me, his voice loud now. "If you don't say anything a minute more, I'm gonna stop!"

My eyes sprung open and I could not help but give way to a smile. He didn't have to say that, you see. He could've, for all intents and purposes, stopped whenever he chose; and yet he aimed the command my way. It was an empty, strategically calculated threat. In the sea of this bliss, James had appointed himself the honorary Coast Guard, but there were always signs that he was caught up in the waters himself.

"No," I managed. James's hands were damp with sweat against me, and by then I couldn't say exactly what my own were doing. Only that I could feel the slipping of my belt at my fingers, the relief of identifying the pocket of give between my hips and the fabric.

James turned his fingers in, watching my eyes and nothing

else. "You know I would never hurt you, Tev," he said low, into my face.

There are only two climaxes that I can remember today with utter clarity. The first is from a blowjob I received in an en suite bathroom during a party, in my eleventh grade of school. The bathroom was attached to the master bedroom of a little house, I recall, and some kid's parents were vacationing in New Brunswick, and some girl and I took the opportunity in the midst of the party. The second is from a time that Cath and I made out for so long with our clothes on that I just let go in my shorts.

In the present moment, there was no en suite bathroom, no clothed Catharine. There was nobody at all. In my mind, and working against my body—James, floating someplace above my shoulder, the ghost of a hand at my beltline, and my back against the mattress—there was nothing. There was nothing else.

Nothing, you see, but me.

This time I meant to, and it would have blown those two preceding memorables right out of the water.

But what happened next was that beneath James's fingers, I felt as though I were drifting off to sleep. James retracted into the distance. Then he disappeared completely.

The next thing I knew, I was on my side and opening my eyes to a shower of firing little lights.

And immediately I heard it—the vague background noise of a belt tine jingling against a loosened notch. The high was gone already, a phenomenon that never ceases to amaze me, not like a spliff that circles your brain and body for hours, and in that instant, released from the mellow-yellow ecstasy of James's stranglehold and God only knows how many moments of unconsciousness, I found myself back in life as I knew it. I heard the belt, jangling and free, and my first response was a shock of suspicion—

Who's there!—

and panic, before I understood that the noise had come from my own clothing. Behind me, his back against the wall, James stared. His eyes were wide and his hands clamped to his knees. There was an expression of dismay and horror upon his face. "Tevan," he managed. "Tevan, we are *never* doing that again."

I nodded, very seriously at first. Hurriedly hiking my belt closed, as though I had no idea what had just happened. And then I started laughing. I rolled up onto my back, clenching my knees to my chest, and I howled. I continued nodding, though, because he was right. Jesus, of course he was right! If I understood anything at all, it was that we should never do that again.

But we did.

Of course we did.

By the end of that week we'd done it twice more—once totally intoxicated and once, incredibly, stone cold sober. It was almost like how we had grown to talk about Mount Rosa's, Betty and Veronica and Bern. Except instead of it being the case that we just couldn't stop fucking talking about it, suddenly James and I just couldn't stop playing it out.

As Keith would put it, *Whuh happens when ya don't understand the lesson the firs' time?*

We didn't stop. There was so much to learn.

James holding long enough that I could lose my mind. Sometimes James constricting and releasing alternately, liberating his grip long enough to breathe into my mouth. His exhalations—guarded, calculated, delicious—becoming my brief, controlled inhalations. There was wariness upon his face too, the look of a child with his hand in the cookie jar

(Kenny's in the convenience store)

someone who's committing an offense and knows it. What offense, I wonder? Information; it was just information. Taking it in was James's right, his to have. I told him so.

"Just don't look," I whispered anytime my hand happened to make its way to that other nebulous dimension below my beltline.

"Okay," he'd agree. He never did, either.

If you're a freethinker or a pervert you might ask why. The

obvious reason is that he simply didn't care to. In this co-facilitation, I believe he understood just as well as I, James and me were not performing a two-man act. We were performing something solitary, private, even within the same cooperative moment. We may have lain in that bed together—but just as at Mount Rosa's, we learned our lessons apart.

James never looked, and I was never scared, and just as he promised, he never hurt me. *If your lungs stop working, somebody can start them up again for you.* When the time came and James realized he could not feel my breath anymore, he tilted my head back, pinched my nose, and breathed until he brought me back to consciousness.

"Just like I did that one time at Mount Rosa's," he said, as though this said it all. He waited a moment. "Don't you remember, Tevan?"

"Yes, James," I said. "I remember that too."

We kept going, and still, to this day, I have difficulty associating those nights with danger or alarm or fear. It never felt close to fear or marked with danger. Not even the time in the dark when I awoke with James at my mouth, vomit on my chest, and an acrid burning running the length of my throat, did I feel alarm. To tell the truth, you had to tempt yourself into wondering: Was there really any danger at all?

Five years we have done this (and this statistic I tell to Shawn Schroeder with some pride): five years, two hands, one breath, countless nights. And only one time where James panicked, breathing so hard down my throat that my stomach clenched, flooding my windpipe with vomit and an unknown expanse of time wherein I became without air at all.

Five years; one mishap.

When you think of it, North Americans have worse odds with condoms, with B-52s, with lung resection fucking surgery.

9

A LONG SILENCE SPREAD OUT BETWEEN SHAWN AND ME WHEN I finished. My mouth had run dry and yet the whole rest of me was sticky with sweat. Shawn lit up a cigarette and breathed the smoke out into the air.

"I don't know about odds," he said finally. "But I can shore see your problem." He shook his head and laughed. "Six times, Tevan? A *night*? Sweet odds or not—man, whichever way you slice it, the chances of things going all fubar increase with every stunt a night you pull. It's too raw. Even *I* know that."

I know, I agreed to myself, though I didn't say a thing out loud. We sat for a while, me not speaking, Shawn squinting into the sky as his cigarette smoke twirled lazily upward, and James watching both of us. After a moment Shawn's lips pursed.

"It's not simply an issue of trickery, Tev," he said. "What I'm seeing for starters is that even when it's real, nobody knows it." He looked at me. "What's the point in being bona fide—specially bona fide to the point of putting your *life* on the line—when the audience can't even tell?"

My brow folded. "How do you mean?"

"I mean," he said, "how do the gawkers know you're not breathing?"

"Because I'm not," I said at once. "I just *told* you the whole business on how it's done, Shawn. I just told you."

"You told *me*," he said. "You've convinced *me*." He held me in a long, weighty gaze. "But you haven't convinced *them* of anything."

I thought of Damon, arranging James and me strategically upon the stage the day before. *All I can see is your back!* he'd bitched. A swell of alarm rippled through me. For the first time I saw that Shawn was right: all the audience was going to see was me going down. The crux of the act—breath—was invisible. Whether or not I was breathing when I dropped was technically irrelevant.

"Well, what am I supposed to do?" I said. "Breathe smoke rings? Put a balloon over my mouth? There isn't really any way to—"

Shawn nodded. "I getcha," he agreed. "And it's exactly my point."

James's eyes slid between Shawn and me as he chewed his fingernails, the look on his face saying that only we could save him. I sat beside Shawn in the grass. All I could hear was my own breathing. *Hear* it. If only I could *see* it.

"I think I got an i-dee-ar," Shawn said after a minute. He rolled onto his belly to look at me. "Damon and his daddy want the marks to see the whole thing, right? And you say you lie there for at least a minute before James brings you back?"

I nodded feverishly.

"Well, there's your opportunity."

I looked at James carefully, then returned to Shawn. "No it isn't, Shawn. In fact I'm starting to think that that minute is going to be my biggest problem. If it weren't for the minute, the delay that's supposed to prove I'm dead"—I rolled my eyes—"I could probably *fake* it six times a night. I could, I don't know, maybe hold my breath. But I'm not so sure I can. That's a long time to hold it. And anyway, who cares?" My voice climbed as I found myself right back at the initial conundrum. "Nobody can see whether I'm breathing or not! *Shit,* I could be dead *for real* and the goddamn audience wouldn't even—"

Shawn put a hand out. It stopped inches from my face. His voice was a slow, cautious tone: "You don't have a lot of experience with this kind of show," he offered. "Do you?"

I dropped my chin into my hand. There was no use saving face now. "I guess it's that obvious."

"No. I only ask because the *solution* as I see it is obvious." Shawn slid the sleeve on his right arm up to reveal a row of shiny gold bracelets. "You prove and misdirect," he said. "Maybe you've seen my magic rings, for instance?" He nudged them off his wrist in one quick movement, arranged them on the grass, and then held them up. "There's five of them and they're made of gold. I'm going to link them all together. But they're solid. So how am I going to do it?"

"They're fake," I said immediately. "Gaffed. There's holes in them. A slit that you use to connect them, say."

"They're not *fake*," Shawn said, feigning indignation. "Why, go on and take a look at 'em, if you don't believe me."

Shawn passed me a ring. He passed James another. He passed me a third when I was satisfied with the first; and when I was satisfied with the third, I passed it along to James for good measure. We went on in this fashion, inspection first by me and then by James, until we had looked over all five.

"Holes?" Shawn asked, his eyebrows high on his forehead.

James and I exchanged a glance. "No," I said.

"No?" Shawn put his hands above his head. He bounced one hand against the other. Then he spread them apart to display five rings linked together. "Then how am I doing *this*?"

James and I stared up in silence. Finally James spoke. "Magic," he breathed.

Shawn grinned. "That's right." He lowered his hands to the grass and set the linked rings upon it. Sitting beside us and whistling to himself, he nonchalantly began to separate the rings. To James's and my dismay, Shawn suddenly had three intertwined, one single, and another single—this last one, indeed, with a slit in it.

James stared. His hand went out, mesmerized.

Shawn snatched the ring away. "Don't touch that!" He raised his eyebrows. "I paid twenty dollars for that one *alone*."

"I didn't see it before," James said, flustered.

"Of course you didn't," I told James. "It's the sixth. There's six rings. He told us there were only *five*."

"Yeah," Shawn agreed. "And you believed me." He reached behind his back and produced a single that I had no idea was hidden there. "Here's the fifth one now, actually."

James started giggling to himself. But me, I couldn't believe my eyes. I felt like an idiot.

"Aw, don't feel bad, Tev," Shawn said, spying my expression. "You didn't stand a chance. Prove and misdirect, man. What I do is prove to you that I'm legitimate through some of my equipment. I let you hold it. Turn it over in your hands, even pass it to your buddy. I swear to you it's real and then I let you judge for yourself. I got nothin' to hide. Then"—his grin grew wide, mischievous—"then I use that very equipment to pull a fast one on you."

"So you're saying," I put in, "you're saying that if we can use some item or other to prove that I'm *breathing*, then all we have to do to fake *not* breathing is—manipulate the item?"

Shawn nodded. "That's exactly what I'm saying. It's that easy."

"But what about the minute?" I asked. "You mean we're going to have to rely on, ah, equipment for a whole minute?"

"That *sucks*," James said. "We don't need equipment! We can really do it."

"I believe you," Shawn put in. "But not six times a day you can't."

I looked from James to Shawn. "I don't know, Shawn," I said warily. "I can't say I'm great at fooling people. And a minute's a long time to misdirect an entire audience—"

"Hey," Shawn cut in. He lit another cigarette and held a finger out at me. "Tev?" His lips spread into a grin. "They're not called *aw-dee-ence*. Here on the sideshow? We call them marks." Shawn retracted his right hand in the air. He squinted at his left, as though marking a bull's-eye visually, before letting an imaginary arrow fly. "A mark is an easy dollar, a sitting duck, ready to believe anything. No, I'm suggesting that your *equipment* manages to give you a little break somewhere in between."

I nodded, reached for Shawn's cigarette, listening. Shawn snatched it back before it even touched my lips.

"Hey," he said in admonition. He held the cigarette away

from me, managing a small *tsk-tsk* through his teeth. "I say, Tevan. I think we ought to consider how long a fellow like you really *can* hold his breath." And a moment later, Shawn Schroeder had it all laid out.

James could drop me like he always did, he said; then we would make sure to demonstrate ("dem-unn-strate," he articulated, slow and laden with meaning) to the spectators that I had indeed quit breathing, using some dupe equipment. Midway through this demonstration, we could cause a diversion of some sort—a little sideshow of the sideshow, the details he'd work out between himself and James and, of course, involving the dupe—to take the pressure off the act. In magician's terminology, this he called sleight of hand. We *could* fake, is what Shawn was saying. But of course Shawn didn't call this faking, either.

"Bamboozling. That's all it is. They want to see the evidence that Tevan's dead—"

"Near-dead," James put in.

"Dead," Shawn reaffirmed. "The crowd wants to see him *dead*. You see, James, my friend, the mark comes to a freak show because he wants to freak out." He nodded. "Here, seeing is believing. And since we know what it is they all come to see, well, we just decided what it is we're going to *show*. We'll use some sort of easy-breezy method to prove you're not breathing. Then we'll just manipulate that particular method of *proof* to fiddle with—you know, whatever the audience sees. Or has an opportunity to see."

I felt the honest raw bloom of partnership between us. This time my paranoid side dwindled to a low pulse. And I didn't fear Shawn Schroeder anymore at all.

"Now here's what I want you to do," Shawn said. "You're gonna need a few props. Nothing complicated, just a little *vis-u-al aid*. Whatchou guys want to do first is go on over to the kootch tent and ask for—"

James nearly jumped right out of his shorts. "You mean the one with the *girls* in it?"

I looked to Shawn. "We were over there the other night," I

told him. "Though we never got to see the show." And then, in James's defense: "It's still sort of a—ah—mystery to him."

Shawn pursed his lips. He looked back and forth between James and me. "On second thought," he said finally, "Tevan, maybe you oughta go on your own. Might need some time with James here to show him"—he winked and I caught it—"a few tricks."

"Now why can't I go?" James bitched.

Shawn put a hand on James's shoulder. "Because I get the feeling you're a little too enthusiastic, my man." He turned back to me. "Some of those girls are lot lizards, Tevan. You understand?"

"What's a lot lizard?" James asked, his nose wrinkled.

Shawn eyed us both. "It's somebody who fucks for pay."

A strange moment of silence overtook James and me. He didn't look at me and I didn't look at him. I had an idea we were both thinking the same thing nonetheless; and this time, it was about me.

"They travel with the show from place to place, just like all the help," Shawn went on. "You both'd be smart to stay away from that." His expression shifted as he watched us. "Oh," he said, his face taking on a combination of amusement and interest. "Oh, you guys have some experience with girls like that?"

My mind swung back in time to the girl we'd seen in her pink bathrobe. I felt an odd, sudden sense of connection to her.

"Which girls?" I said finally.

"Never you *mind* which ones," Shawn said. "You'll know, you dig? You'll know. There'll be no doubt in your mind." He grinned, shaking his head. "I only been here six weeks and I know already, so never you mind. All's you need to do is go on over there and be real nice to them and ask for what you need. They're sweet girls, the whole bunch of them."

"That'll be easy," James said. "Girls really like Tevan."

"I'm not worried about that," Shawn said. "What I'd worry about is how much Tevan likes girls." He cast me a dubious look.

"I do." My mind turned to the long-haired girl from two

days before, the one with the bells at her waist: *Giddyap.* I smiled. "But don't you worry. There's just the one."

I was almost late.

Much as Shawn promised, the kootch girls weren't trouble ("What are you doing tonight, handsome?" a redhead said to me as I turned to leave), and I made my find with ease. I returned across the lot fluttering Shawn's requested article in one hand. Another magician whangdoodle—only I knew exactly what this one was for.

I had a sense that time was getting on by the time I left the girls' tent. It was when I stopped off at our camper and found it empty, however, that I really understood the lateness of the hour. I knew at once that Shawn and James had gone on to the side-show tent without me. I didn't bother hanging around; instead, I paused in the doorway of the camper.

I swept the room with my eyes. I had the feeling I was forgetting something important.

You've got what you need, Tev, something piped up inside me. *All's you need to bring is your neck!*

I spied James's old sweatshirt, flung across his post at the door. I grabbed it and went out the door, tying it about my waist.

The tent was a long rectangle of canvas in the distance, with lights already burning hard in the fading daylight. And the commotion coming from it was loud—a rousing calliope tune and a booming voice that ran clear across the lot. Damon had informed me a day or so before that James and I would be the last of five acts. By the time I trotted off toward the sideshow tent I could hear the sound of our openers.

Now, I'd met the other performers from the show—they were pointed out to me by Schroeder here and there about the grounds—over the last few days. Still, it all sounded so very exciting: the voice, the up-and-down tempo, the confident promise of a thrill. A throng of spectators approached the tent alongside me. I began to wonder what exactly Merit might have on this great show of his to draw such a crowd, as I quickened my step toward it.

I ran around the entire tent skirting the crowd, rapt with attention, their backs facing and huddled together, before I remembered that I was supposed to enter through the secret side entrance. As I completed my loop, I turned to get a quick glimpse of what was taking place in front of the tent. And when I did, I blinked in surprise.

There was nothing taking place in front. There was no spectacle at all but Damon Merit.

The voice over the loudspeaker was convincing, persuasive, charismatic—and coming from greasy-haired, lanky Damon Merit. Damon had become the spur of the performance hidden inside, the go-between: the inside expert as well as the outside persuader. He stood before the sealed curtain tempting all who paused to take him in. I couldn't believe it and yet, in this moment wherein I glanced over my shoulder to watch him talking the talk, I did believe. It was clear, from the spellbound crowd, that everyone else did too.

"We just witnessed Raj, the savage man!" Damon's voice boomed over the speakers. *"Seen him consume all, seen him swallow it down—twelve daggers in all, can you believe it? I'll say! Why, he eats blades like you and I eat a meal."*

That left just Schroeder on the agenda before yours truly. I'd missed the Fat Lady, a guy purported to knock nails up his nostrils and slam his head through a stack of bricks, and now even Raj.

"His stomach can take it all, he has the belly of a monster! You touched that sword, didn't you, sir? Was it sharp? I'll say! None but a man hardened by the wild could live through such a thing! But LOOK INSIDE! What's next, you ask?"

I came around the corner and found both Shawn and James standing outside the side entrance. Shawn was decked out like a king. His hair was styled around a gold headband, and he had on a robe—a sparkling, red, crazy get-up. America would never recognize him for 1-A status now. Just as I began to laugh, raising my finger at him to comment, Damon's intro came to an audible close. We heard the microphone click off on the other side of the tent, a rush of activity in between, and then Damon appeared.

He was huffing and puffing, his forehead gleaming with sweat. "Jesus *Christ,* Tevan!" he boomed, spying me. "Why, I started to think you weren't going to show up!"

I'll say! I was tempted to cry. But I didn't. "Relax, Damon. I'm here." I raised my eyebrows. "I had to stop off and pick up some *vis-u-al* aids, that's all."

"You got it?" Shawn's eyes sparkled along with his mad outfit.

"Yeah, I got it." I put my hand into the kangaroo pouch of my sweatshirt and produced a long, wispy feather. I twirled it around in my fingertips, and it drifted outward like a parasol. "Plucked it right off her boa for me," I said. "The biggest she could find, as promised." I held it out for them like an exotic treasure. "Look, James," I said, grinning. "It's pink."

James laughed. Shawn produced a low whistle. "*Perfect,*" he breathed.

The feather's down fluttered in the night air. He was right— it was perfect. It was almost as big as my forearm in all dimensions. With that size and the airy underside, I could see it would fit the bill just right.

"Fine, yes, very nice, boys," Damon cut in. He turned, looking me up and down. "Are you ready then? Because, after Shawn here, you understand that you're on next."

"I'm ready," I said. "Don't worry about me."

"Good. Then we're all set." Damon put his hands on his hips. He studied me. His upper lip curled. Then he jutted his chin out at my middle. "Take that off," he said, indicating the sweatshirt slung about my hips.

"Why?" I asked. I knew why, of course I did. But by then I'd had plenty of time to think about it, and now I held the opinion that the sweatshirt had been a damn good idea. Plus I'd long grown tired of taking orders from Damon Merit's chin.

"*Why*," Damon scowled. "Don't be a dick, *you* know why. Because I told you to wear all white and it's black, that's why! So take it off!"

"I can't." On the side, my mind giggled silently as it weighed the irony of Damon demanding that I remove it and telling me not to be a dick all in the same breath. I'd picked up that sweatshirt in a brainchild of afterthought, tied it exactly where I'd meant it to go, and walked all the way over here. Color scheme and whatnot notwithstanding, I sure wasn't taking it off now. If I went out on stage without it, the marks might see more dick from Tevan George than they'd ever wanted to see.

Damon huffed impatiently. "Yes, you can. Take it off. You just"—he made a twisting motion with both hands—"untie the little knot there at your—"

I raised my eyebrows. I gave a look partway between bemusement and haughty ennui. *Thing?* is how I would have completed it for him, but I didn't have to. Damon Merit was already thinking it. His eyes bounced past me as though I was something dirty or catching, or maybe both. He waved a hand.

"Take it off, Tevan," he finished. He turned and disappeared through the side entrance without even passing a glance back to ascertain that I'd complied. Which, of course, I hadn't.

Shawn stepped forward. "Well then," he said to me, "guess I'll be seein' ya." He whisked a thin rod through the air with one hand: your household magic wand. "Good luck, huh?" He smiled as he said it, and this bolstered my confidence.

I floated the feather into the air again. "Thanks," I said.

"Hey," James piped up. "Aren't you gonna watch us?"

Shawn stood with his hand on the curtain. He rolled his eyes. "*Of course* I'm gonna watch you. I'll be sitting way in the back, already changed into my civvies! Oh, and James, you be sure to show Tevan what *we* got, hey?" With this, Shawn disappeared into the tent, his smile gleaming.

I turned to James. "What did you get, James?"

Already James was hunched over, pulling what appeared to be a long, dark ribbon from a sack by his feet. He stood and held it out: a black stretch of fabric, tapered at either end. For a moment I thought he had gotten a feather of his own.

"What is that?" I asked.

James didn't say anything. Instead he brought the fabric toward his face, leaned his head in and in and in, until when he looked back at me I saw that he and the cloth had become one and the same.

"Look, Tev," he said, grinning at me. "It's a mask."

A *mask*. It was too, and a neat one at that. It covered the upper portion of his face and forehead. Holes were cut away in the center so that he could peer out from inside. It looked like the mask of Zorro.

"Hey," I said. "*I* want one. Why don't I get a mask?"

"Because I'm evil and you're not. Remember?"

I laughed. "Yeah. Right." I stared at him, tall as ever, black from head to toe, and now weirdly obscured by a swath of cloth. Only his eyes, green and shining, showed through. "That's golden, James. I mean it, you look really cool." And James, with his evil mask, beamed.

I watched as he secured the ties behind his head. He did a really good job of it too. You don't think of such things until later, but this I know. "James," I began. "Are you nervous?"

He blinked, large eyelids encircled in black. "No, Tev. Are you?"

"No." And I wasn't—not at all. "Do you remember what it is you have to do?"

He nodded slowly. "You say when. I drop you. I listen to Damon. He says the word. And then I bring you back."

"That's right," I agreed. "That's good, James." James's part is really quite simple. There's little charisma involved, no speaking at all. Damon had asked that James go all out and holler a bit just to scare the marks, but James had balked, embarrassed. So we decided it wasn't necessary. Growing loud and uncultivated like a psycho works, yes, we agreed; but a quiet, expressionless nutcase can be equally convincing.

"Good, James. There's only one thing you have to remember. Okay? Just one thing, and we've been over it already." I could see that James was listening, his face serious. "Don't stop. Don't stop, okay, James? No matter what. Whether we use Shawn's tricks or not, you'll know. Just don't stop. You keep going until I drop. Got it?"

James bobbed his head again. "I got it, Tev."

Through the curtain of canvas, you could hear the rumbling of the crowd inside. The crowd changed every performance, so I didn't know how big it would be for us. In moments, when I stepped out from behind the curtain after our intro and James's departure, I would find that Damon had drawn close to fifty people. Meanwhile, his voice carried across to us. He was winding down. Winding down . . . and then on to the next act.

"The powers of witchery, the Miracle of Stonehenge!" Damon cried. *"He mystifies us all—how does he do it? Schroeder the Magician and Mentalist, what talent! Ladies and gentlemen, if you would like to try your hand at magic, come to the tent to your left after the show and you can get YOUR VERY OWN magic wand. YOUR VERY OWN, created and consecrated by our Schroeder."* I recalled the unsophisticated look of Shawn's flimsy magic wand as he left us, and shook my head, smiling to myself. *Your own,* I thought. Proof and misdirection: *You can have your very own.*

"Ladies and gentlemen, if you'd like to see your future, do not hesitate to visit our Card Reader and Astrologist just outside this tent. LOOK and one slim half-dollar will divine your path . . ."

Me and James waited in silence. The wind tousled the grass at our feet.

Card Reader, I thought, *ya like seein' the fewchah?* I smiled again to myself, and when Damon's face appeared at the corner of the canvas opening, I was still smiling. "Just a few minutes now," he said, wagging a finger to James.

The feather shuddered in my hand.

"Okay," I returned, and then it was time to giddyap.

10

Now, what I had seen while wandering around the tent like a lost fool just moments prior had not been the show itself. It had been just Damon Merit. What Damon was doing, when my eyes and ears snatched a glimpse of him, is called a ballyhoo. Unlike the performance itself, the ballyhoo takes place before even so much as a dime touches the cashbox floor.

Getting the rocks to hit the cashbox (*Hit where it counts,* as they say) is the gist of Damon's job. The marks stand feet away from the sideshow act, hemming and hawing over whether to part with their change for the sake of believing. In order to get them through the curtain, their change left behind as barter, Damon must use his wit and the promise of a fine attraction. For while the object of the ruse on the inside may be that seeing is believing, the object on the outside is crafting the belief that there's something inside to be seen. On the day before our first performance, we had decided that this attraction would be James.

Between his too-grown-out hair, his empty stare, and his sheer size, James easily looked the part. And so now I stood outside the tent exit alone while James became Damon's ballyhoo.

"See this man?" I heard Damon bellow. *"Tell me, folks, what do you see?"*

The crowd, small though gathering still, rustled.

"A guy in black," came the first wisecracking response. "A masked man!"—another. Then: "The Lone Ranger!" (I could imagine Damon's discontent at that one, so I couldn't help but grin.) Still another, shrill and calling:

"An executioner!"

I thought I recognized the voice as Sandy's, one of Damon's goons—but that couldn't be right, could it? What would Sandy be doing here, hanging around and watching a show, just like one of the marks? And at once I had the answer: Sandy's attendance at me and James's show, like Merit's outdated, leading sign, was part of the rub.

"*An executioner!*" Damon boomed in agreement. "*Why, you could be correct, sir! Well, I'll say! Four men were killed taking this man onto our show. Four men, killed by his bare hands! This man cannot speak with words, yet he speaks with his HANDS! Ladies and gentlemen, come and see the man with no soul! No speech, but evil! If you can stomach the sight of death, step inside for a small price—*"

Outside the tent I paused, running my hand through my hair.

"*See tonight—an innocent killed!*"

On the other side of the tent, the crowd murmured.

"*I promise you, this man has a blood lust,*" Damon continued. "*We know not from where he comes, but we DO know he is a soulless, remorseless man. And tonight—if you can stomach it, if you can stand to watch it—LOOK! Look inside! He will bring death upon another inside this very tent!*"

I couldn't see them, but in my head I could imagine James, silent on the ballyhoo platform. James, standing, like an item for sale as our Talker tempted the crowd with his alleged wickedness, and what small token such wickedness would be worth to see.

"*—twenty-five cents, that's all, folks. Twenty-five cents to witness our soulless Dr. Faustus himself do his horrible deed. Look inside! Why, you couldn't get such a deal on the dead from the county morgue, could you? Oh, I say!*"

Damon's voice rose and fell. It hissed over the loudspeaker, the words themselves—*wicked, remorseless, criminal*—bounding across the lot: "*Do you want to see the deed done? Can you stomach the sight of death itself? MUUURDER?*"

Damon later confirmed that I was right, that James *had* stood and stared, his eyes empty and remote. "Well, he did take a step forward once," Damon admitted. "But that was good."

Good—valuable—for as he had done this, the front row of ballyhoo spectators had actually taken a collective, compensatory
step backward. The front row are the believers, Damon claimed.
They're the ones who have parted with their cash once already,
watched the previous show, then returned with eagerness for
the best seats in the house. Perverts' Row, Damon called it—the
same designation he gave the old, balding enthusiasts who turned
up, up front, at the kootch show to watch the girls take it all off.

"Hey!" Damon yelled. "Hey, you there! Inside, right now!
LOOK INSIDE! Can you stand to look into the eyes of the
innocent? The man to be slain?"

I stared into the curtain covering the exit with deep concentration. I couldn't see a thing beyond the thick, embroidered pleats.
But again I could imagine, and again I was right. I imagined the
coins hitting the floor of the cashbox and the simultaneous shuffle
of purported skeptics inward from the opposite entrance. A herd of
sheep, ambling toward the enclosure of the tent. And as I imagined
this, I heard the low murmuring of bodies, of cynics and believers
alike, creeping toward me. Damon, sounding farther away now
as the spectators entered the tent and marched between us, maintained his tirade: "LOOK inside! Come inside, I hope you're not
faint of heart or a member of the law, because what you are about
to witness is the murder of morals and of law itself!"

The ballyhoo had run its course. This was signaled by a
brief, muffled clunk as Damon abandoned his exterior post and
strode to meet the crowd on the inside. From where I stood, I
could just barely hear the heavy flutter of the canvas curtain as
someone outside, maybe Shawn or Sandy, maybe even John, the
old guy who ran the lights on the lot, closed the entranceway
behind them all.

Now the creak of the sideshow stage as two bodies boarded.
One began to pace, the creaks grinding a circle into the stage just
outside of my field of vision. The other stood solid and continued
to rant.

"Have you yet heard the tale of Dr. Faustus? The hungry

fool who traded his very soul for twenty-four years of immortal power?" Damon sounded like a fanatic now, a psychotic. A psychotic quoting a play, sure, an ecstatic, educated one maybe. "Traded his soul, treated the innocent like his own playthings? Tortured and ruined for his own pleasure? Ladies and gentlemen, keep your children close, but don't worry . . ."

A pause.

Then Damon again, his gaze finally pointed my way: "We have an innocent of our own."

The stage was wide and yet I crossed it with no recollection of moving my feet at all. I heard the eruption of breath taken in around me, and then I saw the look on Damon's face. He turned, at the moment of what was planned as the very zenith of his spiel, and his face nearly fell into complete disgust. If Damon Merit could have mastered the art of stopping time as he had that of presentation, he would have made the T sign with his hands right then and done so: *I thought I told you to take that fuckin' sweatshirt off*, his face said.

Propitiously, Damon recovered. "Seraphim," he proclaimed. "Our martyr."

I took this moment, as instructed, to stare about the crowd. I was surprised to see what Damon had gathered—close to fifty people, all sorts of them too. There were men in hats, boys with their hands slouched into their pockets, women ranging from teenagers to grandmas, and as I assumed my place on stage, I took special pains to connect my gaze with every one of them. On the periphery I noted Sandy standing right in the front row. Way in the back, broadcasted by a bush of coiled hair, was Shawn Schroeder.

Damon took in a long, suspenseful breath. "Abandoned as an infant at a monastery," he said, "our Seraphim was raised by practicing Buddhists in Mexico."

I don't know how Damon said it without laughing. Buddhists don't cater to orphaned children. And even if they did, what in the name of Buddha would they be doing in Mexico? But the marks ate it up. They peered up at me curiously, some of the women craning inward. I, in turn, batted my eyelashes.

"He came to our show as a counselor and spiritual advisor—"

Now that was a laugh and a half. I mean, even if adoptive Buddhist monks from Mexico weren't, that surely was. I steeled myself, nodding solemnly. And still they watched, transfixed. Followed James pacing a circle, and me, quiet and unmoving. They watched as Damon spoke:

"Seraphim volunteered to be the victim—"

If I didn't know better, I'd say they watched *nervously*.

"—of this *monster*!"

The crowd pulled inward, rapt and bewildered. Something was about to happen; Damon hadn't said so, but he didn't need to. Something was going to happen, some connecting—some *clash*—between these purported embodiments of good and evil. And as I caught this in the stifling tent, in the heated scent of their fifty-odd ruminating bodies, their upturned, concentrating eyes, their worried, shuffling steps, I sensed that the moment was right. I *knew* that the moment was right.

I passed my hands before me, displaying the feather (the hootch-kootch *stripper's* feather, but nobody had to know that), and I opened my mouth. The words came from a battered copy of Marlowe's prose. Bored and obstinate, I'd rehearsed them before Damon Merit just that afternoon, but now I delivered them with a combination of dramatically rendered contempt and sad pity.

"O Faustus," I said, "lay that damned book aside and gaze not on it, lest it tempt thy soul and heap God's heavy wrath upon thy head!"

Buddhists don't speak of God or the book either, but no matter. The timing was right and the talk was respectable and the crowd knew it and they believed. Plus the year was 1966, Jesus Christ; and until July, when Lyndon B. Johnson was blamed for the self-immolation of numerous Vietnamese Buddhists halfway across the earth, for all intents and purposes no one knew what a Mexican monastic Buddhist was anyhow.

The timing was right and it was all happening and James heard my voice and he took this moment to turn and spy me—to see me apparently for the first time—and he lunged.

Damon put his arm out and caught James in a beautifully rendered human blockade: as if Damon Merit could block a running house of bricks like James. But still, no matter. The marks shrieked—for a moment, before they regained their senses and dignity. Then they caught themselves at it, and giggled nervously.

I raised my hands again: one in a halting motion to Damon, the other sliding to one side to offer him the feather. My eyes passed over the crowd as I did so. I saw their heads, a multicolored blur topped by upturned faces, follow my movement, mesmerized. The hair on my arms prickled. I breathed in the tent's heavy humidity. And once Damon had taken the pristine whangdoodle from my confident, priestly hand, I stood before James, divided from him by just four feet.

Now James began to circle me. We stood almost as we had in our dry run three days before, closing in on what Damon had so specifically instructed. We looked like an inevitable kill—me a stolid, tiny, defenseless sacrifice and James a mean, stalking animal. Damon, in the meantime, inched off to one side, feigning a horrified look of anticipation that the crowd deftly mirrored. We moved into position, our sides to the lawn and two contours to the wind.

Damon's voice rang out, deafening. "Hey, is he going to run? Is he going to *fight*?"

I shook my head. I spread my arms wide, like a G.I. waving the white flag, like fucking Jesus himself, like a guy demonstrating the size of the one that got away.

"Do you think he's scared!" Damon boomed.

Like a man not scared of anything, I dropped to my knees. James watched me, his eyes bright behind the mask of Zorro.

"NO! Ladies and gentlemen, he's not scared at all!" Damon cried. "Why, I'd be scared, any of us would be! But not this man, no. He's not even afraid to *die*!" And then, Damon to

one side, the crowd leaning in and me looking up from the floor, James attacked.

"Aaauugghh!" I managed, a stifled, wet, gurgling sound as his hands came down on my neck. I didn't have to make that sound, see. James let me. The marks didn't know this, though. They recoiled, horrified.

"Aaauugghh!" A second burbling, surprised cry. James leaned in—one hand into the base of my head, the other into the soft curve under my chin—so that they could all see that he entirely meant for one palm to meet the other. He let up and leaned in more, and this time I let out a snotty, throaty cough. Again the mob withdrew anxiously, as it flitted through their collective brain for perhaps the first time that they might actually get to see what they paid for.

"He's not going to *really*—" Damon shrieked. "He *is*, ladies and gentlemen, *I really think he is*!"

My hands were at my sides and my knees on the floor. My eyes were open, staring wide into James. When the first spasm came, the last breath I'd taken rebounding against the walls of my chest, the spectators witnessed it point-blank. At my periphery I saw them. It was like watching a load of kids on the Scrambler or the Eli Wheel. The mass rolled back as if on a sliding, cock-eyed floor. Then, coming back for a better look, it swung forward again—not all of them, though. Two women to the left shrunk back and never returned. They covered their eyes and, twenty-five-cent down payment or not, slunk out the entrance. Apparently they'd seen enough.

But they hadn't seen enough; in fact, they had hardly seen anything at all. I began to gag for real, soundlessly. My eyes watered as the air caught in my throat, the route closed. Harder doing this upright, harder on the legs. My arms were heavy. My eyes witnessed red flecks of light. My torso thrashed in and out, hammering for air. And suddenly the world about me was retracting. Even the crowd seemed far off and nondescript. My eyelids fluttered of their own accord, and James's face, his swathed and slitted eyes, flickered.

"Does anyone know where the nearest telephone is, ladies and gentlemen?" Damon droned in a voice that seemed to arrive from a thousand miles away. *"Because I daresay that soon enough we might have to call an ambulance—"*

Staring at James. Time running short. I knew inside my head and outside, for once the two agreeing, that I must feign my collapse in the next few moments or else I'd be meeting the real thing. The portrait of Shawn standing in the back row flitted through my brain. Like a string wrapped around my finger, telling me it would not be wise to submit to bona fide unconsciousness at my first of six acts of the night.

The sound of the people below us billowed, close to ecstasy. I peered into James through heavy lids. And here, randomly, I thought of another line of prose. A cheery, ridiculous one too:

And Ma in her kerchief and I in my cap had just settled down for a long winter's—

My eyes blinked and James's portrait blinked along with it; and in my defense, I want to tell you I fully intended on faking it. But then I paused, my head swimming in what seemed a lulling ocean. *James?* I thought for the first time. *Gee, I really wish I could see your face, James.*

And once I thought it, boy, it was too late.

James? I came again inwardly, something strong and bright rising now beneath the thought. *James??*

Some years back, when I was about sixteen and still living with my mother, I caught a fish off a friend's dock up in Algonquin. I brought it home to show it off, telling my mom I'd cook it up for the two of us. I'd have it ready when she got home from work, I told her; and in the evening of that very day, just as the sun was setting in the long twilight of June, I did that very thing and nearly burned the house down. The problem was that I turned the skillet on while I battered the thing—turned it to low, or so I thought—but then I smelled a funny crisp scent in the air.

In my enthusiasm I'd turned the dial to Flame. I remember turning my head, the fillet still draped beautifully across one hand, and witnessing a blue-orange lick of flame circling the perimeter of the pan. As though in acknowledgment of my gaze, the flame uttered a little noise: *Whoosh,* it said to me. *Whoosh,* as it circumnavigated the entire pan. In a comical way, it somehow reminded me of the turning cyclists on the 1950s Wall of Death. Then it exploded into a foot-high fireball right on the stove.

Now, staring at James—James in my shoddy vision, James in his evil mask, James, concealed so that he could very well not be James at all—I felt a similar progression stir within me. The stir of a prickling, encroaching horror

(Whoosh)

with nary a hitch in place to stop it.

James? some interior voice shrieked. *Is that YOU in there, James?*

Calm down, I told myself. *Calm down. It's him in there! Who the hell else could it be?*

James! Heatedly this time nonetheless. *James!*

You know very well who it could be, my head returned, speaking with the black wit of a kid who's been around the block too many times for his own good. *It's Elvis, Tevan, you stupid shit,* it whispered at me. *It's the president of the United fucking States of America. Who do you think it is? You KNOW! It could be—*

I coughed and I sputtered and I wanted to know. A thousand times as a child, I'd wrestled with my brother. I was smaller than Kenny and it was always me who ended up crying Uncle. As an adult, I had a similar repertoire with James. *If you don't let me up now, I'm serious, James,* I'd inevitably announce (most often with my head stuffed under his armpit or pressed to his rib cage), *I will no longer be personally responsible for what I do to you.* What I meant was that if he didn't take my cease-and-desist order to heart, I'd go berserk against my will. I'd go apeshit. Poke his fuckin' eyes out, and James

(If that's you in there, James, let up)

understood this. "I would never hurt you, Tev," he would say, or even "Tell me when you've had enough."

I jerked backward. *Let up!* I commanded inwardly. *If that's you in there, James, let up!*

But we weren't playing; we were in a show for pay. *Don't stop*, I'd instructed James just moments before. *You keep going until I drop.* And so my last attempt at reason became slanted by my first jolt of sheer terror.

If that's you in there, James, let up NOW! I thought, pulling back. But James didn't stop. I wrenched again. I managed a thin gasp of air as his fingers were caught by surprise. And still, James—the *is that James*, then the *perhaps not James*, and now finally the *is not James*—kept on going. The look in his eyes and against his exposed jawline was jovial, amused. Seeing this expression upon him, I was horrified. So I did something I'd never done before: I put my hands out and clamped down on his wrists.

His eyes widened; the room swelled with noise. I could see the surprise on his face. As I witnessed the effectiveness of this jab, my resolve dug in even deeper. I closed my nails in on his knuckles.

Let up! I thought toward the unknown assailant—because by then the thought of James had dwindled away, dwindled like an ethereal mist, like a flush going down the toilet—and so the assailant *was* largely unknown. My hands circled his wrists, and I yanked away from him with all my body weight. This came to no result, other than to send me reeling backward, thudding to the floor on my rump. I came down on the soft cushion of the sweatshirt tied beneath me; but for the life of me I could not think what it was that I'd landed on; could not think why I would tie anything about myself, could not remember even *doing* it—

("You're no use to me now")

could not place myself chronologically *any*where, so that suddenly I was loose and fighting in some nebulous dimension instead, with bits of time fluttering around me like grains of sand through an egg timer, my mind and body in different places—

"No use to either of us now," Catharine says as she leads me into her dormitory, *"wrecked out of your mind."* It's dark and I stumble just inside the doorway, over a pile of crap she has lying there.

Crash! My shoulders landed on the floor and in response the room swelled with noise.

"Watch it!" she hisses. *"And don't step on any of those books! I paid an arm and a leg for those texts. Damn capitalist institution."*

"Oh yeah, Cath," I say, rolling my eyes, *"because communism is SO much better."* I laugh as the bed bends inward under her weight. I'm already—

flat on my back, writhing, twisting

breathing hard in anticipation. I peer down at her, trying to catch sight of her undressing. But it's dark and I can't see and so I just laugh again; the booze is good for that. "It didn't work," I remind her. *"You know, like Kollontai?"*

"It didn't work for Kollontai," she says, *"because she didn't get enough funding, that's all."* She bends her head, tussling with some underthings. *"She ran programs for women, and Marxists weren't interested in women, see."*

"Uh-huh," I say. *"I'm interested in women."*

He came after me. I coughed and bucked and writhed while he

sinks down on her elbows overtop of me. Her hips settle just below my chest. "Sure you are," she says. *Her face is at my temple, her thighs against me, already speaking another language. "Good old democracy. Very egalitarian. You know how it works?" She smiles, watching me fiddle with my belt. "Sometimes it's not so hard to get convinced, baby."*

I smile back, still fiddling. Cath is a left-wing number all right. Man, she's

one tough bitch! *Let up!* My hands clawed at his wrists and I opened my mouth. I would have yelled if I could have, I would have screamed at the top of my lungs. I would have said—

"Help me out here," I murmur. *She smiles, just a shadow in the dark, before she is gone*

two contours to the wind, only I can't—

breathe. "Cath," I breathe, looking to the ceiling. I turn my head against the pillowcase. The room is quiet and the walls are dark. I wonder where I am. Because while her hands are here in present time, the touch itself recalls another in history, and in it, I can't breathe. My fingers clench, tightening against the bedsheets. "Catharine," I say. I put my palms against the mattress near my head, shifting—

backward, my spine hitting the wood floor like I'd been thrown against it. And maybe I had, because he was bigger than me. He could flatten me, sitting against my chest like this! He began pushing me—

in until: "Cath!" Louder this time. I'm calling less for HER than in the way you might call out if you suddenly found yourself lost in the woods. Or if you were skinny-dipping in a dark lake and felt something brush against your leg below the surface. She moves against me with her mouth and in the dark I squeeze my fists open and closed. "Cath—" I say, though instead what I really want to do is scream

WHO'S THERE! I can't breathe! Please stop, I'll do anything! I can't breathe! On the sideshow stage, I became one with the floor. My back scraped against the crummy wood planks. My throat was rubbed so hard it felt like any moment it would catch fire. Just as sure, it seemed to me, was that I wrestled my attacker for hours—but Damon told me later that it all transpired in less than two minutes.

"Say, you didn't tell me you guys were going to scrap it out on the floor like that," he remarked. "Shoot, that was great! I loved it!"

I could only pause, frowning at him. "The crowd," I managed finally. "What did they think?"

Damon turned. He looked at me like I had nine heads. "They hit the roof, Tevan. Didn't you hear them? Man," he said. "Where the hell were you?"

I am in the sanitarium, fourteen years old and with a fever of one hundred and three, when I truly defy death.

This time no *Quiet*, no *Shush*, no niceness to sway me; no *Shut up*, even. Instead, this time Bern lies behind me, takes his elbow and hooks it around my neck. The room watches in silence like animals frozen in dark hiding places, bystanders rubbernecking a car accident, marks watching a show. And what happens next I don't want to say, even though I know exactly what you call it. He said it's called Experience. But really you call it something else. He fucked me inside my head and he moved forward from there. He gave it to me a thousand different ways; I can't remember them all. In the end it doesn't matter. It holds you down all the same.

And it's the opposite of what you read in all the bawdy magazines about taking your clothes off for someone. The more he's turned on, the more our alliance fades. The more he gets, the less he gives a shit about me. He holds me down at the neck and I have to hold my breath. The only recompense is that, for the first time, gray takes me for one swaying moment. And another. And another and another.

I can't breathe; my head blurs. And that is when I forget myself. I begin to fade off. And that is when, suddenly, I spring open at the seams.

It's huge, a dam bursting: there is a sudden, red-hot slide of what feels like a million fire ants making a mad-dash exit through my member. I drank that entire pitcher of water just as the nurse told me to, and now it's making an exodus from the other end of me. The bedding beneath me darkening, spreading, screaming outward in a wet shadow. I can't breathe and I wonder with dismay if the last thing I'll ever see will be this pathetic portrait of my own body pissing itself. The puddle spreads out— streaks out, actually, with fantastic velocity—and gathers at my knees for a hair-thin moment before dribbling down the side of the bed. Tottering off the mattress, and I am watching it, following it with my eyes, until I am looking up.

And across from me, somebody's watching.

His brow is creased and his lips pursed in fury. It's the slowest horse on the track, *when God was handing out brains he thought He said "trains" and asked for a slow one*, Slim Jim, Jimmy Lowe. He stares across the gap in silence while something tinkles to the floor *plinkety-fucking-plink* between us. This boy lying across from me in his hospital bed, watching with calm deliberation, is the last that I see before my head closes

in

on

black.

When the lights go on again, we've all switched places.

We stay that way for years.

It didn't take long for James to bring me back.

Of course I wasn't there to see it. I missed all the parts about contrition and redemption, about Dr. Faustus's attempts to deliver his poor, sullied soul. I missed Damon's blathering on about God and hell, the deliverance of mortals, and Faustus's wish for this. I didn't witness, though he told me it all later, how the throng moaned when seeing the motionlessness of the feather positioned over my nose and mouth, or screamed at James's dive inward to remedy this. And I certainly didn't see the mint of coins and bills that found their way into the cashbox just moments before Damon promised to have me revived. I didn't see *that*, no, but I would later—and that would change everything for James and me in the end.

Instead, the last I remember is the portrait of my own hysterical hands transposed over the looming perpetrator—they tore the mask from his face to reveal no one but James—and the next, I lay gasping on my back like a drowned swimmer just dragged to the beach. I was hauled to my feet and stood with my arm in Damon's grip. The room was a booming, applauding commotion.

When the gaping faces turned into backs, hats, and the

seams of summer jackets, I inched in slow motion toward the tent's back exit. My head felt waterlogged and my knees wobbled. James moved importantly beside me, his long, strong legs pausing and standing, then moving leisurely forward again. He didn't touch me. He didn't ask me anything. If I've told you once, I've told you a million times: for a stupid guy, sometimes he ain't so stupid.

When we finally made it outside, the sky was a blue-black blanket over our heads. James turned his gaze away from me as I leaned over, rubbing my hands on my neck. Minutes of just breathing transpired between us before he spoke.

"I didn't want to get on top of you, just so you know," he said into thin air. "I had to." He waited a moment. "Did you hear me, Tev?"

"Huh?" I looked around at him.

James watched me. He spoke now as though to a small child. "I said I *had* to. Because you started to fight me."

I continued to stare at James. My eyes were glassy with tears wrung from somewhere far inside. Instead of seeing James for what he was today—standing tall, watching me, a span of four feet between the two of us—my mind's eye recalled him leaning back to watch me from no distance at all: the arch of his feet against my ankles, his stomach pressed to mine. His mouth, his eyes round like doorknobs. The James I awoke to the night that Bern set upon me, and I blew some sort of physical fuse; and then I came back.

"No," I managed. But what I wanted to say was *No, I didn't fight you, James: I was weak; I had a fever, remember?* I wanted to tell him that when he leaned in for the first resuscitation effort of his life that night in the san, what probably happened was that I began to have a seizure. I wanted to remind him that grand mal seizures are common in children with heavy fevers, and he can count himself lucky he wasn't still on my mouth when it hit. *I hear a guy can bite down fifty pounds of pressure when he pitches a fit. And for a fellow who's never French-kissed before, that would've been a pretty lousy return, wouldn't it, James?*

But I didn't say any of this. It was as though we were reviewing two different events inside one confounded moment. I watched James as though searching his face for some indicator of which one he'd been at. Here on the sideshow just now, Damon and me alongside him?

Or back in time, on the night that Bern took me?

James pointed his thumb over his shoulder, back toward the sideshow tent. "Yes," he reaffirmed. "I was there. You started to fight me, Tev."

I had no explanation for him. Wait, yes, I did. I took in a few breaths. When I spoke, this time my voice sounded small and perplexed. "When I saw you I got scared," I said. "I thought you were going to get me. I didn't know what you were doing. I thought you were like—"

James's eyes slid in my direction. When he spoke, his tone was one of dismayed honesty. "You know I would never hurt you, Tev."

"He wasn't there anymore, you know," I whispered in a rush. The disclosure sounded at once amazed and indignant, no different from how it had felt to me nearly ten years before. "When I woke up. He had me by the neck. And then he left me lying there—"

In the dark James only continued to watch me. He gave way to a solemn nod. "And you know, Tev," he said finally, "that's something I would never do either."

The air outside was beautifully cool. I heaved in and out in slow deliberate breaths. Within minutes Shawn rounded the corner.

He tossed a cigarette butt aside and spread his hands. "You never used the magic!" he said, wide-eyed and panting as though he'd galloped full-length around the tent with the smoke in his mouth. I could commiserate with him on that. My throat felt like a bloody track of sawdust, with my head a hunk of rubber sitting on top.

"I know," James said. He cast a look my way. "I didn't need to."

Damon appeared next. He came at a full run, eyes gleaming

and his hands gripping a rectangular box. By the strain on his arms you could tell that box was full to bursting. *"Take a look at this!"* he cried.

He took me by the shoulder, gave me a little shake, and then Damon Merit made the biggest gaffe I imagine he ever came up with in his sideshow-management career. He bent inward, displaying a box filled to the tits with *money.*

I stared into it, blinking. Damon waited for my reaction. He actually gripped the box in both hands, as if for my viewing pleasure, and shook it around a little. Coins rattled against one another; bills shuttled back and forth like boats atop an ocean. It was more cash than I'd ever seen in my life. I looked, slow-witted and confused, for what seemed like an entire minute.

"That's a lot of dough, man," I managed finally.

"Isn't it?" Damon said. *"Isn't* it? And I didn't even call a blow-off, Tevan, I never even asked for it. I asked if they wanted you revived, that's all, and they just—just started emptying their pockets!" He grinned. "Do you see, Tevan? A fool and his money are soon parted." Damon gave a whoop of glee, spinning his fingers through the stash.

"Did you see it?" James asked Shawn.

"Oh, God yeah," Damon answered instead. "We saw it. We *all* saw. Even my dad was out there."

"Your dad?" I said, looking up.

"Hot dog, yeah. Shit, he was practically coming in his pants when he saw all that dough dropping in." He grinned wickedly. And suddenly, inwardly, so did I.

"How much do you figure is in there, Damon?" I asked carefully.

"Oh fuck!" he raved. *"Look* at it. Fifty? Easily close to eighty? *Eighty damn dollars,* Tevan, and they went willingly. Mark my words!"

That may not sound a large sum by today's standards, but in the year 1966 and for a relative cottage industry's one-night take, it was tantamount to a king's ransom. Shawn blinked, putting a fresh cigarette to his lips. "Geez, Tevan," he said, his voice low and alarmed. "That's as much as I make in a week."

And he was right. I was doing the math inside my head: twenty-five cents a pop, over fifty heads in the tent. Plus some undisclosed, apparently magnanimous amount for a blow-off stunt that neither Damon nor I had anticipated.

I looked at the bin of money and I looked at James. *A fool and his money are soon parted*? Whether Damon ever recalled those words as ironic, I don't know, but I'm willing to place my bets.

"Then I'm not doing it," I announced.

Damon's face came up, the smile frozen upon his face. "What?"

"You heard me." I gestured toward the box. He began to retract it inward for the first time, like a child just learning the merits of hoarding his allowance. "I'm not doing it."

Damon stared, his fanatical expression dropping. "What do you mean?"

"I don't need to do this six times a night when I earn you twice my salary in one go. I think I'll go on twice a night. Maybe once, even! If you don't like it, me and James can go find another show." And here, as I used Buddy Merit's own greedy asshole words, I couldn't help but grin. "Working acts cost more to run, of course—but more value for your money too."

Damon gaped, his mouth poised between speaking heat-edly and utter speechlessness. I looked to James again. I noticed for the first time that his hands were white and flaked, the knuckles blooming with specks of blood.

I cleared my throat. "And you might want to think about upping his pay, Damon." I pointed a finger at James. "He gets as much as me now, fair and square."

Damon exploded. "Upping his pay!" he bellowed. "For *what*? Anybody could do what he does. It's not"—he sputtered, staggered—"*skilled workmanship* or anything! Jesus Christ, Tevan!"

"*Anyone* could do it?" I said, getting loud. "*Anyone*? I

doubt it." Unbidden, I thought once again of James pressing his mouth to mine in a roomful of his peers in a hospital ward. I thought of him doing the same before a turning crowd of strangers. "Maybe *you* want to be the one to give me mouth-to-mouth up there. Do you, Damon?"

Damon's expression turned to ice. His eyes passed quickly between James, Shawn, and me. A long moment ran out between us.

"Okay," he said finally. "Okay, you want to do this twice a night? And more pay for your donkey here? Fine, make it worth my while, then! Hell, make it worth the *marks'* while, and all their piddly dimes." Damon gestured at James. "If they're shelling out for some big end-of-night show, you're going to have to pull some serious stunt—"

"I'm game," I cut in. "You've seen it. James is game."

"—and marketing!" Damon sputtered on. "No doubt, your fans may demand a little more proof regarding how deadly he is . . ."

"So *prove* it," I said. "*Go on!* Go on, you're the talker! I've pulled myself together, how about you? Your talk says that I'm the only"—I waggled my fingers in the air—"death-defying survivor, Damon! Your talk says the rest of James's victims are all fucking *dead*—"

And then Damon had me right where he wanted me again. He raised an eyebrow. "Yes," he said, "but your talk with *me* didn't say that."

I stood in silence. My gaze dared Damon to say more; his dared me to dissent. Finally, Damon came right out and made his request. "You're going to dig up some kind of papers for me. Something with his name on it." Damon nodded to James, but the next words were aimed at me. "From what I understand, he's got a stack of them." He grinned. "I'm sure you can stand to part with just one."

Out of the corner of my eye, I saw James's eyes widen for a sliver of an instant; and within that sliver I hated Damon more than the devil himself.

"We'll use it for the show," Damon went on. "It'll work strong, I know it will. Then I'll raise his pay to match yours." He surveyed James and gave up a laugh. "Hell," he said. "Maybe I'll even pay to bail him out next time, George."

I watched Damon, hating him all over again: it was a mean stunt to pull and he knew it. The hell if I wanted James's history displayed all over the midway for any mark or cop or who-knows-who to mull over as they munched away on their stupid candy apple. Even worse, I hated him for calling me by my last name like his father would, and guffawing at our state of affairs. But more than any of these, I hated to see Damon Merit satisfied.

I nodded, giving no indication that his demand had ruffled me at all. Damon Merit had no clout in this, I told myself. Nobody was going to knock me out and resuscitate but James. Nobody.

And besides—well, we *did* have papers.

Damon clutched the hold of money to his chest. "I see we're in agreement then," he said. "Anything else for you, smartass?"

I glowered in response. I reached out and snatched Shawn's cigarette from his fingers. Shawn gave it up with no dissent. I hauled off hard on the cigarette before passing it back. Then I nodded at Damon.

"Yeah, actually there is." *I'm the King of the Castle*, my tone sang. *Nanner nanner boo boo.* "James is never wearing that fuckin' mask again."

And just as I said it I had to close my eyes. Damon went gray in my field of vision. And then the King of the Castle fainted for the second time in an hour.

11

ME AND JAMES WERE RICH FOR A WEEK.

At the time it seemed a plenty that would last forever. We did our two acts a night, the marks came, and Damon talked them into an enthusiastic frenzy. Damon upped James's pay directly on account of this regularity and, I suppose, in seeing no immediate reason to act miserly, gave us a week's grace to produce James's paperwork.

I saw no reason to act miserly, either. James didn't have a lot to lord over—I didn't let him drive my car, nor did I trust him to change his underwear without my perseverance on the issue—but his money, now that we had some, was his. "You count it up, though, James," I said when the first wages came to our hands. "I don't put it past Merit to think us too dumb to check if it adds up straight." But mine added up straight all right, and between this and the extra cash we were making on Keith's machines, I came to believe that James and I would be comfortable for a long time.

Within that first week, James and I became familiar with the sideshow just as we had the midway rides. James mastered his diversionary magic trick so well that Damon shifted the stunt to the marks' favor. Each round, he invited a member of the audience—a female member, always—onto the stage to preside over the feather. "Let's make things look more legitimate," Damon declared. But this wasn't all. It also bought James a flawless opportunity to implement his diversion. James did this strategically throughout each act: once just after he laid me to the ground, and a second time during Damon's repentance speech.

James's diversion was neither complex nor contrived. Shawn's mentoring helped; but mostly, James's mastery of our ruse came from gifts that he was naturally predisposed toward.

For a guy as big as a bear and now with an alleged reputation as a killer, all James had to do to jolt the girl (and, in this, the proverbial tell-all feather tip) was *move*. He did this easily in reality, and in sudden, homicidal afterthought within the overactive imagination. Over and over again, James created our opportunity to defy death: he lunged at my "dead" body lying on stage, alarmed the appointed mortician/feather-bearer, and gave me the fleeting opportunity to draw a breath. "Predictable," Damon assessed. "Man, girls love to freak out. You should see the looks on their faces while you're holding your breath."

Of course, I never did see their faces. This wasn't because I was down for the count—that veracity hadn't occurred again since me and James's maiden performance—more, it was simply that I always had my eyes closed. But I heard them ("No sir, he's not breathing," they'd say when Damon posed the question, or "The feather's not moving, not one bit"; one time the girl even shrieked, "He's *dead*," her voice a shrill cry inside the silent sideshow tent). I heard them all. Even more than this, within my two allotted gasps of breath, I could smell them. Girls, their faces above my head and their sweet summertime sweat finding my body in different places. Girls, scrutinizing my face for any telltale sign of life, pressing inward, inward, inward—

"Closer," Damon would coax. "You're the judge now, sweetheart."

—and so they *would* go closer, smelling of grass and cotton candy and perfume. "Was she cute?" I always asked Damon afterward. "Hey, was she a brunette? Blonde?" Each time Damon gave me a bewildered look: "Who?" But a few times girls gathered and waited around after the show, near the exit and in the dark, where they accosted him. They asked for autographs, and when he brought them back behind the tent they found me rubbing my neck, hot from James's attack, and still feeling some storm inside me. Those times I French-kissed more than I autographed. Damon stood aside, watching, some combination of disgust and aloofness drawn across his own lips each time.

He never took on any of them.

Though I bet he could have, if he had wanted to.

"You're supposed to be a *monk*," he muttered at me afterward, as we made our way back to the campers through the grass.

"I am. In fact, I'm thinking to start a new religion. With them," I said, indicating the direction the girls went off in, and beginning to laugh. "You want in, Damon?"

"Fuck off," he told me. And so I just laughed again.

At the close of that first week, James and I took time off of working the Roundup and Scrambler for an afternoon. This meant little to James, who did just basic maintenance. But for me, who'd been working eight hours a day turning the lineups and the ride itself, it meant a day of near-ecstatic nothingness. Me and James spent that entire day on the fair lot, just like a couple of marks.

We watched Schroeder's daytime show and perused the long, sweaty lines of concessions. We stood around near the game joints eating greasy potato chips and smoking hand-rolled cigarettes. James and I were no longer destitute vagrants, biding our time away from a Chevy called home without so much as an interior light bulb. Now we had clean clothes, full stomachs, and plenty of change rolling in our pockets.

I'd seen the Card Reader sitting at her parasoled table every afternoon. I watched her pass by the rides twice a day and disappear into John Hadley's girls' quarters each time. On this day, me and James turned up at the hootchy-kootchy show much wealthier than we had upon our first appearance; and when Sandy announced the outside ballyhoo performer as the Queen of Old Argyle, I saw her there too. She wore a veil and danced like a lick of flame; her decorated belt tinkled. *Queen of Old Argyle,* I said to myself over and over as I watched: *Queen of Old Argyle.* It lasted all of five minutes, but I knew it would replay in my head for a lot longer. And I bet James felt the same about the show that followed *inside* the tent.

Me and James had scarcely spent any time in the car since

we joined the sideshow. Just as Keith called his Scrambler—a piece of metal—his worldly possession, the car served a similar function for me and James. Over the years, as we had moved from place to place, the Chevy served as a makeshift safe-deposit box. Our stashed-away wealth consisted mostly of paper, and the document Damon wanted was in there somewhere too. Although I'd have preferred to never look at any of the papers again, me and James had fairly whittled down our week to produce it. We made out to the car, parked in the furthest reaches of the parking lot beyond the grounds, late in the afternoon of our day off.

"Here somewhere," James grunted, his back hitched over the rear seat. Papers and whatnot scuffled against his fingertips. "This look right?"

I looked up from the Chevy's console. "Yeah, that's them."

I fiddled with the radio while James produced a cigarette. "Gotta match?" he asked, arranging himself in the back seat.

"My ass and your face. Here. Then pass it over."

James took the match from me, lit up, and gave me a non-plussed look. "You're not supposed to be smoking much, you know, Tev."

"I know," I said. "Shut up and pass it over."

He passed it, as he did the collection of papers.

"Christ, this place's a dump," I bitched. "And what's this garbage all over the radio knobs?"

I returned the cigarette to James's hand while he said nothing—likely because it was his garbage and he knew it, or maybe because he was still eyeing his papers. I settled them in my lap.

"Which one are we gonna give to Damon?" James asked.

I turned my eyes away from the paperwork and breathed out in a rush. In the distance, the midway lights lay against the thinning daylight. The sunrays had shifted and painted low streaks across the interior of the car. It was evening, but now that we were near high summer, twilight seemed to last forever. I was ignoring the papers more than I'd intended to.

James's arm inched over the seat. "Which one are we gonna

give Damon?" he asked again. "This one?" He lifted the top page from its resting place upon my knees.

"No," I said. I snapped it from his grip like it was on fire and stuffed it at the bottom of the stack. "No. Please, not that one." It wasn't much of a stack really, with just four *(five, actually)* notices composing the whole breadth of it. Then again, when you're talking about a criminal record, anything more than one is a stack.

"Why not?" James tried carefully. "Why, Tev? It's got my name on it. It's got my name and y—"

"No, James, not that one!" I spat. "Jesus, I already told you once!"

"Okay." James backed away. He was wondering when we were going to talk about the one I'd just vetoed, no doubt. It was about six weeks old now. But he let me get away with it. He retracted over the seat in silence. "Okay, Tev."

I took in another deep breath. I pulled up the next document in line. "What do you say, huh?" I held up a page. "How about this one?"

James leaned forward. "Father's Day," he said, reading the page, tentative, gauging my reaction now.

The spring of '65—yes, the Friday before Father's Day. "Yeah," I said. "Yeah, James, that's right." Warm and sunny out, yes; the kind of day where you'd have thrown pants and a sweater on in the cool breath of dawn and then regretted it come noon. College and St. George streets, just east of where me and James met every day after work back then. Friday, the sun gleaming; I remember it had been a payday too. And here was this guy sitting on the corner, surrounded by buckets of cut green.

"Father's Day!" he plugged. *"Wouldn'tcha like to bring home some flowers for Father's Day!"*

And I, in my pleasant mood, had returned to him sardonically, "My father's dead," as we verged upon him.

"Your brother, then," the man amended. "Flowers for Father's Day!"

"He's dead too."

"How 'bout for yer friend there," the guy said this time, his eyes gleaming. James's gaze came up at for a moment, we went on walking, and I believe the fellow would have gone home that night with his face intact if he'd shut up right then. But like I'd come to say of him, the guy had it coming. The next zinger hit us at our backs: "Yeh, yeh, forget it," he said. "Your buddy's too stupid to know a lay if one sat right down on his face."

His first mistake was making a judgment on the tall, quiet ox that was my accompanying sidekick. His second was turning his back at a critical moment, right after he had made his first. Suddenly James wasn't beside me anymore. It was the middle of the day, rush hour, with an ever-increasing population gliding back and forth on the sidewalk, and as I whirled to see him, snatching the vendor up by his collar, pulling his fist back, I was stunned to understand what James meant to do before tens of milling people:

Pow!

—landing the guy full in the face. I heard the crack, but James seemed not to sense a thing. He broke his nose with that and it gushed, James getting it on him as he dove in for a second and third bomb. By then I was screaming, my arms across his chest and trying to hold him off. Passers-by staring, gape-mouthed and bewildered. *James*, I screamed, *James, what the fuck, what in the holy name of God, Jesus Christ, James, what are you DOING?* And when I finally got him turned around *(Hold it, James, what are you DOING?)*, his elbows were still pounding the air like pistons and his eyes blazed. He whirled and spied me like a little bug that's been buzzing around your neck for no good reason other than to irritate you; and for a second there I thought he was going to swat me.

Let me give you the simplified version of how it all shakes out. I can; after all, me and James are experts by now. The cops came, our old daffodil purveyor laid a charge, and I drained most of my bank account signing James out of the can. So much for payday.

"What got into you?" I said a day later, plunging his shirt in the bathtub. It would soak for a week, but I'd never get the stains out.

"He made me mad," James said. "He said I didn't know what a lay was, Tevan. But I do."

The hell you do! I almost snapped back, because, to add insult to injury, the old flower coot had actually been right. Then I'd peered over at James and understood. James knew. Of course he did. He knew, as my mother would say, "when a fellow shouldn't know at all," at the age of fifteen.

And now he had the papers to prove it.

Inside the car now, I heaved in a long breath. The sun stretched across the interior seats like a great spill of paint. I looked down at the document in my hand.

```
Whereas on September 21st, 1965 at The City
of Toronto, James Daniel Rowley, date of
birth September 8, 1941 in the said region
hereinafter called the offender was convicted
on the charge that (1) Assault, June 16th,
1965 CONTRARY TO THE CRIMINAL CODE
```

"That guy had it coming. Didn't he, Tev?" James declared from behind me. He nodded toward the paper, as though he had just been reading my thoughts. But really he hadn't read a thing. I just said that line out loud one too many times, trying to get James off the hook when the authorities showed up at my apartment that night. God, for all the times I've told James to cork his hole, I really need to watch my own sometimes.

"Had it coming, James," I said. "Yes." And then: "Don't let me hear you saying that too much, though, now." I looked down at my hands again:

```
From the date that this order is
applicable, comply with the following
```

```
conditions, namely that: the said offender
shall:
I. keep the peace and be of good behavior
II. appear before the court when required
to do so
```

I pulled my eyes away. I didn't want to think about James's charges. But here we were, and now I was thinking of them, every one. And in this I could not help but pass a glance toward James, there in the Chevy, not a foot away from me.

```
AND IN ADDITION
III. NOT TO ASSOCIATE, CONTACT, or hold
any communication directly or indirectly
with . . .
```

After this document, there was no more meeting at the corner of St. George and College anymore, I can tell you that much. No more walking like free, democratic human beings down the sidewalk past an old man selling his hawk either. The document specified that James Daniel Rowley *not come within 200 feet* of the man or his place of business. In fact, the Crown Attorney who represented our flower peddler claimed that the man was afraid of James.

I sighed, staring into the paper: the no-contact provision upon it always filled me with an angry sort of exasperation. James might not be the quickest horse on the track, but for a stupid guy, he ain't so stupid. Should James have ever met the man on the street again by chance, I suspect he would have just crossed the street and steered clear of him. Would have left him alone. Would have said nothing. Would have said, if anything—

(I'm not supposed to come near you, Tev. It says so all over my papers)

—well, I don't know what, exactly.

But probably, James would have apologized.

"Come on, James," I said finally. "This will do. I'll pass it over to Damon when I see him next."

James nodded, tossed his cigarette through the window, and unfurled himself from the back bench. I stuffed the paper into my pocket. We made it back to the midway for sundown.

Keith was in his usual spot at the rides. The sky hung deep blue, the shade of bright new denim, and the Scrambler was a reach of metal limbs against it. "Come on, Tevan, let's go!" James cried, pointing and tugging my arm.

"Come on up, son," Keith said, grinning. "No charge for ya's. This tairn's on me." He paused, his lips twitching to one side as he watched my expression. "Whatsits, boy? Not a puker, are ya?"

So I moved in toward the monster. James yanked me up the metal step, then into the tub beside him.

"Just lift yer arms up and wave them aroond if yuh wanna git off," Keith hollered as he hit the pedal. And she started up and we were off—James and I the lone rangers, the only guys at all sitting on the ride in the last wink of a summer night. And it spun its first tepid round, a round I'd facilitated a hundred times or more myself by now, despite the fact that I'd never actually ridden it. I held my breath, my fingers clamped to the metal rungs so tightly that my knuckles went white against them. For a moment—the first moment that the arm upon which our tub was situated swung into the lawn and, I believed, into certain oblivion—I yanked one hand from its death grip and began to inch it into the air. James grabbed it, and as I turned, I saw him grinning, laughing, watching me, his green eyes glittering.

"Aaaauuuggh!" he hollered, into the air. His voice, his call of the wild, ripped through the air, an insane, laughing release.

Oh boy, it came to me, *I'm going to scream now.*

"*Aaaauuuggh!*" I yelled after him, my eyes streaming from the wind, the rest of me swinging side to side with the tub's motion. My lungs felt full to bursting and ripe with laughter and so I laughed and said it again—"*Aaaauuuggh!*"—as the tub extended outward. Again and again; faster, faster, dizzying, ecstatic. And as we punched back and forth, I caught sight of Keith on the forward swing, standing and smiling before the machine controls. He was laughing. James was laughing. And I screamed and I laughed too. Laughed until the tears streamed down my face.

James sat beside me and his paperwork sat inside my back pocket. I handed it over to Damon the next day. The rest I left pressed into the deepest recesses of my mind. For the sixth week in a row, I forgot all about the fifth paper with James's name upon it.

It would be the last of it I could forget.

12

IN LATE JUNE, THE MIDWAY SAW A WET STRING OF DAYS. I begged Keith to give me more hours on the rides, on the rigs, on the grounds, on *anything,* but he didn't need me. While this gave me more time to do as I pleased, it also put less capital in our pockets. Keith nabbed me one afternoon just as I opened my door, offering to pay me a tip to run him an errand. It was his wife's birthday and he wanted a bottle of wine. I jumped at the opportunity.

"What kind?" I asked as we arrived at his trailer.

"Cheap!" Keith flipped me a few bills. "Whatever you can find. Quantity is more than quality in this family, see?" I laughed and pocketed the cash. But I sobered as I left him. I could commiserate.

James and I had been rich for a week, but already that status was dwindling. My pay made ends (read "dings") meet fair enough, though James's contribution was straggling. We pooled our income, and understandably, he earned less on Keith's machinery than I did. Still, I couldn't figure out where all his cash was going. "Please, James," I had said to him just that morning, steeling myself against irritation as he came up dry for the grocery fund. "You have to watch where you're spending."

I toyed with the idea of retracting my promise that Death-Defying would occur only twice nightly. I could have, and I knew that Damon would fall all over himself allowing it. The problem was that by now I had an idea that defying death might be a stunt that a man could pull off only twice a night. I never told anyone this (and when I reflect back, I can only assume that Damon and his management team were either too stupid or too greedy to ask), but the act was proving to be physically strenuous. Just three weeks into performing on the sideshow—and at my negotiated low quota, too—I had already gone to my bed with the skin circling my Adam's apple aching like an Indian sunburn. I prayed that I wouldn't awaken to a collar the color of a sunset. Unconsciousness we could fake, but having James at my throat we could not. We never spoke of it. But me, James, and Damon all understood that it was the brutality that was drawing in the crowds.

I crossed the grounds in the spitting rain ruminating, Keith's cash in one hand, the other rubbing unconsciously at my neck. I stopped off to buy cigarette paper and to haggle for a bag of cherries at the concessions. The air was sweaty and humid. You could see the clouds, gray and thick, swallowing the midway lot for the third day in a row. It was bad news for me and James. There was hardly a crowd on site, and those who stood under umbrellas would undoubtedly make off toward the shelter of their cars soon enough. Even the Card Reader's sunshade sat empty, aside from the girl herself.

I stood with my eye on her, chewing cherries and spitting the pits between my teeth. I made a little pile on the ground, I watched for so long. Then I mussed my hair up a little and walked over.

The girl looked up immediately. She smiled. "Do you have a question?" she asked.

This surprised me—I did, in fact, have a question. I'd thought one up just before I walked over. "Yes," I said. *Maybe she really does know the future*, I thought, fascinated.

Before I could open my mouth she drew a finger into the air and tapped the box in front of her on the table. I recognized it as one of the show's cashboxes, just like the one Damon carried into our venue. I knew what *that* was for. And like a stupefied, full-of-fuck dimwit, I stuck my hand in my pocket and dropped her a quarter.

The girl nodded approvingly. "What is your question?"

I fluttered my eyelashes. "Why are you the Queen of Old Argyle?"

The girl stared at me a moment. Her hand went to her mouth. Then she just busted up laughing. "Christ," she managed. "You didn't have to pay for *that* one, honey. I thought you wanted a reading."

"Oh," I said, as though I had shit for brains. "Well, come on, then. I want to know. I paid, didn't I?"

"You've seen the show," she said.

For a second I worried she might take me for a pervert if I said yes. But I'd already admitted that I'd seen the ballyhoo, and what the hell would it mean about a man if he skipped the show after that? "Yes," I told her. "It was very nice."

She grinned. Her eyes were green like James's. "It's the name of the song I dance to. You want a reading?" She indicated the cards before her. "You already paid."

"Oh, no," I said. "Sorry. I don't, ah, really believe in that sort of shit."

"No need to apologize." She studied me as though I were someone she knew but couldn't quite place. And then, finally, she did. "So," she said. "Why are you Death-Defying?"

"You've seen my show," I said.

"No, actually." She cut me a shrewd look. "I don't really believe in that sort of shit."

I narrowed my eyes. "Look, it's real." I puffed out my chest at her. "If you don't believe me, you should come see it sometime." *I'll let you hold my feather*, I thought. "Yes," I added, on a whim.

She looked about. "Yes, what?"

"Yes, I'll take a reading."

"Well . . ." She paused, studying her fingernails. "A reading's actually *fifty* cents."

And again I dug into my pockets. "Fine, fine. What do I do?"

"It's easy." She was smiling again as she took up a stack of cards. "All's you have to do is sit down here"—she laid the cards neatly before me on the table—"and wash the deck."

I cast her a dubious look. I considered her carefully. "Say, well, why don't *you* do it?"

She giggled. "Wash," she repeated, slowly this time. "That means *cleanse*. You have to mix the cards up with your hands, honey, that's all." The smirk lingered on her lips and she spoke as you would to an idiot. "I can't do it because they need your energy in them. That is the purpose of the exercise."

"Oh." The *cards*. I peered down at them. "All right." I sat in the chair in front of her. Then I plunked the bag of cherries onto the table in between. "Want my cherry?" I asked.

The girl's eyebrows rose. "Thanks," she said, dropping one into her mouth. "Didn't think a fellow like you would have one for me."

I made a face. "Quiet, please," I said. "I'm trying to wash the deck here."

A few moments passed as I shuffled the cards from hand to hand. I noticed that each backside showed a picture of two cats, their beady eyes simpering up at me, and I scowled back at them. I wasn't sure exactly what to do.

"Set them before me when you're done," she offered. "Horizontally."

When I did, she dealt them out in a hexagon formation: four rows, ten cards, the first set in dead center and overlaid with the second.

"Hmmm," she murmured, surveying the spread. "Interesting."

"What?" I had a chance to take a good look at her as she turned her eyes to the table. I noticed the pink of her lips and the splash of freckles spattering her nose. "What do you see?"

"Well, it's just that you have six out of ten Higher Arcana here. It's unusual, that's all. Very unusual. *Higher Arcana*," she said again. "It's a force, you could say, higher than the self. What a reading does is tell us what will happen if we continue on the path that we are currently on. However, the Higher Arcana are a little more divine—external. I call it *That which must be*."

"Huh," I said. I couldn't help but feel impressed with my energy. "Go on, then. What's it say about me?"

She shuffled forward in her seat, lifting the crossed card to reveal the one in the center. "Let's begin. Your Atmosphere. This is the general impression of your current situation, you see?" The card showed a couple of cats, just as on the back, but these ones were surrounded by a number of sticks. "You ready?" she asked.

"Ready," I said. And what happened next is something I'm never going to forget for as long as I live:

"The Eight of Wands, reversed," she announced. "Stagnation. Quarrels. Dispute, harassment, jealousy."

My blood ran cold. For one unmistakable moment I believed—no, I *knew*—that her sentence was accurate. At first this brought an unusually nervy sensation to my stomach. A moment later, it brought me to something else.

"Now just what in hell is that supposed to mean?" I said, getting pissed.

"It means what it says," she told me. "The card indicates that you're in a crisis of standstill. Upright it means the opposite, a process of moving forward." She eyed me frankly. "*Yours* is reversed."

"Reversed," I said, indignant.

"Hey, I just read what the card says, is all." She put another cherry into her mouth and said, "I thought you didn't believe in this shit anyway," then spit the pit over her shoulder.

"I *don't*." I paused, deliberating. "What about that one on top?"

She returned the card to its intersecting position. "Better," she agreed. "This is the Knight of Cups. The placement within the spread represents what's crossing your Atmosphere. For good or bad, the force working against it." I nodded and so she went on. "The Knight of Cups is a mature and wise man. He's ready for a challenge. A warrior, an invitation. He usually appears in the form of a young male adult." She looked up at me. "Does that sound like anyone you know?"

Mature? Wise? Well, scratch James. "No," I said dryly.

"Well, how old are you?"

"Twenty-three," I admitted, not seeing what the hell this had to do with anything. And anyhow, I was still buggered by those damn Wands.

"The Knight represents a person under the age of thirty. Perhaps," she offered, "it could be you."

She moved on to the third card. "This one indicates your Higher Self. That is, what the self knows on an unconscious level. Yours is the Page of Cups, reversed. It's quite fitting, actually. The Page represents a child. Pubescent or pre-pubescent." She looked at me, delicately this time. "This is what your Higher Self knows: Inclination. Deviation, flattery, susceptibility, vulnerability. And seduction."

I drew my head back.

"Feel free to add in at any time," she said.

I didn't have anything to add in. Or, on the contrary, I had a whole lot to add in. All at once I could feel myself starting to sweat. "What do you *mean*, it's fitting?" I said.

She shrugged. "I don't know. A page, historically, was the assistant to a knight. If he was a good assistant, he went on to become"—she put a finger to the previous card—"a knight himself."

"Oh," I managed. *This is a joke*, I told myself. *This is just another bamboozle, like Shawn said. Relax, Tevan. It's a ruse.* Even so, I decided I'd better get a handle on the situation. I put my hand up. "Wait. Just hold on a second here. So if that's my Higher Self"—I put a finger to another card farther up the line—"what's *this* one?"

She slid me a look, as if to question what it was I had in mind. But she didn't ask. Instead she simply looked down into the spread. "The Future."

"Uh-huh." The *do-you-really-want-to-know* category, I reckoned. "And this?" I indicated another card.

She rattled them off—Recent Past, Quierant, Hopes and

Fears—one after the other after the other. The cards were all starting to look the same to me, the cats appearing uniformly accusing. My plan was to avoid the ones that were alleged to have a lot to say about me; but, unlucky for me, that accounted for a whole lot of them.

"Great," I said finally. "Fine. Fuck this going in order. Let's start . . ." I gazed about the table and chose the card farthest from me. "Here."

"Culmination?" She looked at me, a smile playing at the corner of her lips. She looked to the card. "Oh, you don't want to hear *that* one."

"I don't?" I asked, alarmed.

She didn't launch into any sermon about how we were going about it all wrong, how I wasn't playing the game correctly, or how I was screwing up energies. She simply looked back at me matter-of-factly. "No," she said. "You don't. I suggest you pick another."

"Okay." I peered about the spread nervously. I chose the Quierant. This card was quite encouraging (aside from the fact that the card in question, the Empress, designated that a female relative weighs heavily on your mind. I cringed: it had been weeks since I last called my mother). On to the Future, which was the most positive of the entire sweep: Approaching the end of a problem. Progression. Beginning of an end. The reading was getting better and better. I should've started at the middle right in the beginning.

"So I'm no longer stagnating, am I?" I said to the girl.

"Mmmm. Sounds like it," she agreed.

"You like men who are progressive?"

"I like men who don't ask so many questions. Should we move on to your Environment?" she asked, then did so without waiting for a response. "The card in your Environment is also reversed. It's the Hierophant, which means the Wounded Healer. It represents a man of wisdom or knowledge, though of little practical experience. Dogmatic, fixed though highly compassionate.

"The placement of the card—Environment—represents

surroundings. Maybe some context in your life, or more likely a person. A friend or family member close to you just now."

I hardly had *any* family members, I thought wryly, much less any close to me.

"Does it sound like anyone you know?" she pressed.

A man of knowledge, though of little experience: *He said I didn't know what a lay was, Tevan, but I do.*

"Yeah," I said suddenly, getting a little excited. "Yeah, actually it kind of does."

"Hmm." She nodded. "This person displays over-kindness. Generosity. Susceptibility. Foolishness. And vulnerability." She paused and screwed her face up at me. "Poor guy, eh?"

"Yeah," I agreed. *You don't know the half of it*, I thought.

She nodded, sighed, and stretched her arms up above her head. I noticed the slim curve of her muscles as they drew into her sleeves and disappeared. I glimpsed the tiny swell of her breasts against her shirt. I was busy watching all these minutiae; and then before I knew what was happening, she reached her arm out and made to sweep the cards right off the table.

"Wait!" I grabbed her elbow just as the cats' eyes nearest me began to slide away. "What are you doing?"

She stopped, lifting the crook of her arm. "That's it, honey," she said. "That's the reading." She looked down at the remnants, the top row already cockeyed and overlapping the second. "Other than the cards you skipped, that is. The ones you didn't want."

"But I *want* them," I bleated. I noticed my fingers around her arm, how I was touching her, speaking into her face; the closest I'd ever come to her. "Please," I said, leaning in. The girl gazed past me into the lot.

I looked too—and as I'd predicted, it was now clear of anyone at all, save the few staff picking their way through wet sod. She turned and looked right at me. "Shove off, pal," she said. "No whining, either."

"I'm not whining," I said, though even that came out sounding like a whine, and now she was pissed at me.

"Recent Past?" she said, her voice shrill. "Ah, that's right. This is where we were, weren't we? Before you got all fuckin' uptight on me?"

"Wait a second," I returned, in my defense. "I didn't get uptight on you."

"Yes you did," she countered.

"No I didn't." *Oh great, I thought: another one of these.* "I just told you we'd get back to it. That's all."

She gave me a dry look. "Your Recent Past." She sighed and began again. "This is something that happened roughly six weeks prior to today, and is now in the process of slipping away. The card is Strength, reversed." She studied me matter-of-factly. "Boy. You have a lot of reversals, you know."

I, not knowing anything about anything, had not known.

"Strength, reversed," she began. "It is precisely as it sounds: the opposite of true, honest strength. That is to say, it represents an exploitation of strength, or brute strength directed at an innocent party. An accident of domination. Pettiness," the Card Reader said. "Tyranny. Sickness. Abuse of power. Succumbing to temptation. Indifference."

"Man," I breathed, horrified. I thought, unbidden, of the paper that me and James had left hidden in the back seat of the car: the one now about six weeks old. "Did you say—"

"Six weeks ago, give or take." She nodded. "Yeah." She glanced at the card again. "Leave it to reversals. It sounds really awful, doesn't it?"

And this time I winced as her words brought to mind something James had said to me, almost word for word: *It looked really awful, Tev,* he had managed in a whisper. *Man, I thought you were dead.* I watched the girl but said none of this aloud. *You ever done this before for show?* I recalled Buddy Merit's question.

And my own response: *Yes.*

I'd pushed it from my mind for that long, and yet she got it right on the dot: six weeks before. Four criminal charges for

James; five, actually, if you count this last time, wherein the guy he'd knocked out refused to talk even after the fuzz showed up. The guy who'd shook his head and offered repeatedly, *Nah, he didn't know what he was doing, he musta got mixed up; no, the man didn't know who he was! Look at him, look at him, sorry, stupid dipshit, I think he's retarded! Come on, let it rest, man: there's something wrong with him! He didn't mean it, come on.*

The lousy guy in the bar who lay unconscious long enough for the girl behind the counter to become hysterical and call the ambulance, who in turn called the cops, who in turn laid a charge whether the guy wanted them to or not.

Six weeks past or not, I still can't help but hate myself for it all.

Before me, the Card Reader shook her head. "A troublesome card, I agree. But like I said, don't worry. This is something in your past." She shifted in her seat, waiting for me to say something. "Your, ah, cherries are getting sweaty." The bag of fruit stood, paper wilting onto the wood table: I'd long forgotten all about it.

She tried a grin, raising one eyebrow. "Who are you here with?" She righted the bag with one hand, tapping the card with the other. "You staying with family on the show or something? What did you do before this?" She cast me a look. "I mean, you haven't been Death-Defying forever."

I looked up, distracted. "I—turned up with this buddy of mine." My voice sounded small, somehow; and speaking of James now, it grew smaller still. *Look at him,* my head repeated back at me, my own words: *Look at him, sorry, stupid dipshit, I think he's—* "No family," I told her. "That's all. I'm just here with my friend." I hesitated. "I was—unemployed before this."

She smiled. "Hey. Ain't that the truth for all of us." She took the remaining cards, still neatly stacked to one side. "That's pretty much it. Unless you want your life card. Do you want your life card?" She shrugged toward the cashbox. "I have a special on. Two for one."

"A special for nice boys like me?" I managed.

"A special for twenty-five cents."

And I, Tevan George, not made of money and yet made on seeing this slippery girl outside of her card table some way somehow, bombed another quarter into the box. "Okay," I said. "But I'll get mine later. I want you to read my friend's." I'd had just about enough of my own mysteries for one day. "I'll pass along what you tell me," I offered, though I had no intention of doing any such thing.

"Birthday?" she asked.

I deliberated briefly before coming up with James's birth date. "September eighth, 1941."

She scribbled it down and went to task adding up the numbers. "The date's coming up," she mused, peering down. "You shopping for her yet?"

"It's a him," I corrected.

"Huh," she said, staring down at her work. "Well, well. That's certainly interesting."

I looked at her, my eyes questioning.

"Your friend's life card," the girl said. She turned the page around. The number that she had tallied and circled at the bottom read:

"Five," I said. "What of it?"

She picked up one of the cards from my previous reading and placed it beside the page. And when I looked down I saw what it was that she had found so interesting. "Your friend's life is represented by the Hierophant," the Card Reader said. The number at the bottom of the card read 5 as well. "And that same person represents your Environment."

A man of wisdom or knowledge, though of little experience, I thought. *Dogmatic, fixed though compassionate. Over-kindness, generosity, foolishness, vulnerability.*

She shrugged. "Thanks for coming by," she said, collecting

her cards. She watched me, waiting. When I didn't move she grinned awkwardly, as though uncertain what to do with me.

I opened my mouth. "Please. Come out with me sometime."

Her eyebrows rose on her forehead.

"Please," I said again. "You can show me—that crazy dance you do. And I swear I won't bug you about cherries."

She grinned, looked at the card table. "I would," she said. "But you have a very poor Culmination."

I remained in my seat. Still, suddenly I found I had to turn my head and put my eyes away from her. I wasn't too used to getting turned down, no; but it wasn't this. It was more that I believed her. And worse, I didn't blame her either: I didn't want hang with somebody damned like me any more than she did.

I stood and offered a smile. I took up the bag of cherries. I started away. But then I paused some five feet away and turned to face her.

"Hey," I said at her, standing there. "If it's going to stand in my way. What was my Culmination, anyhow?"

She answered as though it had never left her mind: "Nine of Pentacles, reversed," she said. "Years culminate to create a masterpiece. But—threat to safety. Danger. Bad faith. Possible loss of a treasured belonging or friend."

I stared at the girl, silent. Though

(I'm not supposed to come near you, Tev. It says so all over)

somehow, not surprised at all.

"Come back and let me know if it pans out at all like I said," she offered. "You know, I always like to see if I'm right in the end."

I stood watching her, wishing she'd said nothing this time. Her comment told me that she really was a soothsayer, a reader: a woman just telling it as she saw it. She had no control over the cards. Instead, those cards had come to me.

"Say hi to your friend for me," she said carefully.

I waved, jingling Keith's change in my pocket.

Me and James delivered Mrs. Cruikshane's birthday gift later that evening. Although I haven't been much of a wine drinker since my sangria days, we took Keith up on his offer to join them. I swung mine back in minutes; and then me and James headed to the Chevy. There was a bottle of Four Roses waiting in the back seat, thanks to the errand I'd run for Keith. Four Roses—*gag*. I guess you could say me and James were turning into a little *quantity is more than quality* family ourselves. We sat inside and passed the bottle back and forth between us.

In the dark, I turned and eyed James in silence. His eyes were as wide and dilated as those of a cat watching a sparrow through a screened window as he swished the contents around the bottle. *Stagnation*, my head recalled. *Quarrels. Dispute, harassment, jealousy. Threat to safety. Danger. Bad faith. Possible loss of a treasured belonging. Or friend.*

"James," I said. "Do you like it here?"

"Like it where?" James held the bottle up to the windshield as though measuring its color and weight.

"Here," I said. "On the show."

James peered over at me in the dimness of the car interior. "Sure, Tev," he said. "Sure I do."

"What do you like?" I asked.

James gazed through the bottle again. He pursed his lips, weighing the question. "I like being sort of famous," he said finally. "Powerful, big, like Damon's talk says." He thought some more. "I like Sandy and the dog. Keith. And Shawn." He smiled. "Yeah, Shawn. He's like my friend. You know?"

In the dark, I closed my teeth tight together. I felt something sour bloom inside myself: some combination of hatred and mourning. I breathed in, shaking my head. I breathed out again.

"And so," I tried carefully. "So—you want to stay?"

"Yes," he said. "Yes. Sure. I'll stay."

I placed one arm against the window ledge. I put my chin upon it and peered into the darkness, where the midway and sideshow tents were dead giants against the sky. "What if we needed to leave?" I said suddenly. It arrived as a whisper, swift and abrupt; in the absence of light it sounded near-hysterical. And although I hadn't meant it that way, I admit it was how I felt just then.

James turned. He appraised me, his eyes calm and cautious. "Don't be scared, Tev," he said.

"I'm not scared," I told him fiercely. "I'm just *ask*ing, is all."

We drank the whole bottle in under an hour. It left me with no feeling in my extremities and no memories at all. We left the car in the swaying moonlit grass and the next thing I remember is John finding us watering the bushes up along the highway overpass. He dragged us, staggering and laughing, back to Keith's place.

"Found these two out past the lot and thought you wouldn't want them to get into any trouble." He paused, looking us over. "The big one's fine," he said. "But the littler one . . ."

"You shore like yer drink, dontcha, boy," Keith said, lifting my feet onto my bunk some time later. He grinned, even though his eyes looked tired and irritated.

"Runs in the family," I mumbled. And that's the closest I ever came to saying out loud that my brother had been a drunk.

"Yeh, yeh," Keith murmured. He pulled my shirt right off me with my back splayed across the bunk. "Got a feelin' yer gonna fit in just fine around here."

He turned out the lights to lessen the battle against the ever-loving fucking dings. He even locked the door behind him. He placed James and me in separate bunks, though. How was he to know?

I awoke to the first needling of the next morning's light. My head pounded and my eyes stung at the memory of the evil Four Roses. I awoke in the exact same position that Keith had left me in. I squinted across the room: James was curled and sleeping on the floor.

I didn't tell James hi for the Card Reader, and I didn't tell him about his life card. I certainly didn't tell him about my Recent Past—how the girl had professed that something terrible had happened six weeks ago. But then again, James already knew all about that.

No. I didn't tell him. I believed the Card Reader would never know James—or me, really—at all.

But I didn't have magic cards to read the future with. And so I was wrong about all that too.

13

IT WAS A HOT, SWEATY FRIDAY WHEN I MADE MY DEAL WITH the devil. It was payday, so I was actually in a good mood as I wiped down Keith's equipment that afternoon. James was there too, doing the kind of work that any ten-year-old with muscles can do. I'd hardly said a word to him all day.

"Merit!" I yelled, spying Damon walking up the lot. "Just the man I want to see!" I climbed over the sweeps of the Scrambler and he met me on the ground.

"Got your beauty sleep, I see," he quipped, looking me over. "I imagine you want your upshot. Your sidekick already showed up this morning for his."

Our outfit had set up on an outskirt of the city—Halton region—the day before, and Damon was referring to the preceding hairy night on the road. I'd followed Damon's taillights the whole way to our destination, like a bug wacked out on caffeine and caught in the drawing beam of a hurricane lamp. "You okay?" he'd said, looking me over when we stopped for fuel in the first misty light of dawn. "You look half-dead, man. More dead than usual, actually."

"You'd be the one to know it," James had managed under his breath in reply.

Still, Damon had been right: I was so tired I *felt* half-dead. And when we'd finally reached our location, I passed into sleep the way a man clubbed on the head passes into unconsciousness—that is, with a sudden drop, following a long surge of his own adrenaline. I hadn't opened my eyes until noon.

"Yeah, sure," I said to Damon now. Then I turned and hollered to James that I'd be back in a minute and to finish up without me. I actually hollered a bunch of times. When James didn't seem to hear me and otherwise appeared to be minding the machinery like a deaf shepherd tending the holy flock of Jesus Christ, I turned back to Damon. "Ah, who cares," I said. "He's driving me crazy anyhow. Let's go."

We walked over to Merit's Winnebago together, hardly a word between us. I was thrilled to have run into Damon, antsy to get inside and paid; maybe even considering asking for a little optimistic advance on the upcoming week so that James and I could douse our stomachs with something other than beans, coffee, and cigarettes. It never even crossed my mind that I was just the man Damon had wanted to see too.

"By the way," he said as we came up the steps, "my father wants to see you."

I marched in ahead of him. Buddy Merit was waiting inside his stinky little office. He nodded as I came through the doorway. He had a pile of papers before him along with his cashbox.

"Going well out there, George?" he asked. Buddy never called me by any normal names, never "Tevan," never "son" or even Keith's endearing "boy." Instead, like a military officer or a commander on a SWAT team, he only referred to me by my family name.

"Yes, sir," I answered.

Buddy pulled out a stack and licked off a few bills. He totted them up and placed them before me. I, in turn, gave him two-thirds of it straight back: rent, weekly dings, plus a portion of the cost for a trailer hitch that he'd bought and I installed, which would come to sit on my Chevy Nomad like a vestigial appendage for the next five years. I paid for it all right then myself. I figured, confidently, that James could get back to me on his end later, even though this was his current express means of driving me crazy. James had lit out for Merit's office at the crack of dawn like Damon said, but by the time all hands were on deck at noon he'd had all of ten dollars left. He couldn't explain to me where it had gone, either. I'd barely said a word to him since. But there in the office with the debts momentarily square and the diddly-squat left over in my hand, I felt pretty cheerful. I'd worry about groceries later, I even thought. This optimism lasted all of three seconds.

"You're not going on this week, George," Buddy announced.

I turned my eyes up. "What?"

"I think you heard him," Damon said. "You and your jackass aren't going on. Sorry."

"Don't call him that," I said at once, even though a minute before I'd hardly been in any mood to shore up for James. My gaze found Damon standing in the doorway. "What do you mean, not going on?" I said.

Buddy spread his hands. "The venue. I just spoke to the fair head that operates the space, and because—"

No, I thought at once. *No, we're hardly making any money as it is.* A kind of unbidden inventory sprang into my head on the spot: me and James had a bag of frozen vegetables, a few cans of soup, and a piddling amount of anything else left.

"Because *shit*," I said. "I don't care about the reason. You hired us on. We're *on* your venue." *Please, James, watch what you're spending*, some inside voice was already blasting, *don't think that comes for free* . . . "Are you firing us?" I sounded incredulous now, and for good reason. James and I were bringing in more money in two acts nightly than Shawn Schroeder or Rajid did in a week.

"No," Buddy said. "I'm not firing you."

"You're saying," I tried, "that there's no sideshow, then?"

"Oh, there's a sideshow, George," he returned. "It just doesn't include you."

I stared, confounded. I saw Damon, his chin lowered toward me in its most self-righteous posture. My eyes went back and forth between Buddy and Damon. "Who else isn't going on?"

"Well, nobody," Buddy replied. "Nobody from the sideshow isn't going on, really. Only the kootch girls are cut." He paused, looked at me meaningfully: "And you."

"You can't bump us off," I started. "Please. No. No, you have a"—I hesitated, floundering—"a Ten in One."

That was a mistake; I knew it the moment it left my lips. But I was thinking of a week without pay, a week full of dings, a week of poverty that James and I couldn't afford. I was thinking of James, shining up the Roundup like an idiot, dreaming of returning to his camper at nightfall to at least a peanut butter sandwich. I was thinking of me, who'd drunk nothing but black coffee for a fortnight and had woken up this morning to the first familiar sting of a urinary tract infection.

"No," Buddy said. "I don't. I have a venue without a skin show and a gasper or else I have nothing at this location at all. Do you understand me?"

I stared at Buddy. I looked to Damon. *You're not sorry,* I thought directly at him. And then I lost my bearings completely.

"*You're going on without us?*" I shrieked. "Why? *Why?*"

"Calm down, Tevan," Damon murmured. His tone held a combination of apology and disgust.

"I *am* calm!" I said, heatedly.

"Well, you sure don't sound it," Damon cut in. "You ask me, you sure sound—"

"I sound *what?*" I screamed. "What, Damon? How did you expect me to sound? Tell me, just—"

His father's voice boomed, cutting between us: "*You're not going on, George, because your act is racy.*"

Damon and I stood blinking at each other.

"It is not," I said, for the sake of saying something, anything, anything at all.

"Oh, I think it is." Buddy folded his hands and sighed. "The protocol on a carnival—like that which you are now enjoying the pleasure of traveling with, George—is that the showman pays a ding. A *sizable* ding, to secure a place on the fairground itself." He eyed me as though this were some grand favor he'd been paying me over the last few weeks. "You are familiar with dings by now, aren't you, George?"

I nodded.

"The showman—myself, that is—describes his wares to

the ground's fair committee," Buddy went on. "The committee sets a price depending on the size of the space needed for the show. Now, normally, such a price is simply monetary: I pay the fee, my show sets up shop, we go on. See?"

Buddy's face took on a sorrowful look. "This is your average vanilla, upper-class community here, George. They don't want any carnal acts or hookers or perverts on their family venue." His shoulders heaved up and down. "I'm surprised this hasn't happened already, really. This time the price listed on the contract, among the usual bucks, is that I drop my punks from the show or I don't go on. And that"—Buddy tapped the papers in front of him—"is what I've decided to do."

He took a pen into his fat little fingers and leaned over the document. *We don't want any carnal acts or hookers or perverts,* my brain spat back at me as I watched him. The year was 1966: a year in which Jeannie herself continued to appear on television with a jewel tucked into the profanity of her navel, a year in which skin mags still ran relatively underground and K-Y Jelly, by God, was *not* found in the open aisles of your corner drugstore. Ten long years before Trudeau stood up on Parliament Hill and officially legalized the birth control pill. When Merit reached the CNE in Toronto come August, he would find that Conklin Shows had a sideshow flagrantly titled "Striporama." But even that consisted of just swimsuit models.

I saw Buddy's predicament, the fact that some meddling conservative provisos were standing in the way of his capital, but I didn't care. I flailed, frantic for a compromise.

"But we make more principal than any other show you've got here, Merit!" I tried, to which Buddy replied that he wouldn't generate a damn cent if he didn't abide by the terms. "We need the money," I pleaded, to which Buddy put forward that maybe I should go tell my problems to Jesus. "How about talking to the fairground management—I'll even do it myself," I suggested— which, in the end, nobody would let me get close to.

All I got was a copy of Merit's contract, listing the seven

or so acts that would go on without Death-Defying. The papers were of no use to James and me unless, say, we baked them over a fire and ate them. I crumpled them into a little ball right there in the office and threw it away.

"Eat shit, Merit," I said under my breath, and which I suspect he heard anyhow. "Your show's the bum's rush, isn't it?"

He did hear it—I know because Damon told me later. What Buddy said in response (and which I *didn't* hear at all) was that James would be smart to find himself his own act for the week. And as for the other one? Well, he'd known from the moment he set eyes on that little faggot that he'd be trouble.

If I had been wise to it, I think I'd have taken James and cut myself loose from Merit right then. But I wasn't. And so Buddy's next design proved just as effective as his strategy in laying Death-Defying off the show: he made a pricey offer in the interest of salvaging the bigger picture. Moments after I stormed out of his trailer, he sent a handful of cash and his son after me.

Not that that money was meant to reach my hands, no. Buddy only needed the dough to patch things up a little—just so's I wouldn't get my shit wound so tight that I'd pack my bags and cut out on the sideshow completely. Damon called his offer a drink for a friend down on his luck. On a carnival, the official name for this sort of money-for-forgiveness strategy is "icing things over."

I admit, I accepted Buddy's ice without difficulty. In the position he'd put me in, what other choice did I have?

Known from the moment he set eyes on that little faggot that he'd be trouble.

At least I have the satisfaction of knowing that Buddy Merit in his mean, bigoted assessment never came to know the half of it.

Damon wasn't my friend and I knew Merit had sent him after me purposefully—but neither of these gave me any reason to resist him. I could scarcely stand to look at Damon's face after the stunt he and his father had pulled, but I could imagine returning to James with the news even less. I allowed Damon to talk me down; then walk me off the lot, down the road, and toward a pub he said he knew of, about a ten-minute jaunt away. He tried to sell me on the virtues of patience and good faith in Merit's business the whole while, of course. I wasn't interested in anything Damon had to say. The only thing that sounded good to me was a stiff drink.

"Keep 'em coming, sugar daddy," I directed, dangling my empty glass before Damon. That drink for a friend down on his luck easily swelled to a second and a third. Soon we'd been sitting there so long that the offer extended to dinner. When I ordered my spaghetti, I began to calculate that if Damon's motivations— either guilt or familial—were stout enough, I might be able to wheedle enough of a gratuity out of him to carry James home a doggie bag. Besides, Damon was proving to be a fine conversationalist, and an amusingly easy target to niggle, once he'd put a few beers in him.

"Don't call me that again," he muttered, "and maybe I will."

I grinned. "I'm an expensive date, you'll find." I caught the unnerved look in Damon's eye. "Maybe another for you too, then," I added. "It was a joke. Christ, you're uptight."

"I'm not uptight," Damon said, though his expression was wary. I caught him passing a fleeting gaze about the room as he lowered his voice. "What with how often you make those kind of remarks at a man, a person would think my dad was right about you."

"Heaven forbid." I made a face. "And so what if he was."

Damon turned his head and scouted the room a second time. Satisfied, he leaned back in his seat. "You? A problematic little faggot?" He gave a derisive laugh. "If that were the case and he knew it, my father would have vetoed you long ago. Death-Defying's as close as the man's gonna come to it. One big lug"— Damon paused to study me—"who attacks this good-looking thing with long eyelashes? He roughs you up, then brings you back with a soul kiss? Boy, if it weren't for the money, my dad would be putting you and your jackass friend in Hoover's fruit machine."

"Oh God," I said. "It's *resuscitation*, Damon. You're hard up if you think that's sex. Faggoty or otherwise."

"No," he agreed. "But you have to admit it's erotic."

"No. I don't. I think the word you're looking for is *violent*."

"In your show, Tevan," he told me, "I think they're the same thing."

I shot him a dubious look but had no retort. It's not like the thought had never trickled through my brain. The truth was that the act had been getting weirder ever since its inception. Damon had deliberated, for instance, ways in which Faustus could tie Seraphim up before knocking him down—"You know, with a scarf of some sort," he had offered up. "Or wait, if only we could get hold of some handcuffs"—and everyone had heartily agreed. I'd already appeared on stage in a toga (Sandy had gotten it off the kootch girls in some adventure that he wouldn't disclose), and more than twice, when I'd shown up to the tent in a shirt of the wrong color, I'd just whipped it off and gone on topless. As each funny add-on was conjured up it just seemed somehow appropriate for Death-Defying. The fact that me and James were both male didn't seem to dampen anyone's enthusiasm. But it merited saying that no one ever proposed that Shawn appear on stage topless or in handcuffs.

Damon shook his head at me over his glass. "Tevan, this is why your show brings in the rocks," he said. "There's a saying, you know: sex is the currency of love. But it's also true that, under some circumstances, sex can be the currency of power, the juice that makes it go. You're showing something on stage that we all know about but pretend we don't see. Death-Defying sells for the same reasons that it got the boot here in Halton—because its violence is sexy."

I shook my head. Then I pointed my chin upward and spoke in a low, dramatic tone. "Yeah, yeah: *Have you yet heard the tale of Dr. Faustus? The hungry fool who traded his very soul for twenty-four years of immortal power?"*

"Well, that's exactly what I mean," he said. "Know what a 'double veteran' is, Tevan? It's a sort of slang term from the army. It's a term for a woman who gets laid and then killed by a soldier. That's what they call it in Nam. Shawn told me." He paused, watching me. "Isn't that awful?"

I gazed across at him. I didn't say anything at all this time. I'm sure he had no idea; but the truth is, Damon was preaching to the choir.

Finally he gave a grim smile. "They have a word for it, and so do we. Here on the sideshow, we call it Death-Defying." Damon flagged the waitress and held up two fingers. When he turned back to me, he rubbed his thumb against the four fingers of his hand. "Money talks. What people spend their cash on says a whole lot about what they want to see. Or what they wouldn't admit an attraction to otherwise." He held his glass to his lips. "Oh I'm not saying it's a good thing, Tevan. I'm just saying. And if we keep on like this . . ." Damon paused, shook his head. "Mark my words, in twenty years bigots like my father'll probably be able to come to a midway and shoot M16s at hookers and queers for their one slim half-dollar. Today we have the same effect on a show like yours."

Damon waited for me to appear either surprised or appalled. Instead, I found myself nodding. "Money is surety," I said.

"How do you mean?" he asked.

"Surety," I repeated. "It's something that monitors an agreement. You know, like a security against loss or damages. Something put in place to ensure that the parties involved both abide by the conditions."

"What kind of conditions?" Damon asked.

I shrugged. "Whatever," I said. "Whatever's needed to make the deal acceptable. Silence, for instance. Anonymity. Tolerance. Shoot, for Death-Defying, you get all that for your half-dollar. You pay for a service; that makes it feel normal." I looked at

Damon and slowly grinned. Then I tipped my glass to him. "You sure are talkative when you're soused. I like it."

Damon scrubbed at his eyes with his palm. "Yeah." He gave a laugh. For the first time in the evening, it was genuine. "What were we talking about again?"

"Your father hates queers," I said.

"Oh," Damon murmured. "Right." His eyes narrowed and his lips drew into a thin line.

New glasses arrived at the table, and the empty ones went. Something had quashed him and now we sat in silence. I just can't stand sitting around with nobody saying shit. I swished my drink around the inside of the glass; I put my fingertips against the sweat on the outside.

"Come on, Damon," I said. "Don't be a drag. Speak freely."

"Speak freely," Damon said. I watched him turn to survey the room. "About what?"

I experienced a raw pang of sympathy for him; it was there, and then it was gone. This is the moment when me and Damon could've actually begun to behave respectfully toward each other. But the booze had gone down smooth. And anyway, I was still angry at him for throwing me off the show. I just couldn't stop myself.

"I'm not sure," I quipped in a low, breathy voice. "But we can talk about whatever you want—"

Damon jumped back in his chair. "Knock it off. Stop doing that. Christ, anybody ever beat you up for that mouth of yours?"

I began to laugh. "Oh yeah, sure. Once, actually, you know? Once a guy said he'd get a mob to kill me if I didn't keep my trap closed. And"—I raised an eyebrow—"hey, stop doing what?"

Damon glared. "*You* know what," he said. "*You* know. You're hitting on me, trying to get to me. Whether I love it or hate it, you think that'll get things going your way, don't you." He watched me warily. "And I bet you do it to everyone. I bet—"

He stopped just there. But his earlier remarks rebounded in my head: *Under some circumstances, sex can be the currency of power, the juice that makes it go.* And that's when I knew two things about Damon Merit. The first was that he was right: I was goading him in the most effective way I knew of. I hadn't had to touch him to do it, but it was filled with heat and brawn nonetheless. And the second was that Damon was afraid of me for it. And even though I knew he was right on both counts, I opened my mouth to dissent; and he leaned forward in his seat to stop me.

"You know what your problem is?" he hissed. "You're like a fucking walking hard-on. I knew it the moment I first saw you."

I stared at him, amazed. "Yeah, and you know what your problem is? I think you're like James. So afraid of the fire that burns within that you let it eat you from the inside instead." My brow creased. "What's your story, anyway? You get rubbed the wrong way? Or just nobody's come along to teach you how to fuck yet?"

"Wouldn't you just love to know it."

"No," I said. "I wouldn't, actually. But I'm sure there's a nice girl out there somewhere who'd be willing to come to your bed and ease you of that burden for fifty bucks."

Damon looked ready to lean over the table and swat me. The bill arrived just in the nick of time. The waitress set it before me, and I, in turn, passed it to Damon.

"No thanks," I said, catching sight of the total as I slid it across the table. "I'd have to sell my ass to pay off this tab."

Damon picked up the note and studied it. I watched him scowl, put a hand to his pocket, and pat down for his wallet. A tiny image of James, back at the camper by now and sitting beside an empty icebox, sailed through my consciousness. James *(watched me from under his eyelids. "He keeps staring at you")* with ten crummy dollars in his pocket, nothing inside him, and probably wondering where in hell I'd gotten off to by now.

Then something came into my head. I think it was see-ing the ding on the bill that did it. It occurred to me that talk was cheap and words were clumsy. It occurred to me that I was hammered and time was short; and although money was even shorter at this moment in time, this was the factor that would stick around unless I had some sort of plan, and fast. It came to me that Damon was a reasonable try—one who had said a substantial amount, I weighed, by merit of his saying his usual, informative nothing. Last, it came to me that Damon was full of surety this night. He was full of it *all*: booze, money, want—and a fear so strong that it would certainly make for firm collateral.

Next, something strange came out of my mouth. Something strange and strategic and evocative in a way meant to please instead of harass him this time. "Fifty bucks."

Damon's eyes came up, preoccupied. "What do you mean?" he asked, unfurling a bill from his hand.

"Well, you heard me, right?" I asked. "Fifty bucks?"

"For *what*?" Damon sounded disgusted with me; as though he believed this to be a suggestion regarding our waitress's tip, despite all the dough our event had already run him. But that wasn't the case. In fact, I was quoting him the highest price I'd ever been paid for a service of any kind.

"For someone to teach you how to fuck," I said.

Damon sat stop-motioned in time. The bills stood still in his hand. "Are you trying to sell me a woman?"

I shrugged. "Do you see one before you?"

This time his eyes narrowed. And he really did sound offended. "Are you propositioning me?" he said, incredulous. "Have you gone deaf as well as wasted to the breath? Christ, what in *hell* are you saying?"

"If you have to ask the question," I said steadily, "then forget I said anything at all."

Damon waited. Around us, the room bustled with activity. Off in the distance, two men at the bar burst into gales of laughter; behind us, the waitress slipped past as though on silent wheels. He didn't turn his head this time. Instead he watched me with a great and speculative interest. Finally he spoke. "You're like them," he said softly. "A lizard off the lot." He shook his head; his lips turned slightly. "Holy Moses, you got a lot of tricks up your sleeve, Tevan. I can't believe my ears." He stopped short of *How'd you boys figger out you could do this trick* as he continued to count his cash onto the table. He paused a few moments later and looked up again.

And next he said something I will never forget: "Are we talking about the same thing, you and I?"

"I think so," I said. "Fifty dollars. Surety. And—well, best say two more shots from the hair of the dog that bit me. That ought to do it."

Damon's mouth opened very slowly. He raised one finger. His voice was nearly a whisper. "Do you have any idea what would happen if the old man heard you talking like that? To me?"

"Yes," I said. "We'd both be double veterans."

Neither of us said anything. I gazed down into my hands and saw that my glass was empty. I pressed a finger into the rim, spinning the glass on its base.

"But let's be honest here, Damon. I mean, hypothetically. What is this, George fuckin' Orwell?

"For starters, I said I'm an expensive date. If the price is right, I can be a real quiet one too. I mean forever. Second, you're drunk. Which means if anyone asked, you wouldn't remember a thing. And third, well, shit, who's gonna *know* any—"

The glass, one moment gyrating around my fingertips, curled up on one tottering edge. It hit the floor and detonated. And I, drunk and dimwitted as anything, started to laugh.

"Whoops," I said.

The waitress hurried over, favoring us with a nonplussed look. "Had enough then, boys?" she offered, leaning over with a dishcloth. She looked to Damon and nudged her chin in my direction. "Whaddya say, is your friend cut off for the night?"

Damon paused, watching the girl's smile. His face held an expression of strange, steady resolve. "Before we call it a night," he said, "actually I think my friend here said he'd like two more."

・ ・ ・

Me and Damon returned to the midway lot with the tables completely turned. I didn't just get two more shots: I got whatever I wanted.

"I want a pack of cigarettes," I announced. "Flip-top. King." And Damon, the first person I ever knew to be thoroughly, outspokenly disgusted with the habit, stopped at a gas station, spun open his wallet, and put out.

There was no question as to location. I hauled on a cigarette the whole way there, Damon trailing beside me. When I was done with the first, I tossed it into the grass and sparked up another. *You're not supposed to be smoking much, you know, Tev,* my brain railed at me. *I know,* I told it back. But I kept going anyway, and by the time we reached me and James's camper I'd maxed out my body with so much substance that I could sense it hitching in revolt.

"Wait a second," I said as we stood at the front steps. "Wait a second, I'm going to throw up." *Need to* was more the appropriate term, but *going to* made it sound like I was somehow in agreement with the event.

Damon didn't hear me either way: he was barely paying attention. He stood at my back, his eyes scanning obsessively. He looked like one of those gophers in a Whack 'Em game, poking their questioning heads around in one tentative, paranoid circle. "What?" he said.

I put two fingers into my throat: "*Blaaagghhh.*" Man, I never forgot that spaghetti.

"Jesus Christ, Tevan!" Damon hissed.

I leaned over and hucked off into the grass. As I did this, I felt a vague, moaning ache emit from my groin. I should've taken a piss right then so as not to encourage the situation further, but I opted not to. You know what they say about breaking the seal— go once and you'll be over the trough all night.

"Don't worry about me," I said to Damon. "I'm fine. I'm done now." Though in my experience, a person can go on vomiting long after he believes he's finished. I looked over to catch Damon's worried expression. Inspired by what I can only call some sudden, wayward stab of sympathy for him, I offered in hurried afterthought: "Oh, it's not you." Then I reeled up, pulling my hands off my thighs. "Come on."

We entered the camper one after the other. I flipped a switch by the door to illuminate the room. *Don't think that comes for free,* something inside me chided. *Who cares?* I returned. Soon enough we'd have finance enough to cover the next rent; electric and gas I'd worry about later. And then, in innocent irony, came another thought: What was it that Damon had said again?

Sex is the currency of love; it's also true that sex can be the currency of power, the juice that—

What was it now?

The camper, my addled brain told me. *The juice that powers the camper. Right?*

Right, I agreed.

"Have you a sit-down," I said to Damon. I turned to the washbasin, and he followed my instruction without question.

I heard the soft creak of springs. "Where's James?" he asked.

I turned to note Damon sitting—coincidentally—upon James's sentinel perch by the door. "I don't know," I said. With that thought, I spanned the floor in three steps and turned the deadbolt. "Don't care much, either." James wouldn't be coming in any time soon, though, that was for certain. And if he did turn up, I knew what I'd say:

Get lost. I'm busy.

I scraped about our little kitchen for what seemed like an eternity. I only found half of what I was hunting for. When I grew irritated (and anxiously conscious of the time), I threw in the towel on the second half of the search and took up the partial rescue in one hand. I set my burden down—and a burden it was, in my state—a huge amber glass ashtray. Shawn had lent it to James some weeks before. James, who had said *You're not supposed to be smoking much, you know, Tev* and yet had been smoking like a demon himself of late, cheerfully filled it to the brim each day. He had a particularly irritating penchant for kicking back with a cigarette (or even one of its more interesting and expensive cousins, for that matter) before sacking out at night. The ashtray was one of those immense dealies that kids made in art class. I dragged a kitchen chair out from one corner and positioned it beside Damon's left arm. I didn't sit on the chair, though: I left it all to the ashtray. Instead I put my shins on the floor and slung my elbows atop his knees.

Damon's eyes flickered in quick, startled understanding. He tried to hide this, but I caught it.

"So." I shot him a grin. "Need a little help getting your motor started? You know, telling you you've got a nice fat one and all that crap?"

Damon looked appalled. "Oh that's really cute, Tevan. Real endearing."

I shrugged, bent slightly, and found the pack of smokes inside my back pocket. I slid it out and laid it next to the ashtray.

Damon executed a curiously worried expression. "You gonna . . . smoke that at the same time?"

"No," I said, petulant. Though I realized maybe I *had* been intending to do that very thing. At least lighting it; at least *that*. Because I knew for certain if I'd had a drink on hand (which I usually did in such situations), I'd be swinging it back before and after (especially before); but now we'd left all the fucking drinks back at the fucking *bar,* and smoking a cigarette—I hadn't been able to find one of James's bedtime pardners, one of them pricey relatives I've alluded to, wherever the hell he stashed them, I'm not picky, but, Jesus, he hadn't even left me a *roach* at the bottom of the ashtray—was the next best thing.

I still had my hand on the pack and I shoved it an inch to the right, as if to demonstrate I'd simply been emptying my pockets. Damon looked relieved, and seeing this, I suffered a momentary, stinging urge to kill him. It passed graciously. Between the puking, the smoke, and where I intended to put my chops next, I admit you could hardly blame the guy. But, *Jesus*, I wasn't asking for much. Jesus, once you were right there, surety didn't feel like much to go on.

I shook my head, steeling myself against this thought.

Get lost, I told it. *I'm busy.*

Then I put my hand where it should go. Damon uttered a little hiss. His spine straightened as though he were a puppet on a network of strings. His left foot bounced, shuffled close to my knee. In my head, his movements barely registered. I told you things had been getting weirder lately; and as I sat between Damon's knees with my hand upon the family jewels, I accepted the odd feeling of events somehow just unfolding in an organic, timely manner. I could say I simply felt like a man doing his job. If you have trouble believing this, I'll add that I'm pretty sure slaughterhouse workers or gynecologists or the man who flips the switch on the fucking electric *chair*, for that matter, feel average in their duties too. My head bowed and my fingers spread out into their five distinct directions. I felt sort of like a little Indian, hunkered down and trying to pipe up a campfire so that he could get cooking. Or at least I did at first.

But I didn't find what I'd been expecting.

"Oh come *on*, Damon," I exploded. "Jesus, you want me to light it and smoke it for you too?"

"*Sorry*," Damon managed through his teeth. His voice sounded both cross and mortified, the tone of a man looking to drop a load in a public restroom and finding the only stall occupied.

"You're still thinking of your father," I said. "Aren't you." Looking at Damon's expression, you didn't even need to ask. "Stop it, Damon. Stop thinking it right now. Think about some-one else. Little minute of this and then you can get right back to spending the rest of your life sucking *his* dick. Get what I mean?"

I hadn't meant it as a joke exactly, but Damon let loose a laugh. It was genuine, dry, and above all in agreement. And in this I suddenly felt I understood something very interesting. Regardless of any disclosures he would ever deign to offer me about himself, I believed that Damon Merit was getting off more on the notion of defying his father alone than he was on anything we might do together.

"Just wait a minute," he said to me. "Please, wait a minute for me."

He didn't look to be in any position to give orders—and me in no mood to go on being courteous—so I took my chance. My free hand shot out like a striking snake and pounced upon the pack of cigarettes. "Sure." I took up a cigarette, lit it. "Whatever. My business is your business."

So I waited. My hands felt cold, heavy. I was conscious of the fact that I was wildly intoxicated, impaired to the point that I could not even wager a guess at what quantity I'd had and how much of it was responsible for where Damon and I currently stood. Worse than this, there was uncertainty, an awareness that I could suddenly and without warning lose the buzz at this capacity. When that's the truth in such cases, well, as the saying goes, time really is money.

I waited as long as I could. And when I was afraid to wait any longer, I got to my feet and I crept up beside Damon's neck. I put my forehead there. Then my mouth, gently; then hard, pulling at the skin, sucking, bursting the blood vessels and leaving him two bruises, side by side, and each in the shape of a kiss. And then, although he'd called it cute and endearing—had saved me the hell of it all just moments prior—I opened my mouth, the cigarette stooping as though in shame between my lips now, and I began to say it all anyway.

I spoke a stream of adjectives and body parts and evocative swears, parried into desperate, reaching sentences. All lies, too. All damned lies.

There was one horrible moment in the middle of this filth when I thought I was going to be sick again. And, unwitting, I thought of the night I'd gotten James out of the cooler the last time; the night he'd passed the fifty-dollar bill into my hand and yet I'd continued throwing up the upshot until the wee hours of the next morning. "Wait, I've got an idea," I'd said after three unplanned pit stops (and one near miss out the window) as James tried to navigate the Chevy down side roads at my instruction. He drove at a miserly thirty kilometers an hour. "I'll get out of the car," I suggested, "and stand about a hundred meters down the road. Then you turn out the headlights and drive at me as fast as you can."

He hadn't done it, of course. I'm not even sure he understood what I meant, and come to think of it, I can't be certain whether or not I'd been joking. I'd drunk so much poison that night that I believed I must be dying slowly. The only way I could calculate my escape of that misery was to finish it up as quick as possible. James running me down with my own car sounded a good solution to—well, brother, to *a lot* of things that night.

When I was finished talking, Damon stared at me, his jaw slung open. "You know," he said, "you really *are* fucked up. Aren't you?"

But I didn't feel fucked up. I felt largely successful. I ignored his sentiment. "Now we're cooking with gas," I said. "You take your end out of your pocket now."

His eyes met mine in disbelief: for half a second there, I think he thought I meant his prick. He surveyed me, arms hung over his knees again and waiting, then nodded in comprehension. Because for the other half-second, Damon Merit knew with unwavering clarity that I was actually going to do it for fifty fuckin' dollars.

When I was eight and Kenny was fourteen, he snagged a job after school as a dishpig in Style's Bakery, just down the road from our home. The job, his first, was a novelty to both of us: he always came home with all these fantastic stories. Stories about cooks tossing pizza dough and waitresses who swore like truckers. But the story I remember best is the one about the butter at the bottom of the garlic bread trays. Maure Style made the best garlic bread, infamously so because he soaked the dough in butter before he cooked it: *heart attack in a basket*, he used to call it. One night when Kenny and Maure's niece were closing up shop, she'd stopped and studied the remnants of the tray. "Say," she began, offhand. "How much'd it take to get you to drink this, Kenny?"

Kenny had shrugged. "Let's say five bucks." And he'd done it.

"Five *bucks*, Tevan," he repeated to me later, as though the explanation could not be more obvious. "I'll shit it out in two days, but I'll spend that dough for more than a week."

Minimum wage was a dollar Canadian those days, which brought my one-shot compensation to more than the salary of an entire work week. I watched Damon peel the bills off with great care: two twenties, one ten. His breathing was low and choppy, his hands shaking. I don't think it was parting with the dough that did it. I don't think it was his glands either. There aren't too many times in my life I seen a guy that scared.

At the end of this he paused—and then, in a flurry of seemingly electric postscript, he slicked off an additional ten. I saw him do it. He saw me see him do it. His gaze rested upon that final bill long enough for me to see that he had placed it there strategically. I looked at the money. Looked at him. A laugh sputtered out of me.

"What's the matter with you, Damon?" I managed. "Are you playing for the wrong team?"

But Damon didn't laugh. His expression was blank, fixed. "I swear to you, Tevan," he breathed. "If you let fly a word of this to anyone, I don't know what will happen to me."

I'd been warily digging for that kind of information the whole time I'd known Damon Merit. Now I was sorry I'd asked. I felt the hair stand up on the back of my neck.

"Damon," I started. "Hey, listen—"

"No, Tevan George. *You* listen. If you open that big mouth of yours, this time you'll be sorry you ever did. First you'll have the entire lot after you for coming on to me and then lying. Which is what I'll have to tell them, I'm sorry. Then I'll have to kick your ass so hard that you'll taste it in the back of your throat for the next ten years." Damon's eyes were fiery. "And then, George, I'll see that ass of yours in hell. Because if my father hears so much as a breath out of either of us on this, I swear to God that's where both of us will be."

I nodded. Because he was right. Right, and I'd gone incognito for far less before. I'd shut up for *If you ever see me again, you don't know me.* For *If anyone finds out about this, my life will be over*; and, in trying moments of fear, *We could get ratted out to the cops for this, you know.* And they were true; the worst of it, as James likes to say, all true. Because there was a whole world living with fear of their desire, just like me and James lived in fear of the sanitarium. Because people outside of it feared men and women with particular desires; and with that fear coursing through their veins like poison, they'd call them sick or fucked up or perverted, or threaten them, or even hurt them, with impunity. It had happened before. The year was 1966: a year in which—although nobody believed that James Daniel Rowley had been preyed upon as a boy in a place where he hid under his bed for months and yet still found no escape—consensual same-sex acts were against the law.

Damon was right. And although I did not like the way he'd turned this into an exchange that hinged on threat, did not miss or discount the fact that he had, without even noticing, called me by my last name like his father would have, I could not dissent.

I sat watching the sweat standing out on his forehead. Adrenaline coursed through my blood like a shot of morphine, and for a moment I worried I might just freeze up, congeal, in reactionary fear. But instead of fear, what I found in myself was white-hot anger.

I looked at Damon steadily. "You know that guy I told you about when we were at the bar, Damon?" I asked. "That guy I said told me he'd find some big goon to wipe my face across the pavement if I didn't shut my mouth?"

Damon's eyelid twitched. His look was one of wary confusion. But he nodded very slowly.

"He did find somebody, you know," I said. "Got the biggest fuckin' person he could find, actually, just some dude sharpening up a pool cue alone in a pub one night, a complete stranger. He told him he'd pay him fifty bucks to knock out that pretty boy sitting at the bar, talking to the waitress." I smiled. "The dude who took the fifty agreed. He thought maybe that pretty boy was knocking on the man's girl or something, thought it was a joke. Cute kid like that, he looked the type to be hitting on another man's prize." James told me that that's what he'd guessed as the guy's sore spot right from the get-go. *Here, Tevan,* he would say to me later. *I only did it to give you the money. I did it for you.* That's why, for the first time in his natural life, James had feigned stupidity and agreed.

"So he took the guy's money, fifty bucks." I motioned to the bills, furled against the chair seat and curling upward against Damon's drying sweat. "Fifty bucks and he nearly killed me. Right here."

I moved a hand. Damon, frozen with apprehension, did not resist. I took his hands from his knees, placing the two longest fingers against the sides of my neck—and as I did this, I was nearly blindsided by a clear, coherent recollection:

"If I recall, Pretty, you said you COULDN'T—but then you went ahead and did it anyway, didn't you?"

And then, wildly, randomly:

"O Faustus, lay that damned book aside and gaze not on it, lest it tempt thy soul and heap God's heavy wrath upon thy head!"

Between the booze, this reel of memory, and the returning portrait of the present—myself with knees on the floor and fifty, wait, *sixty* filthy dollars at my shoulder—it all suddenly felt concisely unambiguous.

For the first time in my life I wondered what I was *doing.*

"Right here, Damon," I whispered. "Bruises up the fuckin'

wazoo, hear? Man, I had a hell of a sore throat the next day. Right here, like he said. That guy had a hate-on for queers or anybody who hung with them, and when he found out what exactly I did for money he told me he'd cut my throat. And the goon he paid to send the message home to me, when he got round to it, came pretty close, too."

Damon said nothing. He only breathed softly, his fingers laid against the cords of my neck.

"I'm—God, I'm sorry," he managed finally.

"Don't be sorry. No, don't be sorry at all. Wasn't you, was it?" But that wasn't exactly what I was asking him. *Wasn't you and WON'T be, will it? I was saying. Don't ever say something like that to me again. Don't you ever. Especially when I'm sitting here like this, my head between your knees and defenseless as the day I was born. Don't you ever, hear? I may be rent and I may be fucked up, yes; but sex is not the currency of love—or the sidearm of any boss, either.*

You're not Bern, it came to me with perfect, unstippled clarity. *You're not Bern, and I'm not Pretty.*

I watched his eyes a moment, then turned to survey Shawn's ashtray. "Hey, Damon." Looking away from him, I found I could muster a smart little laugh.

"Huh?" His voice sounded small and far away.

"Close your eyes, man," I said. "And think of England."

I crushed the cigarette expertly against the amber rim—and that is the last thing I remember.

Oh, I was there. There the whole while, thinking of Elvis and Betty and Veronica and the way that my brother made me laugh when he set upon me and pinned me down. I was there when James arrived at the door outside, found it locked, and sat down unquestioningly upon the front stoop to wait. I was there on my knees as, halfway across the world, U.S. jets attacked two South Vietnamese villages in error, killing over fifty civilians and wounding a hundred others. And I was there as Damon gritted his teeth for three sweet seconds and felt convinced, just as I'd been convinced by countless women, that he was in love.

I was there, convinced myself—not of love, but that this would be the last I'd ever know of this deal between myself and Damon Merit. But I was wrong about that. Once I performed that underworld sideshow for Damon, word got out. And I was dead wrong about Damon, me, and surety: after that night, although no word was ever said aloud, it seemed to be all that the two of us could speak to one another about at all.

I was there. I sold my soul.

It was, in fact, like drifting into a coma.

14

IT TAKES A LOT OF CONTRIBUTING FACTORS TO BRING YOU TO your worst. Me and James would know it because we'd come close before. James is in fact a self-professed expert at worsts, but he was of no use to me during the week most aptly described as the worst we had on Merit's show. Within days of my appointment with Damon Merit, James simply quit talking.

It began when I awoke at the light of midday to Keith banging on the side of the camper. This type of wake-up call wasn't unusual; but as my senses focused upon the room about me, I noticed something that was. On the floor, folded in a lump of blankets, James, the early riser you could practically set your watch by, was still there. I might have known it was to be a rough day for James from this evidence alone. James went on to say nothing at all as we dressed, combed our hair, and walked toward the midway. He would not speak a word for close to forty-eight hours.

I spent the day working Keith's rides in dead silence alongside James, his brow hunched overtop his eyes as he circled the Roundup replacing light bulbs. A scowl covered his features like a coat of armor. He only shrugged in response to the greasy envelope of French fries that I'd altruistically haggled for both of us at the concessions. When a pair of men from the sideshow appeared, making their way up the causeway toward us in the late afternoon, I found myself uncommonly grateful for the company. I wasn't too friendly with Rajid the famed sword swallower, and not particularly fond of the Human Blockhead (a large, tattooed beast of a fellow, affectionately called Butch), but James's quiet had near driven me up the wall by then. I waved and Butch waved back.

The two paused on the grass, waiting until I'd churned the

Scrambler well into motion before approaching. Keith didn't like the performers fraternizing about his machinery during the day—*Bad for tha business,* he said; *scares all tha kids away*—and he sort of had a point. The Human Blockhead appeared just as bizarre offstage as he did on, and Rajid with his chocolate skin, long, pointed mustache, and wild hair looked a sore thumb amid the humdrum upper-class midway patrons. Sales went down when you had a human oddity hanging around. "Who owns that green Chevy out there?" Butch asked me, leaning up against the fence. "The big'un with all the shit in the back seats?"

"That's me," I said. "There a problem?"

He aimed a thumb over his shoulder. "We're trying to get the jenny torn down for tonight and there's a coupla vehicles standing in the way of the rig. It'd be quicker if we could just drive them round to the other side of the lot." He gazed past me to the girls twirling around on the ride. His mouth formed a lazy, wistful smile as he watched. "The green one," he said, turning back to me. "Damon said you might know about it."

That was a laugh and a half—Damon *knew* I'd know about it. Damon knew it was *my car.* But since our recent midnight séance, making contact with our ghosts, or whatever you want to call it, Damon was scared to even lay eyes on me.

"Yeah, it's mine," I said. "If you want it moved, you'll have to do the job yourself, though." I raised an eyebrow at him, at the girls now slowing in the tubs. They giggled and cast curious stares at us as they brushed their hair back. "I'm stuck here until evening."

Butch rolled his eyes. "My heart bleeds for you, fella."

I fished around in my pockets. The keys were easy to find. As expected, I didn't have any money on me. In fact, beneath my pockets I wasn't even wearing any underwear. Stuff cost money to wash, and me and James were pinching pennies. We'd also taken to cheapskating when it came to supplies. Just the day before, we'd shored up to buy ourselves a small store of provisions: potatoes, canned whatnot, and a frozen bag of vegetables.

"We'll split this even like, okay, James?" I'd said to him. "You can have the beans and I'll have the peas." James, James-like, had agreed. "Sure, Tev," he'd agreed. "Beans."

Standing here and calling it up in memory, our little last night's negotiation suddenly felt a thousand years ago. I wondered, with some combination of dismay and misery, if the last word I'd ever hear James say would be *beans*.

I *hate* beans.

I shook my head, turned to Butch, and flipped him the keys. "She's all yours," I offered. "Just come back and let me know where you've moved her to."

But there was no need for anybody to tell me where they'd moved her to. Rajid trotted up the grass a short five minutes later.

He put his hands on his hips, hesitating. "Problem now, son," he said finally. "Your car is—what do you call it, *la merde*." He dangled the keys in front of me. "*Il ne marche pas*, see?"

I didn't speak a word of French, but I understood his assessment nonetheless. After all, by 1966 the thing was over ten years old; the Nomad was, in any language, a piece of shit. A horrible awareness began to dawn upon me: James wasn't the only thing that quit on me. Now my car was a blank too.

"You better take some time off from your girlies here, I think—yes?" Rajid offered. He handed me the keys and tipped his head toward the ride—toward the whole midway lot. "We move off tonight."

When Keith relieved me that evening, I made straight for the parking lot. I already had an idea that my juice was screwed, and I can tell you I hated being proven right for once in my life. Even with a boost from some country bumpkin I found eating Tiny Tom's doughnuts in his pickup while waiting for his wife, all I got from that Chevrolet bitch was a soft, deathly click. *Click*, that was all. No sputter, no cough, no *rhooooooomm*—and so much as I might've cringed at those sounds before, I swear I would've sold my soul to hear it in the fairground parking lot that day.

We move off tonight, Rajid had reminded me, which I

needed no reminding of, thank you very much. I, Tevan George, had been personally counting the days until Merit's sideshow departed the conservative, non-Death-Defying region of Halton. Now, it came to me bitterly, I'd be blessed if we only stayed one more lousy day. As things stood—with my vehicle a boat-sized paperweight and my personal savings account a big fat zero—it all at once appeared that James and I might be trapped here forever.

Oh, I tried to tell James. Tried to get the words out of my mouth and into his ear, hoping that this would at least catapult him back into life as we know it. Tried to explain to him, as the We Five put it, we *got troubles, whoa-oh.* But James, in his shroud of silence, had the luxury of not hearing it. I didn't have *anyone* to tell my troubles to, unless you count Jesus, who Buddy Merit himself never failed to recommend in times like these, and which was basically his way of saying "Nobody here gives a rat's ass." Keith was busy readying to haul his machines off the lot. Damon was busy being afraid of me. And James, well, he was busy proving he was impervious to us all. Despite the July heat, a cold kind of prickliness fell over me as I sat there inside my decrepit Chevy. It wasn't my bladder acting up. It wasn't the sun coming down. It was a sense of being suddenly, completely, and painfully alone.

The sun dipped lower and lower in the sky; I must've turned the ignition fifty times. And when I got tired of doing that, I began to turn the day's curses over in my mind instead: First James. Then the car.

Jesus, I brooded. *What next?*

The worst. And the last contributing factor toward that, of course, was the girl.

Now, the Card Reader was what one would call an "independent"—a concessionaire who produced and sold her own wares on the show. However, she had also arranged, much the same as me and James had in setting ourselves up with Keith and his rides, to moonlight on John Hadley's dance troupe. John Hadley managed a company of dancers, also known in the civilized world as strippers, and I knew very little of John Hadley other than that he had found James and me out irrigating the fauna one fine and intoxicated night some weeks before.

There were other things I knew about John Hadley. But those things were relegated into the bowels of my subconscious, just as any good fragments of gossip are. John Hadley, I had learned from Shawn, had also served a short stint with the call of duty. Thus, John loved and hated Shawn in the same breath. He hated him for shirking his duty and yet found him irresistible for the same reason. I suppose this is what they call patriotism in some weird, upended sort of way. John had served in Korea in 1951—a year in which I was just eight years old—and this had functioned to change the entire world for John, himself then twenty-something years young.

"Eighth Army, March of '51," he'd put forward when he met Shawn, green to the lot, back in April. "Twenty-fifth Infantry Division. You?"

"Me, nothin'," Shawn had told me, recalling this interaction. "*Me Tarzan. You Jane.* What the hell was I supposed to say to *that*? Sweet Jeeee-sus."

But John Hadley didn't say much about it all either. He'd served his tour, been rotated out of service in '53, then gone on to work on the trains with Strates. Not too long after that, John became a showman: he shored up enough to buy a truck and a trailer-version stage, and from here he came to recruit and manage his dancing girls. Of course the cast of women shifted over the years. But in the mid-1950s, hootchy-kootchy shows were a marvelous spectacle to have roll into town—the show was titillating and the dough was hot. As he progressed from managing the Dance of the Seven Veils to Salome to his present Stage Girls, John did well for himself. He had plenty of company by the time he reached Merit and our Home and Native Land.

But on the show, it was only Shawn that he talked to.

Shawn who he told about the busted hip with the shrapnel in it, for instance. How the shrapnel had caused a later infection, but the *hip* had nearly killed him by immobilizing him inside a place where it was best to keep moving. How the matter had complicated itself as he lay along the edge of the North Korean Han waiting for a medic ("That hip still moans like a bitch in negative temperatures, like she got a memory of it herself"), in an operation evocatively named Ripper.

Shawn, who had himself nursed a broken ankle over the course of a long Maine winter as a kid (and not knowing what else to say, Sweet Jesus), had attempted to sympathize: "My, that shore musta hurt, John. Nothin like cold to point out the wear of a man!"

No, John had amended. It wasn't the cold. What he recalled most was what he *saw* when he was there—hot, as being in action was called in the military—while out in the cold.

John didn't give up all his information. The rest was filled in by his girls. Some of his girls were peelers; some, like the Card Reader, were simply ballyhoo dancers looking for extra cash. Some of his girls were lot lizards. Most of the girls he'd picked out of trouble someplace. In that, they all owed him favors, and they knew it, too.

Damon had informed me a long time ago that John Hadley was not the fellow to be fucked around with. "Not only has he got the chutzpah and mind to get his way round here," he'd specified, "but he's also got a gaggle of goons to do his dirty work."

Gaggle of goons? I'd laughed. John Hadley had Sandy, maybe two green grunts who moved metal for him on weekends, and a collection of prostitutes. That hardly qualified as a thug squad, I said.

"It's enough," Damon avowed. And then he told me about the time, about a year prior, when old man Merit decided to start dinging John for electricity.

John didn't like that. John Hadley was the lot electrician: the guy you wanted to get friendly with if you'd like the lights turned on in good time once your show rolled onto a site. The girls always had their power on first. Fellows like James and me, on the other hand, had to sit around in the dark like we had during the November 1965 blackout. John didn't appreciate the fee. Since the whole goddamn lot would be powerless *without* his skilled craftsmanship, John felt that he should ride on the house—"and with a little more fuckin' gratefulness from you, too, Merit," he had added.

Merit didn't bend. In usual form, he delivered a generic, unassented-to bill in its place. Damon knew all about it: he had typed the bill, at his father's instruction, himself. *John Hadley will pay said amount to the undersigned by the first of August, 1965;* on paper we can substantiate your financial delinquency, tell your problems to Jesus, Buddy capital A. H. Merit, blah blah de blah. And that's when the feud really began.

On the first of August, the hell if John Hadley had gotten square on his invoice. That was no surprise, Damon said. What *was* a surprise was that the midway began suffering rolling brownouts past call.

"Why, I'm rationing on your behalf, Merit," John had said with unnerving calm upon Buddy's inquiry. "Don't want your staff racking up the dings! Do ya now?"

Buddy had figured on insubordination as temporary and anticipated—John taking his time with the land lines, Sandy showing up at the office trailer dead last with the connection. But no power past showtime? And that smart-ass remark he'd made when asked—well, that sounded a whole lot more like John's gratefulness stipulation than like anything to do with money. John was getting dirty. John was getting philosophical.

To make matters worse, John was like a bat, or one of those moles that have acquired the skill to see in the dark. He was long used to working in pitch black. That's how, as per Damon's testimony, the trickery came to a head. "Dog shit," he clarified when I asked what he meant by tricks. "You know that mangy mutt Sandy's got at his heels all day and night?"

The first night dung turned up on the admin trailer lawn, Buddy won out. He spied it, sitting in the grass like an ostensibly benign alien landmark, and so he had the opportunity (probably grinning self-righteously as he did so) to skirt it completely. The second time, however, Buddy had made the mistake of departing his sanctuary in both the John Hadley-induced dark of night and—though Damon had no real proof of this, only his father's own raging deposition as Damon later picked him up off the ground—in his own Jim Beam-induced stupor. This time he planted his heel right into it.

It must have still been steaming, Damon said, because it sent old man Merit right into the atmosphere on what you could only call a kind of shit-generated slipstream. He hit it once with the sole of his shoe, zipped backward, and then bombed down flat on his back.

Man, what I would have paid to see that in person. What then? I'd asked Damon, thrilled.

Damon said he supposed they could've squarely fought crapola with crapola if it had been two years earlier, before the Merit minion, a half-shepherd named Frank, sat out in the lot at exactly the wrong time of day and got nailed by the face painter's rig. But that was years ago, years since they'd been Frank-less, and so any chance for a comparable contest evaded the Merits. Instead Buddy decided right then (*shit on this,* Damon recalled as being his father's exact words, and despite the glaring irony of them, Damon had not dared laugh) to concede the whole business. John got his electricity for free. A gratuity, they called it, for his kind service.

I'd have expected Merit to be a little more creative, resilient even. And about the dog shit, it could have been anyone who put it there, I added. We had mutts around the midway nearly every day, eating the popcorn, snuffling the little goldfish at the hanky-panks, pissing on the sides of the canvas. "Plus that dog of Sandy's looks three hundred years old," I said. "It probably feels the call of nature at least that many times a day."

Damon made a face. "Poo, Tevan?" he said. "Twice in one week? It's more than just a coincidence."

John knew the score. He didn't smoke weed like Sandy or shoot up like some of his girls. He didn't have that pining drive for coffee brandy at six in the morning anymore, but if his workers did he knew all about it. He didn't even access the services of his girls as much as you might think. ("He's a veteran," the girl who'd introduced Shawn to her wares on the lot had told him, "but his own thing got some trouble standin' at attention.") John didn't participate in many of these things; he only watched and provided for them. I can't tell if that's evil or empathetic in the end: in any case, call it what you want, but John Hadley just called them as he saw them. The midway lot was *full* of people looking for opportunity amid their own cold troubles. And John Hadley simply knew how to make a deal.

As for me? Well, I guess by the time I got up close to John, I was ready to negotiate too.

I came upon the girlie show just before dusk. I'd already spent over an hour ruminating in my car, and time no longer seemed to be of the essence. My mind was filled with things I didn't want to think about, yet couldn't avoid—like what I'd tell James and how I'd explain it all to Keith—and so I sat myself down in the grass before the stage and I simply ruminated some more.

There was no risqué show to be had—*no hookers, strippers, or perverts,* as per the regional requirements—and I couldn't have afforded any anyway. There was a dancing-girl show, though, and the usual freebie ballyhoo. I lay down in the grass, before the stage. I had a George Orwell paperback in my hands. I'd found it in the back seat of the car and picked it up, considering it good procrastination material, but I didn't open it. To be perfectly honest, in hindsight I think I stopped there because I figured it might be some time before I had the chance to lay eyes on my girl again. I'd already riffled through my options as I'd watched the sun go down—pay for the car with our rent money and lose the camper, for instance; or leave the car behind for the sake of keeping the job—and none of them were appealing.

I watched Sandy and John move about the base of the stage for a while. John's hair was short and prematurely gray, and he walked with his distinctive limp. Sandy wiped sweat from his brow, looking a little the worse for wear in the heat. Sandy spied me sitting, exchanged a grinning word with John, and waved. Instead of waving back, I opened my paperback and buried a scowl inside it. *I could do work like that*, I thought bitterly. Even dumb nit *James* could do it, and with *a little more fuckin' gratefulness*, too. The next time I peered up, a collection of colorfully decorated girls was beginning to gather to the left of the stage. And the next time I looked, I saw John Hadley's black engineer boots coming toward me.

He stopped, towering six feet above me. "Son," he said. "How goes it."

That sounded like a rhetorical question, the type you weren't meant to answer. But I liked the gentle "son" that prefaced it, and the question itself suited me fine, on account of I wasn't in any mood to reply honestly. "It's going," I said. "You?" I didn't require a straight response to that either, of course, so it didn't surprise me that he didn't answer me. Still, he did offer up something reasonably kind in its place.

"I hear," John said, "you had some troubles this week."

Now, I hardly knew John, as I've said; but I knew his game and I believed I knew at least what he was referring to. His girls weren't taking their clothes off and I wasn't gasping, that's what.

"Ain't that the truth," I said, my eyes down, but giving up a wry, commiserating smile nonetheless. Under such circumstances, you couldn't help but kind of like the guy.

"Thatsa boy," John smiled. "And I hear you like your drink."

A second time I turned to look up at him. It suddenly occurred to me that John and Sandy were going to ask me to tip the crowd for them before the show. *I'll find you a few dollars if you run around and shill for the show. Before we head off, you know.* Or even *I'll buy you a six if you round up a few pervs to watch the girls this time around.* Shit, money would've been better than beer; but beer was better than nothing. It sounded fair, an unproblematic wage for a fellow like John, him being the hub of all substance on the lot in general. And with the day I'd had and no wits about me, it didn't even register that John had yet to state his offer aloud.

"Sure," I said. "I got time. Whatever you need."

John nodded, his hip to one side and his left toe tapping. He lit a cigarette, passed it to me real friendly-like, and a moment later he nudged the book in my hands with the toe of his boot. I remember turning the cover over so that he could see it: ironically, *1984*, the very one I'd paraphrased to Damon before we set our little deal nearly a week before. And as though he were reading that very transaction inside my mind, that's when John did something that made little sense to me just yet, but would become important down the road: he took the sleeve of my left arm and tugged it upward.

Then he hunkered down on his knees. He leaned in over me. "Is there anything else I can do for you?" he asked. "I hear you've had some troubles this week. In fact . . ."

And then he said something low under his breath. At first I thought he'd asked me if I *liked corndogs,* if I *hiked snowballs,* or maybe if I *waited at bus stops,* because that, phonetically, is what it sounded like. And anyhow, in the span of about the last ten seconds, John Hadley had already hit the bull's-eye on rumors he'd heard, assessed, and deftly surmised as true. A slipstream of a second later, my ears registered what he had really said:

I hear you like blowjobs.

And then there were just three things in my mind: James, the car, and the girl.

On the side, however, two words hammered in the sane side of my brain: *Damon Merit. Damon Merit,* my mind sputtered. *That fucking Damon Merit! Damon If-you-breathe-a-word-of-this-I-swear-I'll-kill-you Merit.*

I drove my car off the lot that night. John Hadley fixed it.

15

I DROVE MY CAR OFF THE LOT THAT NIGHT. NO DOWN PAYMENT, no questions, no complaints from John as to the wiring harness that he had to dig up from his equipment store and wiggle into the Chevy's engine networks. "You're lucky it wasn't your alternator, boy," he told me, wiping a wrist across his forehead. "Now *that* I couldn'ta helped you with. No, just stripped the harness and saw the tickler wire was barely making a connection, like." He grinned. "For a carb'd car all's you need is gas, compression, and spark. Hot wire's all you were missing." He furrowed his brow down at the Chevy. "How'd you afford a baby like this anyhow, son?"

"My brother," I said. "Call it the Ontario Studebaker Assistance Program. Only he bought a Nomad."

"Nice," John commented, impressed. "Well, now she's cooking." *Cooking with gas,* I revised to myself.

That night, I merged onto the highway behind John, who waited while we started our engines; John drove off behind Sandy, who towed the racked hootchy-kootchy stage; and Sandy, in turn, drove off behind Damon, who, for the record, had yet to speak to me since the previous week. I rolled down my window. Beside me, James fell into sleep with his face pressed against a balled-up sweatshirt on the windowsill.

We were still aligned in our conga line—racked rides ahead, trailer-rigged vehicles at the end, painted boxcars in the middle— when Damon signaled to hang left. I put my blinker on, and John, between us, burned off the road without using his brakes. He'd spied the diner off the highway with the *Open 24 hours* sign, and by then all of us were half-starved. I roused James as we pulled into the parking lot. He got out of the passenger seat, the imprint of his makeshift pillow still pressed upon his cheek.

Our company congregated around the diner's front: Damon, Butch, and Rajid; John and a collection of four of his girls (the Card Reader among them), and Shawn. Me and James came in behind them. But they halted like a stew reaching a bottleneck just before the front doors. James, bleary-eyed, nearly walked right into them. I grabbed at his elbow.

"Hold up, hold up," a voice barked, and my grip on James tightened. "What's this now?" Eclipsing Damon in height stood a man with chest and gut draped in a wide white apron. His eyes scurried over us one and all.

I quickly gazed down at my sneakers, as though in doing this I'd fall right down into them. Out of the corner of my eye I caught Rajid and the girls doing the same. Damon took a step forward.

"We're stopping by for something to eat," he offered. "That's all. Then we'll be on our way, friend." Beside me, a blonde who chummed around with Shawn bit down hard on her lip. Nobody grumbled about Damon electing himself our spokesperson. Nobody said anything. On average we're a noisy bunch, but this time we all just shut our traps. "We won't be any trouble," Damon said.

The man's eyes waited on Damon, then rolled over our party. "Look," he said. "I run this place with my wife and two boys, you understand." The next words came in short, stunted bursts. "I don't want this kind. Not here."

Damon paused, breathed. At the words *this kind*, I caught his brow twisting into a little knot. Now he turned his head to survey the rest of us, still standing in our silent semicircle. He turned back to the man at the door. "There's no place else open at this late hour," Damon told him. "We want to give you our business."

The man's heavy expression flickered over our posse now, east to west: James, his brow cinched in concentration. Butch, mouth drawn and the bare bulb over the 24-hour sign glinting off his balding, tattooed head. The four girls, huddled together with their hair flapping in the midnight breeze. This time I noticed how the man's gaze banked at length to the right: Shawn, his eyes downcast beneath a mop-top of hair.

The asphalt squeaked a cautionary note beneath the man's feet: "No." His head switched to the one side again. He barked suddenly in his favored direction: "*I don't like the looks of some of you, you hear?*" The girls, the two in front of the Card Reader, shuffled a compensatory step backward. But behind them, Shawn seemed to grow taller. His mouth contorted into a scowl.

"Well, let the rest of them at least, will you!" Shawn hollered. He wheeled on one foot and stomped off.

Damon watched him go, blinking. He had taken the wife-and-kids bit respectfully; had swallowed *this kind* with patience. But the sight of Shawn storming off seemed to batter all the pleasantry out of him. "Anyone else, then?" Damon demanded. "Anyone else you don't want in your fine establishment? Go on, then!" He stood back and waved a hand. "Go on, pick 'em out. Pick 'em out and let the rest of us in!"

With Damon clearing the passage, we all got a look at the guy. He stood with his body set inside the doorway like the stone at the tomb of Jesus Christ, and his fists clenched. His cheeks were a pair of flaming stop signs. Over his shoulder, I could just see into the adjoining room beyond, and from inside the dining room, heads peered out at us like rubberneckers passing a highway accident. Their expressions were some combination of fear, disgust, and amusement. I could no longer sense the faintest trace of my hunger.

"Fine," the man in the doorway said. His eyes left Damon's face. They narrowed, scanning the rest of us one by one, like the scope on a rifle. "You," he said after hardly a moment.

Butch, slouched beside John, harrumphed. He took a step backward.

"You, neither."

Heads turned. Butch never stood a chance with all those tattoos; but this time, as the Card Reader shrank back and dissolved from our group through the rear, my stomach turned over. The gatekeeper's eyes passed my way, and as I felt James's elbow in my side, I felt a sudden, momentary stab of sympathy for him. *So long, James,* I thought wistfully as a pointed finger aimed our way.

"And you," the man said. I looked up to find myself staring straight at him.

Me! I nearly squawked in indignation, but I was too embarrassed to say anything at all. James's eyes met mine, and I saw my own surprise mirrored upon his face: for a second, I thought he might break his nonverbal streak on account of it all. But as the rest of the party began to file into the building, I understood he wasn't going to say anything. Worse than this, I realized, James was going in, and I wasn't. It was Damon who turned toward us.

"Don't worry," he said. "Us guys'll take care of you. Okay?" He looked to the Card Reader, and then to Butch, who was already waving a hand and muttering as he headed off. The management fellow stood watching from the door, and for the first time in days, Damon's gaze came right to me.

You're like them, my head hammered as our eyes met. *A lizard off the lot. Holy Moses, you got a lot of tricks up your sleeve, Tevan.*

His brow bent as he studied me. "We'll see you outside in less than half an hour."

I kicked a pile of stones to one side as I started back to the car. The girl—the Card Reader—stood wrapped up in her own elbows twenty feet away. I could hear Butch clambering about his abode, the jaunty bannered outfit three cars down, and Shawn complaining about the state of the world that we live in from roundabout the same location.

As for me, I roosted down on the curb before my headlights. From this position, parallel to the diner, I could see our party holed up inside.

The thought of my mother passed into my mind. The thought of her alone, in Hamilton, likely asleep in her bed by now. My mother, turning in her slumber, having no idea that her only living son was too crude to be permitted service in some crapola greasy spoon, and inside a house I hadn't visited in months. My chest ached just thinking about it. *Where are you, Tevan?* she'd ask if I called. *Why don't you tell me anything?* Staring down into the gritty half-eaten-away hems of my jeans, I understood the twisting inside my guts for what it was: secret stuff. Sideshow stuff. I decided what it was I meant to show to my mother a long time ago. The problem was, it wasn't a lot.

"It's not what it sounds like," a voice said into the darkness.

I pulled my gaze up. The Card Reader, her shoulders clenched but bolt upright, sat to my right on the curb. Her arms were covered in a kind of wispy shawl.

"Don't worry about it, I said," she went on, not looking at me. "It's not what it sounds like. He was just taking you for first impressions. Haven't you ever made a bad first impression before, honey?" Her eyes remained fixed upon the crowded windows of the diner. When I didn't know if this was some sort of a lead-in or joke at my expense or what, I did not reply; and she huffed a laugh. "Look at them all in there. God, don't you just hate them all right now?"

I snorted. "Or hate that guy who told us to hit the road." I cradled my chin in one hand. "Lousy prick."

"Bah." She waved a hand. "He just thinks we're a bunch of troublemakers. You know, hobos, hookers, and all the rest?" Her hand rose, then paused, indicating the loud, colorful airbrushed trailers some feet away: *The Human Blockhead!* one read. *Stage Girls,* coaxed the other. "Well, *that* sure helped matters, I bet." She seemed to spy her own hand outstretched in the air and hurriedly returned it to herself. "But he had a good eye," she mused, peering into her arms. "I'll give him that."

I frowned into the ground. "What do you mean, had a good eye?"

The girl looked surprised but did her best to hide it. "Well," she said slowly. "He picked us out just by looking." The air smelled like asphalt, and her shawl fluttered lightly inside it.

"Butch, for those long pinkie nails he's got. Well, we all know what those are for. Shawn because he's black. You, because of those—" A pause. "You know, those—"

The girl held her breath this time, then stopped completely. A moment too late she read her own gaffe right off my expression. I knew what she had been on the cusp of saying: *Those marks on your face.*

Those marks on my face had not escaped my eyes either. Red, pinhole-sized speckles about the eyes, a smattering of rose-colored stains along the cheekbones. I knew they were there, but I didn't know what they *were;* and as with the thin ring of yellow I'd found crossing my throat more than once, I didn't want to know either. Years later I'd learn that these little spots are called petetiae. It's a harmless condition, little more than a bruise— burst blood vessels, to be exact, from heightened blood pressure inside the head. It's a phenomenon most common in bulimics, who spend much of their time retching over toilets; heavy coke users, who spend their social hours holding their breath over lines like the ones that Butch's pinkies were so good at making; and scuba divers. If I had known then, I suppose I could simply have called it a work hazard on the Death-Defying circuit. The only other people who ever wake up to such constellations cir- cling their faces in reality are probably strangulation victims who live to see their next day.

The girl watched me warily. The smile she tried was strained. "Well," she amended. "Well, he—probably picked you off just, maybe for good measure. I mean, like I said, he picked Shawn first, and only because—"

I nodded. Quickly, to shut her up, but I didn't believe her.

"Listen, don't worry," she said, speaking fast now. "Christ, we aren't going to starve. Like Damon said, your friends will get something for you."

"I'm not worried," I told her, a lie. "It's just—my friend. I just remembered. He's on his own and I forgot to send him in with any money. That's all." Which was true; I had forgotten.

But James had his trusty ten rocks on him, and I knew that. The real truth was that I couldn't shake the idea that I had been picked off for other reasons. Reasons established way before
(You're like them. Holy Moses, you got a lot of tricks)
some stranger had the opportunity to inspect my complexion.

The girl leaned in, studying me. Her hair hung down, some of it dusting the tops of her knees like delicate fingers. Her brow furrowed as she watched me. A brief longing to reach out and touch her fired through my body and then crept mercifully away. She produced a cigarette from her belt, stood, cupped her hands, and lit it. We said nothing more to one another.

Within minutes the rest of our troupe emerged from the restaurant. I noted James among them and could not help but wonder if he'd spoken aloud during dinner. I hoped not. If *I* had to put up with his nonsense, I thought, I fucking hoped everyone else did too. I unlocked the passenger door and waited for him to get inside. When he did, he put a hand out to me. He held out a brown paper bag. It was hot and smelled good, and I could see the steam wafting up inside the confines of the car.

James's eyes held an expression of gentle inquiry. But in the moment, I looked at the bag and found it to be an insult.

"I don't want it," I spat. "Leave it! Jesus, my stomach feels like I already ate a fuckin' brick."

The engine roared at the first try.

And so I was scheduled for two performances Friday night upcoming: the first, the usual Death-Defying on the midway, and the second, the recompense that I owed John.

16

THE SKY GREW DIM BETWEEN THE FIRST ACT AND THE SECOND. Me and James's Death-Defying took place near eight o'clock Friday night, and by the time we exited the sideshow tent—the last bodies to leave, as always—the wide, cloudless ceiling outdoors had faded to deep indigo.

I hadn't said a word to James at all that day (not counting the old *O Faustus, lay that damned book aside* rhyme) and he was still going strong on his mute streak. When we hit the camper, however, I found myself again doing what I did best, which is talking.

"When's the last time you washed, James?" From where I stood at the kitchen basin, I could see his reflection in the window. "Because you're smelling kind of ripe, friend. As only a friend has the luxury to say to a friend, that is."

James, James-like, said nothing.

I huffed a weary breath. "When, huh? Last week maybe?"

I don't know, I answered myself inwardly in James's slow, deliberating tone. James, behind me, stared into the back of my head and took a seat at the foldout card table. Keith had lent it to us: "No sense eatin' off tha floor!" he'd cried, setting it beside the far bunk two weeks back. "Course you'll hafta move her come bedtime to reach yer bunk, James, but she's easy 'nuff to set." He'd popped the folding legs up and out demonstratively, set the table where he meant for it to go, and spread his hands, satisfied: "Got that?" Me and James nodded politely, but we hadn't paid any attention. We never used that bunk anyhow.

"I'm going out," I announced at James. "I might be gone late."

Where you going? Again, in James's phantom voice.

Hot date, I answered to myself.

The girl? Is it that girl you're meeting, Tev?

I paused, wringing the soap from my hands. *Shut the fuck up, James.*

"What are you doing tonight, James?" I asked aloud. "You going to see Shawn?" I ran my fingers through my hair, slicking the sides back. "You staying here?"

I don't know. James sat with his height bowed inward, his hair in his face. His fingers leafed listlessly through the pages of a book he had found on the table. There was no expression on his face and so there was nothing to look at. But it was my paperback, I noticed. George frigging Orwell.

"Don't read that, James," I said. "It'll make you paranoid."

Fuckin' A, you're a bossy little shit tonight, aren't you, Tev?

I stared, but James hadn't moved. And so I bet myself, just to shift my mind off of things, ten dollars and a pack of Player's that after two solid days of inertia his breath was as rank as a dead prostitute's. Then I told myself that it was only by coincidence that I'd come up with that particular analogy. I was disgusted with myself.

"Don't wait up," I muttered.

I opened the trailer door, stepped out, shut it heartily behind me, and set off for my second performance of the night. I knew where I was going—John had told me the specs the night he fixed the car—but I wasn't thinking much about it. I passed the sideshow tent as I went, only slowing to pass my eyes over the brilliant, scripted banner proclaiming *Death-Defying!* and pausing only slightly more to peruse the glass-cased, eight-and-a-half-by-fourteen certificate (*legitimate legal document!* this one professed) identifying James Daniel Rowley as an assuredly convicted assailant. As I continued across the lawn, the words (*Death-Defying! Murder and Divine Intervention, Live!*) were stippled by the lilting passage of my shadow.

I found myself humming a little tune, the popular one from the radio about the bus stop and the umbrella (*I hear you like corndogs, I hear you wait at bus stops*), as I went. I noted the weather as clear and cool, no umbrellas necessary for me, no sir, thank you very much. I heard the sound of my own whistling, tasted the damp air that threaded through my lips; and, to my satisfaction, found if I concentrated just so, I could remember each and every word to the song: *Bus stop, bus go; she stays, love grows. Under my umbrella.*

I don't remember what I wore that night, though, when I reflect back upon it. I don't recall what I ate for dinner before I left James either. I don't even remember whether my bladder was still niggling at me, typically a very salient consideration. *But who cares?* you might wonder.

I do. When I call it up, I can scarcely remember how I got to John Hadley's at all. It was this performance, really, that resonated as death-defying—a trick that was undefined, eerie, dangerous; a question mark, unanswerable, and, whether I liked it or not, directly determining my survival. Today, that daunting thought is now so indivisible from the act that came to be that I can scarcely imagine how I made it to John's. I walked over in a state of suppressed terror—a numb automaton, a thing disguised as me, deciding carefully what it was that I wanted to show.

Don't wait up, I'd said to James as I left. He hadn't answered me, of course. In my usual bitter silent rejoinder, I guessed he wasn't listening. But you want to know something funny?

Listening or not, James did wait up.

I found the hootchy-kootchy trailer just past the sideshow home base where me and James performed every night. As usual, it looked gaudy and ancient, a portable stage closed over for the night with reels of heavy canvas. A pair of girls stood to the left of a side entrance, speaking in low tones and sharing a joint. One of them I recognized as the Lady in Pink from ages before, and the other, the blond friend of Shawn's.

The lights were on inside, and as I closed the distance, two things occurred to me. One, I hadn't been inside since James and I had watched the skin show for our viewing pleasure a week into June. And two, it sounded as though there were plenty more people inside than just John Hadley.

I was right. I came up the metal rung stairs and opened the door to find a room—the wooden, splintery floor of the stage itself, now set with a smattering of chairs and card tables—packed with people. Okay, maybe not *packed*: but there were a good nine or ten guys in there. They sat holding drinks, trading cards back and forth, laughing and shooting the breeze. The ceiling was a blue haze of cigarette smoke. It gave the place a tight, claustrophobic feel, and to my adjusting eyes the handful of men within it appeared to teem. Maybe that sounds dramatic, paranoid even. But when you're arriving at a place to provide a private service of undisclosed parameters, I can tell you this: any more than one in a room feels packed.

John looked up to spot me in the doorway. "How's the car running?" he called across the room.

"Fine," I said. "Cooking with gas."

John parted a collection of guys standing in work shirts and Levi's as he came toward me. I recognized them all: a couple of guys from the hoop-shot and hanky-panky joints, and a couple of guys who moved steel alongside James when we shifted sites.

"You drink scotch, son?" John asked, gesturing at me with an empty glass. "Not too hard for you, is it?"

I continued to stare past John and the glass in his hand, and a funny thought went through my brain: I wondered if all these guys knew what I was doing here. A simultaneous, equally terrible notion accompanied this: wouldn't it be smarter of me to keep my head screwed on straight and sober under the circumstances? The circumstances, being that perhaps—

Scotch? My head said at me suddenly, in Steve Orono's timbre: *A big'un too, you don't want any piddly little jug!*

"Scotch is okay," I told John.

John nodded, motioning me away from the gathering. I didn't hesitate to put some space between the crowd and myself. He led me toward the back of the stage and to the right, where there was a small vestibule. I had no idea where I was going. Back and to the *left,* I was familiar with—to the left stood a darkened, private room where you could go following the hootchy dance routine during the day, should you be one of the lucky SOBs to afford the blow-off stunt. In that private room, you and a handful of genuine gawkers had the privilege of paying fifty cents each for every article of clothing the dancer removed. A dollar for the last article, most certainly her panties. In any case, John didn't bring me in that direction. I fumbled along behind him in the dark. Nobody from his party seemed to see us go.

Once we had stepped through the vestibule, we found another door. John paused before the door, passed me a grin, and gave the panel a rap. The door opened up to display a dim little enclosure—and Sandy.

Sandy stood with his hand on the doorknob, blinking at us. His eyes were wide and sheepish, his retinas stark with tiny firing veins. Looking back, it doesn't take a brain surgeon to figure out what he was doing in there. The place even smelled like a holy heave-ho. But at the time the only thing that registered in me was that Sandy had been found in this private suite to which John Hadley happened to be directing me, alone.

"Clear out," John instructed. "We'll let you know when you're needed."

We made a switch: John and I, for Sandy. "Hey there, Tev," Sandy said, smiling as he passed. And as I looked at him over my shoulder, bewildered and half-wild with sensory input already, without even having seen the little room beyond, I decided it was high time to get to the point. I turned on my heel as the door closed.

"Who's the beneficiary?" I said. My voice sounded loud and defensive in the little room, an effect I hadn't meant.

John bent one eyebrow. "Pardon?"

"You heard me." I looked about warily. "Who's getting it tonight?" And in the instant in which I said this—just as it occurred to me that I really had no clue how much a Chevrolet wiring harness might run a fellow (*Just what could one of those things possibly cost anyhow?* a prickly inside voice wanted to know. *Imagine it was a hundred dollars, Tevan? Two? Just how many corndogs*)—it came to me that perhaps I didn't want to know the answer. "You heard me," I said again nonetheless. "I just want to know who."

John put a hand on his hip. He dispatched an expression of genuine, amused confusion. "You do . . . understand why you're here tonight, don't you?"

"Yes," I said steadily. "Like you said. You want me to do you a favor and to keep my mouth shut in the meantime."

John broke into a relieved grin. "That's right. Good. Geez, thought I read ya all wrong for a second there." He waved a hand. "I'll answer your question, then," he said with a laugh. "Don't worry. Why, it's you, of course."

My jaw felt like it was cemented in place. And despite what he'd just said, suddenly I *was* worried.

John still had one hand on the doorknob. He twisted the knob rightward, cracked the door two inches, and yelled out just what in hell did a coupla guys have to do to get a goddamned shot around here. Sandy, on the blind side of the door, acceded.

"Me," I repeated. I began to get a creepy, nauseous sensation. Then the thought of James trickled unbidden through my mind. *But then again,* I thought—

"Hey, where's that scotch?" I said, wheeling my head around.

John laughed. A second time, he launched his head out the door and yelled, bringing Sandy running. He consulted through the cracked door, slammed it in the kid's face, and returned to me with a glass. By God, with the biggest fuckin' shot of scotch I ever seen in my life. I stared at it, uncertain whether to feel frightened or impressed.

"Shit, son." John snorted as I chose to feel neither and instead downed a quarter in one swift gulp. "What do you think? I'm gonna be performing? That's the case, I think you'd be paying me. Right?"

I smiled, not shifting my gaze from him in the slightest. "In your wettest fucking dreams, John." Though an odd thought crossed my mind as I said this: if I was here to perform a service, then why did he call me the beneficiary? For the first time, things felt enormously undefined, weirdly off-kilter. And for the hundredth time my mind returned to the crowd gathered in the front room.

John returned the smile. His own was deliberating, scrutinizing. "I like you, son," he said. "Moody little thing, aren't you? Worse than the girls, even." He hunted in his breast pocket for a pack of cigarettes. "You can take turns complaining soon enough, I guess." He grinned again. "That's fine with me, if it suits you."

What girls? I nearly trumpeted, but that sounded so much like a thing James would say that it wouldn't leave my lips. It also sounded too much like how I felt. I couldn't deny it now: I was totally confused. Something funny was happening between me and John. Some sort of confusion on both of our parts. Twice now, we'd barely been able to follow each other. There was some sort of miscommunication, maybe some mistake as to the terms of the deal. I suddenly wished I could consult with Damon on the problem—pause, scoot out of the room, hunt him down, and find out just what exactly that little snitch had *said.*

"I know you got some troubles, son," John began. I put the glass to my lips and began concentrating very hard on his words, in hopes of making sense of just what in the Sam Hill was going on. Already my skin felt cold. My pulse was beginning to clack in my ears like a bicycle running down an incline with the Ace of Spades taped to its axle: fast, faster, faster still—

I'll just listen, I told myself. *Listen to his agenda and make a calm, rational decision. That's all.* If I didn't like it, I could change my mind. If I didn't want to, I'd—

(But you told me all those things. I know you want to)

I'd leave. Yeah, that's what I'd do.

John puffed on his cigarette, watching me. And although my brain had just told me it had a plan, I knew full well that my body was beginning to gather other ideas. I hoped he couldn't see the perspiration starting to stand out at my temples. My heart was hammering in my chest.

"Allow me to explain," John said. "I've got a nice one of my ladies coming to visit tonight, been paid to give me a good time. I just have a little show I want her to perform first. And that's where you come in, son." He shook the cigarette pack at me. I put a hand out and took one. "You're on the sideshow, I hear. Familiar with shows, aren't you?"

"Yes," I told him, glad to have a point that we could finally converge on.

John nodded. "Good, then. That's all you need to know. Now what *I* need to know is that you can shut up, listen, and follow instructions to get your end. Can you?"

"Yes," I said again, when suddenly it occurred to me that I had no idea what he was referring to. I'd already gotten my end. He'd fixed my car. Just what in the hell end was John talking about? "Yes. Yes, but—"

"There's no buts, son," John interrupted. He smiled, but his expression looked forbidding. "It's a yes-or-no question."

No, it wasn't, not exactly, I considered. But my conviction of this was at once wishy-washy, uncertain. Time was beginning to speed up, and something random fluttered into my consciousness:

You know how this works? Sometimes it's not so hard to get convinced, baby.

It was the words of my old beau, Catharine—Christ, it even came in her voice. *What is she doing in there?* I demanded at my brain. *Get lost! I'm busy!* In this hurried moment I grew so confounded, panicked, that I didn't dare think to answer John's question outside of the basics. "Yes," I said. And as the word left my lips I at once understood what Cath was doing inside my head: I was convincing myself yes. I was lying.

"Good." John put his glass aside. "The first thing you're going to do, then, Tevan, is take a seat."

My eyes fixed on him, as though I thought he might spring

and wrestle me down if I didn't keep watch. This was a paranoid notion, a ridiculous way of thinking—John had yet to do a single physical thing to make me feel detained. Yet with him telling me what to do and the clear acknowledgment that I had no blink of an idea of *what* he intended to do with me, an ancient creature within me had begun to awaken.

"I don't fuck," I managed. I know that's not the sort of thing you usually do sitting down—not unless you're getting creative, anyway—but it was my only shot at clarification. I mean, so far as I could figure.

"I never asked you to. On the contrary—" John's tone grew strident: "I told you to *SIT THE FUCK DOWN*."

It's a wonder I didn't wind up on the floor. My ass hit the seat before I even chanced a look around to calculate the chair's geography against where I was going to land. As I did, with a soft thump, my eyes began to focus upon the room for the first time. At first I saw nothing, and next I saw short glimpses, and then, in a matter of spliced, negligibly-accounted-for seconds, I spied something pastel and airy slung upon a peg across the room. I remember it very clearly as though it were today. It was a horrible sight.

It was the pink feather boa.

I sat in the chair, and as my eyes met the boa's ugly, ostensibly benign fluffiness, my veins pulsed with terror. For one stark instant I grew scared—no, I grew *convinced*—that John Hadley was going to make me put it on. I don't mention this because pink feather boas are the things that nightmares are made of. I mention it because this was the first moment I understood what would happen the next time John opened his mouth. And the next time, and the next time, and the next after that.

Whatever it was, whatever he asked for, I was going to do it.

My mind exited and only a body remained in the chair. And as I sat—breathing in and out, whitening my knuckles against the fuzzy, threadbare patchwork beneath one hand and that motherfucker of a shot glass in the other—I understood that I was nothing more than a dry mouth and a pair of eyeballs inside an empty space. Time seemed to accelerate, faster and faster still, like a losing game of strip poker, moving, moving now toward its nasty, inevitable end.

"You sink that down, son," John says. This is the third time in the span of about ten minutes that John has encouraged me to drink up and be merry. It's very questionable, and yet I swiftly ignore it and do as I'm told. What John Hadley gave me is enough alcohol to drop a horse, but I drink it like water. As I do, I begin to peer carefully around the room. I see the gauzy robes dangling from a row of pegs alongside the boa, the warped heart-shaped vanity mirror standing against the far wall. The vanity top is cluttered with tiny bottles and tubes that bring my mother, vaguely, painfully, to mind. I comprehend for the first time that I'm in a ladies' dressing room.

This resonates in me as reasonable. But why am *I* here? It's reasonable, except for the fact that there aren't any ladies for what appears to be a country mile from where I sit. Why?

Don't you ask why, Tevan. Don't you even.

No, I don't dare. No sir, do I. I comply.

And in the same average, sensible fashion—again the odd feeling of events just unfolding in an organic, timely manner, as always seems to happen to me—the question is answered. John reaches for the door and consults with the outside, and a girl steps in.

My eyes follow her as she follows John, just like that neat little conga we perform upon the highway every time the mid-way moves locations: steel following campers following *(Human Blockhead!)* rigs. I see how her hair is long and full down her back. Her skirt falls in long, wispy layers right down to her bare, sweet ankles. I am the Human Blockhead. I am immobile, a use-less body of concrete in my chair, performing a trick. It's not just any girl, my eyes transmit. Oh no. Oh Jesus Christ, oh fucked if I know it, oh hardee-har and hidey-ho—

It's the girl.

The *girl*. The Card Reader. The belly dancer, the cat's-eyes soothsayer, the *honey-that's-a-dime* persuader. Though I have an idea that she ain't here to read my future or teach me how to tango, no sir. She's here for the show.

"This is my friend Taiva," John tells me.

I sit, a frozen lump of human indolence, staring. Defenseless and without agency. A memory enters my mind. It's funny and yet it's terrible. It's of James and me, singing along to Paul and Paula in the car: *What hawk, that'd be like you, James, falling for a chick named Jamie or . . . Jamesette or something. Me, I'd have to hook up with a girl with a name like—like—*

Taiva. It is the first time I know her name. I wish I'd never come to know it at all. *Never mind, there's no hope for me.*

The girl follows instructions. She approaches, gathers her skirt in one hand, and settles at my feet. I stare upward as she roosts at my knees like the fine concubine of Rasputin. Calm, she just sits. She's sitting and all of a sudden I know what she's doing there. Oh I know, all right. I know because I sat down like that before Damon a week ago to the day. *You're like them,* Damon's voice says inside of me. *A lizard right off the lot.* I have a dismal, loathing feeling that I know exactly what *I'm* doing here.

"The lady wants to know if you're ready," John says. I wonder if John's ready. What it is that *he's* doing here, that is. The creature at my feet coughs. Somewhere in the deep, untainted recesses of my brain where I can still feel sympathy, I suddenly feel profoundly, heartbreakingly sorry for her. "Is there anything that you want, son?"

I look at the ceiling and I look fleetingly at my lap: *A dollar for the last article,* my brain sings out to me, *most certainly her panties—*

Jesus *Christ!* it hits me. I'm not wearing any underwear!

"Yes," I say, pointing to John's untouched pint of scotch. A voice comes into my head, something like a cross between comedic relief and a smarmy sports broadcaster: *Tevan drank the scotch. It was his only defense.* "I want that."

John leans in and passes it across the void. I go for it. Then I go for my belt.

"Don't," he admonishes. "She's a professional. You let her do the work."

I breathe, seething. I make one calculated, begrudging concession: I take her fingers to the belt. "It's hard to undo," I tell her—which it is, and I would know: I've wrestled with it a hundred times as James has grappled with the muscles of my throat. It crosses my mind that I've known this all along, just never spoken it out loud. I think maybe I bought that particular belt—a thick braid of leather, the metal pin wide and clumsy—to function as a sort of weir wall, in the hope that it would stop me from fulfilling my end of that awful thing that James and I do.

The girl meets my eye and nods. Now there is a sensation of skin meeting first fleshy humidity, then rain. And a compensatory moan from somewhere in the system that has no name and yet within which my eyes are somehow still embedded. They witness John Hadley's sharp, aroused amusement, his mistaking the reverberation of pain for one of pleasure, and for this I hate him.

I see him and I am enraged but still I don't move. In this horrid, hazy-yet-omniscient moment, I am able to glimpse myself through his eyes. It's like watching a skin flick from the seedy chaise of one of those inner-city underground theaters. I see myself, frozen and trapped in the lounge chair: a cigarette in one hand, a kickass glass of gold in the other, and the girl down my pants. And I understand with plain, nonjudgmental nonchalance what John is doing here. Some fellows like *free love,* you know: fucking at no beyond-anatomy cost. Some fellows like *swinging.* Some men are gaspers. And some men, I realize, just like to watch. It's no crime. I can't hate him for this. And yet I remember—animals frozen in hiding places; bystanders rubbernecking a car accident; marks watching a show—and I do.

John generates a haze of smoke. I see the cherry burning, a fiery eyeball across the room. The smell is sharp, organic like the breath of an herb greenhouse or the first drag of a Camel. I have the idea that it's not a cigarette he's smoking. It's one of those incestuous cousins that cost James an arm and a leg, perhaps even the entire wage of what got me into this chair in the first place—

"Some of this, son?" Now he's offering me that little blazing wand, like a comrade tendering a reward. But—*ahh*, it's no reward. It's protection against—

(Remembering)

something . . . I can't recall exactly what. But who cares anyway? I take it in my fingers, John standing courteously to bridge the gap. I don't think; I simply

(Comply a thousand different ways, I can't remember them all; it doesn't matter, it holds you down all the same)

inhale; as I do, tiny ashes flutter, snowflake-like, into her hair.

I try not to look. And it hits me: the scotch from Sandy, the warm-up from John, the cigarette, and now this. It mashes my brain thoroughly, thankfully, squelchingly. I depart from all the places where I've been touched or jammed or accessed like bottles of pop clunked out of a soda machine, and I thank God for this. I feel nothing and I thank—

Jesus, it takes a long time to get home! Longer than I expected. The holdup is mostly my fault. I leave Mount Rosa's at one in the afternoon, catch the 1:43 train into Burlington, arrive at Hamilton Central at half past four . . . and then I simply stand around, waiting.

I stand at the window of the bus station, my bags neatly organized at my feet, my nose pressed to the glass. My heart beats in anticipation, and I wait.

Wait for what? I'm almost embarrassed to say. But as the final straggling passengers stroll into the January chill air to meet their correspondents and I remain unclaimed, it finally dawns on me: I'm waiting for Kenny.

Before the dismay hits, this strikes me as funny. A blasting, stupid oversight on my part, since my mother never drove a day in her life. Not before, not on this day, January third, 1958, and not after. Who the hell do I think will come and pick me up?

You thought he was coming, my brain says to me. Didn't you?

Yes. No. I don't know. I turn a dime out of my pocket. "Hi, Ma. It's me," *I say into the pay telephone.* "I'm here, at the station."

"But heaven, it's taking you a long time to get home!" *my mother exclaims.* "Why are you calling, Tevan?" *That will probably be about the last time she asks me why I'm calling; afterward, she'll only ask why I'm NOT.* "I thought you'd be on the town bus by now."

"That's why I'm calling," *I tell her.* "I just missed the bus."

"I see. Well, I suppose you can catch the next one in half an hour, can't you? You still have your ticket?" *With a train ticket the local bus is free. I, of course, in my sanguine enthusiasm, launched it into the trash as I came up off the tracks. And given the stupidity I already feel at this juncture in time, I'm not about to go rooting around in the garbage can like some kind of wayward hobo, looking for it.*

"I got it," *I say. Because I do, got the cash to pay for a transfer, although I see no need to clarify the details. And thank God no need, too. I'd hate to have to explain what I did with the first ticket.*

"All right then, Tevan," *she says.* "Get home soon. We can't wait to see you."

I never tell her why I turn up later than expected. I don't know if she ever suspected. I think she might've, though.

"Get home soon. We can't wait to see you."

She even phrased it that way: We

are here in this room and my eyelids part. I've opened the window blinds. I am looking down and the girl comes into view, yet what I see I at first don't understand.

I miss the worst of it—the central undertaking itself, that is. Yet transposed like an eerie backdrop behind my right hand, midair and clenching the spliff, is the girl's elbow. The wispy shawl that she carries about her arms has fallen away. The joint of an arm is against my knee. But as my eyes sink into the portrait, I notice something upon it that I've never seen on a woman before:

Upon the intersection of forearm and bicep, there is a smattering of color.

Purplish, pink, and gray. Indented, vicious dimples in which these colors are pooled. The skin is closed, and yet I see the hues of fissures that have been and then moved on, like measles that once roosted and have since been medicated away. It is not unlike what I have envisioned my own battered and healed lungs to look like.

My brow creases unconsciously. *What*, I think, *is that?*

Nothing. It's nothing. You're stoned, Tevan.

Yes, but—

Watch out a that'un, my mind recalls Keith's voice. *Medicated, she is.* I continue to stare at her, at them, bewildered. For a minute I have no idea what I am looking at. Then I remember something else. Not from another time in my life or another dimension, but from just a few weeks before: the girl and I, outside the diner that turned her away. *But he had a good eye,* she'd said of the authority, her arms wrapped tight around her. *I'll give him that.*

I am not incredibly naïve. I have a roommate who smokes dope and a dead brother who drank like a fish and I know that guys use pointed pinkies like Butch's to draw lines of powder. I think of the strep needles I received at the san and I stare at the girl's arm and now I know.

"What day is it tomorrow?" my mother asks me from the doorway of my room.

It's evening. I've already unpacked my bags and laid each belonging into its proper place after nine months of absence. The snow patters down outside amid the eaves, like salt sprinkled from a shaker. My mother waits. And so I answer her.

"January," I say. "It's January fourth."

She smiles again. "You'll find not much has changed round here. But you, Tevan—" She studies me carefully, approaches, puts a hand to my hair. "Now, how old are you tomorrow?"

She already knows how old I'm turning, just as she knew I was fourteen years old the day I left her. Just the same as she knows that Kenny was a fine, promising twenty when he left us both and knocked off for good.

"Fifteen," I say.

She returns the favor. "Get some sleep, sweetheart. We—" Fuck, there it is again! She amends: "I'll see you in the morning."

I slip between the blankets that she laid out for me. I sleep almost instantaneously. But I jump back to life within a short few hours. My eyelids spring open and my heart pounds—to nothing. I sit for a moment, my eyes open. As they focus into the dim countenance of a familiar bedroom, my own legs against the side of the bed, the hands of the clock across the room stand out:

It is a quarter past midnight.

I stare at it for a very long time. The wind outside hoots around the skinny wooden eaves; the clock ticks onward. I wait. I'm not sure what I'm waiting for.

You thought he was coming, my brain says to me, this time a whisper. Didn't you?

It's the second time in a day that this sentence has danced through my head. Yes, I'm waiting.

Though not for Kenny.

Alone in the dark, close to a hundred kilometers from Mount Rosa's, I have the luxury of understanding for the first time what I felt throughout the months that I was there: this feeling like wanting to run for your life. Like wanting to disappear from your own head or body, just to save yourself. Like wanting to crawl under your bed. And it is when I am thinking exactly this that something appears in the doorway.

It yanks a curt, anxious whoop from my throat: the snort of a surprised horse combined with the hiss of a frightened cat.

And there is my mother, no one but my mother, just a shadow in the doorway, in her nightgown. There—

they are. They're old, the skin sealing history into her body like Bern's touch is soldered into me. But I see them and they're there. The girl has *had some troubles.* For one indignant instant, I understand how it is that she got here. Got here on this side-show of trouble. Got here on John's show. Got here, down on her knees. It is a comprehension that, like her name, I will never forget. And one that I am equally sorry for knowing.

"What's your name, son?" John says.

A brilliant cramp clenches my lower half. The physical sensation is great—and worse, I know what it is. And so the sound I make in response is like a cross between a hiss and a moan, the respiratory equivalent of the Minotaur: half man, half beast. For the hundredth time in my life, I wonder how it is that something so sweet as an impending orgasm can feel so doomsayingly vile.

I'm going to heaven now. I drag on the joint and it picks away at what's left of my brain.

"Well, then. I think you're ready for your end now, son," John says. "Do you think?"

I nod, dumbly. Because I can't quite recall what he's talking about. I can't remember where I am; I can't remember my name. I don't think about the girl. I think about the song with the bus stops and umbrellas in it. I think about Elvis and I think about Betty and Veronica. I think about Kenny. I think that pink is my favorite color—

"Take off your shirt, son."

I think that sex is the currency of love. I think I'm not feeling so hot. I think I bought that belt for a reason. I think you ought to be quiet now. I think you ought to shut up—

My head bows into a nod; and when I feel the tiny tug at the corner of one sleeve, I see that I've got my shirt halfway off my shoulder already. The girl is below this and I behold a strange, bottlenecked vision of her: her face is upturned. I could count her freckles. At first I believe she's looking at me because she's annoyed. I've been breathing like a marathon-running asthmatic: I have to concentrate to keep my knees from squeezing her shoulders like a vise. Instead her eyes meet mine:

No, they say. *Don't.*

My brow caves into a militant pose. I have no idea what she's on about. I've already forgotten about those dots on her arms. I've already discounted those dots upon my face. And I've most certainly forgotten the thrust John Hadley made at my own elbow two days prior, saying *I hear you had some troubles, son.*

My end, you see. I've forgotten my end. So what do you do, Tev?

I comply. I shrug at her, as if staving off some small and irritating creature. And then my arm is there and John is there, out of his seat, and it's all there. There is a sound of a man near my neck, and this is so familiar to me that it scarcely registers as relevant. Then there is a sting. A physical, seemingly *teensy* sting. Upon the heels of it, crowding overtop it like a bugling revelation, I hear a voice from the dead:

What are you, dead, boy? Kenny says inside my head. *You dead now? Don't you use those eyes that God put in your head?*

I furrow my brow. There it is again: *Don't fall asleep now, Tev! Keep those fuckin' eyes open,* Kenny says. Within this moment, the sting in the fold of my skin recedes, the fog in my brain suspends, the clench of my guts thickens—and my eyes fly open.

I almost expect to see him. See my brother, *Death and Divine Intervention, Live!,* sitting at my feet. I can picture him as I require him, placed in this room and watching with wise, protective eyes. I nearly *believe* I see him for a moment. But of course I don't. Instead, I see there are two at my knees. The girl, inclined toward my groin as instructed; and John, poised beside my right wrist. This is not problematic in general. I understand that I've expected him to come for me. But John Hadley is nowhere near the part of me that I thought he'd come for. Instead, I see he's come for my arm.

The chair cradles my forearm; the forearm rests against John. In between, above the lounge chair, bridging my body and his, is a clear plastic syringe.

It's my end.

And it's in my fucking arm.

A sound escapes me. As my breath leaves my nostrils, an indomitable force is loud inside my head—half Kenny, half me—and it says without any hesitation:

Oh boy, I'm going to scream now.

But I don't say anything just yet. And still, and somehow, the look on his brow reading that he's not sure what exactly he is looking over for, slowly, John looks up. Our eyes meet: mine, I'm sure are wide, wild with terror; watching him I see that his are completely bewildered. His is an expression I am familiar with. I've seen it thousands of times, in thousands of social situations, over the last five years, but until now I have seen it only upon the face of one other person. It is the look James wears as he is watching, concentrating, deliberating so diligently every damn day, and missing it all nonetheless.

John recoils, the needle cocked in his grip. One eyebrow bends. And although we sit on opposing polarities, a transient moment transpires between John Hadley and me, and amid our silence it's as though thousands of words are spoken. It is the sideshow, for the first time, dead center in my head. A spray of random, firing bullets, made up of John

(*What I remember most is what I saw*),

James

(*Tell me, what did you do, Tev?*),

and Kenny

(*I'm going to scream now*).

At first nothing emerges from my throat at all. My feet lose contact with the floor. James started getting out of his bed at night, and what have I done?

I complied.

John continues to stare at me until his features show comprehension. "Holy Mary, son," John says. "Wait. Don't move. Don't move or I'll break the stem right off in your vein."

In the second between his words and movement, my eyes fix upon the syringe. I see the silver pin halfway buried in my flesh and I see the red tinge floating inside its body. I recognize this as my own fluids mixing with poison, and am brought to an ecstatic, nearly hypnotic level of terror. And in this instant, between misunderstanding concession for threat and the slivering departure of steel from skin, I believe that my mind has finally cracked.

Cracked; broken completely.

In reality, it has done nothing of the kind. Maybe at fourteen I was broken—driven mad with the incongruity between the way a body could at once feel and not be felt—but not here.

Here I open my mouth, close it. And after?

Just a wash. A succession of divine, God-given minutes where I scarcely recall a thing.

At the sanitarium, the inmates wore pajamas day and night. On account of this, I would never wear pajamas again. At the san, we were served beans six days out of every seven; and I haven't eaten them since. At the san, I got a needle once every two weeks—streptomycin, shot indelicately between the fibers of pubescent muscles—and I can't stand the sight of the sheer point of a pin pressed to my skin to this very day.

That's the funny thing about remembering. Sometimes it's less like recalling, and more like being, than you might think. *There it is again. Fuck, there it is.*

I return to this place, this walk-the-plank, this *Death and Divine Intervention, Live!*, this place that convinces

(Sometimes it's not so hard to get convinced, baby)

all the time. Every time I am in it, I see him. In my mind and in my back, and the threads of my urinary tract and my throat, in all the places where he

(broke it off right in your vein)

had me. But still I see him as I did the night he bent over the push-pedal faucet and splashed water on my face. His eyes, his hair dripping and slick in a forward peak. There is a sheet of pain stippled with pleasure in this knowing. I cannot divide the horror from the allure. It's always this way. Always

(the Worst.)

here, I have no words to describe it.

(Yes No Tev, was Bern your friend did you hate?)

Bern has even fewer. He never explains anything to me. His eyes wait and his lips do not move. When he does get to words, they are always the same. *You,* he says:

Shut up! Then to John: "Christ, can't you just tell him to shut the fuck up, Boss?" John Hadley enlisted the help of Sandy in order to secure a room for our endeavor; he called on Sandy to supply me with the necessary warm-up tipple of scotch. Now Sandy reappears at John's bidding. This time his task is to dispose of me.

"Say, you, shut up!" Sandy yells, taking me by one arm as he tries to see me out the back. He roughs me up a bit doing so, but it's still a kind favor: getting launched out the back sure beats having to thread your way to the front of the building. They aren't just saving me the embarrassment of waltzing out through a crowded room, either. John knows I won't make it through that roomful of guys even if they carry me. The only thing that my eyes commit to memory is the thin smile that crosses John Hadley's face.

"No, Sandy," he says, "I'm not going to tell him to shut up. I think that's the first thing he's managed here all night that he actually means." It's the truth. John's learned something of me here in this room

(I say though my voice sounds rusty and my breath shuddery, like it does before you begin to cry; and whuh happens when ya don't understand the lesson the firs' time?)

What lesson? There is no lesson here! I go to Bern honestly, with no judgment! Just as I went to my brother moments after he slapped my face for hollering about the nail in my foot (*I had to get you composed*); just as James continues to follow me after the many times I've told him *Fuck off* and *Shut the hell up* and *You sorry stupid dipshit.* I go to him like the marks set out to the sideshow—with faith in the amazing possibility that they will in fact see something worth their dime.

But then I find, like the marks upon arriving at the show, that I must pay a price. That the rate is not necessarily equal to the act. That it is a cheap grind that keeps repeating and repeating all day without end. That I must contend with the growing suspicion, and then the certainty, that what I see is a ruse. That

(the sign is old, Tevan George)

I find, oh yes: always with the same dismayed, unsurprised misery that it's too late. I judged his intentions latently. A jagged slash of fear arrives like a temperature or a color—a swath of emotion so sudden that I am nothing but a

(whangdoodle)

body set upon my sideshow stage. It's too late to renege. The sign is old and yet here I took the glass from his hands and drank again. My eyes glance at the stage.

Still frozen, I spy another actor in my show. I am not

(Please share my umbrella)

alone. Here, slightly off-center, yet very surely on the interior too, stands

"—my friend. Please, I'm staying with my friend," I say. These are first words I am able to formulate since Sandy toted me from the hootchy-kootchy trailer on John's behalf. To the only other person present.

"Your friend," she replies carefully. "You mean the other guy from your show? Big guy, right? The Hierophant?" And for the first time synapses in my brain fire correctly and I wager a tentative attempt at understanding

(The Page represents a child. Pubescent or pre-pubescent. Inclination. Deviation, flattery, susceptibility, vulnerability. Seduction)

she is bringing me home. "Yes," I say.

Once she identifies James in her mind, the Card Reader is able to bring us swiftly to the camper. James appears in the doorway. But when he gets me inside, I land on my knees. Worse, I can't stop talking. On and on, crazy, nonsensical;

(Bus stop, bus go; she stays, love grows. Under my umbrella)
even watching is embarrassing.

"He had a lot to drink," she tells James, by way of explanation. "I don't know what exactly, I'm sorry. It's a holy wonder he remembered where he's staying. He was screaming and yelling, and he hoofed John right in the chest." She pauses, watching. "What's he going on—"

"I don't know," James says; and yet I suspect maybe he does. I am amped on two pints of scotch, six hauls of marijuana, and God knows what else, which I witnessed John Hadley level into my arm.

(What do you know, James? Do you know?)
I don't know anything. I am trapped, stuck, gibbering—
(Remembering)

"I hear you, Tev. I hear." He peers down at me, his expression one of calm though perplexed analysis. We are now speaking a different language. James watches with careful eyes and I can only

(choke, he takes my throat, see, and I choke. Understand, I take it I take it! Did I ask for it and say nothing and what is coming next I know too? I can't breathe, my friend, yet I know I)
hate you.

(I choke and I take it and I say nothing, my friend, nothing and I say, Aw you want this? Aw you like this? Why don't you take it, take this take it! You want to)
comply, Tevan, it's not like it hurts. And I know what to do. My end. My hand lands on James. I find programmed action in old instructions. I find contact. I find I draw a staggered little yelp from him. I find parts of his body that will inevitably find parts to

(Aw you want this? Take it and let me)
try to take me! Why not! James shrugs me off. He looks

surprised; embarrassed. Sorry he even asked. "He doesn't know where he is," James says in my defense.

This is the line I've told him a thousand times, waking him off the floor to the first indistinct light of day. The line that I've repeated, trying to draw him back to now. The line that I needed to speak aloud in order to live and breathe and feel somehow safe. Bern was after me, I know; no, James, he wasn't; yes he was; no he wasn't;

(Yes he is and THEY ALL KNOW IT)

and I feel smugly satisfied to speak the truth. I put my hand on him, but this time he lays a fist over it. "Stop it, Tev," he says. After the passing of two or three seconds, I come to understand that he is holding me in place. My eyes alight as I stare, not seeing. I actually feel the fire beneath them. He pins my hands down and holds his breath. He presses my back to the soft spring of the bunk. This is the worst coming, it's the worst! You asked for it, it's the worst! I am outraged that he can

(Hold me down and make me)

do this. My teeth clench, and as I catch sight of my arms pinned above my head I grow ecstatic and I culminate the only way that is natural to me:

(I hold my nose I close my eyes I take a drink)

screaming.

"Auuuugggghhh! Auuuugggghhh!" Spittle sprays from my teeth. A wire of snot exits my nostrils and stretches itself like an umbilicus, joining my head to the face of the mattress. And although I've thrashed in bed for nearly half my lifetime now, I understand I've never done it like this before—that is,

(shut up you've got to shut it)

before God and everyone.

James holds me down. The girl steps back. "That's what happened before," she says.

James nods. "Sorry." He grants me one small, polite gesture—he looks away. "Sorry, Tev," he tells me.

I see James. And in this I understand the division between

past and present; the split between resolution and damned, fixed history. I wonder, just as I did on the floor before Damon, what the hell I am doing here.

It may be impossible for me to perform the perjury of my sideshow again. I see James and yet

(You're never going to get free of this place. Never never)

I understand for the first time why it is I keep going back there. Staring at James with wild, grieving eyes, I turn my head and begin to cry.

17

I AWOKE SATURDAY MORNING, ALONE INSIDE THE BUNK THAT James had wrestled me into, with a mother of a headache and a memory just as damning. I couldn't remember it all, but what I did was enough to leave me wishing the vaults of my brain had held on to none of it. The week progressed, Death-Defying rejoined the sideshow's roster; and still, the events of that night wouldn't let go of me.

If you can't forget the past, I decided, the next best thing is to fitfully dull any reminders of it. And so it was around this time that I began to incorporate a new trick into me and James's current practice: a half-hour before each performance, I slid a bottle from its paper sleeve and tipped myself a good, hearty dose. *Medicating, warming up, going in on the nod*: you heard it termed a few different ways around the midway—though only as a joke when a worker showed up for his shift, bleary-eyed; or in the pejorative, when applied to guys like Sandy; or, as Keith had once implied, girls like Taiva. The drink struck my tongue like a bee sting and hit my guts like a bomb. Each time, a frenzied, hopeful beam of faith glanced through me—faith in a trick that you don't need any magician to teach you.

James had found his own method of coping too. With Damon's assistance, he'd started moonlighting, taking on various other tasks about the lot, as per Buddy's suggestion some weeks before. Within days of my ill-fated transaction with John Hadley, me and James were hardly seeing each other at all anymore. He left the camper close to six in the evening, thanks to Damon Merit's make-work projects. I was keeping my nose to the grindstone too. I ran Keith's rides, by then with the hand of a seasoned pro, and for as many hours as possible.

The following Saturday I arrived home in the late afternoon

with the splendid intention of doing nothing but sleeping into evening.

"What's Damon got you doing tonight, James?" I asked as he and I crossed paths at the camper door. James had, thus far, acted on stage as Rajid's minion; had refurbished some of the splintery planks of the sideshow stage itself; and, during a particularly slow day, scrubbed the floors of each and every can in the stinking lot.

"I'm going to be the geek," James said.

"Cherry," I put forward, yawning lustily, my eyes already trained on the bunk. "Good on you, James. See you."

I dropped into bed, then awoke to the muted light of late evening two hours later. I lay there for a minute or two, lazily incoherent. *What's a geek?* I wondered to myself, mulling James's words. And as though an answer to myself, something hit me with a jolt. It was a recollection of me and James's first meeting with Buddy Merit:

Geek's a sideshow performer. A loser. Nobody. A person no one will miss.

And then: *Don't ask, James. Probably the crummiest job on the whole damn fairgrounds, by the looks of the guy.*

An edgy shard of unease tinkled up my spine. I stepped out of the bunk in a hurry. I pulled James's sweatshirt off a hook and slipped it over my head. Then I went out the door— and although I verged on the sideshow tent still assuring myself that no job could be worse than the outhouse digging James had done in the summer of '61, I knew in my gut that I believed otherwise. I'd done worse than outhouse digging for a little extra cash.

I'd gotten a wage that had left me screaming.

I trotted up the sawdust walkway and found Sandy at the mouth of the tent. "Hey," I said, breathless. "Show's not started yet, is it?"

"Nope." Sandy grinned. "Just in time. That'd be a quarter for you, Tev."

I looked at the cashbox in Sandy's hands. I gave him a patronizing look. "Quarter if you'd stuff it up your ass, maybe."

I was one of the last to filter onto the scene, so I didn't get a great seat. That was no skin off my back; I wasn't certain I wanted James to spot me in the crowd anyhow. As I saw him waiting behind Damon, already onstage and addressing the crowd, I made the flash, inexplicable decision to flip the hood of my sweatshirt onto my head.

"This is just an ordinary man, yes?" Damon bugled.

I had to weave my head for a good line of sight. James stood in silence, tall but slouching, looking expectantly to Damon.

"Yes, a man. But is this man civilized as you and I? Does he LOOK civilized? Refined . . . ?" Damon paused, his timbre dwindling to a whisper. The collected crowd quieted.

"SANE?" Damon erupted. As he did so, James came forward. The throng, like a human demonstration of dynamic equilibrium, jumped back a pace. *"We have tried to civilize this man, ladies and gentleman!"* Damon cried. *"He comes from a land far away and speaks not a word of English!"*

Here, as though to fortify the point, James uttered an unintelligible, throaty snarl. I couldn't help but smile.

So did Damon. *"But is he not a man like you or I, a human being who—"*

The crowd's collective gaze traveled back and forth between Damon and James. James to Damon, Damon to James; James to—wait a second. Here transpired a funny bit of movement from behind James's back.

"What's this?" Damon interjected, pointing, and now James held a box out in invitation. Damon stepped back, his face an expression of utter bewilderment. *"What have you got there?"*

As if he doesn't know, I thought to myself. But the crowd, as anticipated, rolled inward. Curious now, *I* rolled inward. James shoulders bowed forward, hiding his revelation. From the bottom of the box, he swirled his hand up and outward to show us his catch.

And it was moving.

And he dropped the box on the floor. And there it was:

It was a rat. What James held in his fingers was a rat.

Damon's face at once conveyed the crowd's response: *"What are you going to do with that?"* It was a flawless re-creation: his nose wrinkled and his lips curled in disgust. I heard a muted huff of disgust slip through my own lips. *"What are you going to do with that"*—Damon paused—*"THING?"*

James gripped the coiling mass. He dangled it by its tail, fluttering it overhead. The thing spun and squirmed; it was impossible to tell if this was the animal's own hysterical reaction or simply the doing of James's expert wrist.

"What are you going to do?" Damon cried.

Women in the throng howled. James grinned. His teeth looked suddenly huge, ominous inside his mouth. He grasped the animal in both hands. His eyes rolled across the sea of staring faces. His mouth opened—

and for the first moment in my life, I understood what a geek's skill to be—

as Damon gasped. *"You're not really going to—!"*

I turned my head and clenched my eyes shut, steeling myself; but the screams that I expected from the people about me did not occur. A moment later I opened one eyelid, then the other. And when I did, the rat was still intact in James's hand. And I saw the Card Reader, her expression grim but her eyes trained in my direction, standing just five paces away.

"A man who works, eats, and sleeps, just like the rest of us?" Damon screeched. *"NO!"*

My eyes slid from the girl's and hypnotically toward the stage. James opened his mouth and bit down. A low, gritty sound emitted from the connection. Something spurted. In the instant that I saw it—the horror of teeth meeting nebulous fuzz, the insanity of lips clamping over scampering claws—I had the unwitting, unbidden opportunity to imagine what it might feel like inside James's mouth. The grainy crunching of incisor joining gristle, gums stroked by tiny, coarse hairs, molars encountering the creature's own crushed, busted teeth.

My next rejoinder was pure, involuntary biology: I bent over my knees and I retched.

I made it outside—grateful, now, for my crummy seat at the back of the room—and stood gasping. I wasn't the only one, either. I tried to differentiate myself by moving a few paces away, but there had to be a good half-dozen marks to count myself among, all gagging in the dark. I could just make out Taiva's outline against the opening in the tent's canvas. She watched me from this distance. But she made after me when I started toward the back entrance.

"Where you going?" she said, matching my pace. "Where you going to, huh?" *To find James!* I nearly shrieked. But she got in front of me, slowing us both, until I understood what she meant: To what purpose?

I tried to picture myself meeting James on the other side of the canvas and couldn't. "I don't know," I managed. In fact, thinking on it, I found myself hoping that James had no idea I'd been there at all.

"You didn't pay to see that, I hope," she said, "did you?"

"No," I said. "Thank God. I batted my eyelashes at Sandy, and he—you know, let me in for free."

So we turned in the opposite direction of Sandy. We walked through the throng gathering outside the sideshow exit. In the open, parting from the crowd, we walked on without saying much to each other. We passed the hootchy-kootchy trailer and the rows of lit-up concessions. The lawn grew up wild beyond the tracks of sawdust in the lot. Somewhere close to the car lot beyond this, I spied a pair of wooden parking partitions dragged onto the grass. They appeared deliberately set, as though they were meant to separate the carnival from the rest of the world.

"Ladies first," I offered, putting my hand out.

"No really, you." She gestured to me. "I mean, age before

beauty." She smirked at the ground, at her own joke: I witnessed the bend of her cheekbone, the freckles running up and down her nose. Now that we had stopped walking, she held her arms tight across her chest. "And if I join you, I sure hope you're going to be nice to me."

I jiggled the sweatshirt from my shoulders. "Here," I said, holding it at her. "How's this? I've been warming it up for you on this fine piece of machinery all night."

Her expression read that this was not exactly what she meant. I watched her put a tentative hand forward. She tugged the shirt over her head nonetheless, and sat. "Thanks."

I sat down beside her. "Perish the thought," I said, fastening the top button of my shirt against the cold. "Don't thank me. It's James's sweatshirt. But he won't mind, I don't think. He's got bigger fish to fry tonight, as the saying goes."

"Bigger rats to eat." Taiva grinned.

"I could kill Damon for that," I said. "If he expects James to pull that kind of crap around here on a regular basis, I can tell you . . . tell you—well, fuck it, we'll blow this shitass pop stand!"

"Yeah?" she said.

"Oh yeah, in a *minute*," I promised.

Taiva looked away. She smiled wanly. "Sure, same here. You think?"

A moment of silence ran between us. I knew what she was suggesting: Within our lowly, disenfranchised existence upon the show, the only power me and James had was our hanging threat to dissent and resign. But still, we couldn't even do that.

"Yeah, I think," I said nonetheless. "Of course that's what I think. You figure this is what James wants to *do* for the rest of his life? Bite the heads off fucking rats?" I shook my head. "Jesus, I been around the guy long enough to know him better than that."

"I can tell." Taiva smiled, genuine this time. She nodded at me to go on. "How long now?"

"Oh boy." I gazed into the dark. Tall, shadowy cedars swayed beyond the parked cars: it reminded me of the night that

James and I had sat in the car, making love to the Four Roses. "At least five years," I said. "Well . . ." I reflected. "Well, actually, we met far before that. When we were kids, practically."

"Kids?" she repeated.

"I was fourteen. But that was just the start. Truth, him and me been going on over five years now, hanging together just us. Man, that's long enough to start speaking the same language. Even with a sort like James." I laughed and so did she.

"Boy," she said then. "I've been meaning to tell you. Boy, you sure can scream."

"Aw, thanks." I gave her a sardonic look. "Did we sleep together that night too?"

"No." Her lips bent upward. A few moments passed as she stared off, as though deliberating whether to speak the next part out loud or not. "But I think you might have, you know, made a go at your friend there if I hadn't been around."

I resisted the drive to change the subject; correct her, in my best Damon-Merit-I'm-Bigger-Than-Thou tone, that his name was *James*, thank you very much. *James*, not *jackass*, not *that one*, and certainly not *my friend*. But I knew she already understood this. She meant no disrespect. I'd called James my friend a thousand times to her and other people; I'd called James this a thousand times a week ago, Friday night alone. *My friend, you want this; my friend, you like that.*

My friend one; my friend all.

Finally I dredged up something witty. "I guess I must've mistook him for you then. I don't really remember."

She rolled her eyes. A moment later she breathed in, long and full. "John is not a bad guy," she said into the air. "He helped me out with a few things when I needed it. Felt like a favor at the time. It turned into a debt." She sounded as though she were trying to justify something to me. When she spoke again, I could barely read her face. "I thought maybe you had a—situation like that?"

I looked over at her. Now it was my turn to try to explain

myself. "Yes," I said finally. "And no. He helped me out with something, yeah. He fixed my car, and so I owed him."

Taiva looked at me. "Fixed your car," she repeated. "That's it?" She lifted the sweatshirt hood over her ears. It made a peak just over her forehead so that her expression was hidden. But from here she gave a little laugh. "Be thankful you didn't want the sort of fix he thought you did, then," she submitted. "Like the rest of us."

We sat for a while, as her eyes scanned the midway in the distance.

"It looks really pretty from back here, doesn't it?" she remarked. "But I been here a long time now. Too long, I think. John's not a bad guy, you should know," she said again. Then she shook her head. "But like Merit himself, it's to his benefit that some of us are just surviving, needing, stuck in the same place."

"Needing," I put in. "Hey, listen. I don't *need* anything from Merit."

She turned and looked at me. "No? No fame, income without a social insurance number, no money under the table? Booze, powder, weed, whatever—a place that'll take you on no matter how many cuts you put on your own skin, no matter what you look like, no matter what color you are, no matter who you fucked or who you pay to fuck you? You don't want any of those things?"

By now she was studying me. "Sure you do," she continued. "This place takes on all of us. The sideshow will repeat its cheap little tricks forever. When you remain on the show, you get caught up in the act. Survival tricks. Hear the ballyhoo and keep on getting drawn back—" She halted, like her voice had caught in her throat.

A moment later, she recovered. "Do you ever think about cutting loose?"

Her question surprised me, then frightened me; then, on the heels of these, it brought me a sudden, profound sense of yearning. It was like being both free, yet in sudden, consequential mourning. Mourning what, I was not exactly certain. Or wait—

maybe I was. For here I used James's own signature words:

"I don't know," I said.

Her hand came out and clasped mine. She offered a wry little smile. "Sure you do," she said. "Either you think it's safer to stay, or you believe it's a fairer shot to move on."

"Yes." I turned her hand over in mine. "But no. This show, it's—like an old sweater, you know? Old and prickly and ugly, but you don't want to throw it away. It's familiar. Real. Comfortable, I suppose."

"You mean it's something you know," she said. "And you think it looks good on you."

I shrugged. "People keep telling me it does."

"They tell you that," she said to me, "because it makes you stay right where you are."

"There's nothing wrong with me," I cut in, firm this time.

"I know," she said, turning to look at me. "I know that. That's why I keep asking what it is you're doing here." When I had absolutely nothing to say to this, she went on: "I guess I'm wondering if there's better sweaters to be afforded. Because looking good on me or not, there is something on this sideshow that I've grown very tired of. You?"

I stared at her. I hardly knew the girl, but for some reason she had just said aloud that there was more to me than some titillating trick. And as with the horror card reading she had given me a few weeks before, for a stark, bright moment I actually believed her. I had the sudden sense of being completely prepared for something big, intermingled with the young impotency of being unable to act upon it.

"Where would we go?" I whispered.

"We," she scoffed. "I don't remember mentioning any *we* in my plans. You had a bad Culmination, you'll recall. I'm leaving myself out of it." But she smiled when she said it, and warmth stirred in places all over my body in response. Her faith in me from a moment before and this physical feeling swam there, confounded, inside me; a spaghetti plate of emotions.

I put her hand to the neckline of my shirt. "I thought we were going to be nice to each other," I said.

She grinned. "I *am* being nice to you—"

And the next thing I knew, my mouth was on her throat. It was on her lips, where I felt her warmth and her tongue. I can't say how long it went on. I became optimistic, convinced that in minutes we'd be doing it on the ground. Then the next thing I knew, a shuffling sputtered up out of the darkness. Actually crashing was more like it.

We split like teenagers jumping off one another at the sound of a key in the front door. I turned just as a body materialized out of the black.

"Tev? That you?"

Sandy. That dumb fuck! And don't you know—like the proverbial I'm-with-stupid compatriot—the damn dog was trotting right along with him. He paused there in the grass, some fifteen feet away and squinting into the darkness.

"Yeah," I returned through gritted teeth. "It's me all right." I turned to Taiva. "Excuse me," I offered. "Sorry"—and Jesus, I really meant it—and got to my feet. I reached Sandy in three determined strides.

"What you doing?" he asked conversationally. I doubted he'd strolled his can, to say nothing of his three-thousand-year-old dog's, all the way out here just to ask that kind of a question. I mean, for Christ's sake—he *better* not have.

"Nothing." *I'm getting on with a woman, you dumb nit.* "Nothing. What's up?"

"Aw, all's aces now that I found you two." Sandy's eyes flickered past me, across Taiva's seated figure, then back to me in earnest. "Fight broke out on the lot, eh? Big'un too." He waited. "James there started it," he said.

"James! Oh, fuck me. What happened?"

"Yeah." Sandy nodded. "Didn't tell you? Went nuclear on some mark down near Merit's home base. Then the cops showed up and—"

"*The cops!*" I practically yelled. "What the—I mean, where—"

Sandy held a hand up. "Hold on. Hold on, I says. All's aces." He put a finger to his hair and produced a cigarette. "Hold it, don't get shook. When it happened we all just up and scattered, like." He held out a match, put the spark to the cigarette. "The fellas wanted to be sure that it wasn't our guy, that's all. And now I sees we're all accounted for."

I breathed a sigh of relief. "Thank God." And then: "Wait. Wasn't our guy?"

"This is why I come all the way out here looking for you guys." Sandy waved a hand. "See, Butch seen the heat taking some dude into the trailer, that's all. He says he was *sure* he saw it, but you know Butch, that wack, always smokin' this and that, his brain fried. Geez, I dunno what he's on tonight, but I think he's seein' things. Maybe summa those mushrooms or I dunno?"

A guy like Sandy could go on forever and a fellow like me could have an aneurysm waiting it out. I began nodding frenetically.

"So he seen the cops take a fella into the trailer, but *I says* we're all accounted for. He says no we're not. So I says yeah we are. So he says okay, then where in the name of Jehovah's fuckin' book is Tev—"

"And you said you'd come out and look for us," I finished.

"Yeah." Sandy grinned. "That's exactly what I says." He nodded, slow and thoughtful. He passed over his cigarette. "I see we're on the same page here, Tev."

I offered his smoke back after a breath, so wholly grateful that I didn't even hog it. "Cool," I said. "Golden. That's good news, Sandy. So where's James now?"

The smoke wafted upward. Sandy blinked. "Huh?"

His eyes passed over my shoulder again, this time in a perplexed, weighted manner. I turned my head to follow. "I said, where's James now?"

Taiva sat watching us. She was far enough away to be deaf

to the conversation, but as she saw us turn in her direction she raised one questioning eyebrow. She put a hand to the hood of the sweatshirt and tugged it off her ears.

"Huh?" Sandy managed, still staring. Now at the sweat-shirt, staring. James's sweatshirt, staring hard. "Well, whaddya mean, Tev? If you're out here, then who the hell is—"

And before he could finish the question, I was halfway across the lawn.

18

I LOCKED MY KEYS IN THE CAR THE FIRST AUTUMN THAT JAMES and I lived together. I pulled off on a side street to chisel the windshield off, slammed the driver's side, retrieved the scraper from the back, then slammed that closed too. Next I recall peering noncommittally into the frosty etching of the driver's side window: to my dismay, the lock button was down on my side. In fact, it was down *all around*. I have no idea how I did it—maybe hit it by accident on the way out, maybe bopped it down unconsciously as I stood, maybe I don't know. But at that point there was neither purpose nor time for speculation. I had locked the keys inside the car—and the damn thing was still running.

I remember how adrenaline burst into my veins. I think my mother had something to do with it. *That tank was meant to last me a week, I've piddled away my pay on beer and takeout, I'm scheduled to drive down to see Ma on Sunday and the hell if I can tell her that I'm too broke to make the trip*—she was already on my back about the infrequency of my visits as it was. I flailed against the handle for about ten seconds—if anybody spotted me at it, I imagine I looked like a man glued to his car through some wayward jolt of electricity—before I simply turned and broke out running. The only spare set of keys I knew of in existence was back at the apartment; and even though I couldn't say exactly where they were in there, my only choice was to look, and fast. I ran like my ass was on fire the whole way. When I returned, the car was warm. I didn't even need the scraper anymore.

A similar phenomenon occurred when Sandy caught up to me out in the field: I was on my feet and running before I even knew one hundred percent where I was going.

When I came through the gates to the pavilion, I still didn't have a plan of action. The psychological directive inside my mind had at first been simply *Find James.* But the closer I got to the lights and throngs of people, the more it mushroomed: *Find James,* and *Hide James,* and *Take James and run. Help James* alongside *Don't be seen with James,* clearly incompatible objectives. And so I stood inside the midway for a few moments; stop-motioned, in the middle of a near kilometer of popcorn, candy apples, and blinking lights. Finally I made off toward Buddy's trailer.

I breathed a sigh of relief when I saw lights on inside. It was a Tuesday, Buddy's poker night with the old-timer fellas, but that was fine with me. Any designated acting jack—Damon, Keith, hell, even John Hadley—to ally with me would do. And as I approached, watching the lit interior and mulling this over, I spied Damon standing outside.

"Damon!" I managed, trotting toward him. It came out in a breathy, ridiculous kind of stage whisper. "Damon! Is James in there?"

Damon turned, spotted me. His eyes narrowed. He gave a resigned nod.

My eyes glanced to the lighted windows. Damon surveyed me, his expression guarded, and so I simply went on. "Boy, am I glad to find you! I might need your help. If the police find out his name, you see, if they see—

James Daniel Rowley, in the said region hereinafter called the offender, my brain trickled out, *was convicted on the charge—*

"—his track record, that he's done it before . . . well, Jesus, I don't know what will happen!" I put a hand to my brow. "So listen, here's what I need you to—"

I stopped, watching Damon watch me. I was almost moved to wave a summoning hand before his eyes: his expression had not budged. Instead, it remained an eerie blanket of tired indifference.

"Why are you looking at me like that?" I said.

Damon eyed me. Finally he spoke. "Well, I'm just trying to decide, Tevan, if you're the first or the last person I want to see."

His words arrived in the same absurd undertone as my own, only the inflection was tantamount to a hiss. "Because I'm in a bloody amount of trouble just now." He pointed a finger. "And not only are you the only guy who will bother to shore up for that jackass—which could be helpful to me right now—but you're also the one who brought him in the first place"—his tone grew high, strident—"*to this fucking show!*"

I took a step back. "I did, but—I can't shore up for him, Damon. I can't, not right—"

"Well, that's good!" Damon hissed. "Because I've decided, just now looking at you, that I couldn't give a rat's ass! If they take his name tonight, well, maybe that's all for the best!"

"For the best?" My voice was a dry, whistling squawk. "No, you can't say—"

"Can't I!" His hands on his hips, he nearly towered over me. "Why in the hell not?"

"Because he'll wind up in the cooler, that's why!" I said. "Man, this is what I'm trying to *tell* you!"

Damon leaned in. He pointed a finger. "Have you gone deaf as well as stupid, Tevan? I said I'm not getting involved. And if you thought otherwise, well, then you can go tell your problems to—"

"Jesus *Christ,* Damon, *I can't do it!* He's got a criminal record! Do you understand? Somebody needs to go in there, keep shut on his I.D., and ice it over!"

Damon chuckled. "Oh, *I'm* not icing anything over." His eyes fled to the light in the window. "Guy's got an impulse control problem. A memory problem, if he's managed to get strung this many times—"

"Ice it over!" I said. "Go in and tell them you'll keep an eye on him. That's all I'm asking!"

Damon waved his arms in a circle. "I'm not his mother, Tevan! If you feel so optimistic about him, *you do it!*"

I breathed in, seething. It had all funneled down to a certain, miserable point now. And although I'd rather have dropped dead than lay myself bare for the likes of Damon Merit, I knew I was in no position to stand proud anymore. *I'm not supposed to come near you, Tev,* something in my head reminded me. *It says so all over my papers.*

"I can't go in, Damon." I practically spoke into the ground. "Even if I wanted to. James has got a charge pending against him and I'm the injured party."

Damon blinked. He forgot all about whispering. His voice was a dumb bleat in the darkness: "What?"

"I said I can't!" I told him. "He's got a recognizance of bail that states he's not supposed to be anyplace near me." In the wake of Damon's silence, I continued: "A no-contact order," I said. "Don't you understand?"

Damon's brow caved. "Are you saying—? You're *not* saying—" His brow smoothed suddenly in one swift motion. "He has a charge against *you?*"

"Yes," I told him. "That's exactly what I'm saying."

Damon rotated on his heel. He peered at the trailer window, then looked back at me. "Oh," he breathed. "No. No way now, Tevan. God, I'm not even going to apologize for it!"

"Oh Damon, come on. It's standard. It's *standard,* they put it in those papers every time to ensure the safety of the—" *Victim,* my head completed in traitorous fashion, but I didn't state that part out loud. "I should know, he's got a stack of them in my car. Look, I'm not afraid of him! He didn't even really mean—"

"Oh, sure, sure. He didn't *mean to.*" Damon floated a hand. "He has an *assault* charge against you, Tevan, and he didn't *mean to?* Oh, that's rich. I saw him hightail it tonight—he went fucking bugshit! And I'm to understand he did the same once to you? His"—he paused, searching for the correct words, then gave a short laugh as he came upon them—"better half? I have over forty staff here under my supervision. You want me to back that sort of thing? No, count me out."

I shook my head, trying to make myself understood. "But it wasn't his fault, Damon," I said. "He didn't do it on purpose.

It was on a bet. These guys, this guy—" I shook my head. Inside, tucked far into my consciousness, I could almost hear James's seconds ticking away. "This guy who found out about what kind of favors I did for pay. You know what I'm talking about, Damon. Don't you?"

Damon, who knew far more than he wished he ever had, only continued to stare at me. It was the first either one of us had said aloud about our own arrangement some weeks before, directly or indirectly. Damon didn't nod, he didn't shake his head. His face was blank, uncommitted. So fuck it, I decided: why not concede the whole sordid business?

"Yeah," I said. "Yeah, you know how I mean. Well, the guy saw me in a bar, after hearing some things about me on the down low. James was there too, playing pool or something, I don't really remember—" That was a lie. The memory of it all remained in my consciousness, more so than I wanted. I didn't like the bar much. I hardly ever went there. I didn't even *play* pool. Still, James had wanted to go.

"So the guy saw me there and started talking trash with all his friends. Telling them he knew all about that kid sitting at the bar, that young, pretty-looking guy. That guy sucks the root and that guy shakes off for cash. That guy's a faggot and a trip and who knows what else." I stole a glance up at the trailer window. For the first time I noted the police car, parked, half-visible beyond the building.

"Didn't tell James what he knew, though; just offered to pay him fifty up front to straighten the kid out and get rid of him. James didn't ask any questions. They's just these guys he's playing pool with who don't have a kind word to say about me, see." I eyed Damon carefully. "You know that trick we do, Damon. Onstage? Yeah, you know it and maybe you ought to know this—me and James, we been practicing that trick for years.

"They probably meant for him to hit me, but what they said was to knock me flat, and James, well, he figured he didn't have to let them in on the history. It was to his—our—advantage.

He figured he could play along and make a pretty decent end." I laughed here, because still it was a little funny. "Show those fuckin' hoods who to make fun of, too."

Damon had watched me in silence the whole while, but right here he opened his mouth: "Those queer-fearing *bastards*," he said, incredulous.

I nodded feverishly. "Damon, I didn't even know the guy," I continued. "I didn't know what he was saying to James. Only next thing I know, James is tearing me off the barstool and I don't even have the breath to ask him what in hell's going on. They didn't let him revive me. As I figure you can guess. James never guessed it, unlucky for him. Then comes the ambulance, the cops, the whole damn row—"

Damon turned his face abruptly. In a state of mounting terror, my voice rose. "I'm sure you can figure the rest out from here, Damon, I'm sure—please," I said. "*Please!* It's not complicated! Just walk in and see what you can do, this is all I'm asking!" I caught his arm. "Please, Damon, I'm begging you, please—"

I'm all he's got.

It's what I meant to say. One time I ran into an old high school girlfriend in Hamilton. Not only had she added about twenty pounds to the body I'd once pressed myself against at the Five Drive-in, but she was wearing the most ungainly ski hat I'd ever seen. *Nice fat,* I'd offered. Aside from that, I believe that this is the biggest Freudian slip I ever made in my life:

"Please, Damon," I said. "He's all I've got."

Damon took his arm from my grip. What followed was a distant shake of the head; and then what I saw was his back moving away. My stomach knotted up against my throat.

"*You're just like them!*" I exploded. "Just like them, you know! You pay him to kick ass, and then when he gets in trouble for it, you sit hard on your own! Don't you! *Don't you, you lousy fuck! Don't*—"

Damon stopped in his tracks. Turned. Then suddenly he was marching back at me. His strides were resolute and businesslike, his face set like stone. For a minute I thought he was going to haul up and hit me. He came to a halt inches from where I stood.

"No," Damon said, pointing a finger into my face. "I'm not like them. And you, for one, should know it."

I said nothing. My gaze darted between Damon and the cruiser jutting out from the trailer.

Finally Damon huffed. "Where are you going to be?"

"What?"

Damon huffed again. I wasn't trying to be obtuse; I honestly had no idea what he was getting at. But Damon had come to the furthest reaches of his patience—or maybe, in truth, he was already miles beyond it. "I mean," he said. *"Where—the hell—are you going—to BE!"*

"Here, just here! Probably—" I looked around, considered all the places I might position myself for the precarious wait for James. I didn't want to get too far away in case something terrible happened without me. But I didn't want to get too close *(that James Daniel Rowley not come within 200 feet)* for fear of making things worse. In the moment, it seemed imperative that I get as far away from James as possible and spare him any further contamination from me. "I could wait at my camper," I said. *I mean*, I thought to myself, *that looks at least two hundred feet from here.*

"Fine," Damon harrumphed. "You go and do that. Go and do it, Tevan, *right now.* If what you told me is true, don't hang around here."

He turned away a second time. When I was finally able to find my voice, it came out sounding bewildered: the tone of a child just waking up in the middle of the night.

"Hey," I said. "Are you—going in to get my friend?"

Damon stopped. "No." He cast a look back over his shoulder at me. "No, asshole. I'm going in to get my geek."

It was only when I reached the camper that it occurred to me that I had, in effect, abandoned Taiva. If I had a dollar for every time I made an ass of myself before that girl, I'd be a rich man by now. I'd left her in the middle of a field with Sandy, inside James's sweatshirt, and likely in some indignant state of confusion, too.

In April, just ten weeks shy of where I now sat, James had left me with a fractured thyroid cartilage, superficial abrasions of the right anterior neck, and hemorrhage to soft neck tissues. The attendant who brought me into the ambulance, and then the doctor who attended to me, relayed this information. The officer who interviewed me in the hospital later on imparted even more: "Yeah, I did it," James had offered up, the officer told me. "Those guys bet me, and so I did it."

What guys?

US guys? a threesome of hoo-haws had cried when asked. *Not us, no sir. Sheesh, Officer, we never seen that fellow before in our lives!*

Okay, I put the *sheesh* in there myself, I admit it. But the rest, I'm willing to conjecture, is stone-cold accurate. This is what they told me, see. In any case, it's all I know.

But by the time I reached my apartment the following morning, however, it seemed I knew even less. My brain was frazzled with questions and my mouth exhausted from pumping sterile answers. As if I needed another challenge, I returned home to a space fraught with James. The place was tidy, quiet; his and my clothes, strewn here and there. A few vinyls lay out on the table; the packaging to a razorblade sat beside the garbage bin. A shave for James, I remembered, that I had mandated: "What you feel like doing tonight, James?" I had offered him as quick collateral. "Anything you want."

James had thought on it. "I dunno—wanna shoot pool, that place down by Sherbourne?"

Had I dissented? *Aw, James, I suck at pool;* or *That joint charges to the nuts for beer;* or maybe even *That might not be such a good idea, James. I met a guy down there. And that led to another guy. He's paying my way in rent this month and people are starting to talk—*

It doesn't matter. I don't really care. The place was exactly as we'd left it, only James was gone. I would have cried if it didn't hurt my throat so much to do so.

Instead I circled the place like a weird, polite sort of poltergeist, picking up socks here, moving cutlery off a table there, and marinating for hours in my own state of shellshock. Little by little, the predicament—or predicaments, brother, there was more than one at this stage; knotting themselves with one another, like a crossword puzzle with only the one-syllables filled in—grew clear to me. After that, the solutions came quickly. I got a plan in order.

The last thing I did before I left the apartment that morning was step into the bathroom. It was a surefire case of *you don't want to know*, yes, but by then half the morning had slipped away and part of me was adamant that it would do us well to know it in the long run. A cased bulb sat above the sink, and so I pulled the cord. Light sprung into the room and I stood blinking into my own reflection. A nurse had advised me that the fractured cartilage was the one to keep a cautious eye on—but by the time I'd written a check to her hospital, made my way away from it via taxicab, and stepped inside my apartment, hear you me, that *hemorrhage to soft tissues* had evolved into the most salient of all the injuries.

The portrait was grim, gruesome. The front, the facing-most portion of my neck, was only spattered; it could have passed for dirt or even pigment to an undiscriminating eye. But on each side, spanning two inches vertically and at least that across, stood a succession of stormy, fierce dappling. The right side was by far the worst. It was dark, shaded, literally black-and-blue, and it was difficult to tell where one bruise ended and another began.

Oh yes, I thought, tilting my head gingerly into the mirror. *Yes, this cannot be missed for what it is.*

It was James's handprints. They didn't look precisely like handprints, but you didn't have to be a doctor to guess what had soldered those kind of marks into that kind of a place: bloody, painted spots. Angry, crescent-shaped cuts framing each edge.

It came to me that in some bizarre, covert reality, those marks had been there all along. Had been there, moody and hurting for years; had begun as well as ended in some hospital that I would never frequent again. This was merely the first time that they had manifested themselves visibly, that's all. In this moment I saw them truthfully—that is, not as *James*'s handprints at all.

A squelched place in my consciousness seemed to crack. My fingers danced above the blots, afraid to touch them. My mind churned; what crossed it was the most concise thought I believe I'd had in close to ten years:

I hate you, I thought at Bern. *You ruined my life.*

And here—I don't remember exactly—but I presume I probably did cry.

Those marks came up somewhat handy in the end. We were renting the basement of a two-story at that time, placing the lady of the house right over our heads. In other circumstances this had been a detriment—having to keep it down when you came in the door late at night, for example, or having to share a laundry room—but in this case it worked to my advantage. If memory serves me correctly, it was this particular place that had taken my king mattress as collateral for first and last month's rent. On this day in April, I promised the landlady that James and I would make tracks as soon as that weekend if she agreed to return our last month's down payment in cash. This was a breach of our contract, technically. But she scarcely winked. Instead, the landlady only nodded and smiled politely as she listened to me plead my case; in fact, she concurred with every measure I suggested. Sometimes a bare apartment is better than one occupied by a guy who looks like he's got the mafia after him. She took one look at that track around my neck and agreed to see me out as soon as I said the word.

Moving on made sense on a lot of theoretical grounds as well as technical. Sure, I needed that cash—needed it fast, if I wanted James to see the light of day anytime soon—but relocating was also a thing that I orchestrated anytime James ended up in the can anyhow. Can't have that Ministry of Health finding a paper trail to your doorstep, you know. Shawn called it paranoid, but at the time I simply called myself resourceful; after all, I'd had to tell the nurse who I was and where I was staying. I'd decided on the taxi ride home that this admission alone was enough to necessitate a clean break. In those days, histories were kept in locked vaults or basement clerk rooms, instead of upon instantly accessible computers. Still, four hours in the local hospital after giving up my name had been enough to keep me shaking in my boots, wondering when the police or Men in White Coats or NATO or Buck Rogers would come tramping into my triage cubicle. Come in, accost me, demand to know where I'd been since I split on my TB reassessment in '61 like some kind of wayward criminal.

Hysterical? Yes. Insane? No. I can't, with clear conscience, call any act of survival insanity. As far as I was concerned, James and I were hitting the streets even before I loosened up that last month's rent. Only I never expected we'd be on the streets for weeks, until we spotted Merit's sideshow and . . . well, never mind. The landlord—landlady, as it turned out—never needed to know all this. I had the money on hand now, and I'd covered my ass. The only remaining trick on the roster to absolving this terrible disaster was retrieving James. I did that through the assistance of Steve Orono, my old moonshine buddy who I had now known since a lad of eighteen, who signed on as James's surety.

"That's like a person who takes responsibility for a loss, Tev," he told me when I rang him up to ask if he could help me out on the matter. "Put in place to ensure that the parties involved both abide by the conditions. Like an overseer. A surety is the guy who rats you out if you fail to follow your conditions of release."

You can't have a rap yourself to be one, he added, which he and I were left to finger as the unsaid detail that took me out of the running for this particular duty. In truth, having a record was not what stood between me and my ability to stand up for

James—and my intention had not been to lie to Steve—but it was better than telling him I was the victim, wasn't it? The victim, under James's offense and not allowed *within 200 feet* of him; the guy who could hardly go marching into the Don Jail to sign off on release papers himself. "Thanks for shoring us up," I told Steve, no details necessary. I hadn't even seen James's release papers, but I'd seen all the ones that had come before. You didn't have to be a lawyer to guess they'd probably stipulate about the same.

Within two hours of soliciting Steve's assistance, James, his release papers, and the dirty fifty bucks we got as reward for his knocking me out were nowhere near *200 feet* away from me. I picked him up from Steve's place that very day.

"I'm not supposed to come near you, Tev," I remember James whispering after long minutes of silence between us. "It says so all over my papers."

When I gave no reply and instead continued to drive, staring straight ahead of me, as though he had uttered no word at all, he faltered. "Where are we going?"

I've been driving James around for years now. I don't know if that qualifies me as a leader. It felt dangerous to watch him follow my instructions this day; but at the same time it felt so very safe to have him sitting there, letting me take the driver's seat again. I guess maybe it's like that old sweater that me and Taiva talked about: familiar, reliable, even if in a nasty way. I wanted to tell James that it was okay now, that things would work themselves out. That the stripes across my throat were no matter, that we'd both seen how those sorts of things could grow invisible after a while. "Home," I said finally. "You're going to get your stuff."

"Oh."

"I already got mine together," I told him. "I told them we'd haul out by the weekend, if that's okay with you." I happened to glance over as I said this. As I did I witnessed the metamorphosis of James's expression: crestfallen, forsaken—to sheer, surprised gratitude.

"*Oh*," he said again, and I realized that James had fully expected me to throw him out on his can.

I suffered a stab of sympathy for him. But worse, I felt nothing but relief for me. For the truth is that while denying what had happened at Mount Rosa's had become me and James's collaborative life's work by then, the notion of losing each other meant mislaying our only—albeit sick, backward, and underground—voice in validating it, too.

James stood by me as I proceeded through those years as though Bern had never touched me, you see. Yet he stood just as firm as I repeated it, or cried, or screamed in an inebriated rampage about the horror of it all, just the same. He was my most staid and honest ally. And he would do this with me for as long as I needed him to.

Today I believe James would have gone on doing so, if I asked him to, forever.

I never saw the face of the constable who met my James that night on Merit's show. Damon simply returned James to me around midnight. His expression was tired and irritated as he stood at the front steps and waved James up through the camper door. "Said this was just some green grunt we picked up a few days ago, he didn't have any I.D. on him," Damon told me, the abridged version of what had transpired in my absence. "Everything's fine. I made out like I was on the cop's side. You know, real suspicious and condescending of the help." Damon raised an amused eyebrow as he stood on the step, watching me. "Told him we only knew him as Jack, by the way."

I nodded, saying nothing.

Damon smiled thinly. "*Jack*, I said. The next part starts with an *A*," he offered, deadpan. "Don't you want to know what his last name is?"

Jack and the next part starts with an *A*. "That's really funny, Damon," I said. "Aren't you just the sweetest talker on the lot?" What I didn't know—*wouldn't*, until at least three days later, when me and James were back on speaking terms and I could no longer stand to coexist alongside him without knowing the details—was that Damon had in fact sweet-talked that police officer into a deal. I don't know how much that ran him; I'm very curious, but he never said a word to me about it. In fact, I have an idea he didn't want me to know.

So as John Hadley likes to put it, sometimes a person ought to be a little more grateful. I never asked. I bade Damon good night and turned in almost immediately, and we never spoke of it again.

As for James and me, we kept going as we always had.

James had stood firm by me; in exchange, I'd done what I could for him. I'd brought him to his court appearances every month. I'd kept an eye on him, making sure he stayed out of trouble. I found us work and a place to stay, didn't I? I did what I had to do, the best way I knew how. Perhaps the law may have seen our continued association as a blanket breach on James's behalf; but to us, on the contrary, it felt compulsory, regulated, and disciplined.

We were frozen in time.

We'd gone through the necessary motions as obediently as possible. We'd done what they told us to do, but we didn't know why and we hadn't known how; and worst of all, we didn't know when it would end, either. We were scared, you see; for years, petrified in a state of emergency.

We sat pretty and we waited. We shut up about it. We did so together, James and me. But we were scarcely adults ourselves as we complied.

19

As was tradition between James and me, we barely revisited that night in talk at all. In its place, we got out of bed the following morning as though none of it had transpired.

Oh, we did debate the geek act that he had performed. James conceded to me that, no, he had not liked biting the heads off rats, had not *wanted* to do it, and never wished to do it again. He was so irked by the act that he could only refer to it by its locus of horror: *the rat's head*, or simply *the head*. I told him, in best commiserating fashion, that I hadn't appreciated *the head* either. But the important things—James's brawl on the lot, his near arrest, me and Damon's frenetic shot at freeing him—sat tepid, silent at the back of our throats. And so I did the only thing I could think to do to clear myself of this gloom: I went out shopping for James's birthday.

On the last Friday in August—payday, that would be, before the cash burned its usual hole in my pocket—I went out to find James a gift. There were a million things to choose from. That week, Merit's midway settled into the biggest show this side of the Great Lakes. In the summer of 1966, the Canadian National Exhibition, also known as the CNE or The Ex, ran from late August until the fifth of September, Labor Day. No sooner had I stepped out of the midway than I came upon a notice:

Labor Day Weekend Fireworks Under the Lakeshore!

I filed this away in my memory as a decent venue for a celebration. Other than that, I perused the entire CNE pavilion with James in mind, and I couldn't find a damn thing. I was at the end of the concessions when I met up with Taiva. She was looking over the wares of a kiosk run by a small, red-haired teenager.

"A birthday," she remarked when I told her of my objective. "Yes, I think I know it . . ." She smiled, closed her eyes, then put her hand out, drawing a line across the eclectic medallions and dream catchers hanging from the roll-top veranda. "The eighth of September—if I recall correctly?"

"You do." I grinned. I took a piece of jewelry into my hand, fingered it absent-mindedly, then replaced it. "I hope your eye's as good as your memory. I can't find a bloody thing in all these rows of slum."

The boy behind the counter glanced up to make a face at us. Taiva caught sight of this and laughed. "Then you aren't looking hard enough."

She was right. There was plenty there—parakeets in cages, quart-sized bottles of pop, acres of cigarettes and candy. I just couldn't make up my mind. We walked around the booth, touching items made of leather and fur. I leaned over the glass cases, letting my eyes dance over the prizes displayed within them. Taiva did the same. After a while, something rough and silvery caught my eye. "Say, I'd like a look at this," I said.

The redhead swung his feet off the counter. He jangled a set of keys from his hip, then switched the lock off the box. A moment later he stood before me, a tiny droplet of gray nestled in the palm of his hand.

"That's a nice one there." He turned his hand over and the pendant sunk into my palm. "Made of pewter, that's why it's so dark," he said. "Ostrich feather, that is."

I touched the silvery piece with my finger: it was tiny, tear-drop-shaped, a small replica of a feather. I never would have identified it precisely as a take on an *ostrich* feather—hell, all feathers looked alike to me—but now that I did, I reasoned that this might be just what I wanted. Incidentally, ostrich feathers are what feather boas are made out of.

"Hey," the kid said, his eyes upon Taiva. "I know you. You're in the titty show, just inside the midway. Aren't you?"

Taiva raised her eyebrows. "You must not be very good

with faces. Because I'm not in the titty show, sweetie. I dance the ballyhoo."

"Oh, that's right!" He grinned, slapping a hand to his forehead. "I knew I seen you somewhere." He turned to me. "Hey buddy, you want that one there? I'll wrap it up for you on the house if you'll buy the chain too."

I seesawed the pendant in my palm. Its spine winked in the sun. "Sure, okay."

The kid nodded. He took the silver drop and laid it against a sheet of gauzy paper. He folded this into a three-inch square with a complicated flurry of his fingertips.

"What is it that you make here, anyhow?" I asked, watching. "It's, ah, Navajo or something?"

The boy passed the parcel over the counter. His expression was a combination of tired and haughty amusement. "Don't make me bust a gut. I'm Canadian. More than you, say. Navajos are American, didn't you know that?" I shook my head, because I hadn't, and the kid shrugged. "This here's my dad's shop. He's helping out at the bingo." He pointed across the sea of concession booths: "Haven't you all played bingo yet?"

Taiva shook her head, and I grinned. The boy went on: "Mississaugas—that is, Anishinaabe—but we didn't make that feather. It's Egyptian, I think. Feather of Ma'at. You know of it?" I shook my head and so he continued. "Ma'at. When somebody dies, she weighs his soul on a scale against the feather. If the soul is lighter than her feather"—he shaped the two longest fingers of his right hand into a pair of tiny legs, and ran them up into the sky, as though ascending a flight of stairs—"he goes on off to heaven." The boy studied us a moment before letting go a sharp bark of laughter. "Don't leave much room for error for any of us, does it now?"

I smiled. "I don't suppose it does."

He watched me a minute, a half-smirk painted upon his face. As we walked away, he called at our backs to go and try our luck at bingo.

Taiva and I stepped into the walkway. I carried James's packet like a prize in the palm of my hand. I was already picturing him, snicking the chain's catch around his neck, the feather swinging, light as anything. Feather for a feather, I reasoned: James would certainly pass the test to heaven.

"There's fireworks on Friday night," I said. "Me, James, and Shawn can make it if we leave the show and head right over. It'll be on the Lakeshore. I was thinking for James's birthday, you know?"

Taiva peered down at her fingertips, then back at me. "Your friend like fireworks?"

"Oh, sure," I said. "He'll be crazy about it!"

Taiva grinned, surveying me. "Well, then. The only way to make fireworks better is to bring a date."

"Oh boy," I said. "It might be too late to start looking, Taiva. For James, I'd have to find somebody with a really good amount of patience. And a serious sense of humor."

Taiva smiled. We continued to walk through the pavilion, the world wild and loud about us. My eyes slipped across to Taiva as we walked in silence.

"You want to come watch fireworks with us too?" I said tentatively. In the subsequent moment of silence, I quickly amended the proposition. "I mean, I was thinking a *bunch* of us could go. James and whoever; Shawn and me. That is, if you want to join"—then revised a second time—"ah, us."

Taiva looked up and around, though not at me. "Sounds like it could be a time."

"Aw, you know us," I agreed. "It'll be a real hoot."

Her eyes ran over to meet mine, then hurried away. She waited, as if considering something for a long moment. "What kind of date? For James, you said. What kind of a date?"

I shrugged. "I don't know. Why?"

"You said he likes fireworks." Taiva watched me. "So I'm asking, does he need the kind of date you invite," she said, "or the kind you pay for?"

"Oh," I said, surprised. "*Oh*." For a second I wondered if this was a trap, if there was something impolite about such a request; she had yet to answer my question to her. Then a moment later I found I could hardly contain my excitement. I started giggling, just thinking about it. "Say, do you have somebody in mind? You know, ah, some—"

"Connections?" she put in.

"Right." I tried to look serious, but I couldn't help it. The idea of such a scheming plan for James just made me bust up laughing.

Taiva rolled her eyes. I had the sense to rethink my request once again. But then it was too late, and she answered me anyway. "You good to your word?"

"What—" I started, bewildered. "Well, yes."

"You show up front?"

"Yes," I said again. "God, of course!"

"Good." She nodded. "Because I'd hate to have to send John Hadley after you on behalf of one of our girls. I mean, I know how you love that guy."

This time it was me who nodded, vigorously so. "Man, you don't have to tell me twice," I said. "What do you have in mind?"

She didn't respond. Instead she just looked across the park. I caught her eyeing the bulletin tacked to a post some feet away: *Fireworks! Under the Lakeshore!*

"Patience and a sense of humor," she mused. "Yes, I think I can dredge someone up for you. As for me—" She considered again. "Ah, to hell with it. Pick me up on your way."

My face bloomed in a grand smile. I gave way to a laugh. She offered just the tiniest one in response. "I've got a feeling," she said, "this is going to be a real hoot after all."

Me, James, and Shawn met up a half-hour after our last show. That was just enough time for me to harangue James into shaving his face, combing his hair, and putting on clean clothes. As he buttoned a shirt up the front of his chest, it occurred to me that

James hadn't looked so presentable since his last trip to court. Even Shawn noticed the change when we joined him outside.

"*Woo-hoo*, lookit this thing!" he remarked. "James, you getting just as cute as your little friend Tev here."

"Aw, thanks." I rolled my eyes.

"Best be careful now," Shawn said. "You might end up with his woman by ac-ci-dent, looking so fine."

He laughed, and James did too. I'd told them both Taiva was coming along, but I didn't have an inkling of who else might be joining us for the sake of James. So I simply said the rest of our party would meet us just outside John Hadley's. But as we drew closer, there was only one person waiting outside for us. It was Taiva.

She spotted us coming up the walk and stood. Her skirt swung to her ankles and her blouse hung in a V about her neck. Her feet were clad in sandals, freckles lay upon her cheeks, and I would've bet my heart and my ass that when she walked her waist would jingle. She waved and ran to join our party.

When we set off walking, I slowed down with her beside me. "Hey," I said, low under my breath. "Where's the girl?"

Taiva looked around. "Last time I checked, I *was* one."

"No," I said. "For *James*. You know, the one I—"

"You paid," Taiva began, "and the service will deliver." She cast a glimmer of a smile at me and reached into her handbag. "Here." She produced a silver flask and handed it to me. "Quit worrying."

People strolled in droves, a wide, slow-moving stream, and all headed in the direction of the lakefront. We bumped elbows with them, now just another party of convivial marks amid the throng. I noticed their faces, split with grins; their arms were filled with packages they'd haggled over in the concessions. You couldn't help but smile as you watched them. Even Taiva's cheeks filled out while we weaved between the crowds.

There was scarcely a place to sit when we arrived. We passed the peace monument and the clock tower as we crowded toward the waterfront. You could see a barge set hundreds of meters out. The water beneath it twinkled like rich oil. The four of us huddled together on the lawn: Taiva to my left, James to my right, and Shawn beyond him. We passed Taiva's bottle back and forth until the first rocket fired off. "Schnapps," she told us. "Peach, I think. The girls gave it to me in Gibton for Christmas. Thought I'd share the wealth, see."

"Thanks for thinking of us," I said.

She smiled. And somewhere between this remark and the straggling sparks fired into the sky, her hand found its way inside of mine.

The first few shot up tentatively: a green sparkle here, a white popper there. The next few came bunched together and quickly consecutive. James's face lit up in time to the explosions. With each crack, I turned and watched him laugh. As the fireworks accelerated into a climactic frenzy I found myself glancing over at him more and more: he had the look of a man applauding a theater show, or the expression of a child in the dark as you flickered her bedroom light switch up and down before she lay down in her bed. The light show tapered like the denouement of a spent lover. It was all over before you knew it.

We left the Lakeshore, laughing and remarking upon the show—our favorite colored sparkles, what it felt like to look straight up yet see the glittering streaks bend like an overturned chalice in the sky—and paused at the living quarters just beyond the midway rides. Shawn parted ways with us then, reminding us not to drink all that schnapps without him. But I wasn't thinking of schnapps at all. I looked around and saw that Shawn was out of our hair, Taiva was walking up the steps of our camper before us, and James was too stupid to think twice about it all.

"I have fireworks every year, just before my birthday," James said to Taiva as he threw himself against the bunk, his hands above his head. "It's like a party just for me." His face bowed with a wide smile. It made me grin just to look at him.

"Is she meeting us here?" I managed under my breath as Taiva stood beside me. "Should I leave the door unlocked?"

"Do whatever you'd like," she told me. I nodded, but still watched the door. "Go on and give him his present," she said. "I'll wait."

So I did. "Take your shoes off," I said to James. "And scoot over."

"Why, Tev?" James did as he was told anyway, pressing against the far wall at my instruction.

"Because you want your present, don't you?" I already had James's present on me. I'd had it stuffed down into the bowels of my right pocket all night. Taiva perched at the foot of the mattress to watch.

"Sure, Tev," James agreed. "Sure I do. But—don't you want to wait until the eighth?"

"No." I turned, striking a match, and grinned overtop of the flame. I felt the first twinge of wild, scheming enthusiasm flutter within me. "I can't wait any longer, James." I reached the bunk in two steps, clamped a cigarette between my lips, and hoisted myself up. "So neither can you."

When I held the package out to him, James snatched it without a word. He looked at it, rotated it in his hands. He shook it in the air like a castanet. Then he held it at a distance. Jesus, I almost expected him to sniff it next.

"It's a *car*, James," I said, exasperated. "It's a fucking Bel Air. Come on now. Open it up!"

James held it between two fingers—it was thin enough, scarcely wider than an envelope—and tore the paper off in one quick strip. He unfolded a flat piece of cardboard underneath to reveal the tiny piece of silver, and here Taiva and I leaned in. It really was pretty.

James studied it, his lips parted.

"It's a feather!" I burst forth.

James nodded. He hooked the chain under one finger. He poised the chain above his nose and looked up from underneath.

"A *feather*, James!" I said again.

The pendant orbited like a hanging top. Watching it turn,

I could scarcely contain myself. "You know, James! You know! Just like in—"

"The show," he finished. He slid his palm under the twirling end and gazed reverently. "It's—man, Tev. It's really nice." His eyes darted to mine. "Just like in the show."

"That's why I picked it," I rambled. "The guy said—the guy who sold it to me, that is, he said there's this chick, Ma'at, you see. She's like some kind of a special thing. She's—"

"An *Egyptian*," Taiva put in. "She's an Egyptian woman."

"Yeah, yeah, an Egyptian lady," I agreed, nodding frenetically. "When people die she weighs their soul against the feather. In order to go to heaven your soul has to be lighter than the feather. See, and then—"

James turned his eyes to me. "Oh, I don't care, Tev," he said, grinning. "I don't care. I just like it because of the show. That's all." He paused, looking at us, shining. "Should I put it on?"

"Yes," I said, thrilled. Taiva nodded.

James bowed his head, shaking his hair from his neck. When he passed me the chain I fingered the catch, snapped it open and swung it under his throat. A second time, both me and Taiva bent in to watch. When James lifted his head he was smiling. He cocked his head sideways, like a model showing off some rare jewel. Taiva smiled and clapped her hands, and when she did my heart thumped out a single cymbal's crash in reply.

I sensed that it was time.

I looked to the door, then to Taiva. I just couldn't hold it from him any longer.

"Taiva has something for you too, James."

James blinked. "Yeah?"

"Yeah. That necklace, it's just from me, see. She—" I paused, considering that I wasn't sure what to call this particular bequest. So I simply repeated myself. "I asked her to find something you'd really like. And so she—you know, looked around a bit. She's got something planned for you too." I looked to Taiva carefully. "I mean, I think."

James looked to Taiva; Taiva looked at him. She grinned and nodded sagely.

"Is it here?" James said, looking about. "Here now?"

"Not exactly," I said. "It's—it's coming up." A smartass smile sprung from the corners of my lips. "In the meantime, I think you ought to guess what it is."

"Guess?" James repeated.

"Guess," I said.

James's eyes circled the room. He gazed about the bunk with one fishy-eyed sweep. "Is it—is it something you drink?"

"Wrong!" I shrieked triumphantly.

He craned his neck toward the washbasin, as though he thought we'd left evidence lying out or had placed it in the room for his discovery. James frowned. "Something I can eat?"

"Nup." I bared my teeth, grinning. "It's none of those things! Guess again."

James turned to me. He smiled unabashedly. *I have no idea,* his smile read.

Taiva put her hand to her mouth and started to laugh. I joggled her with my elbow. "Think, James, think! I know you know it! Something from *Taiva.* It's something only girls can give you. For your birthday! Something I can't do. You know it?"

The confounded look again; a mild trace of frustration.

"Yes you *do,* James! Yes, you know it! I'll give you a hint—" I bobbed my head. "It's something pink, James! You remember?" It almost made it more fun that James was such a dummy he'd never guess correctly. "*Pink,* your favorite color . . ."

And speaking of dummies, here came the first moment that I considered a thin, wild possibility. It was concerning the night's events, James's ostensible date, and the now-indisputable fact that the scene still remained just the three of us, despite the late hour. It was an awful, honest possibility. Yet somehow it was the first time I'd considered it at all.

Patience and a sense of humor, she had said to me days before. *Yes, I think I can dredge someone up for you.*

Something touched my shoulder. I turned my head to see Taiva's hand retracting from me. The next thing I knew, the hand had disappeared into the sleeve of her blouse. And then the next thing I knew, the blouse itself had disappeared completely. It lay puddled at her knees, an arbitrary pond of discretion, entirely abandoned.

One stark, silent moment passed us by. James and I stared with our mouths unhinged. She sat at the foot of the bunk, inches away, her shirt at her lap and her breasts shadowed in the moonlight. Part of me didn't want to look, but the other part couldn't seem to stop itself: my eyes fled over her body. In the milky light, I saw how her freckles fell from her cheeks and neck, splashing onto her parts like a spill of sand. And in this awed yet pained moment, I knew for certain who it was that Taiva's judgment had selected for tonight. James was near hypnotized.

"Oh," he said reverently. "Oh *shit*."

I looked down to see the two of us clinging to each other like two old ladies watching a horror flick.

"Oh shit is right," I said. "Your time has come, James."

To my left, James uttered an astounded, choked little laugh. He could not tear his eyes away from her.

"We can do anything you want, James," Taiva said softly. "All I need to know is if you want to."

"Yes," James whispered immediately, his eyes still fixed upon her.

"Do you know what to do?" she said.

"Yes," immediate again. His eyes ran fleetingly to mine. "Yes," he said—and in this I caught a glimpse of something. Something I could not quite put my finger on. "Oh yes, I know."

Taiva's eyes shot in my direction. It was a small, cloaked signal—a sublime, communicative gesture, sort of like what one driver bestows another at a four-way intersection, *Your turn, buddy*, and I understood her without question. I got to my feet.

"I know what you mean," James went on. "And I know

what to—" His voice paused, held; then, out of nowhere, behind me now, gathered steam: *"Wait, Tev! Where are you going!"*

I glanced down to see my feet, poised and ready to make good their escape. "Why, I'm leaving," I said. I pronounced the last word slowly as I turned to look at him. "I'm going to—" I poked two fingers out, much as the jewelry seller had to demonstrate ascending to heaven, and walked them away from my body. "And you're going to—" I met the fingers from one hand with those from the other and then laced them together. "I'm no John Hadley, James," I offered. "I'll see you later."

As I turned away from him, I again caught a strange note upon his face. And then James erupted:

"Wait, Tev!" he shrieked. *"I'll steal your girl!"*

My back was facing him; I had my eyes on the door. It wasn't the *threat* that touched me, partway across the little room, intent on the exit and half-wild with squelched wanting myself; it wasn't his words, themselves a logistical equivalent to Shawn's joke a few hours before. I turned. Taiva sat before him—but James's eyes were fixed on me.

James had the look of the person who I so often picked off the floor in the morning. He had the eyes of a boy stepping onto the Scrambler for the first time: his knuckles white and his face clenched, wondering if he was going to have the time of his life as promised, or be driven to scream for his life instead. And what came next I could've guessed, word for word, even if the Card Reader could not:

"Tevan," he said. "Bern was after me."

Out of the corner of my eye I spied Taiva, still at the foot of the bed. She didn't move or speak a word.

"In that little room," James went on, his voice a whisper. "That room. You know. That's how I know what to do. But when I was sleeping. In my—"

The girl waited beside him, watching me now. And so I did the only thing that seemed right to do. I began my way back to both of them. "I know, James," I said. "I believe you."

"I didn't want to," he said, nodding. He passed a fleeting gaze in Taiva's direction, bounced off, and returned to me. The next part, I suspected, was aimed at her nonetheless. "It happened in my bed."

"I know," I said again.

James nodded. "You know, Tev. I know you do. Because you got it—" *No, don't say it, James. Please. There is no—* "The worst." James continued, his eyes in her direction: "So I know what to do, yes," he said. "Yes. But that time, you should know I didn't want to."

Silence ran out between the three of us after this. I sat on the edge of the bunk. Taiva, beside me, waited. I put my hand out to James. I gripped his knee and held it. After a long moment, I shook him. "What is it you say before you drop me on the show, James?" I asked. "Before any time you do it?"

James's eyes came up to meet mine. "That I would never hurt you, Tev."

I nodded. "You know that's why I let you do it."

"Yes," James whispered. "Because I would never, Tev."

"Because it's different," I said, and James nodded his agreement.

"There is something different about this too," I said. My eyes shifted to Taiva's. "Isn't there?"

James blinked. Beneath, his cheeks were streaked and shining.

"Didn't you hear it?" I asked him. "What you just said, James. Just now, what did you say about Bern?"

"That he was after me. And I didn't want to."

"Right. And"—I motioned to Taiva—"what did *you* say?"

Taiva's eyes came up. It had been a while since either of us spoke to her. She looked uncertain, wondering whether or not this was her place.

"Just now," I said. "What did you say you were going to do?"

Her expression was at first confused; then it cleared completely. "I'll do whatever you want," she said.

"Did you hear?" I said. "Say it again, James."

"I didn't want to," he put in.

"Uh-huh. And—"

Taiva looked to James. "I'll do whatever you want."

I put my hand out. I pressed my finger into his knee again. "I want you to say it. You say it all together, James."

James, for the first time in minutes, moved to meet Taiva's eye. The words came quickly, in one breathless rush: "I didn't want to do it. And you'll do whatever I want." Now he watched Taiva a deliberating second longer. It was as though he were making a calculation in his head, a complex one too. Only it really wasn't that complex at all. It's just that we had the wrong equation burned into our heads for so long.

"So think of something you want to do," I said. "And you know, if there isn't anything? Then I guess you won't do anything at all."

James didn't answer. His face was immobilized in a wary expression. He bowed his head, his hair over his features. He sat a while, as though considering all of this. Then he put his hand out and onto my knee, just as I had done to him a moment before. I turned. And within the split second before I could wonder if he had missed—had landed upon me instead of the girl by accident, with his eyes closed—James pressed a kiss into my cheek. I pulled back, throwing him a bewildered look.

James looked back at me. And then I got one of those mute little signals. It didn't come from Taiva this time: this one came to me right from James.

I understood it instantaneously: it was time for me to leave.

I slid off the bunk, and this time nobody stopped me. I made my way across the room. When I did, I stole Taiva's cigarettes off the card table and tucked those into my back pocket. And then I opened the door and I slipped outside.

I lit up and sat down on the front steps. I would just wait, I decided. Out here, I would wait. I didn't care for how long.

• • •

Long? Man, they were done in ten minutes.

I stubbed out my first smoke and was halfway down the second when the door opened. Taiva emerged, bag in hand and nearly knocking my can square off the steps. We waited for a moment—her, watching me with indifference; myself, staring back.

"How'd it go?" I managed finally.

She raised an eyebrow. "Now just how am I supposed to answer a question like that?"

"I don't know. I just—I mean, were there any problems?"

"No." She leaned over, spied her cigarettes lying there, and picked them off the steps. She waggled them in the air as if to show she'd caught me and tucked them into her handbag. She smiled. "Good night, Tevan."

"Good night," I returned.

She turned to leave but accomplished only three steps. She stopped then, her eyes speculative. "Hey," she offered finally. "I—got my period."

I've learned better than to respond to that kind of a statement with *I see,* or *How terrible for you,* or, worse, with a noncommittal *So?* I watched her a minute longer before it occurred to me that whatever biological moment she happened to be in within her cycle had no bearing on me. She wasn't my girlfriend. She wasn't even my lover. "What do you mean?" I asked.

"I mean I got it." She paused for emphasis. "I mean I got it *just now.*"

"Oh," I said. "*Oh.* I hope—that went over okay?"

"Yeah." She looked to the ground, then back at me. "He does—ah, know what that is, doesn't he?"

"Yeah." I grinned. "James knows enough to see that it's a woman that brings babies, not the stork."

"That's what I thought." Taiva smiled. A moment later she began to move away.

"Well, wait! What— Did you have to explain?"

"Oh, he seemed to understand." A careful look crossed her features. "He was just worried for a second there. That's all."

I didn't say anything to that. I wasn't quite sure what she meant.

She put a finger to her lips and a long silence drew out between us. "He said that he knew that sometimes a person bleeds when somebody gives it to them when they don't want it," she said. "He said he didn't know that personally." She enunciated carefully, slow and specific, and I understood that she was repeating this to me word for word from James. "But he said you might know, Tevan. Because you got it the worst."

I sat on the steps looking at her. I tried to be angry with James for a minute there. But the truth is I just didn't have it in me.

I breathed out a small laugh. "What the fuck am I supposed to say to that?"

"I didn't ask you to say anything. What I just did in there with your friend?" She pointed a finger. "That was sex. What he was talking about before? That was rape." She paused, watching me. "You do know there's a difference, don't you?"

My brow folded. "Yes." My voice lowered to a near whisper. "Didn't you hear in there, Taiva? Don't you see I know the difference?"

She crossed her arms over her chest. "Then I was just wondering," she said. "To myself, really, not to anyone in particular. I was just wondering"—she turned and spoke this last part over her shoulder—"why it is that you're still going over it every day on that show of yours, then."

She gathered her skirt in her hand. She hadn't given me a chance to respond, but even so it didn't really vex me; I didn't have any response. Instead I watched her move away into the lot. But as I pressed the cigarette butt into the ground, a rejoinder of some sort did come to me, truth.

For the second time in weeks I couldn't say how much longer I could go on with the show.

20

I DID GO ON WITH THE SHOW, OF COURSE. THERE WAS SCARCELY any question if we wanted to continue making ends meet. I continued to work Keith's rides from noon onward; I continued to return to the camper, dropping thankfully into my bunk after each shift. And last but not least, I continued to wake up to the sounds of the midway around me every evening, dress, and walk over to Merit's sideshow tent. The only thing different was that each time now, I did so with an ominous, heavy weight in my gut.

On the Monday evening following James's birthday celebration, I awoke; then found myself dismantling the cupboard under the washbasin, hunting for a bottle I had stashed strategically that I'd told myself I'd never go looking for again. I found it nonetheless. I spent the next hour nonchalantly reading every word of the newspaper that Keith had left upon our front step. I didn't notice until my teeth clinked against a dry rim, roundabout when I reached the funnies, that I'd downed the whole works. I didn't care, either. Like the death-defying automaton I had become, I left the camper soon afterward. I walked toward the sideshow tent in the waning daylight. I caught up with James and Shawn halfway there.

"Hey, Shawn," I called, jogging up to them. "So did you read the latest—that crazy president of yours? Charles de Gaulle calls for him to withdraw from Nam and he refuses!"

Shawn sighed. "Yeah, I heard. Mark my words, Tevan"— he shook his head—"the guy who dethrones Johnson is the guy I'll take in as my own."

James knocked Shawn in the behind with the heel of one boot. "I'll dethrone Johnson for ya." James knocked me with the heel of the other: I spun, nearly hitting the deck, then recovered.

Shawn smiled. "Ah, thanks, James," he offered. "You's a real pal."

A crowd strong enough to start an army already stood in front of the tent. We weaved our way around back and stood outside the side entrance. Shawn upended a knapsack, picked the resultant sparkling material from the ground, and shrugged his way into his robes. Soon enough, Damon popped his head out. He waved Shawn in, and as Shawn disappeared behind the curtain, Damon's gaze halted at James. His face erupted in disgust.

"Say, what do you think you're doing, jackass?" he exploded. "Trading places tonight?"

I looked across to see James in a white shirt. I peered down to see myself in black. "Oh *shit*," I started. I couldn't believe such a stupid detail had escaped me. I mean, Jesus: where was my head? "Let's switch, James."

James nodded, pulling his shirt from his shoulders. We made a trade as Damon stood glaring at us—his shirt for mine, and vice versa. Mine was a bit tight around the chest on James. His fit me all around, only it was a little

(*You know where your head's at*, my brain seethed at me. *It's medicating! It's going in on the nod! It's in the—*)

baggy. I held my arms out at Damon. "Better?"

Damon nodded. He motioned to James. "I suppose. Come on, you."

And so, on the heels of Shawn's garnered applause, erupting beyond my field of vision, James followed Damon through the curtain. I watched him go, the star of the show, the evil Faustus, the black of my T-shirt melting into the sideshow tent along with the rest of him.

Alone on the outside, my hands were all over my body: fluttering, wandering, adjusting nervously. I put a hand to my neck. I pulled another through my bangs. Then I touched my chest, smoothing the wrinkles from James's shirt. That old recollection came to me, the bartender's way of telling when people have reached their limit. *Men always laugh and women always touch their hair.*

I tried to tuck James's shirt in. As I leaned back and forward trying to accomplish this, I had to grab at a support beam to keep from tipping right over. The notion of bringing the entire tent crashing down by accident ran through my head; and I would have laughed aloud at such a prospect if it wouldn't have proved, once and for all, that I was truly soused. Instead I did my best to stand solidly in place, waiting for Damon's cue. For outside the tent, Damon's rant—

"LOOK! Look inside!"—

had, as usual, begun.

I guess I can begin with just this—what happened *as usual* during this particular performance. I can, because there are a lot of things: Damon said his usual fantastic ditty, James enacted his usual glorified eeriness, and the crowd succumbed to its usual horrified supposition. As for me, I executed my usual march onto center stage—women whispering, men craning in to watch, the sideshow version of walking the plank. I carried the feather with me as I did so, holding it aloft in one hand as though it were the Maltese Falcon or some other royal bullshit. This all happened, as usual, for the umpteenth time. I strode across the stage and came to a stop opposite James.

The noise, in response to my appearance, was fantastic. At the CNE, the population was enormous and Death-Defying was a hit, and so the assembly below us was crowded, boisterous, packed into every corner of the crummy canvas walls. Damon looked to me expectantly, and I handed the feather off to him.

"Ladies and gentlemen, *look at him!*" Damon howled, waving the feather. "He's not scared at all! Why, I'd be scared, any of us would be! But not this man, no. *He's not even afraid to die!*"

I looked across at James. The throng uttered its collective hiss. I could see the front row. Faces: wide-eyed, a strange alien gaze aimed at me. Their countenance was blank and riveted at the same time, the eyes transfixed. At the sight of them, a heaviness rolled inside of me like a tide coming up a beach. And I spoke my line about Faustus anyway. And James turned and ran at me. And then I was on the ground.

I exhaled hard in response. My back hit the floor, and a breath of air pressed from my chest and into James's face. And that was the end of usual, boys and girls. For right then, something really weird *did* happen:

James's head cranked back, he made a face, and then he turned away.

It was the face you made on the hottest day in July when someone took their shoes and socks off indoors, the gesture you made when somebody let one go in a crowded room. I recognized the face on James and I knew

(That's called "drinking on the job," Tevan)

that James knew what I'd been up to, too. James's elbow flew through the air and my hair splayed across the splintery stage floor. James's palm over my neck, fingers reaching across my chin. That look on his face, eyebrows bent as though he were adding two plus two plus . . .

"Nothing," I whispered. This is what I said as he had me on the ground, choking me: a lie. *It's nothing.* And as though the universe felt I needed a dose of instant karma for this transgression, what came upon me next was sensorily enormous, terrifying—and decidedly unordinary. Out of nowhere, an immense pulse beat in my ears. It sounded like a gong: a throbbing, hot bang. If I had been spry enough to sit up and look around right then, I might have done so: *Say, what was that!* Instead I only furrowed my brow, a mirror of James's own expression of confusion.

Today I know what that sound is. It's the sound I associate with Death-Defying's crossing over; the fateful clang of "gone wrong"; the hammer marking a serious degree of separation. We kept going: James's fingers, slippery, against my sweaty neck; me with my mouth open. But once I heard that gong go off, things fell apart.

They fell apart fast.

Within minutes Damon witnessed, to his infernal outrage, James beginning to resuscitate before the cashbox returned to his hands. Damon didn't waste much time being pissed, though:

Shawn, toward the exit and stage right, saw Damon turn his back to the audience and put his head to his knees. And James, tying the whole chain of events together, reported a funny gawping noise from behind him the instant before all hell broke loose.

What kind of noise? I asked him. "Well. You know," James said. "A sort of ralphy noise." He held his breath and reproduced it: *Gaaaaaaak.* "It was Damon, Tev," he told me. "Damon we heard. When he saw what happened to you, Tev? Well, he just turned around and gagged."

I have no recollection of this. My auditory input went from "gong," the sound of my own pulse laboring inside my veins, to flat within the span of three seconds. It was like stepping onto a skateboard for the first time: one moment you're on it, standing, steering, flying; the next you're on the floor, completely horizontal, your ass singing "The Battle Hymn of the Republic."

It was like a story my friend Steve Orono told me, of the time he had his appendix excised in a state of emergency. They'd wheeled him down the hallway in a hurry, delivering him to the room wherein he and his appendix would be parted once and for all, in the company of a pretty red-haired nurse. The nurse leaned over him with a mask and told him to count to ten backwards. "By the time you reach five, I promise you'll be out," she said.

Steve felt his appendix ready to pop right through his stomach, with his guts heading it like a parade on its way out, but right then he laughed. Steve weighed close to two-fifty, you see. He could put away Southern Comfort like a full-grown Saint Bernard puts away chow.

Yeah right, sweetheart, he thought, inhaling into the mask. *That'll be the goddamned day.*

Ten, he thought.

Nine.

BAM.

When I next opened my eyes, it was to a very strange portrait. The floor was a sidelong slant with my body streamlined along it, and what had previously been a canvas wall was now sky. Amid this, spread out like a horizontal sprinkle of 3-D puzzle pieces, was what first appeared to be a map of the continents. I noted my own arm extended toward them. I wiggled my fingers around. Just before I reached out to touch them, a funny memory spun through my mind.

It was an old memory from grade school. In it, me and Kenny found a little rock, black and round, in the snow on our way to school. We kicked it back and forth enthusiastically, scooting it along before us on the ice-kissed road. When we reached the schoolyard, I paused to take my mitts off: I had the idea to pick it up and pocket it for the way home. That's when Kenny put his hand out and snatched my arm: *Don't touch it, Tevan*, he huffed with a laugh. *It's dogshit.*

I halted an inch away from the stuff on the floor. It occurred to me I couldn't remember putting my arm out like this. In fact, I couldn't even recall lying down. I waited, listening: the air around me was silent, as though the room had run empty. And as these notions took shape inside my mind, a terrible comprehension came into view:

(Gong)

(don't touch it Tevan it's—)

It was chuck. It was heave. My chest felt wet beneath my chin. Breathing quicker now, I could feel the telltale smoldering inside my throat.

The stuff on the wooden stage slats was puke. *My* puke.

I hauled myself into a sitting position and whipped the shirt off in one quick motion. My senses spun, and as I moved, my neck felt like the hinges of an accordion. Shawn, Damon, and James appeared, jumbled together like a gaggle of scared animals. My throat stung like a wound scrubbed with a scouring pad as I stared up at them. It hurt so bad I would've paid money just to drink a glass of their spit. When I tore my eyes from them, I took in the tent with one wild, disbelieving sweep of the eyes. Whoever thought a room full of nothing could be so telling? But even as I got to my knees, then stood to gather the sight head on, there it was: the room was empty, save four. And of us, none said a word.

Now I'm going to be square here and say something, something that should have been said a long time ago. It's a fact that had been wafting around the whole while, but we all deftly pinched our noses to it. It suffices to say that there are very few sideshows in operation today. It's not just that we can gawk at the TV set instead. The real truth is that busted limbs and injured parties can pile up high and fast on a show, as can bad insurance. So I'm going to come right out and say it now.

The show was ludicrous.

James and I were ludicrous to think to perform such a stunt. Damon was ludicrous to take us on. I'd like to call people stupid for paying money to see that kind of trick, but we were collectively stupid to offer it. We were all stupid, see. There's no one person to take the fault for that in the end; no one to clear the air. And so we did the only thing we could think of—four men, staring dumbfaced about a tent, nothing but the wind and our own stupidity hooting through it. We all started yelling at one another.

"What the *fuck*?" I hollered. "What did you do to me?"

The three lurched backward: Damon, his face contorted in revulsion, Shawn, wide-eyed. You'd think I was a corpse, suddenly standing and drawing its first rickety, death-defying breath. James cringed. My eyes honed right in on him.

"What'd you do, you dumb fuck, huh?" I shrieked. "Choke? Lose your balls? Forget your lines? Huh? What'd you—"

"Knock it off." Shawn's tone was one of incensed indignation. "Take a breath before you chew him out. Please." His eyes were filled with regret. "He saved your ass, you know that? He kept going. Going even after you—you—" His gaze spread out, unbidden, toward my feet. He tried to stop himself, but he couldn't resist looking: splotches of spit and shit and God knows what else lay scattered about the stage. Resigned, Shawn simply repeated himself: "He kept on it."

"Yeah," Damon managed. Then a garbled muttered

undertone: something that sounded like *mutter mutter kept going all right.*

"What?" I interjected. Because I thought that was pretty snotty of him, under the circumstances. "What was that? Come on now—say it out loud so we can all hear!"

Damon lifted his head. "I *said* he kept going, all right. He *started* before he was even *supposed* to. *That's* what! Got it?"

A second before, I'd been convinced that this was all James's fault; but as my eyes found Damon glaring at me, I made a clear about-face. "Supposed to!" I bellowed. "What do you know about *supposed to?*" James's head turned from side to side as he watched. He looked like a man with a pair of bounty hunters fighting over him, the prize.

Damon scowled. "I'll tell you what I know." He aimed his chin in James's direction. "I know we just had a show that *over fifty damn people* watched your friend botch, for starters."

"I passed out, Damon!" I said, incredulous. "How long do you expect him to wait? Till I'm dead?"

"That's not the way it's supposed to work!" Damon said. "You're paid to do this show a certain way! We had a design. Remember? And now this? Tevan, this?" Damon spread his hands. "I've got Sandy outside handing money back to the *goddamned MARKS!"*

"Good!" I screeched. "Because I don't get paid to get killed!" Now, that sounded funny: because if you want to get technical, I sort of do.

Damon didn't catch the goof in semantics. In its place, his face went redder than a sunburn. "I see," he quipped. "So I pay you to come in here wasted?"

I took in a quick breath. "Pardon me?"

"I said do I pay you to come in here wrecked."

I huffed a laugh but on the side my eyes darted to James. "Now what the hell is that supposed to mean?"

"I mean—" Damon's index finger shot out. He pointed it at the floor. "It smells like you yarfed a keg in here. That's what."

I took a step forward. Nobody seemed to want to get near me. I kept coming closer and closer, my shoes creaking upon the wooden stage slats. The threesome parted like Moses' sea until I was practically in Damon's face.

"How long'd he leave me lying there, passed out, James?" I said. James's eyes flitted toward the floor. "How long, James? How long, Damon?" I yelled. *"How long'd you leave me on the floor?"* I pointed sideways at James. "He's not stupid, you know! He can do it! *He can count!"*

"He can't count," Damon scoffed, yet his eyes did not dare sway in my direction. "He nearly killed you." He leaned away from me as he uttered the last part: "You're pissed off that you trusted this jackass in the first place—"

"His name is James!" I shrieked. "He didn't screw up, it was you! How long did you leave me on the floor, Damon? You waited too long, and I was out, and—"

"Why would he do that, Tevan?" Shawn asked. "Come on, why? Cut us all some slack. None of us knew what was going on."

My eyes bounced among the three of them. Perhaps Damon and Shawn hadn't understood, but *I* knew what had happened here; and so, I'm willing to guess, did James. James had gone in for the kill, I'd dropped like a hot rock, and James had huffed and puffed a redemption that my stomach had refused to take. Stupid, again: ludicrous. Painfully anatomical, completely reasonable, and yet so damned damning that we'd not cared to have seen it coming. In this instant, I understood the stunned trepidation in their faces each time I moved toward them—it's nothing short of a miracle that I'm still alive today. How many times had we pulled this stunt? Fifty times? Seventy? A *hundred?* The absurd urge to apologize darted through me. I didn't get the chance to say it. Damon's voice emitted in a low, angry spurt:

"My old man's going to have a *bird* when he hears about this, you know it?" he hissed. "He's going to have my hide. He's going to shit a brick, thanks to you!"

"Aw, thank yourself," I said, spitting off to one side. Shawn and James observed this in silence: just another physical manifestation of the should-have-been-dead.

But Damon's eyes narrowed; his fists were clenched to his sides. "No," he said matter-of-factly, "I can thank *you*, you smart-mouthed fucking lush."

They say the truth hurts more than a lie. I was outraged. "Oh *suck it up*, Damon," I spat. *"My old man this, my old man that! My old man's gonna whip my ass, my old man's gonna tear me to pieces!* You ever sit back and listen to yourself? Pathetic! Shit! Next thing you know, we're gonna hear you pissing your pants about the fact that you like—"

I can't remember what I intended to say. I was hitting below the belt, yes, but I never planned on spilling Damon's information: we had a deal, see. We had surety. It—*you like corndogs, you like snowballs*, whatever you want to call it—never even crossed my mind. I have a vague recollection I was going to offer something juvenile like *You like your chin*, but I never got to speak it out loud. Something flew through the air and rocked my cheek so hard that my teeth rattled inside my head.

Tears sprung in my eyes and my mouth suddenly welled with so much saliva that I had to lean over and let it roll off my bottom lip. There are only three people who have ever hit me in my entire life; for a mouthy sonofabitch like myself, perhaps that's pretty slim. The instances upon which each occurred are wildly divergent, the men themselves—Kenny, Bern, and Damon Merit—even more so. Yet here I knew them all, unvarying. For each of them hit me with the same message in mind

(Shut up!)

and each time I obeyed.

It didn't help matters that I was practically half-naked when Damon did it. I nearly burst out crying. A second later, James had Damon by the collar; and a second after that, Shawn stood between them, waving his arms and yelling.

When the scuffle abated, Shawn was wide-eyed and panting and James glaring hard at Damon. His lips curled up over his teeth as he stood back, wringing Shawn from his arm.

Damon, in response, stuck a finger into his collar. He took one large, cautious step about James, his eyes dancing among the three of us. He continued to back away until he reached the lip of the stage. Here he paused to cast us one last angry look.

"You really are fucked up," he said directly to me, wringing his right hand. "And he can't count." He turned on one heel and stalked out.

I was next to follow. Inside, I felt conflicted, wanting to apologize to James and Shawn and at the same time inclined to kill them. I had no intention of chasing Damon down; on the contrary, I didn't want to be around another human being for as long as I lived. My throat felt bruised and tight and my arms were shaking. I left the sideshow tent without speaking a word.

I stamped back to the camper, half-dressed and brooding. I should have done as Shawn had told me and taken a few good deep breaths. I should have thanked God I was still alive. Instead, I admit my first plan was to fish my bottle out from under the cabinet again. But I didn't have to fish it out. When I opened the door to the camper it was right where I'd left it—on the counter, beside the newspaper, and completely empty.

I lost all my bearings. I really did start crying. Once I got going, I was frightened I might never stop. My breath hitched and my nose ran. I cried like a kid lost in a shopping plaza; I cried like I should have a long time before. I even had to take it outside just so I could get ahold of myself, and this is where James found me some time later. I was sitting on the steps and facing the Canadian National Exhibition with my eyes emptying out.

He took up the seat beside me. The two of us had to squash in close together in order to keep from tipping off either end. I put my face in my hands and he cast his gaze politely outward. He slipped his shoes off and wriggled his toes in the evening air.

After a while I decided I'd better think something up to explain myself. I didn't want James to worry I'd finally dropped off the deep end like I suspected I might've. But in the end I was dry, and so I resorted to the only measures I knew of. I told him the truth.

"James," I said. "He's right. I really am just fucked up."

"No," James said.

Well, that just got me going even harder. I mean, the *audacity*—contradicting me, and on such a difficult admission, too! He'd be lucky if he ever heard it again. "Yes," I said anyway. "It's true."

"No," James said again. He continued to gaze off into the distance. Then he did something completely unexpected: he cleared his throat and his voice plummeted an octave, the way it does before he winds up bawling. "Oh, Tev—" he warbled.

Oh boy, I thought to myself. *Look what I've started. Time to call the funny farm.*

"Man, Tev," James began again. "I have to tell you—something really awful, Tev."

I turned my head to the side. My arms were slumped and my nose was gushing like a blown pipe. I shrugged my shoulders at him: *What now?*

James cleared his throat a second time. He spoke with the most concise sincerity: "He's right, you know. I'm too stupid to count."

I sniffled. "What?"

This time James did join me, his brow crumpling. "Damon was r-r-*right*!" he cried. "He said I was too stupid. *You* said I'd be stupid! Too st-st-st-stupid to c-c-*count*!"

I said—what?

"Count what, James?" I said, my forehead wrinkling.

"The *money*, Tev! The money! When he paid us, you said!" James wiped his hand across his cheek. "You said count it, that he'd take us to be too stupid to count it. Check if it was square! And I—*didn't*. I didn't, I just thought—I thought—" James cut off. But I began to raise my head slowly from my lap.

"You thought . . . ?" I prompted.

"I thought it was *square*," James repeated. "I gave him my papers and so I thought it was square! And then last week, or the week before, or—man, geez. I can't *remember*, Tev—"

Something very important was happening. "*Remember, James.*" I put my hand on his wrist. "You remember. Right now. When?"

It burst out in a rush: "When I did the head?" he said. "The *head*, Tevan, the rat! You remember it?"

"Yeah." *Two weeks ago. Jesus.*

"Well, that's the first time I counted—and it was *wrong*." James made a face. "Wrong that week. Wrong the week after. It's less, Tev. It's less than yours . . ."

"What"—my words were curt now, hard like bullets— "exactly do you mean by *less*?"

James sniffled. "About h-h-half—"

I was going to scream. I felt it in there, burbling around like a bad rye and ginger that you downed before appetizers. The only thing that held me back, truth, was the ache in my throat.

"You see?" James wailed. "You see? I'm sorry, Tev!" He was crying again, leaning in on my arm and moaning. "It really *is* awful, I'm sorry. I'm sorry I'm so—"

"You ain't stupid."

James looked up. "B-but you're *mad!*"

"Of course." Man, I didn't know what to call it. Mad wasn't adequate. Mad wasn't even *half* of it. "You bet your sweet ass I'm mad, James." Things had begun trickling into my head. The tens of expenses that James and me had grappled with since arriving here, for instance. The dings and the monthlies; the bills and the nut that we were still slogging to make. The extra time we put in trying to make up for debts.

"I'm sorry, Tev," James gibbered.

The *car*! The Christly car repair! John Hadley and his end! The *weight* I'd lost. The socks and underwear that we might have been able to afford to wash at the coin laundry!

"I'm sor—"

"*You got nothing to be sorry about!*" I said. "And don't you even let me *hear* you say you're stupid!"

I turned away from James. I was mad, sure. But within this, somehow a little ray of light glimmered in the corner of my thoughts. Here I'd been busting my balls to make ends meet, wondering where on earth all James's money was going, wondering what in hell I thought I was doing. It was all coming together now. It all made sense. I really ought to thank Damon Merit one day.

"Do you remember what you did to make up that money, James?" I mused. "What you did because we were broke?"

"Yes." His voice trembled, a mixture of fury and shame.

Damon did me a big favor. Screwed me over, yes, but paid me a wayward act of kindness too. The truth descended upon me like a warm blanket: *It's not my fault.*

"And," I began, "do you know what *I* did for that money?" I shook my head. "Put your shoes on, James. We're going for a walk."

21

THERE WAS NO PLAN IN MY MIND AS I STALKED TOWARD Merit's admin trailer. Knowing James as well as I do, I'd guess that there was absolutely nothing inside of his either. We didn't discuss anything. We didn't speak. I was so mad I don't even *remember* walking over there. I hit the door like a shower of bullets.

The lights were shining through the front window and I knew he was in there. I rapped again. This time the door cracked open and Damon's face appeared.

"You again," he said at once, spying me. "I should have thought as much! Why, you're the last person I want to—"

I stuck my foot in the door. A stream of light fell across us as I did it. Inside I saw two additional faces, upturned and staring from their seats behind Damon: Sandy, and one of the fellows I'd seen about the lot—at John Hadley's some weeks back, incidentally, who operated the hoop shot.

"Sorry," I said. "I must've missed it, Damon. Somebody ask what you wanted?"

Damon's eyes shifted. He had no idea what we were doing there, but he didn't need much of an idea. He owned the good sense to know pissed off when he saw it.

"Open the door," I said.

"What do you want?" Damon asked.

"I said I want you to open this fuckin' door."

"You got something you want to talk about? The boss isn't in." Damon grinned. "Come back tomorr—"

James's elbow shot over my shoulder, and the gap between Damon and me grew as the door swung full-tilt. It's a wonder Damon didn't wind up on the floor with his face a pulp upon it. His guests popped out of their seats as though sprung from a toaster. Damon's eyes widened, the knob no longer in his grip and his hand suddenly an empty fist.

"Wha—" he began, then regained himself. "Well, now. See you brought your mule along too, huh?" Damon turned his face to James's. His expression folded into a scowl. "You got something you want to talk about too, jackass?"

That was pretty smart-lipped of him; Damon knew as well as I that James never had a damn word to say. I opened my mouth: "Yeah. He wants to tell you that—" James's hand came down on my shoulder and I halted mid-sentence.

"Give me my money, Merit," James said. "You con sack of shit."

There was an instant of staggered silence. The hoop-shot guy looked at Damon, and Damon looked at Sandy. Sandy blinked. As if in comical backdrop—like something right out of Wayne and Shuster—a dog yipped twice in the distance.

Damon looked dumbstruck, weirdly off-kilter. "What the hell is he talking about?" he said to me. "What m—"

"The *money*," James reaffirmed. "You know what I mean." He stamped his foot and the rest of us vibrated. James's voice came again, this time in an eerie calm. "From the show." He paused. "From all those guys on my papers. The papers I gave you. You know. Those guys who had it *coming*."

It couldn't have been better if James had screamed it. At once, the three men began exchanging anxious glances. James's papers had been displayed to the public for some three months now, see. And although the effect those papers had been designed to instill was meant for the marks, it now bled vicariously into the architects instead. Even Damon appeared apprehensive. His own words from days before fled like shadows across his face: *I saw him hightail it tonight—he went fucking bugshit! And I'm to understand he did the same once to you?*

"You stiffed him," I said. "You ripped us off. You're in arrears, you tight fuck."

Damon's forehead crowded in upon his features. It was a recalcitrant expression. In his indignation, in his faith in James's threat, he didn't even try to disagree. "I paid him what I measured was owed," he said superciliously. "Nothing more for a grunt like him." Damon's gaze spread warily to James. He took a preemptive step backward. "And after tonight, I think you'll agree I was right."

"Spare me," I said to Damon. "We had a deal."

The look again to James. "*He* sure didn't seem to miss it."

"Bullshit," I said.

"*Nobody* seemed to miss it—"

"*That's bullshit!*" I hollered. I could scarcely contain myself. Now it was James holding *me* back. "*We had a deal!*"

"Tell your problems to Jesus!" Damon said. "Bring it to the unemployment office! I don't owe you a red cent, Tevan George!" Damon was screaming now. "The boss isn't here! *Now get out of here before I have you thrown out!*"

Sandy and the hoop guy began to move toward us. "You heard him," the second guy said. "Haul out yourselves. Go home before we do it for you." He pushed up one sleeve as he said it, and in this I understood something: me and James weren't getting what was owed us. I nearly went ballistic.

"*Tell him what we did to make up that money, James!*" I shouted. "Tell him what we had to do! The work we had to pull off because he doesn't know how to count!"

The door was against my shoulder; James stood behind me, and Damon's cronies loomed before us. James had already begun to back away. But here he faltered.

"Uhh," James began. I've said that we never planned or discussed anything. He was really just answering the question. James peered at me, then over to Damon.

"You mean," James said, "the head?"

It was awful. It was perfect. In retrospect I believe that none of them—Sandy, the hoop guy, even James—comprehended what in fact had just been said. James had spoken with the figurative language that he always did; but from the expression on Damon's face, I knew he heard it literally.

Damon's jaw dropped. For a moment I waited for him to

power up and cuff me like he had inside the tent. For another, I expected him to foam and sputter like Donald Duck. Finally, there came a terrible moment wherein Damon's continued silence caused me to believe he might crumple to the floor in some self-loathing disclosure. *Sex is not the currency of love,* my mind put forward, watching him. *The sidearm of the boss, neither.*

And suddenly Damon had his wallet out.

"Take it," he spat. "Take what's yours and get the hell out. Here. Take it—" He ripped a bill from the pocket. And another and another. His tone was strained and a vein pulsed upon his forehead. Damon Merit kept counting them out—bills upon bills, reams of colored paper, not even seeming to notice what they totaled. The stack of bills piled into my palm. I felt divided: I had to fight the drive to drop my hand and let them all flutter to the floor. Instead I folded my hand over each bill and passed it over to James. James accepted this gift wordlessly. As Damon handed over the last of them, I opened my mouth to thank him—or apologize, I'm not sure which.

"Shut up," he said, cutting me off. "Shut up and keep it shut. Is that enough for you? Does that do it? Go on and count it." He put his hands to his hips. "After that you can count yourself lucky I'm in such a charitable mood, too. Or else maybe you'd find tomorrow morning that Buddy Merit has no need for a tenth act on his show after all."

I could say I was astounded. He let us stay on the show, which, under the circumstances—after the disastrous *mishap* we'd had—was nothing less than a miracle. But I wasn't astounded. On the contrary, I was miserable. Damon wasn't feeling charitable. Damon was making a deal. He was afraid of what I'd say if he cut me loose. He said yes because he believed no wasn't an option, which is the worst kind of agreement to make. Trust me—I would know it.

"I don't need to count it," I began. "But—"

Damon gave me a grim, miserable smile. "So much for surety. Get out," he said. "Leave me alone."

We did as instructed. Damon's men stood watching as James reversed slowly down the steps. I followed, and when I did, Damon slammed the door magnificently against my back.

James came up beside me. His hands were still working to stuff bills into his pockets. Twenties and fives draped from the seams like a dog with its tongue hanging out.

"Tev," he said after a while. "Hey, Tev. You okay?"

I nodded, knowing it was a lie.

"Boy, we really upset him," James put in. "How?"

I looked sideways at James. The truth seemed so self-evident that at first his question surprised me. But when I had offered surety to Damon a few weeks before, I had meant it. And so, with James, I made my way around that particular truth by simply bringing up another.

"*I* didn't do anything," I said. "What about you, James?" I grinned. "Man, you really told them. Con sack of shit and all the rest, huh? You're the one who got us paid."

James returned the smile. He shrugged at his feet. "Maybe," he offered. Then he wriggled his fingers inside his pockets. Peering down, his face morphed to astonishment. "Look at all *this*, huh, Tev?" His teeth gleamed as he surfaced with two fat wads of cash, one in each hand. He studied them for a second or two, a cross between awestruck and disbelieving, before glancing up at me. "Oh, you ought to hold on to it, though, I think. For us, for now, you know. Hold on to it."

I looked at James, standing there in his ruddy jeans and the T-shirt I'd handed over to him earlier that evening. For perhaps the first time, in the place of tired, overprotective paternalism, what I felt was a semblance of partnership between us. Sure, Damon had ripped James off and he had fallen for it; but both of us knew that Merit had duped me just as fair—in cutting our act in Halton, in selling me off to John Hadley, in plugging me on his Ten in One the day we arrived, for God's sake—and James had never held any of this against me. Nor my decision, again and again and again, to hang tough with the show, despite it all.

"You're not stupid, James," I said finally. Maybe he'd been waiting for this. Because he answered me just the same.

"I know." He held the cash out to me in two fists. "Hold on to it."

I didn't disagree this time. He watched as I took the folded bills and worked them into my pockets.

"So," I said. "Anything in particular you want to do with all this money? I mean, you want to do anything tonight with a bit of it?" I wasn't interested in drinking myself into oblivion, as I had been a few hours before, but we could easily get drunk as lords just for the fun of it. "It's up to you," I said. "If you want to—you know, celebrate or anything." I grinned.

James smiled as he cast a look about the lot. "You know, Tev," he said. "You know, I'm actually feeling kind of tired just now. Aren't you?"

I shrugged. So much had happened so fast, I wasn't sure how I felt.

"Well," James offered, "if you want to go on without me, I don't mind it." His eyes lilted. "Maybe you want to go find that girl of yours. Go and buy her a drink, say."

My lips spread into a smile. I laughed. "Maybe," I said.

James nodded. He turned and contemplated the darkened midway. "Later, Tev."

"Bye." I walked out to the pavilion, plucking a five from the mass and considering where I might find her. I stepped onto the asphalt, and James, behind me, walked off toward our camper. He paused and lit a cigarette as he made his way. I watched him take the rickety front stairs in one grand step.

He shut the door behind him.

I never spoke to him again.

22

I COULDN'T FIND HER.

I checked all the places I'd known Taiva to spend her time before I gave up on company altogether. What I ended up doing was simply walking the length of the lot, alone. Once, out to the end of the pavilions; and then—as me and James had done the night we'd first arrived upon the show—back again.

The midway had quieted and the concession lights were mostly out. Some of the help milled about and a handful of marks were still here and there, eating cotton candy and hot dogs while sitting on the old wooden benches. I strolled past them, all the way down to the far loop of Ontario Drive, where I found myself overlooking the harbor.

Like the night we had celebrated James's birthday, this night was cool and clear. The path I walked wound in and around a gurgling fountain. I spanned the entire area before pausing at its edge, overlooking the lake. Cars whistled by on the fenced-off road. The water beyond was a black inkblot. I turned. Floating above me, in the center of the fountain itself, stood the Shrine Peace Memorial.

I'd passed by this place a million times before. I'd sat on the park benches and flipped pennies into the fountain with James. Once, before Merit's show had found me, when I was about seventeen, I'd brought a girl here on a date. We'd sat below the skyscraping posture of the statue, a tall, lithe woman who I always reckoned to be an angel, and French-kissed. Now I wandered over and looked up.

The angel herself stood behind a plaque, water burbling about her in an enclosed moat. The moat was frontiered by a semicircle of smooth concrete. And upon the concrete, for the first time, I noted the etchings forming a broad lettered ring:

PEACE, it read.

PEACE BE ON YOU.

For an instant, just as had happened a handful of times in my life, I actually whirled around where I stood, expecting to catch my brother watching me. Standing alone and gazing at the monument, I believed that those words were prophetic. Had been placed there for me alone. For me to *read* upon the close of summer, 1966, today. *Approaching the end of a problem*, as the Card Reader had professed. *Progression. Years culminate to create a masterpiece.*

I had the feeling that if James had come along with me, he might've felt the same way.

PEACE BE ON YOU.

In fact, I believed he might've known it well before me. And although there had been many times over the last five years that such a sage perspective of the world belonging to James had frightened or worried me, this time it didn't.

Standing there before the monument, I thought James deserved as much.

Returning to the camper took me a lot longer. I was cold and my feet ached and by then I was really in touch, physically and otherwise, with what a long day it had been. I made it to the camper well past midnight.

I stepped inside carefully so as not to disturb James. I crept across the floor, my hands turning my pockets out as I went. I paused beside the washbasin to drop my keys onto the countertop, and they landed beside a thin line of silver. James had taken the necklace off before going to bed.

Unconsciously, I turned my head to find him. James was on his side on the bunk, sleeping, his face laid in my direction. Once drawn there, I couldn't tear my eyes off him. There was something *odd* about this, I thought. I'd been with James for a long time; yet it felt as though I was looking at something I'd never seen before. Below me and to my left, I again caught the glancing wink of the necklace out of the corner of my eye.

Him and me been going on over five years now, hanging together just us, my head recalled to me. *Man, that's long enough—*

Long enough to start speaking the same language. I saw him entirely, in his defenselessness as well as his strength. And in the moment, seeing James in this sum, the very same words arrived at me as had the time I'd nearly lost him for good, in April:

I hate you, they said to Bern. *You ruined my life.*

The response came but a beat later. It wasn't *my* response, but it didn't scare me. After all, I'd known that he'd been lurking around in there all the while.

You love me, Bern said to me. *Like you do him.*

What would you know about love? I wondered.

I would, Bern reaffirmed. *Sex is the currency of love? The sidearm of the boss? Oh, I know it. You love me*, he said to me. *Like you would your own brother.*

But my brother is dead, I thought.

There was a pause. Long enough for me to stop and listen harder; long enough to speculate, against my better judgment and with a familiar pang of inexplicable fear, that he had left me this time for good.

You love me, Bern said into my head. *You always will.*

My fists clenched at my sides as I prepared to disagree. But in its place, I found that it was true. I love you, I returned: you mean it is something that I will never be free of.

Yes, Pretty, Bern said. *You're never going to get free. Are you?*

I looked again to James. And as if James had answered for both of us, suddenly I understood what was unusual about watching him. James, his chest pressing rhythmically, the long strands of his bangs dipping onto his lips, was asleep in the bunk alone. How long had I left him there? An hour? Two? It only took James half that long to start shivering under the cold comfort of memory and spring from his mattress to shake it off of him. "I'm actually feeling kind of tired just now," James had said as we parted ways. "Aren't you?"

A thrill of hopefulness

(free of this)

ran through me. *Yes, James,* I thought, inspired and suddenly feeling reckless. Just like Taiva, yes: *There is something about this sideshow that I have grown very tired of.*

My hand shot into my pocket. I started counting out bills, just like Damon had. Counting them furiously, hurriedly, and yet I knew as I did this that I wasn't doing it for the same reasons that Damon had. Damon had seen no as a lesser option to yes, and I—

(What did you do, Tev?)

I had a choice.

I snapped the bills out. I left them in a wrinkled stack next to James's necklace and wallet. I took three bills for me, a total amounting to thirty-five dollars, and when I was done, I thought of something else. I flipped my wallet back and I took out a little white card. The card read *James D. Rowley* followed by nine numbers, and it had kept my own social insurance card company for over five barren years.

I can't remember what I told James about that particular card: *give it to me, you can't use that now!; you don't need it; I'll hold on to it* or *I threw it away,* maybe. I don't know how much was in the handful of cash that Damon gave us, either. But I hoped that in leaving both with James, I could make up for my transgressions a little. I cast one last fleeting glance at him. I set the card upon the counter. When he was through with the cash, I had no doubt James could take over himself. And then I did something that I can be neither proud nor ashamed of. I can't lie about it either, truth. I took the feather pendant up in my fingers and I clipped it around my neck.

I can't say exactly why. I told myself it was mine to steal. And as I stole more—about the room and out the door and then down the steps, that is—I understood that I only had one more place to stop. It was the one place in the world I'd promised myself I'd never frequent again, and so I was nervous. But my work at John Hadley's trailer this night took no pain, barely a word, and all of ten minutes. In fact, I didn't see John at all. But when I left his place, Taiva was with me.

We were making our way down the midway when we caught sight of Damon Merit. He was sitting alone on the front steps of his camper, and when I saw him there I stopped right where I stood.

Damon's gaze rose and met mine across the path. We watched each other, warily, for a long moment. Part of me wanted to approach him. Another part was worried he might renege if I placed myself before him—demand the money back, tell me once again, *Tevan George, you got nothing on me.* I'd have hated to have to tell him that I only had thirty-five of it left, boy. But I was lucky. He never asked for it. He never even asked me where I was going.

I left Taiva there on the asphalt while I stepped onto the sawdust path and walked up in front of him. I stood there with my hands in my pockets. Then I turned my head, scanning the area just to make certain we were out of earshot of any passers-by.

"You know, Damon," I started. "I just wanted to tell you. What happened a while ago, back there in the office? I never told him anything. I know you probably won't believe me, but I swear to it." And then I couldn't help it: out of nowhere, I began to laugh. "Maybe you don't want to hear this. But when James said 'head'? Well, what he really *meant* was—"

"The rat." Damon's tone was a calm deadpan. "Oh yeah. I know." He seemed tired in admitting this to me. "I thought of it later." He looked me up and down, and as he continued to watch me, his lips began to curve into a thin smile. He shook his head.

"You know," he said. "While we're on the subject—" Damon rolled his eyes up, as if uncertain how to phrase the rest. "Whatever John Hadley told you that I—" He hesitated, deliberated.

"Let me help you out," I put in. "You told him I had a few likes and dislikes. Didn't you."

Damon looked apologetic. "The week that his strip show got canned, yes. He wasn't making any cash and he was looking for an easy sale. He asked me if you had your eye on any of his girls."

For a moment this news felt neither appalling nor liberating. It struck me instead as irrelevant, a mismatched piece of a jigsaw puzzle.

Damon barked a laugh. "And I told him if he got a few drinks in you, you'd probably like *anything.*"

I continued to stare at Damon. The notion that John didn't know what had transpired between him and me had never entered my mind. Damon's words came as such cold, latent comfort that for a moment I was afraid to believe him. "Like anything?" I repeated, as if pressing for any detail—snowballs, corndogs, whatever—he might be forgetting. "Is that all?"

"Well," Damon said, "I told him you liked his Card Reader." Damon's gaze passed over my shoulder and onto the asphalt beyond this, as if eyeing an unusual, interesting find there. He raised his eyebrow at me, but I made no immediate reply.

"Yeah," I said, upon impulse a moment later. "I knew that," I lied. "I thought of it later too."

Damon upended his hands. Together we gazed out into the midway. The only lights within it now were those bleeding from the windows of his camper.

"What are you doing out here?" I asked finally.

Damon looked up. "Shawn's showing some of the kids how to make magic out of a little piece of paper you put under your tongue. You wanna get in on it?"

I made a face. "Think I'll pass. You?"

"Bah." Damon waved a hand. "You know I had a bad experience with that crap once? I wouldn't do it again if you paid me."

I looked at him for a long time. I smiled. "See you around, Damon."

"Yeah, good-looking," he returned. "I'll see you."

Me and Taiva continued past the rows of trailers, far into the parking lot. I found my car. We opened all four doors one by one, designating a handful of items into each place. The driver's side was the last to bang closed. I was in my seat and shifting into drive before it occurred to me that Damon had tried out one of my own little tricks on me: he'd called me a pet name.

Jesus, I'd scarcely even noticed. Was it serendipity or surety that had effected that response—that is, no response—in me?

Perhaps I'll never know.

We drove for nearly an hour in silence. We didn't even turn the radio on. It was only when we hit Mississauga that I pulled off the highway to put some gas in the car. I exited onto the Queensway and slowed at a four-way stop just beyond the off-ramp. I paused, looking in all directions, and that's when I noticed the stop sign.

It was the usual type. But this sign stuck out at me like one of Catharine's feminist propaganda posters. Below the white lettering stood one wayward word spray-painted there, probably by some conscientious-objector hippie type. And so the sign read:

I sat for a moment, reading it. Over and over I read it. I gripped the shift stick like I was afraid I might lift off from my seat entirely and float away. *The guy who dethrones Johnson is the guy I'll take in as my own,* my head reiterated.

I'll dethrone Johnson for ya.

And then:

Ahh, thanks, James! You's a real pal.

My vision, wide and staring into the sign, went blurry, crimped by watery waves. I bent into my hands and I started to cry.

We kept going, though. Taiva and I switched seats, and after that she started driving.

23

T<small>HAT IS NOT TO SAY THE GOING WAS EASY.</small>

I held my car keys out to Taiva two nights after we left. "Take them," I said to her. We camped out that evening, I recall, and many others too. Taiva had a sleeping bag, and I had a flashlight from our lack-of-interior-lighting days. Neither of us gave a hoot about sleeping in a car. We agreed we'd both seen worse.

"Why?" She eyed the keys, but she already knew my reasons. I couldn't trust myself with them on my person, was why. I couldn't be sure that I wouldn't find them gripped between my fingers in the dead of night. Find them, floating zombie-like, toward the car's ignition. Find us, in consequence, back on Merit's lot. "Because," I said. "Please."

"No," she said, pushing the keys back at me. "You need them. And if you need to go back there, then we'll go."

But we didn't go. And as I faded into sleep, night after night, the questions ambushed me. Where was James? What was he doing, on his own? What did he suppose had happened to me? When did the moment come that James finally understood that, no, I really wasn't coming back? I had a week's worth of locations that Buddy's sideshow was meant to frequent logged away in my mind, see; and it was this knowledge that kept the questions framed as questions at all. It made an entire week in which I had the chance to change my mind and go back.

But I never did.

After three weeks of weighing up, I put in a call to my mother. It's amazing I still knew the telephone number; it had been six months since I'd last spoken to her. Six months!—and even so, before I could even put forth the question, my mother made the offer. We were at her home within hours. She opened the door to us like she had the day I returned home from the san in 1958: that is, as if nothing of importance had happened during the course of our separation at all.

My mother didn't let Taiva and me sleep in the same room. That's about as funny as one of those big silent farts that go off in a social situation every once in a while, with no one having the guts to laugh outright at it. But Taiva and I took our separate rooms without dispute. Taiva slept an awful lot—and was sick an awful lot—when we first arrived. She stayed in Kenny's room. She said she liked to look up at the hockey pennants and Elvis pinups on the wall and, despite the fact that Kenny had never addressed his addiction, or even called it that, know she was sharing a space that had known such troubles.

As for me, I returned to the little room under the eaves— the very same place where I had slept as a child. My mother held the master bedroom on the first floor. She was an older woman by then, and no longer inclined to stand on the top step and listen for her son to turn restlessly in his bed. I still turned restlessly, though. I still awoke at night to the stroke of midnight upon my old windup clock. I awoke to it more times than I can remember, and after a while, I just threw the thing away. The house was quiet and unquestioning. In time, the years that I had spent avoiding it seemed to whittle down into a vague wonder as to why I hadn't chosen to return sooner.

Sometimes it was Taiva that woke me at night. She would slip into my room, and we would hold each other, then undress in silence. We made love holding our breath so as not to make a sound. But silence and this together is not always so good for a person with a history like mine. Many times, while she was on top of me and my head someplace else, I took her hands and put them down on my neck.

Sometimes, within these moments wherein our eyes met and her fingers remained, I believed that she would do it. But instead, each time she only paused, the light from the window glinting inside her eyes, and shook her head at me.

And the want in me would become a breath, the breath

then becoming some sharp, jagged, grieving voice in the dark. She would slide onto one hip and sit beside me. She rubbed my arm, touched my hair while I faced the wall. "Fuck off," I said to her. "Don't touch me." This is what I said to the woman I love: but I also said it to James, countless times, and I respect him more than anyone else in the world. "It doesn't hurt," I said to her. "I don't know why you won't do it if it doesn't hurt."

"I know," she said. "You told me all about it. You can tell me again if you want."

"There's nothing to tell!" I spat; which was a lie and a verdict that I would retract, often within moments of giving it. After years of killing myself trying to shut up about it all, I was surprised to find that sometimes talking was not so bad in comparison. Because it did hurt, and I knew it.

She wouldn't talk to me about everything, though. Once, after the Christmas parade in Toronto, me and Taiva waited at the doors of the underground behind a crowd of parade watchers near Bloor Street. A guy with long, natty hair stood before us, his back to Taiva; and upon his backpack, stuffed with books, sat one glaring pin among a thousand others like *Make Love Not War* and *Hello, I'm off to see the Wizard.* It read:

I'm shy but I have a big dick

I nudged Taiva and raised my eyebrow. We laughed: and then I could not stop myself from asking her. "Tell me," I said. "What it was like to go to bed with James."

"You first," she shot back. "What was it like to suck off Damon Merit?"

And that told me—reminded me, really—that I didn't really want to know. It wasn't just surety and it wasn't discretion that kept her from telling me. The truth is I had no right to ask.

Me and Taiva married in the summer of 1970. We traveled the east coast by Winnebago on our honeymoon, and sure if the newest Georges of this country didn't get laid every damn night of it too. When Taiva took the third of her seven allotted sick days come July, both of us had an idea of what the deal was: we were expecting. We celebrated by using the fourth of Taiva's sick days and having her call in hooky for me. Then we attended the Canadian National Exhibition.

It had been four years since I'd seen the lineup, but I knew it as soon as we stepped onto the midway: it was Merit's show. Damned if he didn't have the same old trick sign posted out front, too—*Ten in One*. There was very little sideshow, though, nowhere even close to ten; I know, because I made special pains to watch it. What I found instead was a motorcycle show that sold for a whopping dollar a run apiece, a variety act, concessions far more extravagant than I remembered, and a great number of game joints with Merit's name on them.

I didn't see the man himself, though. That's not to say he wasn't there. It was more that, as in the weeks that my hand ached to put my car keys into the ignition, I simply chose not to go looking for him. Later that evening at home, I curled myself about my wife and whatever soul lay growing within her with no regrets. In the tradition of my years with James, I didn't call my mother. I closed my eyes, and I slept.

That night I dreamed of the midway, wild and illuminated about me. The sky hung deep blue, the shade of bright new denim, and the Scrambler overlaid against this. I was behind the fence, my hand on the gearshift. James was in the tub closest to me. And when I spoke, the intonation was low, sage with age:

"No charge for ya's," I said in Keith's voice. "This tairn's on me."

And she started up and they were off—James, his face a stretched idiot's grin, the grin of a kid on the body of a man, traveling faster, faster, dizzying, ecstatic. Back and forth, around and around, until he was just a dash of color inside an immense blurring portrait. Then the tubs slowed again. James came to a halt; he leaned into his knees as he made to get out of his seat. He stood, reaching his full height. He looked around.

"Hey," I said. "Hey, I know you."

James didn't respond. His eyes ran right over my head. I

thought maybe he hadn't heard me. Or perhaps he had no idea who I was. So I leaned in, overtop the fence. "Hey buddy!" I shouted. "*You* know me. You know me, man. It's Tevan. Hey—"

Now James began to walk away from the tub, his back to me, and so I looked around wildly. I turned and spotted Damon Merit among the midway patrons. He was leaning in on the fence, in conversation with a woman beside him, but he was looking right at me. On his neck and facing away from his companion were two bruises—side by side, purple, and each in the shape of a kiss.

"Damon!" I said at him, frenetic. "*Please!* Look!" I pointed to James, heading away from me. "Please, Damon, I'm begging you, please—"

He's all I've got.

It's what I meant to say. But just then a funny thing happened: I stood, my lips parted, with no words upon them at all.

I watched James pause beside the Scrambler. He exited at the far end of the fence enclosure—the Out partition always located on the opposite side of the In—without casting a look in my direction at all. *James,* my head said, as though repeating a code, a secret language, a cryptogram of special meaning: *James.* And then I awoke.

I lay there with my brow knit together. Soon I rolled on my side and put a hand to Taiva. I found she was awake, but I didn't mention to her where I'd been. Instead, I lay beside her awhile. The dream faded from my consciousness. I meant it to, too. And then I fell back into sleep, and awoke again the next morning. And the next morning. And the next morning after that.

I found a place to stay. I held down a job. I had to get a TB skin test in order to do that, by the way. I won't lie and say this was easy, but things had changed over time and I was relieved to find that I didn't have to go to a hospital to do so. I had it done in a clinic—with Taiva outside the door, my tongue between my teeth, and my asshole climbing up into my stomach. Nearly ten years had passed between that test and the one I'd run out on in

'61 with James. I like to tell myself that even if it *had* been in a hospital, I would have been able to do it sober. Ten years, yes—but I won't lie.

Maybe not.

The absurd certainty that Bern's still up there, lurking about on the second floor of every hospital into all perpetuity, has not waned. Ten years or ten million—Jesus, it makes no difference.

I used my social insurance number. I held down a job. I went to a doctor. Nobody came after me. I keep waiting for them to, even until today, but nobody came. Aside from Taiva in her warm nighttime visits, nobody.

Not the san. Not Bern. Not Buck Rogers.

Nobody came after me.

Not even James.

CPSIA information can be obtained at www.ICGtesting.com
Printed in the USA
BVOW03*1433311013

334965BV00001B/5/P